Reconcilable Differences

Reconcilable Differences

Confronting Beauty, Pornography,
and the Future of Feminism

Lynn S. Chancer

UNIVERSITY OF CALIFORNIA PRESS
Berkeley · Los Angeles · London

University of California Press
Berkeley and Los Angeles, California

University of California Press, Ltd.
London, England

Grateful acknowledgment is made to the publishers
for permission to reprint revised versions of the fol-
lowing essays by Lynn S. Chancer:
"Feminist Offensives: Defending Pornography
and the Splitting of Sex from Sexism" from 48
Standford Law Review 739 (1996); © 1996 by the
Board of Trustees of the Leland Stanford Junior Uni-
versity.
"Prostitution, Feminist Theory, and Ambivalence:
Notes from the Sociological Underground," from
Social Text 37 (vol. 11, no. 4, Winter 1993), pp.
143–172; © 1993, Duke University Press.
"The Socialist Future of Radical Feminism" from
Socialism: Renewal and Crisis, edited by Chronis
Polychroniou (Westport, Conn.: Praeger, an imprint
of Greenwood Publishing Group, Inc., 1993).

Library of Congress Cataloging-in-Publication Data

Chancer, Lynn S., 1954–
   Reconcilable differences : confronting beauty,
pornography, and the future of feminism /
Lynn S. Chancer.
     p. cm.
   Includes bibliographic references and index.
   ISBN 0–520–20285–6 (alk. paper). —
ISBN 0–520–20923–0 (pbk. : alk. paper)
   1. Feminism. 2. Sexism. 3. Sex. 4. Sex
role. 5. Pornography. 6. Feminine beauty
(Aesthetics) I. Title.
HQ1150.C48 1998
305.42—dc21   97-38670
                             CIP

Printed in the United States of America
9 8 7 6 5 4 3 2 1

The paper used in this publication meets the minimum requirements of American National Standards
for Information Sciences—Permanence of Paper for
Printed Library Materials, ANSI Z39.48–1984.

Contents

Acknowledgments vii

Introduction: Sex versus Sexism 1

PART 1: FEMINIST DEBATES IN CONTEMPORARY CONTEXT

1. Why Split Sex from Sexism? 17
2. A Problem from Within 28

PART 2: FIVE CASE EXAMPLES

3. Feminist Offensives:
   Beyond Defending Pornography 61
4. The Beauty Context:
   Looks, Social Theory, and Feminism 82
5. Prostitution and Feminist Theory:
   Notes from the Sociological Underground 173
6. Feminism and Sadomasochism:
   Regarding Sadomasochism in Everyday Life 200
7. Victim Feminism or No Feminism?
   The Case of Rape 229

PART 3: FEMINIST FUTURES

8. Beyond Gender versus Class 241
9. Third-Wave Feminisms and Beyond 265

Notes 277

Bibliography 303

Index 313

Acknowledgments

Above all, this volume owes its origins to the inspiration of important persons in my life—teachers, activists, friends—who early on contributed to my becoming passionately interested in and committed to feminism. Because of them, I remain quite proud to call myself a feminist, certainly at least until a time arrives when the feminist movement's more ambitious and inclusive goals have come close enough to realization that the word become superfluous.

To Lila Karp in particular, thank you for becoming the Princeton University Women's Center Coordinator many years ago and for profoundly affecting many young women's lives, including my own. You gave much to feminism from your heart and mind, even at a time when women were not especially recognized or remembered for doing so. To my dear friend Bettine Birge, thank you for many inspirational discussions about feminism from college onward. To Pam Donovan, Bill diFazio, David Forbes, Esther Madriz, Isabel Pinedo, Janet Poppendieck, Leslie Salzman, Ruth Sidel, Kenny Thomas, Suzanna Danuta Walters—all wonderful friends and "role models"—thank you for just being there for me through thick and thin, and now through manuscript after manuscript. I want Bob Alford, Stanley Aronowitz, Jon Rieder, Martha Fineman, friends and colleagues from the Graduate Center and Columbia, to know that their intellectual and political (and, in Martha's case, feminist) support have been important to me. Thanks for many useful comments on the beauty chapter go to Bob Alford, Ayana Byrd, Jessie

Klein, Kelly Moore, Isabel Pinedo, Janet Poppendieck, Joe Schwartz, and Ruth Sidel. Thanks to Judith Lorber, Deborah Rhode, and Lise Vogel for sharing their work, and to Susan Bordo and Patricia Clough as well for their inspiring encouragement.

To Abhaya Kaufman, what can I say? As my ex-student and now friend, you helped out greatly in the capacity of research assistant and reader extraordinaire. Thanks are also due Linda Catalano for her help. And to my many students in feminist theory classes, I hope that I may have motivated even a little of the enthusiasm in you that you have stimulated in me.

My gratitude extends to Naomi Schneider and Will Murphy at the University of California Press for tremendous support and encouragement while I was undertaking and completing this project. I am also grateful to Alice Falk and Sue Heinemann at the Press for their impressive assistance in the copyediting and production process, and I thank Barnard College for a grant that ensured completion.

Once again, I am never sure how to express my affection for Annamarie Morales, from whom I have learned more than ever can be found in books. And for Jackie. And for Michael, whose considerable intelligence and love continue to grace my life.

Sex versus Sexism

For the last decade I have caught myself writing different versions of the same essay about feminism again and again. The topics shifted from one essay to the next, but not each essay's basic argument. Self-satirically at first, I suspected that the problem arose from an occupational hazard, a Freudian-style repetition compulsion to which I had unwittingly succumbed. I was hardly the first academic to find herself rehearsing a similar paper, merely varying a well-worn thesis better discarded long ago. Yet gradually I became convinced that contemporary feminism continues to confront a deeper dilemma than that posed by a tired analytic framework alone.

Even today, the pleasures of sexuality and the pain inflicted by sexism remain stubbornly enmeshed in male-dominated societies like our own; it is difficult to extricate erotic joy from oppressive vulnerability. Although imposed from without, this conundrum may have affected the feminist movement within. During the 1980s and 1990s, a division became apparent within feminist discussions, referred to among feminists, and later in the popular media, as "sex debates" or "sex wars."[1] More precisely, one might describe the problem as a splitting of sex from sexism—an understandable but worrisome tendency, which potentially dilutes the collective power of feminism.

Thus feminist debates, not just my essays about them, have unfolded like variations on a recurrent theme. This theme is the splitting of sex from sexism, a division that makes two valid and related goals seem

mutually exclusive. One feminist goal is the achievement of sexual freedom for women, an aim that reflects feminists' realization that male-
dominated societies characteristically exert power by restricting the expression of women's desires. Sexuality has been permissible only with
certain partners and in certain forms. Heterosexuality is elevated to a
privileged status, of course, a discrimination that affects anyone, male
or female, who is perceived to "deviate." Yet, because tied to a system
of gendered controls overall, the institutionalization of heterosexuality
has had especially damaging effects on women: for example, heterosexual practices have frequently favored men's freedom over women's by
condoning double standards of sexual behavior. This bias has meant
that a diverse range of women's sexual feelings and preferences—to live
with and love other women as lesbians, for example, or to live a bisexual existence that challenges sexual categories usually defined only as
binary, or to live alone (whether celibate or while enjoying multiple
sexual partners)—are, by contrast, demeaned and discouraged. Because
of this history of sexual repression, many feminists feel strongly, and
understandably so, that procuring sexual freedom for all women must
be a central concern of the feminist movement. This goal of sexual freedom is often pursued through individual defiance: here, sexual practices
that challenge traditional constraints become a mode of rebellion and a
quite personal politics. To seek and find physical pleasure is believed to
be a good, even in a sexist present.[2]

One feminist goal, then, is that women be able to enjoy sexual freedom. Another, just as necessary, is that women be able to attain freedom from sexism. Feminists emphasizing this aim are more likely to
discuss the oppressiveness and wide-ranging character of sexism more
than the subversive power of sexuality. This political approach tends to
take shape in protesting inequitable social practices and challenging the
institutional structures of "patriarchy" writ large. Here, feminists express less concern about sexual freedom at an individual level than
about the radical transformations required across a wide range of social
institutions—in the law, say, or at workplaces—where gendered discrimination takes place. This emphasis includes but tends to point past
sexuality: sex itself is less significant than its multifaceted ramifications
in terms of power. Through sexuality, a broad array of relationships of
dominance and subordination, from the economic to the familial, are
maintained because male-dominated societies oppress women overall.[3]

What about these two positions are necessarily in contradiction with
one another? On their face, they do not seem mutually exclusive at all,

but intimately connected. In male-dominated societies, sexuality and sexist discriminations are closely entwined though they are not precisely identical: sexist discriminations include, but are not limited to, the sexual. Yet we have already seen that for lesbian and bisexual women, marginalization has historically resulted from this complicated interrelationship. For many heterosexual women, this unhappy marriage between sex and sexism poses a different but also a distinctively troubling dilemma: can women enjoy heterosexual encounters without sexist subordination, and confront sexism without having to renounce heterosexual pleasures? Given this connection, no reason exists in principle why feminists must choose between devoting political attention to sex or to sexism. Indeed, the even more serious problem is precisely those circumstances that lead women to feel as though a rigid pattern has been set in place, leaving little apparent choice *but* to choose. For, as will be seen through five examples that range from the debate about pornography from the 1970s to a current 1990s debate about beauty, a sense of antagonism developed and often persists between feminists along exactly these lines. The sources of these antagonisms are highly complex, involving intellectual disagreements as well as individuals' very differing psychic approaches to personal and political life. Nor can the reasons for recurrent divides be reduced to essentially a matter of women's divergent social backgrounds. Women of varying classes, races, ages, and sexual orientations have found themselves more in sympathy with one side of a particular debate than another. Regarding sadomasochism, for example, agreement has existed among women who are straight, lesbian, or self-identified as bisexual that judgmental attitudes toward consensual exploration of S/M sex is repressive, contradicting the best interests of the feminist movement overall. Other women, across the same range of sexual orientations, have agreed that sadomasochistic sexuality entails a mode of desire that is basically inseparable from the social and psychic effects of male-dominated societies, and therefore poses a problem for feminist politics.

Equally critical to stress, however, is that such differences of opinion over sex or sexism among feminists have been relative, not absolute; many ideas cannot be neatly assigned to one pole or the other. Increasingly, feminist writings are being penned with the express purpose of bridging this divide.[4] In this vein, feminist scholar Wendy Chapkis argues that under the aegis of "sex radical feminism" (the term she uses to designate those feminists who tend to emphasize, in my usage, sex), viewpoints range from those of individuals who believe that any and all

sex is benign to those for whom sexuality can be oppressive unless a
"victim" status is explicitly rejected. Under the aegis of "radical feminism" (the term she uses to designate those feminists who tend to emphasize, in my usage, sexism), Chapkis differentiates feminists who believe that all sexual expression for women within male-dominated
societies becomes contaminated and those who hold the more common
position that embraces sexuality when mutually and lovingly expressed.[5]

Still, as we are about to see, the "sex debates" have not withered
away. Even though increasingly challenged by feminist scholars, relative
emphases on sex or sexism continue to characterize positions on well-
known feminist issues that dominate the political landscape outside,
and sometimes also within, the academy. By now, these debates may
form a habitual pattern that is difficult to change unless stubbornly confronted again and again, with new feminist approaches building on the
contributions of earlier ones. Yet, in the meantime, feminists cannot
proceed as though the problem simply does not exist. Any historical
tendency to emphasize only two sides is likely to leave a legacy; perhaps
the pattern is less likely to repeat in the future the more we can acknowledge its influence in the past. Note, for example, that Chapkis
was not able to avoid characterizing two "sides"—again, in her terminology, "sex radical" as opposed to "radical" feminists—at the very
same time that she succeeds admirably at introducing considerations of
greater complexity, and multiple viewpoints, into her study of contemporary sex work.[6]

But once we are committed to both acknowledging the past and altering the future, doesn't it become possible to reconcile these two
goals—sexual freedom and the dismantling of sexist inequities (ranging
from the economic to the bodily)—in order that we might attain both?
Clearly, we must find a way to address the melding of sex and sexism
without splitting ourselves asunder in the process. We must avoid feeding the conservative backlash that has been assailing feminism and
other movements over the last few decades, forcing us into a defensive
position as we try to maintain prior gains.[7]

The sex versus sexism divide within feminism can also be viewed as
a particular manifestation of a general social dilemma—the structure
versus agency issue that has been troubling social theorists over the last
several decades.[8] Whether the focus is on discrimination by class, race,
age, sexual preference, or gender, similar problems confront any social

movement seeking to overcome rigidly persistent relations of dominance and subordination. Given all that has happened in the twentieth century, from the social challenges of the 1960s to the downfall of communism and the globalizing of capital by the 1990s, what should we do? Should we concentrate on transforming institutionalized power structures with weighty influence, such as the state or the media? Or is it wiser to "resist" as individual agents,[9] trying to "subvert" power through personal practices? Alternatively, can we direct our efforts toward both transforming social institutions and asserting individual agency—with each dimension related, but not simply equivalent, to the other?

Feminist theorists have already been slowly but steadily learning to think and feel via *both/and* rather than *either/or* conceptions.[10] The advantage of taking several dimensions into account is not a new idea to feminists; indeed, the insistence on recognizing complexities is one of feminism's most important contributions to social theory.[11] Yet, even if feminists oppose dualistic thinking in *theory,* this commitment may be far more difficult to maintain in political *practice,* amid passionate debates and disagreements about concrete strategies and courses of action. After all, dualistic thinking is deeply entrenched in Western civilization.[12] Either/or dichotomies have indeed become habitual—difficult to elude, even seductively familiar.

In some situations, either/or choices are unavoidable: in law, for instance, a decision may have to be made about whether or not to criminalize a particular behavior. Or little room for compromise often exists when deciding which of two competing projects to undertake, especially under conditions of clearly scarce resources of time or money. But sometimes, when circumstances appear to require "either/or" decisions, altering the framework through which the same problem is conceived—for instance, in the above examples, challenging altogether the usually taken-for-granted parameters of legal and budgetary decision-making processes—might have yielded an unforeseen solution. An important challenge for social theory in general, then, is not to erase distinctions altogether—philosophically speaking, this is neither possible nor desirable when dualisms, too, are sometimes based on useful analytic distinctions in language, in life—but to assess where and when distinctions are used to increase human misery rather than to facilitate human happiness.

In the social universe addressed by feminism, of course, specious and unnecessarily restrictive dualisms—"masculinity" versus "femininity"—have historically been at the heart of gender-based discrimination. And, of late, diverse feminisms have arisen directly in response to well-founded concerns that "either/or" conceptual constructs cannot accurately describe the complex character of actually overlapping social discriminations.[13] All too often a woman facing multiple biases feels compelled to choose between, say, gender- and race-affiliated loyalties when the realities of her life demand a far subtler and more intricate framework in order for it to be satisfactorily described. Similarly, in the widespread "race/class" debate, social scientists have argued for the overriding importance of *either* race-based *or* class-based impediments, although this either/or thinking cannot capture the complexity of *both* dimensions as experienced daily by many people.[14]

It is important to stress that despite its theoretical commitment to challenging restrictive either/or divides, feminism has not been alone in suffering them nevertheless—often unwittingly. Radical social movements in the United States have been characterized by a proclivity toward splitting and splintering: from the Old Left of the 1930s to the New Left of the 1960s, and from civil rights through black power.[15] As individuals and groups have zigzagged between the poles of reform and radicalism, splitting has been more the rule than the exception. Sometimes, leftist groups have split over genuine internal debates, but on other occasions, as for instance in the 1960s under J. Edgar Hoover's direction of the FBI, outside forces have deliberately promoted internal dissension.[16] Similarly, we can see how sex versus sexism debates within feminism may reflect broad cultural influences, yet also be just what they seem: differences of opinion that are democratically expressed, rather than being repressed or denied. In other words, the splitting of sex from sexism in the particular context of feminism probably manifests both the presence of genuinely democratic debate and a surfacing of recurring patterns that in themselves deserve intellectual and political analysis, because they are not logically necessary. Without such an analysis, a dissatisfying choice between either democratic diversity or collective political strength may seem inevitable. But, again, aren't there ways of thinking, feeling, realizing, and eventually reaping the benefits of experiencing both? Why does the framework of debate, here as elsewhere, seem almost predictable? Specifically, is the sex versus sexism framework of debate a symptom of power, of a retrenched powerlessness, or of both?

In the first part of this book I explore why a split between sex and sexism has repeatedly characterized debates about a number of feminist issues. Chapter 1 looks at conservative backlash and other factors that have impinged on feminism, contributing to the split between sex and sexism. Chapter 2 turns to a problem feminist theory has always faced because of the ambivalent character of gender subordination as it frequently affects relationships between women and men in male-dominated society. This internal challenge, added to the formidable set of obstacles the feminist movement already faced, might have led to the split, even without the vehement antifeminist reactions that emerged from the Reagan era onward. Let me add in advance that most of the book uses the term "male-dominated societies," as above, in a way similar to what was meant by Kate Millett when she defined "patriarchy." In 1969, Kate Millett described patriarchal societies as those in which a preponderance of social power is concentrated in the hands of men: men control key institutions such as "the military, industry, technology, universities, science, political office, and finance—in short, every avenue of power within the society, including the coercive force of the police." [17] By this definition, the social practices of many contemporary industrial societies, including our own, take place within a larger context that indeed at present remains "patriarchally" organized. As R. W. Connell writes about the "facts of the case," women in advanced industrial nations are still found only in the minority at the upper levels of the state; in wages, jobs, and education, women continue overall to encounter discrimination. [18] But I agree with Judith Lorber that the term patriarchy can also often be used in an overly vague and "slippery" fashion. For this reason, I have usually substituted "male-dominated societies" for "patriarchy" in the chapters that follow. Like Lorber in this sense too, however, I have not rejected the term altogether, especially when used to connote discriminatory attitudes and beliefs—that is, what men often do or think that "subordinates or exploits women." [19]

Part Two continues by bringing the split between sex and sexism into clearer relief by focusing on specific examples, or case studies. Each of the five examples in chapters 3 to 7 are of concern to feminists, incorporating issues about whether women can both enjoy personal sexual freedom and live free from sexist subordination. Nevertheless, each example—concerning pornography, beauty, prostitution, sadomasochism, and violence against women, respectively—illustrates a schism that emerged between considerations of sex and considerations of sexism within contemporary feminism. These issues affect all women similarly to some extent; at the same time, the problems they pose are experienced differently when factors like class, race, age and sexual preference are also taken into account. But all women stand to gain, or lose, depending on how we treat matters entailing sexual expression in pornographic and commercial imagery (both of which also involve questions about looks), and depending on the attitudes we hold about sadomasochistic practices and sex work. Similarly all women stand to gain, or lose, depending on how we treat matters entailing violence and fear of being assaulted or battered. The law does not yet adequately protect women from the male violence and sexual abuse too often experienced on the streets, at workplaces, or in homes (whether at the hands of fathers or boyfriends, husbands or lovers). Some of the examples that follow apply more directly than others to problems encountered by heterosexual women: beauty, for instance, poses particular dilemmas for women involved with men. At the same time, most cultural imagery produced by magazines, advertisers, and movie studios still objectifies an "ideal" woman's body, creating a standard that represses many kinds of diversity in favor of homogeneity. Such discriminatory cultural ideals (revolving, too, around thinness, blondeness, whiteness, and youth), are sometimes internalized by women, and by men, across sexual orientations. In other examples, a wider relevance across sexual orientations may be more obvious at the same time differences, too, exist. Still, pornography affects women of diverse sexual orientations who may be involved with it as consumers and as sex workers; people who work in prostitution are of differing sexual orientations, as are their customers, and will be affected by widespread social attitudes toward this issue. And debates over sadomasochism have clearly involved those who are straight as well as those who are lesbian, gay, and bisexual.

Because each issue involves both sex and sexism, and in so doing poses dilemmas often relevant to some extent across social categories, the chapters also suggests alternative possible conceptions. Each is concerned with forging more synthetic and complex ways of thinking about specific issues than either/or positions can justify. In particular, each argues beyond a consideration of only structure or only agency. Each asserts, but does not limit itself to, women's rights to bodily and sexual freedoms: the rights to enjoy or create pornography if we so choose; to have reproductive choices; to live as heterosexuals, lesbians, or bisexuals; not to feel constrained by bad/good woman dichotomies and myths about women's sexuality. These rights to sexual freedom need to coexist with, and are likely unattainable unless conjoined to, protests against institutionalized sexism. For how can we feel sexually or socioeconomically free when so many of our cultural, political, and familial institutions are still structured around sexism and perpetuate it? How can women attain equality unless the rights to both sexual freedom and freedom from sexism are addressed?

In my first example, in chapter 3, I take on the question of legal restrictions on pornography, which has created a passionate dividing line between feminists since the late 1970s. Pornography was the first "sex debate" to preoccupy second-wave American feminists; it is also the oldest, because it is ongoing. "Feminist Offensives," first published in the *Stanford Law Review,* takes as its occasion the publication of Nadine Strossen's *Defending Pornography* (1995). Strossen, then the president of the New York State Civil Liberties Union, was concerned that debates over pornography had not yet been put to rest; she noted with alarm that in 1992, laws against pornography were affirmed by the Canadian Supreme Court. One side of the sex versus sexism divide on this issue is associated most prominently with Catharine MacKinnon and Andrea Dworkin, who since the late 1970s have consistently argued that pornography comprises and reflects institutionalized sexism. Their well-known advocacy of legal restrictions influenced the Canadian Supreme Court in reaching its decision. On the other side are Alice Echols, Ellen Willis, and Carol Vance, among others, who place greater emphasis on issues of sexual freedom and view legal restrictions on pornography as new forms of sexist oppression.[20] Clearly, it is the latter position with which Strossen sympathizes in *Defending Pornography.* The third possibility I suggest in chapter 3 involves *neither* advocating legal censorship of pornography *nor* holding pornography entirely immune to feminist criticism (e.g., that the male dominance of the pornography industry in terms of ownership and profits accords men greater power to shape images and conceptions of sexuality). Thus, I argue in favor of an alternative option that encompasses aspects of both seemingly irreconcilable positions.

Chapter 4 addresses an issue that has only recently begun to separate feminists in a way reminiscent of other sex versus sexism debates: beauty and its ramifications for women and feminism. For instance, questions about whether Madonna is a feminist, or whether cosmetic surgery empowers or entraps women, suggest polarities strikingly reminiscent of earlier examples. Kathy Davis, in *Reshaping the Female Body*

(1995), argues that cosmetic surgery can sometimes bestow feelings of power in women *and* reflect women's collective powerlessness. But she also reports feeling misunderstood by other feminists because of her belief that more complex positions are possible and needed.

At the heart of this particular debate is uncertainty about how feminists ought to respond to the persistence of beauty expectations. Should we be against such expectations because of sexism and its relationship to discrimination based on "looks" (a typical feminist belief about this topic)? Or does opposition to beauty expectations make women feel guilty about "looking good" (a pleasure to which we should all be entitled)? It makes little sense to judge women for worrying about weight or for turning to cosmetic surgery in a world where sexist and ageist discrimination—often based on looks—has remained commonplace. How can we ask women not to manage in the best way possible under conditions that have not yet been transformed so that other choices are available? But perhaps here too a third position can be entertained, in which we both avoid condemning strategic practices of individual women and at the same time vigorously protest the sexist beauty system as we know it.

What is becoming apparent is that there may be a cost to feminism as we lengthen our list of recurrent divides. And this cost is that *as we splinter among ourselves, sexism may be emboldened in its strength and ability to perpetuate and re-create itself.* We may be weakening our ability to fight back, to turn what Susan Faludi so brilliantly deemed "backlash" on itself. We may become more embroiled in disagreeing among ourselves than in confronting society, in effect recycling sexism. It is also important to be wary about *appearances* of greater change than is actually occurring at deeply rooted psychic and social levels. Transformations may be both significant and yet more superficial than feminists once hoped, and than both women and men deserve.

In chapter 5 I reflect on not only feminism but also sociology, and on relationships between intellectual observers and the intellectually observed. These issues are examined in the context of another issue over which feminists have split: sex work. Prostitution seems to pose an either/or legal dilemma similar to that posed by pornography: should feminists favor the decriminalization of prostitution or concur with its present illegal status? On one side are pro-sex feminists, who believe that sex work can and should be rendered legitimate, and sex workers themselves, whose writings testify to pleasure and pride in their occupation. On the other side are feminists who (somewhat like MacKinnon and Dworkin on pornography) stress prostitution's connection with the oppressive and compulsory character of patriarchal societies.

Once again, I argue for a third possible position. For admitting that the larger social context in which prostitution takes place needs to be transformed (especially since large numbers of women report turning to sex work for economic reasons) does not mean that sex work should remain criminalized and delegitimized. The ongoing criminalization of prostitution reinforces for both sexes the bad/good woman dichotomies that are characteristic of sexist societies. Moreover, it perpetuates a situation in which women are often endangered by laboring with no available legal or medical protections. Moving past the limitations of either/or conceptions can bring theoretical and political advantages to both sides of this apparently unbridgeable feminist divide.

Chapter 6 returns to another well-known "sex debate," one that first exploded in the aftermath of a controversial conference on sexuality held at Barnard College in April 1982. The disagreement revolved around interpretations of sadomasochistic sexual desires as experienced by women across diverse sexual orientations. Again, feminists tended to divide according to whether they stressed sex or sexism. On one side were Gayle Rubin, Pat Califia, and other feminists who argued that freedom to practice sadomasochistic sexuality was a necessary component of ensuring sexual freedom in general. On the other side were feminists such as those who contributed to a volume starkly entitled *Against Sadomasochism* (1982), who linked sadomasochistic desires with gendered relationships structured around experiences of dominance and subordination; thus, being "against sadomasochism" meant being against gendered oppression.[21]

The essay published here, which is based on my book *Sadomasochism in Everyday Life* (1992), views this debate as another case study in the splitting of sex from sexism. I argue that we can both avoid judging individuals and acknowledge that the structure of many social relationships—not just overtly sexual relationships—exposes us to sadomasochistic dynamics. A sadomasochistic psychology is not limited to a few marginal individuals; rather, it is common in our society, given the character of capitalist and other social relations. We are constantly exposed to relationships organized around lines of dominance and subordination, particularly those structured by racism, sexism, age, and class. Such dynamics often define gendered intimacy (even if not overtly sadomasochistic) as well as relationships at the workplace or within educational institutions. Thus, it is absurd to saddle women (or men) with guilt about sadomasochistic desires when societal sadomasochism shapes our social psychology. Like previous chapters, this essay searches for an alternative way of thinking that avoids repressing legitimate consensual desires of individuals while not letting society off the hook.

Chapter 7 is based on a talk first given in the wake of the 1993 publication of Katie Roiphe's book *The Morning After,* which suggested that too much feminist attention has been accorded to the issue of violence against women (although her own linking of violence against women with "sex debates" may have brought her book much attention). For the most part, second-wave feminists associated violence against women with sexism, and certainly not with sex; in fact, many have worked assiduously in the 1980s and 1990s to redefine rape as an act of violence, not of sex. Other issues of violence against women, such as battering and incest, have likewise been explicitly connected with gendered power. Nevertheless, some feminists began to question whether too much emphasis was being placed on rape, as high-profile cases, such as those of William Kennedy Smith and Mike Tyson, reached unprecedented levels of mass-mediated public awareness. It was in this context that Roiphe suggested that some incidents of alleged violence reflect the ambiguities and sometimes even the pleasures of sexual play more than the structures of sexism. Roiphe charged further that feminists treat as omnipotent the issue of violence against women, seeing it everywhere and in the process making essentialist assumptions about the brutish nature of men (as well as the delicate character of women, who need protection)—that is, that feminism has veered too far toward "victim feminism."

But that position itself—ironically, given Roiphe's contrary intentions—creates another either/or division. With little statistical documentation, Roiphe simply dismisses a great deal of evidence that shows violence against women to be disturbingly common. More important, one does not have to deny women's experiences with violence to acknowledge that sexual ambiguities also sometimes exist (although the ambiguous situations Roiphe highlights appear to be statistically rare in rape cases). Roiphe does make astute and interesting points, and it is important to guard against the essentialist assumptions that sometimes slip into feminism (as into other areas). But in raising important issues, she unnecessarily attacks the greater legitimacy finally accorded the issue of violence against women, threatening to erode feminist arguments rather than simply revising them. For this reason, her book is itself a symptom of backlash. In chapter 7 I again argue for a third position, one that acknowledges the urgency of addressing women's experiences with violence but also leaves room for a discussion of women's rape fantasies—without nurturing the "blame the victim" ideology feminists have struggled so hard to uproot.

In Part Three, I return full circle to questions of backlash and historical context as I reflect on the future. Chapter 8 raises the complicated issue of how gender and class interrelate in creating social stratification, and whether feminism's most ambitious goals and dreams could conceivably be met within an unchanged capitalist context. This essay is dedicated to a former student who was interested in why J. Edgar Hoover, while targeting other New Left movements of the 1960s, did not think feminism worth bothering with: what was it about feminism that Hoover perceived to be so unthreatening?

The final chapter, based on a 1991 *Village Voice* editorial in which I proposed the term "third-wave feminism,"[22] calls for both feminism and feminism*s*, for proceeding—politically and intellectually, with our minds as well as our bodies and hearts—on several fronts *simultaneously*. It calls for renewed enthusiasm built around hopes for recognizing the interests and needs of *all* women, across classes, races, ages, and sexual orientations. More men than before, realizing that the strictures of masculinity distort their lives, may also wish to participate. A third wave of feminism needs to be far more inclusive than was the second, without sacrificing the political self-confidence and theoretical boldness of the women who came before us. It is essential to place both commonalities between women who are affected by ongoing structures of gender and the equally legitimate differences between them at the core of third-wave feminism, determining both its strategies and its dreams.

The danger of continuing to split sex from sexism is in sapping our precious collective strength. My goal in calling attention to a recurrent dilemma between feminists is not to add to the forces of backlash (still alive and well at the turn of a new century) but to assist, however slightly, in the revitalization of a social movement in which I strongly believe, one that cannot be declared obsolescent. Sexuality has long been at the heart of gendered analyses; issues of sexuality like those debated within second-wave feminism cannot simply be dismissed, since they continue to affect most women. For example, reproductive rights, including freedom from sterilization abuse, have not yet been assured for women of all classes and races. Issues outside the realm of sexuality also confront us, such as class-based assaults on single mothers and on welfare, and ongoing racism and its complex effects. Thus, we have not been accorded the luxury of being able to ignore either problems directly related to sexuality *or* other important issues that are only indirectly connected with sexuality. There is neither time nor necessity to pit our needs for sexual freedom against our efforts to dismantle sexism in its multiple incarnations. Somehow, however difficult and challenging, a third-wave feminism needs to move beyond a defensive position, to refocus the attention now divided between sex and sexism, to respect and grow beyond our differences if we are to proceed with the realization of earlier feminist hopes and recent feminist dreams.

PART ONE

Feminist Debates in Contemporary Context

Why Split Sex from Sexism?

It is easy to assert that differences in relative emphasis have separated considerations of sex from sexism in contemporary feminism. But to understand why is more difficult, requiring a theoretical explanation. It is not sufficient merely to observe a recurrent divide in second-wave American feminism from the mid-1970s onward. Unless feminism is placed within its own social and historical context, feminists may seem responsible for problems that are not of our own making. Indeed, several broad cultural factors have impinged on feminism's development and contributed to its defensive predicament.

Yet isn't it limiting to focus only on impediments imposed on feminism from outside? Any social movement that fails to recognize that groups of people acting in concert possess *agency* and thus that it is not predestined to proceed in any particular direction may find itself stuck; it may become caught in a historical vise, its changes having little effect, finding solace only by blaming hostile outside forces. Thus in this chapter I identify a set of factors that may have influenced the feminist dilemma depicted in the introduction. For surely a patterned opposition of some feminists to others did not *have* to develop and recur. For instance, feminists could have intensely disagreed, but stayed within their umbrella organization(s) or formed coalitions of diverse feminist groups (representing a broader range of colors and classes, and embracing liberal to radical to socialist to black feminist perspectives). Such an "agreement to disagree" has occurred in the past and is occurring in feminist issues and spokespersons who best fit the media's either/or mold: they supply a ready-made, built-in hook. For example, pornography's status—should it be legal or illegal?—seems to be a feminist issue especially suited for heightened coverage. It is literally as well as figuratively sexy when personified in controversial figures such as Catharine MacKinnon and Andrea Dworkin, who somehow became virtually the sole recognized spokespersons for all radical feminism in the 1980s.[10] Once this "side" had been constructed, perhaps the *New York Times* went in search of the other and became interested in one particular young feminist—making Katie Roiphe and her book *The Morning After* nationally known. By contrast, viewpoints that tend toward the complex, toward three- or four- or even no-sidedness, may seem relatively boring and far too academic. Complexity is clearly out of sync with a growing need to think and speak in sound bites.

In part, then, the conservative antifeminist backlash of the 1980s and 1990s may have been exacerbated by a media culture that still holds to beliefs in objectivity, tends to construct oppositional sides, and values simple presentations over the complex. It follows from this that widely recognized feminist splits may not in fact exist: they may be constructed perceptions. In other words, these divisions may be "real" only insofar as reality is identified with what is *represented*. Feminist splits between sexism and sex, structure and agency, here become dismayingly ironic postmodern conceits; as antagonistic sides become prominent, all dissenting positions drop away. Such representation is de-politicizing indeed. As we have already seen (and as Hall's observations suggest), it is precisely those positions and perspectives that *cannot* or *will not* be split in two that maximize—rather than dilute—feminists' collective ability to challenge continuing discrimination related to gender and other blatant forms of inequity.

But splitting is not simply created by the media, though the media interacts with and likely intensifies the divide both inside feminists' psyches and in the public sphere. As will become clear from the cases described in chapters 3 through 7, however, ample evidence that the media did not conjure the problem all on their own can be gathered by attending conferences and by reading texts written by feminists themselves. Suffice it for now to cite only a few brief examples from among the five more detailed cases that follow. In the case of pornography, Catharine MacKinnon regularly refuses to speak on the same panels with other feminists with whom she disagrees (though, of course, she has far more in common with these feminists than with spokespersons in "either/or" categories;[6] and recent ways of thinking about social change, especially certain aspects of postmodernist theory.

Consider first the conservative antifeminist backlash. Reactions against 1960s social movements slowly but surely strengthened with rising conservatism, even before the Reagan-Bush era officially commenced in 1980. As Susan Faludi has reported in *Backlash* (1991) with encyclopedic thoroughness, antifeminist reactions took a striking array of forms, from the assertion of "family values" to the essentialist tendencies of Robert Bly's version of the "men's movement."[7] The feminist movement was confronted by direct political antagonism in the shape of a highly organized and well-funded antiabortion campaign, including at its margins terrorist acts of violence aimed at closing abortion clinics. This necessitated that feminists devote huge amounts of time and energy to reacting to this reaction, in order to protect a right to choose that was supposed to have been won. Under such circumstances, a defensive posture would have been difficult to avoid indeed. Another, more indirect, manifestation of backlash is especially germane to the specific problem of splits within feminism: it is one of the effects of the news philosophy of U.S. media. Though it refers to tenets that characterize the media in general, not just its actions during the conservative social climate of the 1980s and 1990s, this philosophy may have interacted with backlash in a way which intensified the latter's effects.

For perhaps the feminist movement has *not* really been divided into dual positions, splitting sex from sexism. What we may be seeing instead is the tendency of American mass media to make it *seem* as though only two opposing sides of feminist debates about sexuality are worth bringing to public notice. Typical habits of journalists may have aggravated—or even created—a *perception* of discrete sides that takes its "truth" from media intervention. As Stuart Hall has observed of Britain, conventional beliefs in journalistic objectivity remain very much alive—and they produce conservative effects. Hall and his coauthors describe how British media characteristically oppose two positions and spokespersons, even if both "sides" share an interest in radically challenging society. And once contrary pairs are posited, their opposition works to neutralize the significance of each: Hall calls this a "central element in the repertoire of modern liberalism."[8] There is no reason to expect anything different in the United States, where objectivity and the need to present "two sides to every story" are still commonly held ideas of editors and reporters in mainstream news organizations.[9]

Thus we might expect preferential treatment to be accorded those

feminist issues and spokespersons who best fit the media's either/or
mold: they supply a ready-made, built-in hook. For example, pornography's status—should it be legal or illegal?—seems to be a feminist issue
especially suited for heightened coverage. It is literally as well as figuratively sexy when personified in controversial figures such as Catharine
MacKinnon and Andrea Dworkin, who somehow became virtually the
sole recognized spokespersons for all radical feminism in the 1980s.[10]
Once this "side" had been constructed, perhaps the *New York Times*
went in search of the other and became interested in one particular
young feminist—making Katie Roiphe and her book *The Morning After*
nationally known. By contrast, viewpoints that tend toward the complex, toward three- or four- or even no-sidedness, may seem relatively
boring and far too academic. Complexity is clearly out of sync with a
growing need to think and speak in sound bites.

In part, then, the conservative antifeminist backlash of the 1980s and
1990s may have been exacerbated by a media culture that still holds to
beliefs in objectivity, tends to construct oppositional sides, and values
simple presentations over the complex. It follows from this that widely
recognized feminist splits may not in fact exist: they may be constructed
perceptions. In other words, these divisions may be "real" only insofar
as reality is identified with what is *represented*. Feminist splits between
sexism and sex, structure and agency, here become dismayingly ironic
postmodern conceits; as antagonistic sides become prominent, all dissenting positions drop away. Such representation is de-politicizing indeed. As we have already seen (and as Hall's observations suggest), it is
precisely those positions and perspectives that *cannot* or *will not* be
split in two that maximize—rather than dilute—feminists' collective
ability to challenge continuing discrimination related to gender and
other blatant forms of inequity.

But splitting is not simply created by the media, though the media
interacts with and likely intensifies the divide both inside feminists' psyches and in the public sphere. As will become clear from the cases described in chapters 3 through 7, however, ample evidence that the media did not conjure the problem all on their own can be gathered by
attending conferences and by reading texts written by feminists themselves. Suffice it for now to cite only a few brief examples from among
the five more detailed cases that follow. In the case of pornography,
Catharine MacKinnon regularly refuses to speak on the same panels
with other feminists with whom she disagrees (though, of course, she
has far more in common with these feminists than with spokespersons

Why Split Sex from Sexism?

It is easy to assert that differences in relative emphasis have separated considerations of sex from sexism in contemporary feminism. But to understand why is more difficult, requiring a theoretical explanation. It is not sufficient merely to observe a recurrent divide in second-wave American feminism from the mid-1970s onward. Unless feminism is placed within its own social and historical context, feminists may seem responsible for problems that are not of our own making. Indeed, several broad cultural factors have impinged on feminism's development and contributed to its defensive predicament.

Yet isn't it limiting to focus only on impediments imposed on feminism from outside? Any social movement that fails to recognize that groups of people acting in concert possess *agency* and thus that it is not predestined to proceed in any particular direction may find itself stuck; it may become caught in a historical vise, its changes having little effect, finding solace only by blaming hostile outside forces. Thus in this chapter I identify a set of factors that may have influenced the feminist dilemma depicted in the introduction. For surely a patterned opposition of some feminists to others did not *have* to develop and recur. For instance, feminists could have intensely disagreed, but stayed within their umbrella organization(s) or formed coalitions of diverse feminist groups (representing a broader range of colors and classes, and embracing liberal to radical to socialist to black feminist perspectives). Such an "agreement to disagree" has occurred in the past and is occurring in important respects now.[1] Nevertheless, building coalitions to maximize collective feminist political strength is extremely difficult indeed; it may be harder still to preserve healthy internal debate in an umbrella organization or maintain the autonomy of organizations within a coalition. Another possibility is that for each of the issues on which this volume focuses—pornography, beauty expectations, violence against women— *four* dominant feminist positions would recurrently emerge, or more likely three (as feminists attempt to synthesize apparently unbridgeable gaps separating the other two points of view).

So again, why split—and even more to the point, why split into *two* politically identifiable positions? For there seems to be little question that two-sided debates and the creation of feminist "others" have indeed dominated contemporary feminist politics. As Part Two's well-known case studies make clear, these debates have frequently been highly charged and in some instances highly polarizing. Catharine MacKinnon and Andrea Dworkin have referred to feminists who oppose pornography as "Uncle Toms" of the movement,[2] refusing on many occasions to debate them and engage with their views. On that other "side," Nadine Strossen mockingly refers to the "MacDworkinites" as she defends pornography; the MacDworkinites provide both a real and a straw person argument against which Strossen can define her position.[3] Similarly, philosopher Laurie Schrage has disdainfully referred to sex workers as "Uncle Toms" in collusion with patriarchy; on the other hand, sex workers themselves often conclude that many feminists pay little attention to their immediate interests and concerns as women.[4] More generally, by referring to victim feminists versus power feminists in *Fire with Fire* (1993), Naomi Wolf conveys a decided sense of "them" versus "us" despite her intention to incorporate the strengths and discard the weaknesses of older perspectives.[5]

On issue after issue, we find a tendency toward dichotomies, a polarizing of feminist positions as sexism "versus" sex, structure "versus" agency. Though this phenomenon is partly explicable from within, as we will see in chapter 2, we must also examine it from without. A host of cultural, historical, and social factors have affected the shape of U.S. feminism, adding to the distinctive problems of confronting gendered subordination itself. In this specific setting, there are at least four such outside factors that could easily affect the reactions of the feminist movement itself: the conservative antifeminist backlash; a factionalizing tendency common to numerous social movements in the United States; the cultural habit, deeply engrained even in feminists, of thinking of conservative backlash alluded to above). On the other side of this issue, law professor Nadine Strossen refers more seriously than humorously to the "MacDworkinite" movement in her 1995 book *Defending Pornography.*[11] Even more important for this argument, since these two law professors are figures relatively well-known to the press, similarly structured oppositions have characterized writing by authors who have not been recognized and highly profiled in the media. Lisa Duggan, one of the editors of *Sex Wars: Sexual Dissent and Political Culture* (1995), is relatively less well-known to the media than Catharine MacKinnon. But she expresses a deeply felt concern, one not explicable solely in terms of typifying media practices, about MacKinnon's association with antipornography feeding into an already repressive atmosphere of sexual conservatism and homophobia in the United States of the 1990s.[12] The problem also recurs over issues that hardly interest the media at all. In *Live Sex Acts,* a sympathetic study of sex workers' lives that seeks to avoid usual dichotomies between sex and sexism, women's studies professor Wendy Chapkis writes, "As I began spending more time in the United States in the late 1980s, however, I discovered that reconciliation among feminists appeared as distant as ever. The camps remained firmly in place, and even before I knew exactly where I stood relative to the key issues in the sex debates, other American feminists knew just where to position me."[13]

This, then, makes it necessary to introduce a second explanation of splitting: the tendency toward factionalization common to many U.S. social movements. In this respect, the development of feminism has followed a typical trajectory.

I recall that when writing a senior thesis in college on the American Left, in the days before personal computers, I needed to purchase more and more cardboard sheets to finish diagramming what turned out to be a strikingly fragmented history. Whether the divisions were between Trotskyists and Communists, or within Communists, or within Trotskyists, or within Maoists, or between the more "radical" parties who claimed superiority to democratic socialist parties (sometimes deemed unworthy of any notice), repetitive patterns of splitting have characterized the Left, too. Indeed, differences *between* groups loomed larger than their supposedly common goal of battling capitalism. Such polarized and polarizing dilemmas have also affected groups dedicated to overcoming racism in American society: the split between civil rights reformers and black nationalist radicals has formed a famous fault line since the 1960s (compare the Weathermen's well-known split from the earlier and less revolution-oriented Students for a Democratic Society).[14] These splits were not all spontaneous: disturbing Counter Intelligence Program (COINTELPRO) documents obtained from the FBI under the Freedom of Information Act (FOIA) testify to the savvy of undercover agents whose tactics purposely divided groups, frequently in half.[15]

But would social movement groups have split apart without the help of such insidious infiltrations? Organizations of the American left, groups dedicated to fighting American racism, and more or less radical feminists found themselves in similar circumstances in at least the following respect: facing social subordination and entrenched discriminations, at some point, they were likely to have glimpsed the enormity of the social power that opposed them. This can be a terrifying realization; think how overwhelmingly shocking and anxiety producing it must have been (and must be) for radical feminists to sense the pervasiveness of the patriarchal ideas, institutions, and practices that surround us. (Chapter 2 explores why and how gender subordination quite distinctively produces such anxieties and fears.) At the same time, this realization can produce rage, often quietly simmering beneath the surface.

Splitting, for feminists as well as for those in other groups, may be a way of expressing this shock, anger, and frustration. At once sociologically and psychologically explicable, it creates the feeling that one is fighting back somewhere, somehow, even if the anger is being directed only or mostly at others close at hand. Yet it results simultaneously in the quite effective—and rather insidious—reproduction of powerlessness and hopelessness. Psychologically, one may *feel* better while waging internal struggle rather than confronting a threatening, massive power in the larger world. If anger were directed outward rather than inward (or, at least, aimed in both directions), could it really triumph against various leviathans, whether we call these "patriarchy" or "capitalism"? (The glimpsed enormity to be defeated may also involve an issue—for example, the rigid and ongoing racial segregation that sociologists Douglas Massey and Nancy Denton call "American apartheid.")[16] And what if actual power were won—could one stay right, and righteous? Splitting from within in many ways seems and indeed may be safer; while still marginalized in the larger world, one can at least be relatively powerful in one's own smaller social movement circles. Factionalizing allows those who otherwise are subordinated from without to be the definers rather than the defined; an internalized "other" enables those in the splitting party to gain a sense of themselves as a group from that other "side," rather than feeling only that they are being discriminated against for the benefit of the larger society.[17] After the split, enemies may be easier to target, and angers may be more easily expressed when channeled or displaced from outside the movement to within.

The problem, though, is that all of this can also be a seductive trap for social movements—subtler, even, than the machinations of agents provocateurs in the mold of J. Edgar Hoover. Splitting is *symbolic* and *symptomatic* of powerlessness and fear experienced and encountered in the larger world; but it may then reproduce that very powerlessness and fear, from which more splitting again follows. This analysis—at once political and psychic—suggests there may be a kind of *investment in marginality,* which can itself become self-perpetuating. When surveying the history of the Left in twentieth-century America or simply in the last several decades, we can easily detect an almost strangely stubborn resistance to altering this pattern: with so much invested in the current dynamic, its defenders may find some reason or other to belittle this argument or even to justify factional splits, despite their greatly debilitating effects.

Over the course of the sex versus sexism debates, I have been struck by the excessive and peculiar feminist *demonization* of Catharine MacKinnon (as extreme as MacKinnon's own labeling of opponents as "Uncle Toms"), taking place at the same time that "radical feminists" have become quite noticeably demonized from without.[18] Why such hostility? However annoying Catharine MacKinnon may be to many feminists, they still have more in common with her than with the huge numbers of those whose politics are to her right. Perhaps she provides a more concrete target of frustration over gender inequities than some amorphous notion of "patriarchy." Yet choosing such easy targets can be dangerous. As MacKinnon becomes negatively associated with a now feared and tabooed "radical feminism," protests against male-dominated social practices she objected to may also become delegitimized and harder to conceive. Of course, I do not mean that feminists should not criticize the positions held by MacKinnon and Dworkin, or that MacKinnon and Dworkin should not criticize others in turn. I am, however, insisting that two things must again become possible for feminists: *both* to disagree from within *and* to focus on effecting the desperately needed changes that require collective action.

This tendency to split in the face of overwhelming obstacles, which links feminism with other U.S. social movements of the twentieth century, though important, does not explain the preference for splitting in two. Factionalization can occur in smaller and smaller units, virtually ad infinitum, as the sectarian tendencies of left history have amply demonstrated; yet even sectarian groups have tended to identify *one* "other" as primary antagonist, as *the* major left offender. In addition to the very real ideological and ethical differences that often motivate and maintain divisions, there may *also* be, as we have seen, a psychic and political advantage to shifting anger at a seemingly invincible external opponent onto a single, specific target within the movement (not spread over multiple antagonists).

More important, the third factor comes into play here: the deeply embedded cultural habit of thinking in either/or terms. This bifurcated thinking, shown in the media's fondness for insisting on "two sides" to every story, as well as Americans' fascination with legal cases that reduce events to a question of guilt *or* innocence, affects social movements themselves—even a movement like feminism, which seeks actively to explore complexities and ambiguities. For example, social movements have tended historically to divide gender and race, two overlapping forms of discrimination that we are still struggling to understand in a way that respects their frequent coexistence. Or it may be race and class that have yet to be analyzed in a way that captures these concepts' complex relationships. Thus, in the course of now well-publicized debates, women of color have found themselves arbitrarily split, as though one's experiences *could* be reduced to a framework based on "either/or" alternatives. Women's multidimensional struggles seem often to be artificially framed by recognizing only one of two sides (although an individual may well suffer other forms of discrimination, such as those involving sexual orientation or age).

In our culture, then, it is hardly surprising that feminists have swung back and forth between stressing *either* the structural causes of sexism *or* the advantages of individuals exerting their sexual agency. To be sure, feminist theory as it has developed in the 1980s and the 1990s characteristically advocates consideration of complexities, of thinking in terms of "both/and" rather than "either/or." [19] But the attractions of both/and conceptions in *abstract theory* may not translate into *concretized practice* in political situations, where the psychic seductions of acting out angers through splitting may be quite unconscious and much more powerful when experienced at moments of intense emotional as well as intellectual immediacy. Moreover, feminist splits between sex and sexism reflect a particular gendered duality predating feminism itself: the cultural habit of dividing considerations of mind from body, which reaches beyond a specifically American context to Western patriarchy generally. This bifurcation extends back to ancient philosophical splits: body versus mind, nature versus culture. It is the foundation of, and frequently justification for, constructing gendered poles of "masculinity" and "femininity." This, too, may have been subtly internalized. As we will see, one side of the feminist debate has tended to hardly deal with sex at all. Although discussions of structure provide excellent analyses of how patriarchy deeply affects women's collective situation overall, they nonetheless tend toward the disembodied and conceptually abstract. The other side, which focuses on agency, is more likely to stress patriarchy's effects on our sexuality; but it is less likely to insist on analyzing, say, the political economies of patriarchies in general, or even of pornography in particular.

And so it is likely that a characteristic splitting of sexism from sex, structure from agency, has been strongly influenced by these cultural and historical factors: the pattern cannot be explained merely in terms of problems internal to feminists and feminisms alone. A fourth factor also deserves mention, relating not to long-standing habits of thought or shared circumstance but to contemporary intellectual developments and strains, most notably of postmodernist bent. If feminism is to move toward more effectively incorporating questions of *both* structure and agency, sexism and sex, then it becomes critical that commonalities as well as differences be considered at the same time. Yet some postmodern theory, while undoubtedly containing elements that recommend it— many of its insights have already become part of feminist consciousness for good reason—also makes it more difficult to assert the importance of *commonalities* as well as the need to recognize plurality and differences.

Commonality has become an unpopular concept also because it implies a connection to still more unpopular beliefs that some statements about the world are "truer" about human experience than others. But this connection is not necessarily alarming at all. It has the distinct advantage of opening and potentially legitimizing, rather than (as has characteristically happened in the 1980s and 1990s) foreclosing and stigmatizing, the possibility of making references to *universally* encountered dimensions of life. For just as questions of difference are literally inconceivable except in relation to commonalities, so particulars are unimaginable except in relation to universals. Each dimension loses meaning unless linked to an appreciation of its mutual dependence on the other. Yet, at this historical moment, we tend to believe that it is in the best interests of opposing racism, or class inequalities, or sexist/heterosexist biases, to base such protests *mostly* or *only* on appeals to recognizing particular needs and differing interests alone. But these claims are paradoxically weakened to the extent that, in the process of asserting particulars, the simultaneous validity of universally based assertions becomes repressed or denied. How, for example, is it possible to powerfully oppose racism unless an individual, reasoning alone or in sync with a movement, can insist with confidence that a world without racism would indeed be "better" than the present one in which racism yet runs rampant?

It may be no coincidence that postmodern cynicism toward the possibility of concerted social action around beliefs held in common has been greeted sympathetically at the precise historical moment when social movements have become relatively quiescent and earlier gains, slowly eroding, have been under attack. The two developments may reinforce each other in complicated fashion: social movements become fragmented for historical reasons partly outlined above; aspects of postmodern theory may then provide an ex post facto justification, tending to make a virtue out of necessity.

For there is no longer a historical agent, or so some theorists have opined.[20] Yet class stratification is alive and well, as is the racial discrimination with which economic disparities are so regularly entwined. Moreover, as I will argue later,[21] there cannot be feminism*s* unless there is also *feminism*—unless we simultaneously insist upon both preserving the commonalities that structurally bind us *and* acting upon recognition of diversities between us. If we emphasize diversity too much without continuing to believe in the possibilities of commonality, we may become vulnerable to forms of backlash from within, added to the backlash from without. It may leave us, once more, quite familiarly powerless, filled with self-doubt, unable to assert the ethical necessity and certainty of *anything*. On the other hand, failure to understand the historical significance of battles fought to ensure the recognition of diversity is also unacceptable, threatening to constitute its own after-the-fact justification for maintaining traditional arrangements of power. Unless tied to recognizing differences, asserting commonalities alone can become and has been oppressive as well.

The problem remains of what to do once this set of influences have been identified and analyzed. For we are still left with the same questions: How can feminism be revitalized in a third wave, neither apologetic for its past nor heedless of self-criticism in charting its future? How can the dreams of second-wave feminism come closer to fruition, in such a way that both common hopes and diverse needs are incorporated across diverse classes, races, ethnicities, sexual orientations, and ages? In short, how can feminism learn to do several things *at once*? For learn it must: feminism stands greatly to lose unless, in our vision, we manage to include both structure and agency, sex and sexism, assertions of postmodern differences and particularities as well as very modernist elements of commonalities and universalities. Beyond modernism, beyond postmodernism, eventually beyond even feminism: let us proceed from here by committing ourselves to erasing gendered inequities, a project that is at one and the same time a commitment to human freedom.

CHAPTER TWO

A Problem from Within

It would be preposterous to assert either that feminism has changed the
world enough or that feminism has changed nothing at all. Sharp gendered inequities persist at the same time that the international feminist
movement has been one of the twentieth century's most significant developments. Contemporary feminism has faced complex impediments,
buffeted by reactions and counterclaims emanating from within as well
as without. Yet *even if* the set of cultural and historical factors discussed
in chapter 1 had not shaped and sometimes exacerbated these difficulties in the U.S. context, a basic dilemma confronted the feminist movement here—and likely elsewhere—right from its start. I will now focus
on a problem that arises in feminist theory because of the character of
gendered subordination itself, in order to further explore why recurrent
splits between sex and sexism characterize contemporary U.S. feminism.

I do not wish to forge a new false dichotomy between factors that
divide social movements from the outside, as opposed to those problems that emerge internally. Rather, these dimensions become mutually
reinforcing, so that how a movement is received by the outside society
strongly affects how it reacts to challenges from within. In the case of
feminism, we have just seen that the movement has been touched by a
formidable combination of forces external to it in the form of strong
conservative and antifeminist reactions; historical tendencies in the
United States that make it common for radical movements to fragment,

for reasons that cannot be reduced to a function of individual personalities or internal differences alone; cultural habits of "either/or" thought
that may unwittingly be internalized, despite overt feminist efforts to
avoid such oversimplifications; and, finally, influential critical theories
that emphasize pluralism and differences more than commonalities.

But a problem stemming from the characteristics of gender itself was
likely to have created an obstacle for the feminist movement even without these added difficulties. Politicization is especially challenging to
achieve when a historical consequence of male domination is to tend to
divide women from one another, both physically and psychically: the
ability to develop a feminist "class" consciousness can become easily
diluted, especially when the complexities of diversity (by class, race,
sexual orientation, and age) are respected and taken into account. How
much more daunting, then, does this already complex structural situation become when further complicated by often antagonistic outside
influences! Thus, without a collective movement strong enough to directly address both these external and internal impediments, feminism
runs the risk of remaining at a political and theoretical impasse. Unless
both commonalities and differences can be kept simultaneously in
mind, we are in danger of recycling sexism rather than uprooting it as
we become resigned to a world far less transformed than feminists
boldly dreamed only a few decades ago.

A HISTORICAL CONTEXT

What is this internal problem? Perhaps it can be best defined in the
context of its own development. How did feminism move from a position of greater confidence about the validity of its ideas in the late 1960s
and 1970s to a weakened and defensive posture by the late 1990s? Were
there certain ideas that flourished during the building of feminist
strength, and others that coincided with moments of weakness?

Clearly, there was a time not so long ago when feelings of immense
excitement and discovery about feminism were in the air.[1] Many
women have recalled how an outpouring of feminist activism and theory inspired commitments at once intellectual and political, as the writings of, among others, Shulamith Firestone, Kate Millett, Anne Koedt,
Ellen Willis, Ti-Grace Atkinson, Michele Wallace, and Catharine
MacKinnon slowly gained cultural currency.[2] These theorists were not
spurred by hopes of winning personal recognition—such goals, if they
existed at all, were afterthoughts—but by a sense of participating at

once individually and collectively in something beyond any one social institution's borders, by the feeling of belonging to an incipient collective movement.[3] As feminist scholarship has begun to detail, the social background of participants was also far more diverse than their current depictions as only "white" and "upper middle class" reveal. Indeed, many women of color played important parts not only in sustaining and writing about but also in creating the movement.[4]

Just as important, as we look back, was a wider sense of social ferment—much glorified, in retrospect, but nonetheless genuine. Feminism's own intensity was connected to and matched by the vitality of other social movements, from the causes of the Old Left through the New, including civil rights, black nationalism, gay rights, and environmental activism. Indeed, various movements of the New Left and against racism helped generate, however unintentionally, a particularly radical feminism; if a feminist movement had not already been born, the chances are that women's encounters with sexism in other movements would have inspired its invention rather than simply accelerating its growth.

Many women who became involved with second-wave feminist groups had already participated in radical organizing of other kinds; they had learned through experience that sexism was routinely subordinated to other realities alleged to be more pressing.[5] Without a space, and a movement, of their own, women were told to wait; race and class oppression had to come first. The frustrations this caused have been clearly documented. Sarah Evans's *Personal Politics* (1979), for example, recounted patriarchal habits of the New Left; in *Black Macho and the Myth of the Superwoman* (1979), Michele Wallace courageously called attention to sexism in the writings of Eldridge Cleaver and in the self-presentations of many black nationalists from Stokely Carmichael to Malcolm X. Through these accounts and others can be traced shared resentment at being forced to await a moment that, like Godot, seemed unlikely ever to arrive—the moment when male dominance could finally be placed near or at the center of social movement's agendas.

It is thus no coincidence that second-wave feminist rebellion *in practice* and the assertiveness of radical feminism *in theory* grew in close parallel. As on other occasions, actions began to enrich the content of ideas and to be nourished by ideas in turn. This interplay is precisely the starting point of the present argument, which revisits two ideas particularly significant at the time. For, indeed, certain basic ideas circulating were of such fundamental importance that they could be deemed virtually the sine qua non for second-wave feminism's emergence (chapter 8 elaborates this point in greater detail). The first was the envisioning of women as a class, which allows common interests to be asserted across other social categories. The second was a critique not only of heterosexuality as the primary means through which patriarchy, as an organized system of male domination, controlled women and their bodily freedom, but also of the traditional nuclear family as the institution that most contributed to producing and maintaining gendered power.

Basic to second-wave feminism, then, was the assertion that women as a group were vulnerable to similar oppression, which was structurally based. According to Firestone, women comprised a sex class even before their division along lines of economic class.[6] In particular, reproductive capacities—biological differences—had apparently facilitated the exercise of coercive controls by men over women; restrictions were promulgated thereafter as gender-based subordination permeated a wide range of patriarchal institutions and practices. Most relevant here is not a debate about biological determinism but the simple fact that structural commonalities among women were being asserted at all. In retrospect, it is hard to overestimate this claim's historical importance. In the 1980s and 1990s, fortunately, activists and theorists have called attention to the need for including questions about multiple biases and intersecting discriminations in the perspectives of social theories and political movements. Yet in the late 1960s and 1970s, forms of discrimination by categories like class and race were already recognized; they obviously affected both men and women. These categories were of legitimized concern, if only to progressive men and women working against discrimination and for social justice and change.

Much less obvious at the time was what women had in common with one another. Thus, the notion of women as a class was crucial in expressing the reality of something uniting the category "women" by virtue of collective exposure to biases encountered *within and without* other social categories such as (economic) class and race. Without such a notion, not much separated feminism's particular understanding of the social world from other discriminations that affected persons (men as well as women). Moreover, it would have been impossible to conceive of feminism*s*, once other complex forms—socialist feminist thought or black feminist thought, for instance, or poststructural or psychoanalytically oriented theories—arose. Differences here rely on the coexistence of previously asserted commonalities: the ability to generate feminism*s* depended on something already agreed (however broadly) to constitute feminis*m*.

Therefore, a key early contribution of radical feminism was the insistence that women, though divided in other respects, were still commonly demeaned by birth, by having been classified as female. But the second basic idea was at least as critical. For what was it that women as a class shared across other social divides such as those generated by differences in economic class, race, ethnicity, and sexual orientation? It was generally agreed that male-dominated societies routinely subjected women to controls aimed at *regulating all aspects of women's existence through expectations about, and restrictions on, sexuality* (as the latter term was broadly conceived). This statement—the depiction of patriarchal societies as controlling and subordinating women's very existence—was daring indeed. It prominently included, at the same time that it could not be reduced to, the understanding that women's *bodies* were historically the primary objects of patriarchal wills to power.

Obviously, women's minds were affected by domination as well, so that early radical feminist thought challenged Western civilization's classic dichotomies (including, of course, either/or distinctions). Not only were conventional splits between the mental and physical rendered suspect through patriarchy's imperious reach (and by feminist theories about it), but also conventional divides between the material and the ideological, the sociological and the psychoanalytic, the economic and the cultural. We can easily imagine how the very same sense of excitement felt by early feminists (and others struck by the originality of these ideas) might have slowly begun to create anxieties and discomfiture as well. Uncovering patriarchal structures meant unveiling a leviathan and realizing that women were surrounded by enormous obstacles. In all likelihood, it meant thinking and feeling overwhelmed.

But our initial focus here is that sense of discovery, beginning with its expression in theory: if patriarchal directives were aimed at regulating women's existences overall, then *sexuality and the body became the occasion, and the excuse, for promulgating a world of desired controls.* Even as directives were inclusive of the sexual and bodily, such controls extended well beyond these matters per se. What initially may seem a picayune distinction—between patriarchal desires for control *in general* and for sexual controls *in particular* (desires themselves intimately connected and yet, sometimes, analytically separable)—has, on the contrary, quite significant potential ramifications. For, unless feminists kept the complex relationships between society and sexuality explicitly in mind, they might later tend in their politics to target *either* patriarchal society (a generalized focus that may ignore, relatively speaking, specific issues of sexuality and the bodily) *or* sexual repressiveness (a specifically sexual focus that may ignore, relatively speaking, the exercise of patriarchal power more generally). Yet early radical feminist theory itself seems to have recognized that critical attention must be paid *both* to patriarchal societies' generalized aims in controlling women *and* to desires for controls over sexuality itself—and, most of all, to the pervasive connections between the two. Thus, persons who were female were constructed in gender-divided societies to appear not only different but as though especially connected to "bodily" and "sexual" dimensions of life. This association was insistently cemented even though, in fact, all human beings constantly partake of these aspects of being: physiological and cerebral, bodily and mental, sexual and unsexual. Surely, then, the social world *could* have been organized differently—as it could, and needs to be, still.

Yet divisions between culture and nature, and mind and body, served ex post facto to rationalize women's relative restriction to certain spheres and exclusion from others; thereafter, extensive rules about "proper" and "improper" sexual and bodily behavior for women were promulgated. For instance, Adrienne Rich, in a classic essay, targeted "compulsory heterosexuality": only heterosexuality was permissible for women, certainly not lesbianism, as Rich went on to list the intimating and punitive consequences of women seeking other than prescribed forms of emotional and sexual association.[7] Patriarchal imperatives also subjected not only choice of sexual partner but also questions about women's reproduction (if and how it was to occur) to intensive scrutiny and regulation. For this reason, it was not the least bit surprising that the issue of procuring legal abortions—symbolic of reproductive rights and sexual freedom in the broadest sense—became one of the first political issues around which radical feminism organized en masse. Feminist critiques were aimed at sexist expectations about how women should look, dress, and act; double standards of sexuality that created "madonnas" and "sluts," legitimate and supposedly illegitimate mothers, were decried. This system of imperatives was linked under the rubric of an *ideology of family,* a set of interrelated notions that attributed to nature aspects of being that had been socially constructed. Women were to be specially associated with a domestic sphere (at once glorified and inferiorized for this alleged specialization), in which matters concerning emotionality and the sexual/bodily, reproduction and housework, were thereafter confined and contained.

In this critique of patriarchally organized families, radical feminism was arguably at its most "radical" by the late 1960s and 1970s. Just the decade before, television had commenced wholesale vigorous advertising of the traditional nuclear family, its supposed virtues and typicality; the 1950s sprouted images of conflict-free households, from *Leave It to Beaver* and *Ozzie and Harriet* to *Father Knows Best*. Yet, for Kate Millett, it was precisely this traditional nuclear family that provided the key to how "patriarchal socialization" occurred: it was the place where assumptions about gendered hierarchies incubated and became self-reproducing from generation to generation.[8] For both Millett and Ti-Grace Atkinson, the patriarchally organized traditional family—in which structural inequities still frequently reigned—was perhaps most damaging not in its sometimes coercive and violent abuses, but in its virtually ever-present gendered ideologies about love.[9] Ideas from Simone de Beauvoir's *Second Sex* (1949) were incorporated into later texts that remarked on gendered asymmetries: for little boys, romance might well be part of life, and even a major part; for a girl, fulfillment within a family was regularly held out as a necessary precondition of any and all eventual happiness. Young women accorded greater importance to connections, associations, mergers; one's life would be viewed as meaningless, unfulfilled, and uncomfortably abnormal unless it contained heterosexual attachment, marriage, and children.[10] Thus, prominent in radical feminist theory from its very beginnings were the assertion of commonalities among women and a critique of sexist marriage and family structures.

To be sure, later feminist theorists, noting actual differences that are greatly affected by class and race, have rightly faulted the radical feminist critique of "the" patriarchal family for taking for granted that all families were identically structured. But if we can correct for this mistaken presumption, as this book in its entirety argues feminists must do by incorporating both differences and commonalities into our intellectual and political practices, does the feminist critique still apply? What of the many families that are and have been headed by women, where male father figures may not be present? Here we should be careful not to throw out the proverbial baby with the bath water. While the absence of attention to difference was (and remains) a serious problem, the feminist critique nevertheless contained a certain generalizable va-

lidity in targeting a dominant and hegemonic *ideology* about families—
the ideology that continues to thrive in most patriarchal societies, including the United States.[11]

This ideology, coded in the 1990s via concerns about resuscitating
traditional "family values," holds that men *ought* to be present and
heads of households, whether or not this is possible or actually desired
by the women involved; it still tends to differentially associate women
with allegedly "natural" matters ranging from child care to housework;
it still often places greater emphasis for women on the importance of
finding a partner ("having" a man), and of marrying. And much of this
ideology has at least some applicability *across* class, race, and ethnic
differences, at the very same time that the significance of the specific
variations arising from such differences must be respected. Year after
year, when my students of diverse backgrounds read those chapters of
The Second Sex that describe asymmetries produced inside traditionally
organized families (and inside the gendered culture of which they have
been a part), I am struck by the broad range of young women for whom
this aspect of de Beauvoir's analysis still powerfully resonates. For while
male-dominated societies have certainly been shaken in a so-called post-
feminist era, older structures of power—including the subtle power of
sexist and heterosexist ideologies of family—remain largely in place.[12]
The dominant myths continue to shape reality, even as particular effects
of gender shift greatly depending on the overall context and circumstances of individual women's lives.

On the other hand, if the importance of commonalities were to be
increasingly recognized again, this would have to happen in such a way
that feminists do not veer reactively toward the opposite extreme, com-
promising the equally critical task of incorporating differences simultaneously. For it is also true, in this example, that women's experiences
within families are not simply equatable. In many situations where
women are heads of households themselves, this is likely to have occurred because of class and racial discrimination. Women then find
themselves in powerful roles because men are absent, an absence that
reflects the deep legacy of biases which are not only gendered; only
some men, in particular those who are white and well-to-do, have had
the ability to assume what is undoubtedly a patriarchal head-of-house-
hold role. This leaves a woman head of household who faces class, race
and gendered subordination in an overdetermined situation indeed.

In one respect, this woman has something in common with all
women: patriarchal attitudes do not accord to her the fully equal status

accorded men, in and outside the family. But in another respect, that of difference, contemporary feminist politics may not strike this individual as yet sufficiently sensitive to encompass her fears that protesting gendered subordination will be used in the larger society to reinforce racial and class discrimination against men. And there will be reasons for such fears unless the feminist movement loudly objects en masse, and with a vehemence comparable to that it displays toward gender, to the also systematic character of ongoing racial and class discrimination in the United States. This problem exists and has existed historically, even as its extent has been divisively exaggerated; as noted above, the backgrounds of feminists who began the women's movement were far more diverse, and many of their concerns much broader, than common cultural depictions let on. As a result of this problem, both real and exaggerated, a woman who faces gender, race, and class biases all at once often responds cynically to any categorical claims about the potential of the feminist movement to improve her life. Indeed, many women in this situation believe that more is shared with men of the same race and class than with other women as feminists.

Still, gender bias persists as one component of such multiple experiences of discrimination; for this reason, a basis for commonality also remains. But the degree to which such potential is actualized depends on the depth to which concerns about differences, too, are incorporated into contemporary feminist politics. Without commonalities, the rationale for a diverse feminist movement existing at all may be weakened; without an understanding of difference, large groups of women are likely to continue to feel excluded, so that assertions of commonality ring false. At present, though, the importance of commonalities is the dimension that seems to be relatively less visible and recognized. Most to the point, the theoretical basis of our ability to believe commonality is even possible, and desirable, has been obscured in the 1980s and 1990s. This brings us back to the question of shared concerns across categories of women and, in the process, back to radical feminists' early critiques of intimate relationships within nuclear families that have traditionally taken heterosexuality to be their norm.

AN INTERNAL CONUNDRUM

Let us continue to pursue a connection between these early radical feminist ideas and the splitting of sex from sexism in contemporary feminism. For how these two fundamental ideas were interpreted—women structurally set up as a commonly subordinated class, in such a way that this subordination incubated inside privatized and heterosexual relationships, most particularly within institutionalized family units—may well have affected how later attitudes toward sex and sexism unfolded.

In arguing that traditional family structures and ideologies often produced sexist controls and skewed psychic processes between men and women, radical feminists were in effect declaring that *the very intimacy of heterosexual relations* was what most distinguished gender from other discriminatory realities such as those based on race, class, or ethnicity. This critique enabled radical feminism to explain how gender subordination produced *commonalities* across women's experiences while, at the very same time, allowing that *differences* existed along other social axes. For it tended to be true that no matter how historically diverse and culturally specific were particular women's experiences, most other social categories also still had as their dominant family structure a form that accorded disproportionate power to men.

From this observation, one might or might not have proceeded to the conclusion that Shulamith Firestone and Kate Millett reached in *The Dialectic of Sex* (1970) and *Sexual Politics* (1970), respectively: that gender must be the "deepest" and most primordial form of human oppression.[13] Yet simply because gender cuts across other social categories, it does not logically follow that other forms of discrimination—racism, for instance—are therefore any less serious in their own histories and consequences. To claim that gender is deepest can needlessly encourage counterproductive comparisons, pitting specific types of oppressions against others.

For the specific ramifications of this argument are disturbing enough. If gender bias is particularly rooted and perpetuated through the intimacy of family units, then breaking away from and organizing against this mode of subordination will be distinctly difficult and complex. Here, our concentration need not be on "ranking" oppressions but on understanding precisely how and why diverse discriminations interrelate. Consider class distinctions, which are hugely influential: clearly, workers labor under the capitalist's controlling eye (or the eyes of that owner's representatives) all day or all night long. But during that day or night, possibilities for working-class association are facilitated, at least in theory (and often, throughout U.S. history, in practice). Moreover, the structure of the workplace itself does not diminish the chances of solidarity and class consciousness actually developing. Consider, too, racial discrimination, distinctive in its own ongoing virulence: clearly, U.S. racism in its sometimes genocidal forms has involved systems of surveillance and supervision, from the institutionalization of slavery itself in the nineteenth century to what Douglas Massey and Nancy Denton have called a differently rigid sort of "American apartheid" in the late twentieth. People whose entire existences became arbitrarily devalued because of their skin color have also been forced into segregated spaces. The former apartheid system in South Africa exemplified such forcible separation, of course, as do ongoing controls imposed on ghettoized and "hyperghettoized" areas in the United States today. Such forced separation sometimes facilitates community; it can, and has, created common culture and common cause. Thus political consciousness about racism paradoxically is often fostered (and not simply diluted) by the very conditions of group subjugation.

This is precisely the point at which gender, as analyzed in early radical feminist theory, differentiated itself: its typical locale and operations raise distinctive dilemmas indeed. For what other relationship of subordination is exactly analogous to gender in terms of the closeness that is *supposed* to develop in prescribed heterosexual relationships, and on the basis of pleasure and love? Where else does one—literally, figuratively, as a matter of course—sleep with the person whom the force of history, tradition, and ideology continues to render in many respects more powerful, and in many respects more privileged, than oneself? It would be as though the worker were to arrive home from the factory to unwind in the embrace of the very capitalist with whom in most other regards a class relationship of hierarchy existed. Or as though the person encountering racism not only at work but on the street had to live with the white oppressor, even in bed, even as he or she slept. Slaveowners certainly did rape many black women, and forced many into ongoing sexual relationships. Still, "marriage" or other forms of heterosexual intimacy are not *supposed* to be forms of enslavement ("slavery" being a word that admits, arrogantly and sadistically, to its coercive character) but pleasurable, fulfilling, mutually voluntary.

And so this particular type of power relationship will frequently feature, in its modern form, a modern woman coming home after work to the male partner she lives with, or that partner coming home to her. In either event, between them, a relationship distinctive in its emotional, psychic, and physical intimacy is likely to unfold, and on multiple levels.

Emotionally: there are chores to be done, and matters of shared household and economic concern to be discussed. A universe of day-to-day associations and cares subtly but forcefully bind the couple together in literally millions of cases. Children often cement this familiarity of the routine, these comforts of the habitual. Indeed, what closer tie can one imagine than the joint intimacies that develop through a small person who represents the merged bodies and interests of two partners, providing shared joys in the wondrous course of watching that child grow older? Sexually, bodily (and these levels are often interwoven with the emotional): the relationship may encompass the gentleness of physical tendernesses; the closeness of bodily and intimate recognitions, touches, physical warmth; the passions of sex, of lust, of desires; the intimacy of orgasms given and received, sometimes apart, or perhaps together. To this may be added the knowledge and acceptance of emotional or sexual displeasures and imperfections, the secure belief that satisfactions also often not fully attained need not necessarily lead to rejection or to total loss of love, at least in *this* relationship (even if one can so easily be "fired," left rejected and abandoned, in the larger world beyond one's family).

Here, then, is what I have identified as an "internal" conundrum facing feminism in theory and practice right from its start. For radical feminists were declaring that the most profoundly intimate relationships and places to which women were socialized to turn for diverse emotional, social, and sexual comforts were simultaneously the *same* relationships and places where subordination subtly took hold (as that subordination, too, possibly became habitual, familiar and familial). In other words, *comfort and oppressiveness regularly occurred together,* and in such a way as to seem inextricable, melded together and intimately enmeshed in experience.[14] It followed that if one were to walk away from the oppressive parts of this relation, one might also simultaneously be sacrificing its emotionally comforting parts. And, conversely, if one tried to maintain such basic comforts, one might have to live with degrees of inequity simmering at or beneath the surface of a given intimate relationship.

Put simply, then, that which was "good" and "bad" about many heterosexual relationships in male-dominated societies could not be separated; these aspects coexisted like two sides of a coin. Moreover, and provocatively, this observation recalls how both *pleasures* and *subordinations* have also figured prominently in the concerns and considerations of feminism itself—even though, as we have seen, those most

concerned with each of these two "sides" later came to regard each
other with suspicion or hostility.

Still, this critique of intimacy does not apply to all women in the
same way. How does this analysis affect, if at all, women who are not
involved sexually with men—what about a women who chooses to live
alone? And, of course, what about women who are lesbians? Once
again, answering these questions necessitates incorporating both considerations of difference and those of commonality into feminist theory
and politics at one and the same time. In the case of a woman who is a
lesbian, several differences are obvious. To the extent that the dilemma
just depicted depends on sexual interaction with men, an experience
likely to create contradictory feelings as long as male/female relationships are structurally unequal, our "internal conundrum" does not
apply to a woman who is lesbian in the same way as to a heterosexual
woman. The woman who is heterosexual will suffer from the problem
most intensely, a problem that the lesbian does not face or no longer
encounters. Yet, unlike the heterosexual woman, a woman who is a
lesbian cannot avoid her own structural vulnerability to both sexist and
heterosexist biases; obviously, the latter prejudice affects gay men as
well. This is a significant difference between the two women, which
indeed necessitates feminist support, for a woman who is lesbian regularly feels compelled to devote time and energy to struggling with the
ramifications of two firmly established and overlapping forms of discrimination (and possibly more, since in many cases she will be working
class, poor, and/or a person of color as well).

But there are also simultaneous commonalities: these dual discriminations are intimately linked within a system that has traditionally legitimized only some forms of sexual association and behavior and not
others. After all, the problems of sexism and heterosexism are rooted in
an ancient history of relationships with men inside patriarchally organized societies. Without that history, and the problems it has posed past
and present, no need for feminism or feminisms would have arisen. This
is Judith Levine's point when, in *My Enemy, My Love: Man-Hating
and Ambivalence in Women's Lives* (a title Levine later changed),[15] she
describes a structured and structural contradictoriness, indeed an "internal conundrum," of contemporary gender politics. In Levine's words,
worth quoting at length because she does not limit their applicability
only to straight or lesbian or bisexual women, or only to Latina or
Asian or Caucasian women, or only to working class or wealthy
women:

> Feminists have been accused of hating men all along, and in some sense
> rightly. . . . Man hating isn't a function of feminism; it's a function of the
> *reasons* for feminism. Feminists did not invent man-hating. Women of all
> politics and circumstances carried these feelings into the 1970s and have
> lugged them around ever since. . . . If man-hating is mine, it belongs too to
> my next-door neighbor, my mother, and to the woman standing in front of
> me on line at the post office.
>
> . . . Now you can hate, but what do you do if you also love the hated
> person, need him emotionally, or depend on him materially, if you feel com-
> pelled to placate him or fearful to disturb him? A powerful unspoken theme
> of post–World War II feminism—and women's lives since feminism—is the
> struggle with the enormously disquieting ambivalence accompanying the
> fury of recognized oppression." [16]

In this important sense, the more the vestiges of still dominant patriarchal attitudes and controls are analyzed and dismantled, the more
women overall—and, whether or not directly recognized, surely all human beings, male and female—stand to gain. And, thus, the ability to
criticize what is a structurally rooted sense of ambivalence stemming
from ongoing sexist inequities is likely to be a sign, past and present, of
feminist strength. Conversely, defensiveness about criticizing the inequities structurally bequeathed to heterosexual relationships probably
arises in periods, like our own, during which feminist self-confidence
has been severely weakened and the political legitimacy of expressing
anger tends to become undermined.[17]

But further, not all women who are lesbian are necessarily simply
immune from ambivalent and contradictory feelings toward heterosexual relationships in any event. Here again, a basis for commonality between heterosexual and lesbian women coexists alongside a simultaneous reality of differences. Let us look at various ways, then, in which
the still unequal character of gendered intimacies in male-dominated
societies can create a range of more and less ambivalent reactions in
women across various situations and sexual orientations. Clearly, intimate associations with men inside families that are often still traditionally structured are not limited to women who are actually sleeping with
men as husbands and lovers: not all emotionally powerful relationships
are, or have been, sexual. In some cases, a woman who is a lesbian may
experience deeply ambivalent feelings toward her father, or brother, or
cousin, or childhood friend; later, she may feel intensely toward, perhaps, a business associate. Some relations may have been intense indeed, possibly abusive, but most are likely to have been rife with complex, conflicted feelings from past to present: perhaps love and

resentment, affection and rage. Moreover, in a study of lesbian (and bisexual) women, sociologist Paula Rust reports that although few lesbians questioned were currently involved in heterosexual relationships, 90 percent had been in the past; 44 percent of her lesbian respondents had been involved in serious relationships or marriages with men,[18] and many women were likely to have children from these marriages. For a bisexual woman, a range of possibilities similar and different apply. Again, the gendered conundrum relating to ambivalence may affect relationships with men from her childhood, but also (and thus, possibly, in a distinctively intensified way) as lovers or former lovers. In many cases, a woman who is bisexual may see her primary affiliation to women; in others, ambivalence may manifest itself through a rejection of necessarily dichotomized options.

For heterosexual women, who are most obviously affected by the structural character of ambivalence, degrees of comforts and oppressiveness experienced in relations with men alter from situation to situation, and frequently include both emotional *and* sexual intimacies. Once again, a range of differing experiences are likely to surface, linked by their relative combinations of advantages and disadvantages. At one extreme of this group of experiences exist good and even wonderful relationships between women and men, ones that many women would not think of renouncing. Inside such relationships, comforts outweigh any glimmers of oppressiveness. However, these glimmers may persist because of cultural and historical realities that make it common for a woman's male partner to still possess and occupy (in some respects, at least) the more privileged social position; or somehow the woman finds that, however sophisticated, she is still cast as the "caretaker" or mothering figure in the relationship. At the other extreme of heterosexual women's experiences are relationships in which oppressiveness clearly outweighs comfort. Again, perhaps a given male partner is abusive— emotionally, physically, or both—expressing anger in ways that range from painful to deadly. In such situations, arguments in favor of the woman's leaving are clearly well-founded.

Yet it is critical to emphasize that women in even the most hateful of relationships (where, say, battering takes place) are often convinced that such situations nevertheless contain "good" as well as "bad" aspects. A woman may yet ardently believe that the relationship's pain can be borne or forgotten because of the comforts she recollects from the past and changes she hopes for in the future. Thus, the battered woman is both very different from, but in another sense definitely related to, a woman in "healthier" situations. Both feel deep desires to adjust and to maintain connections (desires that obviously have been influenced by gender socialization itself). Different as they may seem, each heterosexual woman still confronts *some* combination of pleasures and inequities because of ongoing sexism in male-dominated societies like our own.

We can now clearly see that the memorable slogan of radical feminists, "the personal is political," had profound implications for defining the scope of gender. The distinctiveness of this slogan was not only that it forced conceptions of power beyond conventional borders, beyond distinctions between power's public and privatized manifestations. The feminist critique also raised the troubling possibility that the very *fulfillments* and *pleasures* of the personal could also be the *undoing* and *bane* of the political. Gender brought along with it both pleasures and dangers, a range of complex feelings that touch all women to some extent, though in significantly varying ways. Thus, gender posed a distinctive challenge indeed to any movement aimed at altering it.

But how was a collective movement to politically express this wide range of experiences? What strategy could possibly address (hoping to redress as well as encompass) *both* the reality and origins of the contradictions, of this ambivalence, and even (or especially) of the deep anxieties that such a dilemma was likely to cause? Certainly, it is hard to deny that such a conundrum did and does exist for large numbers of women. Life, not just theory, vividly attests to its influence. We may better illuminate this point by examining biographies of feminists involved in heterosexual relationships within clearly sexist contexts.

Take, for example, the life of one of the best-known feminists of all, Simone de Beauvoir, and her much-chronicled forty-year relationship with Jean-Paul Sartre. Clearly, it was Sartre who possessed far greater cultural capital and power in the French intellectual and academic world.[19] Biographers have detailed what amounted to blatantly sexist treatment and insensitivity to her feelings by the more self-confident Sartre; de Beauvoir suffered numerous intellectual injustices and intimate betrayals at the hands of her male partner. At the same time, there is no doubt that she saw the relationship as a conscious experiment in trying to push heterosexual intimacy toward greater equality.

But given the extent of inequity nonetheless, why didn't de Beauvoir break the tie, rather than keeping a strong connection alive until Sartre's dying day? In retrospect, it seems impossible to explain the power of that lifelong intimacy simply by reference to internalized sexism—in this case, of course, Sartre's sexism, without which *The Second Sex* might not have been so persuasively argued (paradoxically enough, Sartre's encouragement was also in part responsible for nudging into being de Beauvoir's magnum opus). Moreover, that we are speaking of the author of *The Second Sex* epitomizes the pointlessness of falling back on simply explaining oppression by "false consciousness" (as though if a woman only intellectually grasped the profound scope of sexism and its systemic effects, she would be able to readily transform her life and emotional reactions shortly thereafter).

I suspect that for de Beauvoir, however sexist Sartre was and could be, there were very genuine pleasures related to his company and to the familiarity of her multidimensional association with him. The balance of pleasures and inequities did not sufficiently tilt toward the latter end of the continuum for her to bear—or wish—to renounce the relationship completely. This seemed to be the case no matter how blatant its subordinating features. Somehow, de Beauvoir was unable to stand the thought of the loss, of sacrificing deeply familiar and intimately intellectual pleasures in the interests of avoiding concomitant pains, even if those pains were worsening.

Poignant compromises, then, are made and lived; indeed, they are to be expected. (This applies distinctively but not only to the case of gender.) Thus, problems may arise for social movements when people's need to live as best and comfortably as possible in the present—even while they may be pursuing some hoped-for future social transformations—is not *adequately anticipated and taken into account explicitly.* When individual martyrdom—or even unrealistic individual consistency—is expected, a collective price may come to be paid. For certainly de Beauvoir was not alone in her human response when faced with such difficulties, at once deeply personal and political. Analogous compromises face women now as then, across differences of sexual orientation and other social differences, and they are likely to continue to confront us so long as sexism remains alive and thriving.

Other examples, too, help bring the issue into clearer focus. Closer to home and to the present are women who seriously hesitate to use the term "feminist" when describing their own attitudes toward gender and interpersonal relationships. Not surprisingly, though with remarkable frequency, often the phrase "I am not a feminist, but . . ." is followed by a list of those aspects of the speaker's life that have nevertheless been strongly influenced by feminist perspectives (wanting a career, for instance, or being troubled about violence against women, or feeling angered at ongoing ramifications of sexual and sexist objectification of women's bodies). My sense is that an association between feminism and "hating men" is at the core of many women's anxieties about labeling oneself—and becoming labeled by others—a "feminist." Women seem to fear that anyone so branded will forever after be seen as necessarily "anti-men."

Yet year after year, in courses I have taught on feminist theory, many of the same students who shy away from calling themselves feminists respond quite viscerally to specifically radical feminist literature containing now decades-old analyses of families and other intimate heterosexual relationships. It is these texts that seem to strike them as most intriguing and provoking. Sometimes, students will comment on the vehemence of their own angry reactions, surprised at how quickly they begin to question whether what they read and learn somehow translates into "Does this mean I have to leave my boyfriend?"

My immediate response is to reassure such students, "of course not." To make a compelling intellectual and political analysis does not mean that it neatly translates into a clear or dogmatic program in terms of its psychic and lived ramifications. At one and the same time de Beauvoir was a feminist (even if she, too avoided the label at first) and lived in a world where the implications of that acknowledgment were often difficult. Moreover, most radical feminist theorists did not propose compelling women to leave their boyfriends. Though some feminists have advocated separatist or countercultural tactics, this portrait is greatly exaggerated in mainstream cultural depictions, contributing to a backlash against feminism in general and against radical feminism in particular.

But the most important response is that at its best, feminism points toward widening the options of women—of people—not toward closing them. Since I first read and was influenced by Simone de Beauvoir's *Second Sex*, my conviction was that feminism's dearest dream was its own obsolescence; ideally, one day, it would no longer be needed. Simultaneously, though, I have wished to ask my students another question in turn. No, of course, you don't have to leave your boyfriend if you don't wish to, but why can't you fulfill two of the needs you are expressing at once? Why not enjoy what you do about your relationship but, at the same time, participate in some way in building a feminism, and feminisms, that would render your nervous doubts irrelevant? For the greater the sense of support, confidence, and self-worth women can gain from strong feminist communities *outside* still structurally ambivalent relationships, the better their chances of feeling happier and more confident *inside* those relationships—and potentially protected from their imbalances. Only then could a concept like "choice" become genuinely applicable to most women's situations. Perhaps only such a two-pronged strategy can maintain the joys, and eventually diminish the chances of reproducing inequities. For, as we have seen, both joys and inequities coexist in many if not all heterosexual relationships, which normally partake of what Ellen Willis has brilliantly called mundane sexism, the "sexism of everyday life." [20]

But if we focus on the dilemma just identified, what indeed is an adequate response to the challenge it poses? How did radical feminism process the *strategic* ramifications of the *theoretical* problem just surveyed—that is, were the potential consequences of that dilemma seriously and systematically thought through? Thus, the question of whether analysis found satisfactory translation into politics as the movement moved from the 1960s and 1970s into the present has brought us back full circle to this chapter's opening query. Is it possible that this internal conundrum, arising from the character of gender itself, contributed to a tendency for sex and sexism to later split, as seen in the "sex debates" that emerged in the 1980s and 1990s? And, if so, how do we respond?

FROM THEORY TO STRATEGY: DIVERSE POSSIBILITIES

Looking back, we can see that incipient radical feminist theory was at its weakest in the realm of political strategy. Given the infancy of the movement, this is of course understandable: my intention here is not to blame radical feminism but to influence conceptions of the future by surveying the past. Yet it appears that the theorists of the 1960s and 1970s wrote little explicitly linking their insights to pragmatic steps; they devoted less attention to studying how feminist means could effect feminist ends and to answering now classic questions concerning what was to be done. Nor was it clear how controls exerted by law or within other largely male-dominated institutions could be fought against, or lived in without co-optation resulting, given the day-to-day practices and needs of individuals.

Thus, after radical feminism's initial creative explosiveness, little progress was made on a theory of individual agency, let alone on linkages between structures and agents. And, as gender studies and systematic feminist writings became increasingly academicized over the course of the 1980s and 1990s—a process that often necessitates the separation, rather than synthesis, of political and intellectual concerns—the chances of theoretical texts being written that were consciously *strategic* receded even further. Still, an internal conundrum was there. It existed, and persisted, even though radical feminism's innovativeness *in theory* was out of sync with the development of concomitant strategies *for practice*. Such disjunctures, and consequent omissions, clearly had serious ramifications.

For one, it became extremely easy to read into the void a series of conclusions that feminists may or may not have intended. At a minimum, confusion remained; questions were left to hang. It appears absurd for feminist theory to even mistakenly seem to demand that women "ought" simply to walk away from relationships of long standing or give up entirely on heterosexual relations. Such relationships often involved complex combinations of pleasures and dependencies; obviously, as feminist theorists themselves had quite astutely observed, gender wove intimate emotional ties into the same fabric with economic ones, and then again added other bonds—psychic, social, sensual, sexual. Where were women to go, if this interpretation was permitted to stand, giving a presumably generalizable directive, neither corrected nor explained; and did a life without men make much sense anyway—at least for some, for many, heterosexual or lesbian or bisexual women? And what about those women who would not choose to walk away, even if they could, even if they had places to go and the means to get there? (In fact, statistics on battering reveal both horrifying frequencies of occurrence and an abysmal lack of resources for women in abusive situations.) Were they to feel beyond the pale of feminism if they did not wish to leave—might they find themselves feeling as though in collusion, literally sleeping with the enemy?

Imagine that anything was, or had been, possible. And then, imagine that anything was, or had been, possible not only *in theory* but correspondingly *in strategy*. What *would* have been a satisfying translation into political terms of the anxiety-causing, because apparently self-contradictory, dilemma we now have identified? If in theory the problem diagnosed was two-sided, a political vision corresponding to it may have to be two-dimensional as well, in order to deal with two aspects of a problem that relate to but are not identical to each other: in this particular case, it may make good sense to concentrate on a dualistic strategy.

Certainly, one dimension of a proposed appropriate strategy would have to be *structurally oriented*. If indeed women have been in at least some senses a constructed and then structured "class," then the feminist movement must be concerned with how social, economic, and cultural resources are allocated and distributed in order to meet the meets of *all* women (see chapter 8). Therefore, on one level, a *collective movement presence* would be required to coordinate, articulate, and make public such needs in the larger world in and beyond feminism: to the media, to government, inside unions, and so on.

Moreover, demands aimed at procuring such structural changes need to consider *both* women's common requirements, as being in certain respects a class, *and* equally significant divergent needs that arise because of experiential differences among women (on the basis of varying economic class, race, and sexual orientation). Thus, such a collective movement strategy based on commonalities as well as differences would have to call—at this first level of a twofold strategy—for providing numerous entitlements, at once particularly feminist and universally social in character. Some likely demands would be for universally available child care; guaranteed incomes (at the least, restoring the minimal social protection against poverty provided until welfare was "reformed" in 1996); jobs for all; and the opening of the media and culture industries including, but not limited to, pornography, so that more power might be concentrated in women's hands (a categorical imperative whether or not women use this power toward feminist goals). Finally, common demands would have to include sexual and reproductive freedoms ranging from abortion to freedom from sterilization abuses, as well as insistent commitment to gay and lesbian rights. Even this inadequate wish list makes clear that basic rights and needs of *all* women are not even close to adequate realization (nor are the rights and needs of many men—again, see the discussion of this relationship with regard to gender and class in chapter 8).

One dimension of this potentially appropriate and effective strategy has to tap and to articulate *collective concerns,* because short of the solidarity gained by strength in vision and in numbers, feminists have little chance to realize social change. But, simultaneously, a strategy built around the distinctive dilemma of gender would also have to encourage and accept diversities in *agency*—the second dimension of my suggested twofold strategy.

This second and interrelated part of the feminist strategy would assume that indeed women's individual experiences (both in and outside of relationships with men, and including lesbian and bisexual orientations) vary greatly among women overall. Among heterosexual women, as already analyzed, such experiences range from those of the woman who feels more satisfied than dissatisfied with her intimate heterosexual relationship to those of a person unable to leave an abusive partner. (In the latter case, a movement capable of making *collective demands* could best ensure that diversities within *this* situation, too, were accounted for—that a woman desiring to depart an oppressive relationship was not prevented from doing so because material resources and social services were not available to her.) By recognizing diversity, this second dimension frees *individuals* from meeting specific demands and expectations, behavioral or psychological, to make a movement successful (after all, a collective movement would still exist and would provide a benchmark of success amid this individual diversity). For, expectations or no expectations, uniform outcomes are unlikely given the individual richness of human agency; such demands virtually set up a movement to fail. Nor are such demands desirable in any event. Potentially depriving individuals of *equally* needed freedoms to explore and grow on their own terms, they are likely to be experienced as antithetical to a genuinely loving and humane vision of personal and political transformation. Indeed, this partly explains why postmodern theorists separated themselves from perspectives and predecessors perceived in retrospect as stiflingly "modern." Modernist "metanarratives," whether Marxism or other post-Enlightenment worldviews, were felt to have become overly self-righteous, incapable of allowing for provisionality, contradictions, nonlinearity—for ebbs and flows of life far too complex to be captured in any totalizing schema.

Some persons, women as well as men, will wish to—and do—live out quite courageous personal and political visions even as these, too, vary in their individual self-definition. Other persons will not manage to challenge conventions, or may not wish to do so. But most germane to our concerns here is the immense potential benefit of a two-dimensional strategy in this particular instance: it allows *two political objectives to be accomplished at once.* For example, the feminist movement's overall sense of solidity need not depend on whether an individual woman likes and is aroused by pornography, or not; whether she loves women, or is attracted to persons of both sexes, or is heterosexual; whether she decides to undertake cosmetic surgery, or not; whether she enjoys sadomasochistic sexual practices, or not; or whether she is a "good feminist" if she is employed or enjoys being employed doing sex work, or not. To the contrary, diversity can be understood and democratically accepted at this second level of individual agency, where it seems neither surprising nor suspect. One need not concentrate energy on judging individuals politically; indeed, to do so is counterproductive and guilt-mongering. Moreover, anticipating such individual diversities of agency would not conflict with an overall political strategy so long as a collective movement is also present to deal with the structural character of gendered troubles, with their origins and effects overall.

Even when there are substantive debates, allowing for diversities in agency would not hinder activism. What individuals like or do not like about (say) pornography need not deflect attention from targeting the structure of sexism in the pornography industry per se. As interested as we may be in the pornography debate, the existence of a collective movement means that we can argue while at the same time challenging institutionally based power and raising questions of political economy. For instance, in this case of pornography, those on all sides of the debate might devote energy and be able to agree about the need to alter who holds the cultural power to create visions of sexuality as well as who benefits disproportionately from the profits of the industry. Analogously, individuals' attitudes and actions regarding cosmetic surgery would have little bearing on the more structural concern: a media industry that still overvalues only thin, young, and mostly white women's bodies, thereby contributing to much human unhappiness (on beauty, see chapter 4). Nor would the decision of an individual woman to engage in sex work deflect our attention toward merely *her* behaviors, *her* actions or inactions—we can continue to concentrate on changing the larger social and economic context that regularly leaves women with no real economic options that could render this decision a genuine choice.

In other words, *diversities of agency* are at once encompassed by and now become (relatively) irrelevant to the insistence on altering the *structural sources* of ongoing sexism. For such a two-dimensional strategy to emerge, however difficult and challenging, both commonalities and differences among women would have to be addressed. This would be a feminist *strategy* purposely aimed at the *theoretical* dilemma that emanates from gender's distinctiveness. But is it fair to put forth this suggestion as though it were novel? Clearly, collective solidarities have been asserted by the feminist movement in the course of its development, as well as by other American social movements. Why else would both Democratic and Republican candidates in the 1990s be anxiously seeking to benefit from a gender gap across categories, carefully noted by pollsters? Just as clearly, the feminist movement did not fall from the outpouring of theoretical creativity traced back to the late 1960s and 1970s into anything approximating an intellectual and political slumber. It has *not* been the case that feminism has been standing still, with no strategies at all forthcoming. On the contrary, feminism and feminisms have grown steadily and thrived. As I noted at the beginning of this chapter, it would be preposterous to assert either that feminism has changed the world enough *or* that feminism has changed nothing at all.

But this is not all that can, or should, be said. While interest in feminism and feminisms has continued, it is still *also* the case that structural changes of the magnitude sketched above have not come close to realization. No feminist movement acted collectively, for example, against the historic dismantling of welfare in 1996 and the huge costs to women (as well, of course, to children and men) of such a horrific abandoning of social responsibility. Nor have the structural roots of the sex debates altered much at all. Ongoing sexism, and continued concentration of socioeconomic power in male hands,[21] remains their contextual backdrop.

Thus even as liberal feminist politics have arguably become more culturally visible, and certainly have not been lost amid the conservative backlash, the more ambitious and radical visions of early feminism have stayed just that—visionary and unrealized dreams. To be sure, we must recognize that it was precisely a dismantling of *liberal feminist accomplishments* that was occurring through the Reagan-Bush years, when even so widely popular a gain as reproductive freedom began to be turned back. This gain was important for all women, so that there is good reason to agree with Zillah Eisenstein's argument in *The Radical Future of Liberal Feminism* (1981) that liberal feminist causes often involve an assertion of demands potentially beneficial to all women, whether or not this was liberal feminists' express intention.[22] Yet liberal feminist progress notwithstanding, we have *not* seen a more radical and collectively oriented movement blossom to assert the needs of all women—a movement dedicated to embracing commonalities *and* differences, understanding *both* the usefulness of some concept of "women as a class" and yet fully aware of the dangers of essentialism. In sum, then, it seems that we have not yet managed to translate the insights of early feminist theoretical observations into appropriate, humane, and far-sighted political strategies that also incorporate later developments.

But if in the past decades feminism has *neither* devised a two-dimensional strategy *nor* stopped growing and self-destructed, then what *did* actually happen? Perhaps our internal dilemma came to express itself in contemporary feminism in a less than fully conscious way: perhaps it manifested itself *through splitting.* Or so it appears, as we retrace a connection one last time between that dilemma, outside influences, and debates pitting "sex" versus "sexism" in the 1980s and 1990s.

SPLITTING AND BEYOND

For indeed, as we have already seen, with intriguing frequency a divide has separated those feminists who emphasize *sexual subordination* and those who emphasize *sexual pleasure,* leading each "side" to often antagonistic political stances on a range of substantive issues and debates—notably pornography, beauty, prostitution, sadomasochism, and violence against women. Moreover, the particular topics debated bring to mind the second fundamental concern that occupied the attention of feminist theorists in the late 1960s and 1970s: how male-dominated societies have maintained control over all aspects of women's lives by controlling sexuality and the body. Thus, the feminist split over *these particular issues*—all of which concern sexuality and the body—was not accidental, but was relevant to the heart of what is distinctive about gender subordination per se.

Still, we need to determine the relationship of our internal conundrum to this pattern of splitting on issue after issue of feminist concern. It is hard to believe that splitting represented a *conscious feminist strategy* to translate theory into political strategy, and there is no evidence of such deliberate division. Of course, it is no longer acceptable to blithely think in terms of one *feminism* rather than varied *feminisms,* a change that reflects increasing sophistication and healthy growth in this social movement. Furthermore, it has not been a negative but an extremely positive and hopeful sign that recent theorists have taken to heart criticisms about the need to incorporate considerations of difference into feminist thought more assiduously than in times before. (From the writings of bell hooks to Nancy Hartsock, Patricia Hill Collins to Iris Young, to cite only a few examples, race and class have quite effectively and aptly been co-emphasized in wide-ranging analyses that simultaneously highlight gender). Nor are feminists likely now to presume that there is only one acceptable position on any particular substantive issue. Debates on these issues are undoubtedly genuine, even as they are sometimes profoundly influenced by the personalities of those involved (e.g., Catharine MacKinnon's disinterest in publicly

debating other feminists has shaped the trajectory of the charged pornography debate).

Yet it seems difficult if not impossible to explain the *pattern* of the
divide solely by referring to substantive disagreements over any *one* issue or to clashes between particular individuals. Nor can the divide be
explained by any one factor alone rather than by a combination to
which this next can be added. For perhaps referencing a kind of *social*
or *sociological unconscious* may help answer the question at the core
of this book, "Why splitting?" What happens if we seek an explanation
of our dilemma not only in chapter 1's cultural and historical factors
but also partly in the more sociopsychological conundrum just surveyed? Feminist history and tradition apart, is it possible that psychoanalytic theory can shed even further light on the subject? In the object
relations tradition of psychoanalysis, some interpret "splitting" as a defense mechanism that becomes operative "in order to separate two currents of strong feelings and urges when these currents would arouse
anxiety if experienced simultaneously toward an object." It is when that
object becomes "the target of intolerable ambivalent trends that its representation is split."[23] Such processes and representations frequently
take place on an individual level: the child who separates "bad" from
"good" impulses; the man who categorizes all women as either "madonnas" or "whores" (apparently unable to tolerate what he sees as
good and bad in the same person). But isn't it possible that similar motivations contribute to similar reactions once individuals are part of
groups as well—specifically, inside social movements?

Indeed, if we substitute the ambivalent character of intimate relations with men in male-dominated societies, as first analyzed in radical
feminist theory, for the word "object" above, we find ourselves with yet
another provocative explanation of why *splitting* was the translation
from theory into strategy. Let us assume that the feminist movement
was not able to find a way to consciously translate psychic experiences
of structured ambivalence into appropriate political language and strategy: that is, language and strategy reflecting the ways that many intimate heterosexual relationships at once encompass experiences of inequities *and* comforts, indignities *and* intimacies, good *and* bad. Again,
these relationships may be emotional, sexual, or both. And assume that
early feminist depictions of patriarchal societies were experienced as
potentially overwhelming and intimidating, even and especially if in
many respects such analyses rang true. Indeed, it would be surprising if

that critique did *not* strike many women as devastating, as so world shattering that individuals might recoil and desire to rebel against it. This reaction might occur to some extent across women's different sexual orientations, again a point that in no way negates the simultaneous significance of such differences. Because of the two-sidedness of relationships between men and women, the feminist critique was likely to have generated enormous *anxiety* about its own object of change—patriarchal society—an anxiety that is at once individual and collective.

If individuals feel such strains, perhaps the social movements in which they participate may *manifest* the dilemma—one could even say "act it out"—by splitting into sides, and into two sides at that. One of these sides might come to emphasize the ongoing legacy of inequities within male-dominated societies (the *sexual subordination* side, taking up structural critiques and concentrating less or not at all on actual sexual expression), the other emphasizing a set of comforts possible even in a sexist present (the *sexual pleasure* side, rebellious against any feminism that would forge another set of sexually repressive behavioral criteria for women, yet concentrating less or not at all on downplaying structural critiques of patriarchy).

Yet, clearly, problems theoretical *and* political would be attached to such a split, insofar as our gender dilemma itself contains both of these sides: the costs might be high. If those on the sexual subordination side kept their vision mostly fixed on the structural enormity of patriarchy, their theories and practices might not be able to capture and express the pleasures and comforts that also characterize many women's experiences (both sexually and emotionally, and across diverse sexual orientations). Conversely, if those on the sexual pleasure side focused mostly on the sexual repressiveness of patriarchy (and of other feminists) in denying women's rights to freedoms and comforts, they risked losing sight of the simultaneously structural character of women's subordination as it affects all women. It was by no means necessary or inevitable that such a splitting process *had* to occur; it was rather one of several possibilities that *might* have unfolded (another being the potentially preferable two-level strategy outlined above).

But we are still left with the question of why events seem to have followed the pattern of a recurrent divide. To answer it, we must go back to review where we began, wary of misleading separations between "outside" and "internal" factors that affect *both* social movements and individuals, individuals and social movements. If we are to understand why splitting rather than a different outcome occurred, we must consider both feminists' own reactions and how those reactions were affected by the larger U.S. social context.

For certainly, the outside world did not passively acquiesce to early feminist critiques with their elaboration of huge social and psychic changes required if gender biases were to be uprooted from nearly all facets of the social world (the cultural to the political, the sexual to the economic). As discussed in chapter 1, Susan Faludi's *Backlash* (1991) became deservedly famous for documenting the rich, multifaceted character not of feminist actions but of *antifeminist* reactions in the 1980s and 1990s. Social conservatism began to flourish; as we have seen, conservatives became and remain preoccupied with the loss of "family values"; gays and lesbians were seen as threatening; Hillary Rodham Clinton was called a "radical feminist," serving to further stigmatize this branch of feminism while also quite inaccurately describing her views, which are much more characteristic of liberal feminism. The breadth and depth of reaction were a paradoxical confirmation of feminism's power, yet hardly welcome: feminists now had to deal with both the global character of gender biases generally and a well-funded and extensive social movement whose agenda more specifically included derailing *it*.

Consequently, what was already daunting was rendered more overwhelming, while the possibilities of radical feminists immediately achieving their goals or even finding short-term gratifications were slim. In such a predicament it would be psychologically seductive—and indeed, as chapter 1 suggests, a reaction quite characteristic of many radical social movements (certainly the American Left illustrates this tendency)—if resultant angers became redirected, subtly and perhaps not consciously, from without to within. As we have seen, such a channeling of anger has certain pleasures, understandable though often counterproductive. Directing anger toward those near one's own social movement is usually less risky, and not as disruptive to one's day-to-day life, as constant engagement with an especially hostile outer world. Yet, to the degree that a movement targets internal antagonists even more energetically than those outside, its chances of actually possessing power recede. And it is actual possession of power that can lead to unanticipated role reversals, to disconcerting discoveries that "we" must now make messy, complicated, and seemingly quite "impure" political decisions. Finally, there are pleasures in finding allies against the internal antagonists, who make possible a sense of recognition and relative success in defining oneself against that "other" side. It may be much easier to achieve, and to maintain, such relative success and recognition than to achieve the movement's larger goals in the outside world.

And if we recall that either/or modes of thought (say, counterposing gender against race, or race against class) have likewise characterized American culture more generally, then these psychic seductions of splitting are even easier to understand: they may become married to our also sometimes unwitting intellectual habits. For it is customary for us to think in divided ways; it is dualisms that are most familiar, not the more complex and synthesis-oriented ways of conceiving the world to which feminist theory has consciously committed itself by now. Moreover, given the added influence of postmodernist thought in the 1980s and 1990s (an influence that happily encouraged respect for pluralism and diversity, if tending to underplay the ongoing and simultaneous importance of commonalities), it is hardly surprising that psychic and intellectual factors slowly but surely began to intertwine and overlap with one another.

Perhaps I need to emphasize one last time that this interpretation of splitting and its seductions in no way denies the *also* autonomous merits of substantive debates, nor the importance simply of principles in fueling unbridgeable disputes between individuals within social movements. But it does suggest that such debates and disputes are not sufficient to explain the strikingly fragmented history of radical movements in the United States, including but not only feminism. And it also suggests that the psychoanalytic concept of splitting may be highly relevant both to feminism and to other U.S. social movements. Perhaps J. Edgar Hoover knew this when, under his long tutelage of the FBI, he quite self-consciously fomented and directly encouraged fragmentation and dissensions: *collective movements* are immensely more powerful when united than when divided.[24] This may be an insight as old as it is elusive in practice.

But finally, a movement's collective presence will only be satisfactory so long as individuals' inner diversities are *also* and *simultaneously* respected and recognized. It would be difficult to overemphasize this challenge to feminism(s) of a focus on doing several things at once. On the one hand, if *only* or *predominantly* structural impediments are emphasized by feminist movement(s), individuals are likely to lack any sense of how they can survive within a male-dominated society's still massively problematic confines (this point also applies to the U.S. Left, within the confines of a capitalist society, and to antiracist politics, within the confines of a still largely racist America). Individual women, as well as men, may indeed feel loathe to renounce whatever comforts, pleasures, recognitions, or sense of personal community they have—however small. Thus, on this side, unless critiques aimed at structural changes consciously leave room for individual contradictions, feminism (like other social movements) *finds itself potentially subject to reactionary backlashes even from within.*

On the other hand, if such individual latitude is incorporated at the price of challenging the larger society, still organized patriarchally (as though considerations of agency are necessarily opposed to those of structure), feminism(s) will again lose. Indeed, the influence of radical feminist analyses of male-dominated societies and their characteristic modes of exerting control grew precisely, and exponentially, because they provided basic ideas that resonated at the level of women as a class. These ideas engaged differing groups *because* they pointed to something common which aligned us all.

Severe political liabilities predictably ensue, then, if *either* in focusing on structure we overlook agency *or* in paying attention to agency we fail to emphasize institutionally structured inequalities. *Both* levels need to be incorporated, and their complex relationship further investigated, if feminism or feminisms are to build, rather than dilute, potential power as a social movement. Moreover, if lasting changes unfold step by step, in a dialectically shaped fashion (as they seem to, pressing two steps forward, and then pulling one step back), this too is a powerful argument that feminisms need to exist on two levels at once. Social movements can then remain *simultaneously* aware of immediate and far-reaching concerns, rather than swinging back and forth reactively between them, in order to maintain historical perspective in the short as well as the longer run.

For how else can we be confident that contemporary interest in issues of agency (which in the 1980s and 1990s indeed have seemed to enjoy relatively greater popularity, perhaps taking the upper hand) is not permeated, and overdetermined in its origins, by a sense of defeat? Is the focus on agency really itself "chosen" freely, or has it resulted in part from feelings of being overwhelmed? How can we make certain that in the process of humanely attending to our own psychic health—supporting individual efforts to live happily in the immediate if imperfect present, and our desires to find comforts and satisfactions *now* rather than only awaiting uncertain and distant pleasures in the future—we will not unwittingly contribute to male-dominated structures of power remaining largely unaltered?

Without explicitly and constantly following a different strategy to confront a particularly complex mode of dominance and subordination, feminists may find ourselves caught in similar struggles again and again. And what radical feminists once dubbed "patriarchy" may remain alive and kicking, while the term "feminism" itself stays insidiously demonized. On the other hand, if feminists possess deliberately thought-out theories as well as strategies, other outcomes become possible—even probable. A commitment to maintaining a multifaceted vision, beyond either/or considerations, may revive earlier ambitions. For then a new wave of feminism is best equipped to pick up where the second wave, with its high expectations, was interrupted and thrown onto the defensive. A third wave has already begun: let us help it take back not only the night but the powerful promise of a movement that can be both solidly diverse and diversely solidified.

PART TWO

Five Case Examples

CHAPTER THREE

Feminist Offensives

Beyond Defending Pornography

In high school in the early 1970s I often felt schizophrenically gendered. During the week, I wore glasses with walnut-colored frames and kept my hair in a severe bun while getting As in math and editing the school newspaper with all the assertiveness of which I was capable. In suburban New Jersey my cowriters and I took what even in those years were iconoclastic positions in favor of "women's liberation" and against war and racism. I was thrilled to read Simone de Beauvoir, Kate Millett, Shulamith Firestone, and Anne Koedt, all the while fearing that the movement would be effectively over by the time I could participate. On the weekends, rebelliously but rather guiltily, I shook out my hair and dressed up in short skirts with plenty of makeup, hoping to "make out" with boys at local parties and dances. These two facets of my adolescent persona cohabited, although not very happily; neither was entirely at ease with the other. A more comfortable coexistence would have required knowing that a woman can feel both forceful and sexual. It would have meant believing that commitment to radical feminism had no cost, and that my dreams of social change could include both my desire to be desired and my will to get beyond typical relationships of dominance and subordination.

But I did not believe those two "sides" could make peace—not then. Now, in a supposedly Madonna-certified and postfeminist age (or post–victim feminism, as Naomi Wolf's *Fire with Fire* maddeningly insists the present juncture ought be designated), I *am* sure that underlying problems symbolized by that gendered schizophrenia are not close to being solved. To challenge sexism and feel sexually free still calls for assiduous negotiations, and often unsatisfactory compromises; many women seem unable to realize a comfortable combination. Through the 1980s and 1990s, the years of Faludi-esque "backlash," it has remained difficult to struggle against sexism while simultaneously embracing sexuality as a crucial dimension of being-in-the-world. Yet, for feminism to meet the challenge posed by this ongoing dilemma, both facets of many women's experiences will have to be recognized.

FRAMING THE PROBLEM

This may seem an odd beginning to a discussion ostensibly about pornography, one that takes its inspiration from the publication of New York State ACLU President Nadine Strossen's well-written and thorough *Defending Pornography: Free Speech, Sex, and the Fight for Women's Rights* (1995), an excellent updating of pornography's controversial legal career.[1] But there is an important sense in which the persistence of a chasm that separates the acts of confronting sexism and liberating sexuality is highly relevant, as will become clear as we consider *Defending Pornography* within a wider framework of contemporary feminist politics.

As Strossen describes, incorporating a good deal of such contextualization herself, since the late 1970s—an era punctuated by now well-known events such as Barnard College's 1982 Scholar and the Feminist Conference, "Towards a Politics of Sexuality"[2] —the feminist movement has splintered over a range of sex-related issues. In the shorthand descriptions embraced by the media, these divisions have sometimes been called feminist "sex debates" or "sex wars," reductive formulations whose exaggerations or too-neat oppositions obscure what may be better described as differences in *relative emphases*. Many feminists who believe that some pornography should be illegal would certainly not characterize themselves (even if others would) as "anti-sex"; many feminists placed in a "pro-sex" camp do not simply celebrate pornography (even if they are against its legal restriction), nor are they blind to or unconcerned about the pervasiveness of sexism.

Nonetheless, in several respects, the sex debates do indeed reflect discrete splits *within* feminism. For one thing, when it comes to disagreements about pornography (or, to take another instance, about decriminalizing prostitution), unambiguous "sides" are bound to develop since either regulation or deregulation by the state is demanded: one is forced to take a stand. When either/or opinions—are we pro- or anti-pornography, for or against legalizing sex work?—are necessarily called forth in a particularly clear-cut *legal* sense, there is little theoretical or political encouragement to develop subtler positions not so easily reflected in such stark oppositions. In this sense, then, the two groups to which Strossen steadily refers—sometimes as the "procensorship" and "anticensorship" feminists, sometimes as parties holding "anti-sex" or "pro-sex" positions (often I had to pause to recall who was who, and which was which)—are more than merely creations of a media unconcerned or ignorant about nuances of feminism.

Drawing on Strossen's terminology (though it, too, tends to be overly reductive),[3] we find on the one hand a *procensorship* faction, familiarly personified in Catharine MacKinnon and Andrea Dworkin and earlier associated with the group Women Against Pornography (WAP). These feminists have tended to emphasize the Leviathan-like characteristics of patriarchy, particularly sexism and its alleged objectification in pornography. At the same time, however, they have left the ambiguities of sexual existence—of women's needs for and rights to desire and pleasure in the present, not only in some utopian future whose arrival cannot be guaranteed—comparatively underexplored and underemphasized. This is the side that might have indeed adjudged my youthful miniskirted activities potentially traitorous to feminist principles; even today, a woman who enjoys pornography, or claims work within the sex industry as a legitimate occupation, may be perceived as betraying her feminist beliefs.

Moreover, this side is prone to underrate both the costs of sexual repressiveness, once the state intervenes to restrict pornography, and the human risks of strict judgmentalism and unquestionable dogmatisms. In sexuality as in other areas, there are problems created simply by the abjuring of flexibility, and even by the potential loss of a sense of the absurd. Once certain sensibilities are jeopardized, at some definite but hard-to-pinpoint moment, movements that originated *against* authoritarian structures paradoxically may begin to resemble their former nemeses. Think, as Strossen in *Defending Pornography* and Ellen Willis much earlier have both observed, of the ironically "strange bedfellows" encountered by MacKinnon and Dworkin as they found themselves allied with otherwise utterly antithetical traditionalists in the interests of

illegalizing pornography.[4] Such alliances happened first in the United
States with the Meese Commission and others hoping to restrict pornography because of the threat it supposedly posed to dominant "family values." They have recurred more recently in Canada, where local
authorities have used MacKinnon-inspired antipornography rulings to
harass gay and lesbian publications that neither she nor Dworkin had
the slightest intention of prohibiting.

On the other hand, we also find an *anticensorship* perspective. This
position has been associated with the Feminist Anti-Censorship Taskforce (FACT), formed to argue that antipornography ordinances passed
in Minneapolis and Indianapolis in the early 1980s were unconstitu-
tional. Carol Vance, Ann Snitow, and Ellen Willis are among the feminist writers and thinkers linked with this side, which stresses civil liberties. This is Strossen's starting point as well, with which she associates
(through quotations) other recent highly publicized books about feminism, including those by Katie Roiphe and Naomi Wolf.[5] Not surprisingly, the relative emphases here are reversed from those of the procensorship faction: there is no problem with asserting sexual freedom,
rights to expression and pleasure, diversity and ambiguities. Rather, on
this side of the not-altogether-spurious political divide sexuality is discussed much more optimistically, less repressively, and with a focus
more on exploration than judgment.

However, these feminists tend not to stress or explain why and how
large numbers of women (though certainly not all) often do feel tremendously alienated by pornography as we know it. Nor does their attention linger on the connections, at once ideological and massively economic, between pornography and the still largely male-dominated
businesses that control and profit from the multifaceted, multinational
sex industry (which links sex, not merely knowledge, with power in
a decidedly Foucaultian fashion). One figure Strossen and others have
quoted, and which has been corroborated by the Justice Department,
estimates the pornography business to be a $10 billion annual enter-
prise.[6] In 1989 Americans bought more than 9 million copies of *Playboy, Penthouse,* and *Hustler* each *month;* more than 400 million X-
rated videos are rented each year, and adult video sales and rentals have
increased 75 percent between 1991 and 1993 in general-interest video
stores alone.[7] Thus, the patriarchally controlled *institutionalization* of
pornography, still largely in place at an overarching, macrocosmic level,
makes a mockery of the assumption that individual men and women
can watch a film—in public or private—*simply* from positions of equiv-

alency, as liberal philosophy insists. It is highly unlikely that sexuality can be explored equally and nonproblematically in a world that remains pervaded by psychological, sexual, and socioeconomic differentials according to gender.

This side would also be *less* apt to emphasize how I, as a dressed-up teenager—hoping both to be desired and to desire—was more likely in her wanderings to encounter relationships that objectified her than ones that fostered mutual recognition, in and beyond sex.[8] Such a teenager now as well as then might also experience eroticism as intimidating, as often haunted by a sense of violence and the coercive; moreover, she might learn to fear loss of conventional heterosexual attractiveness as she aged, because only one type of youthful body is valued in virtually *all* commercial imagery (from *Cosmopolitan* to *Penthouse,* Hollywood to pornography). All these reactions and lessons relate to a discriminatory leviathan indeed. However, this side has been less likely to dwell on institutional factors that militate against women's sexuality being experienced with full freedom and without feelings of fear. Thus these feminists have been less likely to insist on the need for the transformations of *social structures* (and on attendant psychological changes) required to profoundly affect the legacies of the past *at the very same time* that we attempt to seize what pleasures can be taken in the margins and the niches now. While forums have been held at which feelings about desire, sex, and pleasure are discussed, relatively speaking, this side has not provided many outlets in recent years for the expression of anger at the persistence of sex*ism* and the all-too-frequent problems of still male-dominated societies. This is itself a relatively new development. In the 1970s, consciousness-raising groups, a form of small-scale organization critical to feminism's ascendancy as a political movement that stressed expression of a range of emotions, were not associated with any particular "side."

Broadly speaking, these relative emphases, which continue to separate feminist considerations of sex from sexism for reasons and in ways not altogether attributable to external factors, provide the context for Strossen's *Defending Pornography.* In this framing, though, I am by no means trying to avoid taking a position about restricting pornography myself. For I quite agree with Strossen's stance, as will soon become apparent: it is foolhardy at best, and dangerous at worst, to restrict First Amendment liberties and women's sexual prerogatives through vague definitions and censorship of pornography. But even if Strossen succeeds in presenting the issue persuasively both in *principle* and *law,* other *theoretical* and *political* questions about pornography's relationship to feminism remain unsettled and unsettling. Other queries need be posed: for one, how serious are the debates, the relative divides, sketched above? Do they indeed affect, largely or at all, whether feminism(s) can move beyond the defensive and worsening impasse of much of the 1980s and 1990s? Moreover, as some feminists have suggested, it may be absurd and inappropriate to be bothering now with sex debates at all. At a time when poor and minority women are being slashed from welfare rolls, continuing to dwell on sex can seem not only tiresome but insensitive, a sign of a movement devoid of a sense of proportion, still centered only on the pressing needs of those women who can afford—literally as well as figuratively—the intricacies of feminist debates turned inward.

There is a final important point to be considered. While I oppose legal ordinances outlawing certain forms of pornography, I also believe that separating sex from sexism diminishes feminism's continuing effectiveness, its confidence, its ability to project collective strength and purpose from an *offensive* rather than chronically *defensive* posture. Either/or dichotomies need not extend beyond questions of law: one can be both against restrictive censorship and just as passionately in favor of transcending the subtle legacies of male-dominated societies; one can, as a feminist, accord crucial importance to issues both outside and inside the realms of sexuality. With regard to this last supposed antithesis, feminist thought and practices need neither obsess about nor abjure sexuality. But to foreclose the topic entirely, rather than to improve our understanding of how it fits within the larger parameters of a movement, would also entail a loss of collective memory, forcing us to forget how certain prophetic ideas—such as sexual politics—have played a critical role in feminism's partial resonance across class and race over the course of its recent history.

With these thoughts in mind, I have divided the following remarks into three brief sections. I first review Strossen's contribution in *Defending Pornography;* this part treats her book as a thesis before moving in the second section toward an antithesis, namely, the question of *why* MacKinnon and Dworkin have continued to garner support despite the logical arguments of the anticensorship arguments. Third, and finally, I consider how and whether it might be possible to move beyond what is ultimately a self-defeating and much too dichotomized situation for feminists of all persuasions, ages, and backgrounds. MacKinnon and

Dworkin—along with the issues they favor and the positions they adopt—have become too exclusively connected with the vestiges of *radical feminism* from the 1960s and 1970s. Yet, ironically, their anticensorship position may restrict rather than expand that early brand of feminism's initial promises and wide-reaching goals—promises and goals that must be revitalized if any third wave of feminism is to be forthcoming.

THE STRENGTHS OF STROSSEN'S ARGUMENTS: A THESIS

In 1988 I wrote an essay reconsidering the pornography debates after attending an April 1987 conference at New York University, "Sexual Liberals and the Attack on Radical Feminism." The conference had been disturbing: several of its featured speakers, from the procensorship side, denounced those "other" feminists who allegedly colluded with patriarchy by failing to join the campaign against pornography. These feminists were portrayed as traitorous "sexual liberals" who had played into the "enemy's" hands by criticizing aspects of earlier radical feminist practices at the Barnard conference of 1982, thereby dividing the movement. By virtue of their pro-sex position and protest against the illegalization of pornography, the women in FACT as well as certain individuals (Ellen Willis was cited by name) had somehow become seen as *pro*pornography, and indeed propatriarchy. This "reasoning" reached its nadir when Catharine MacKinnon referred to Willis and others as the "Uncle Toms of the movement."[9]

While these intolerant and, ironically, highly divisive comments were troubling enough in themselves, they were also troubling as an argument, for they failed to address at least three cogent "anticensorship" points.[10] The first is the potential abridgment of *civil liberties*: the dangers to First Amendment rights if certain sexual images are censored according to the vague criteria of the proposed ordinances. The second, which draws on Willis's earlier arguments, is a dilemma of *sexual repression*.[11] Even if one grants that pornography frequently contains conventionally sexist images, it remains an overdetermined form. For it also contains imagery arguably freeing in effects, especially since it is generally socially taboo to express and acknowledge sexual feelings: how, then, could antipornography ordinances manage to avoid reinforcing a tradition-bound sexual repressiveness, which has often hurt women? The third is the danger of focusing on a *single issue;* fighting pornography by itself is no panacea for transforming power relations, which are far more multifaceted and complex in their origins.[12]

These critiques from the anticensorship side were hardly new in 1995; indeed, they had long been in circulation by 1987 and 1988, when it might well have appeared to an outside observer that the arguments had put the pornography issue to rest—at minimum, again, in a *legal* sense. As Strossen notes, Dworkin and MacKinnon had drafted their model antipornography law in 1983, when it was adopted twice by the Minneapolis City Council and vetoed both times by then-Mayor Donald Fraser. In 1984 the ordinance was enacted in Indianapolis, only to be quickly struck down in the courts in *American Booksellers Association v. Hudnut,* which was affirmed by the Supreme Court in 1986.[13] Moreover, there was certainly additional irony in the key role played by conservative Republican politicians and right-wing groups (opposed to women's rights in the past) in winning passage of the Indianapolis ordinance. MacKinnon had claimed that the sexual liberal side was stacked with those working against feminist causes, but clearly the accusation could be turned back on her.[14]

Yet as late as 1995, when *Defending Pornography* was published, Strossen does *not* perceive herself as writing about a debate long resolved and past. Quite the contrary. To MacKinnon, the *Hudnut* decision was "the *Dred Scott* of the women's movement" and Strossen describes how it energized her side: "Just as the Supreme Court's 1973 abortion rights ruling in *Roe v. Wade* galvanized the antiabortion movement, so the Court's 1986 ruling in the Indianapolis case motivated the feminist antipornography faction. For the time stymied in the courts, the procensorship feminists redoubled their efforts in other forums."[15] Even following *Hudnut*'s affirmation by the Supreme Court, laws based on the proposed model ordinance were considered in a variety of locations throughout the United States, from Bellingham, Washington, to Cambridge, Massachusetts, and Suffolk County, New York. In 1992 the Senate Judiciary Committee approved the Pornography Victims' Compensation Act, which would have allowed suits against pornographers for alleged damages caused, though it never passed the full Senate. That same year and perhaps most momentously, the Canadian Supreme Court in *Butler v. the Queen*—apparently influenced by a brief MacKinnon coauthored—incorporated the antipornography restrictions written by Dworkin and MacKinnon almost ten years earlier into Canadian obscenity law.[16]

It was as though the issue simply refused to die; obviously, its proponents were far from giving up. Ironically, those fighting pornography
drew continuing strength not only from their desire to surmount legal
defeats, as Strossen suggests, but also from the growing conservatism
of the environment. Rather perversely, the more reactive the cultural
climate was becoming, the likelier it was that some people were swelling
local antipornography campaigns because of their outrage over sexual
promiscuity, not their concern about sexism's ubiquity. In consequence
it was still necessary to "defend pornography," and Strossen proceeds
to do so in an admirably exhaustive fashion. In readable, lucid prose,
Strossen effectively re-presents the cited trio of themes; she expounds
and expands upon them with such care and determination that it is hard
to imagine many anticensorship arguments that were not offered by the
book's denouement.

I can best illustrate Strossen's thoroughness by briefly presenting a
few of her characterizations, as they parallel and embellish those antior-
dinance considerations already mentioned.

Preservation of General Freedoms   This argument, which corresponds to the fear of abridging civil rights, similarly subsumes the pornography issue within the larger context of general First Amendment
rights and freedoms. The now-familiar argument proceeds as follows:
adoption of the antipornography ordinance is likely to incur negative
consequences for social movements *generally* (and thus, of course, for
the women's movement as well) by placing restrictions on *generic* individuals. If one were to restrict sexually explicit speech because of its
sexism, Strossen asks, why "shouldn't we restrict non-sexually explicit
speech" as well? [17]

But there is a related philosophical argument that is perhaps even
more serious. The Supreme Court has ruled that censorship is only justified when a direct causal link can be shown between speech and harm.
However, such causality can be admitted in the case of pornography
only if we accept a decidedly vulgar view of human beings, a deterministic perspective that leaves little room for the possibility of change. Such
existential possibilities arise in what Jean-Paul Sartre in *Being and
Nothingness* (1943) calls a "nothingness" intervening between ideologies to which we have been exposed and our responses. [18] Sexist words
and images—like ideology in general—can thus strongly influence, but
not strictly speaking determine, our reactions. If not for such "nothingnesses" separating the ideas to which we have been exposed from our

reactions, how could feminism or other movements promoting radical social change come about at all? Yet modern positivistic social "science," in its most conservative quantitative guise, seeks to avoid all such questions of indeterminateness by treating the actions of human beings as though they were indeed determined and totally predictable. Unwittingly, then, MacKinnon enters this positivistic social scientific terrain— which, feminist philosophers of science would argue, has also been used to women's detriment—by engaging in a protracted argument about the statistical validity of figures correlating rape and pornography; the deeper question of whether such cause-and-effect relationships are ever definitive is thereby bracketed, presumed to be irrelevant.

Once again, it does not appear logical to accuse anticensorship types of being "patriarchal," as though procensorship types thereby emerge unambiguously profeminist by contrast. Furthermore, Strossen predicts a series of deleterious and antifeminist *effects*—regardless of *intentions*—that are likely to occur should the latter's goals be realized:

> If MacDworkinism should prevail in the courts, it would jeopardize all of the foregoing free speech precedents and principles. The government could outlaw flag burning and the teaching of Marxist doctrine because they might lead to the erosion of patriotism and our capitalist system; white supremacist and black nationalist speeches could be criminalized because they might lead to racial segregation; peaceful demonstrations for (or against) civil rights, women's rights, gay rights, and, indeed, any other potential controversial causes could be banned because they might provoke violent counter-demonstrations. . . . [F]eminist expression could be stifled because it might threaten "traditional family values" and the attendant domestic order and tranquillity; abortion clinic advertising and other prochoice expression could be suppressed because it might lead to the termination of potential life; indeed, feminist antipornography advocacy could itself be suppressed because it could endanger cherished constitutional rights![19]

The argument seems, on its face, to be a strong one. But Strossen's case does not rest there.

Threats to Women's Freedom, Particularly Sexual Freedom   This argument, which broadly corresponds with the dilemma of sexual repression, similarly shifts consideration toward the particular risks that antipornography legislation poses for women. Strossen paints a history of censorship having been used in fact, rather than hypothetically, against women; whenever and wherever enacted, such state-imposed restrictions have also impeded struggles to attain equality and reproductive rights. From the time of the Comstock Laws of the 1870s, through the legal harassment of Margaret Sanger, to charges brought against Emma Goldman for providing information on birth control, Strossen argues, banning written and visual materials concerning sexuality has resulted in the restriction rather than expansion of women's options.[20]

And there is indeed reason for concern that antipornography restrictions, in the name of overcoming women's subordination, will be used to tighten sexual repression. Strossen takes pains to note that while civil liberties in the United States are in general strictly insisted upon, they have been most readily abridged in matters related to sex—that is, in the arena of obscenity law, which specifies permissible exceptions to First Amendment protections. Under such laws, charges have frequently been brought against works by gay, lesbian, and minority artists; Two Live Crew has been prosecuted for rap lyrics, and the Cleveland Art Museum for exhibiting works by Robert Mapplethorpe involving homoerotica and depictions of sadomasochism.[21]

But perhaps the common element in all of these points is that by the criteria of MacKinnon and Dworkin's proposed ordinances, *their own work, images, and efforts to change sexist ideology face censorship.* Thus, the legality of pornography needs to be protected to preserve the very rights that have allowed MacKinnon and Dworkin's views to be expressed.

Paradoxical and Self-Defeating Effects   This argument roughly corresponds to the problem of focusing on a single issue, insofar as it too questions whether targeting pornography *alone* could create benefits that outweigh these other problems, both predicted and actual. But why would regulating pornography necessarily contribute to weakening a still male-dominated society, rather than strengthening the hand of a state that feminists cannot control? And of course, the prospect of some feminists gaining a measure of control poses other problems—for surely other feminists would disagree with their actions. Strossen describes how antipornography restrictions adopted by Canada have been misused by that government: the new regulations are hardly undermining sexually discriminatory controls. Since 1992, in the first few years after *Butler,* over half of Canada's feminist bookstores have had materials confiscated or detained by customs; most of the literature targeted for restriction have been gay, lesbian, and women's literature. Inland Books, a New York–based company that is the largest U.S. exporter of lesbian and gay literature to Canada, had 73 percent of its shipments detained in 1993. Moreover, with a certain poetic justice (or, more aptly, injustice), that most ironic of the ordinance's potential ramifications actually materialized: two books written by Dworkin herself—*Pornography: Men Possessing Women* and *Woman Hating*—were stopped at the U.S.-Canada border because of obscene pornographic descriptions they were alleged to contain.[22]

By this point, the argument seems overwhelming. Yet there is more to be said, and Strossen continues: for the preceding paragraph implies that the desired antipatriarchal effects could have been achieved if only the intended texts (say, misogynist works like Bret Ellis Easton's *American Psycho*) had been seized rather than unintended ones (publications like Dworkin's *Woman Hating*). Let's say for argument's sake, then, that the antipornography ordinances could be ideally interpreted from a profeminist, antipatriarchal perspective; let's say that all *American Psychos* and no works of feminist theory or lesbian/gay eroticism are restricted. But once the censoring of pornographic images has been perfected, what about those of violence in commercial representations outside pornography, many of which regularly feature the injuring, raping, maiming, or killing of women? What about, say, commercial films (from *Basic Instinct* to *Pretty Woman*) and magazines (from *Glamour* to *Essence*) and music (from the Rolling Stones to Public Enemy) that depict women discriminatorily as well—often as objects but sometimes as perpetrators of violence, and quite regularly as predominantly sexualized characters? Would we have to censor *contemporary culture itself* in order to prevent the reproduction of such imagery—and could such censorship even be effective? What about the desires, thoughts, impulses, ideas, feelings that are manifest through cultural artifacts and of which those artifacts are in one respect merely symbolic—would they simply evaporate, too, or resurface in altered forms unless they were themselves first comprehended more profoundly and addressed? With this, we return once more to general questions relevant but not limited to the context of feminism: the complicated issues of how targeted symptoms and underlying causes interrelate, and the broader problem of seeking a balance between proposing reforms and maintaining radical visions.

But it is also at this juncture in the *present* argument that another puzzle, a political/intellectual conundrum, becomes perceptible. It ought be obvious from my admiring recapitulation of Strossen's case that on logical grounds alone, I believe she "wins" the debate: if I were a judge rather than a sociologist, I would see little choice but to rule in Strossen's favor. Even if one agreed entirely with MacKinnon and Dworkin's concerns about the damaging contents and effects of pornography, it is not at all clear how already-noted objections could be answered or the anticipated pitfalls forestalled. This itself is a legalistic assessment; such a ruling would, once again, arise from the practical necessity of thinking in terms of either/ors. And even assuming such a necessity, winning a legal battle is not the same as triumphing in an ideological war: I use such language now deliberately and somewhat sardonically, insofar as these words' own militaristic connotations oversimplify issues much more complex than can be explained in terms of either/or logic alone.

For something else must be going on beside merely logic—or perhaps there are other logics, and additional considerations—to explain the surfacing again and again of antipornography feelings and ordinances. These acknowledged resurgences, as we have seen, explicitly motivated the writing of Strossen's book; yet even though the resultant text is exhaustive, they also augur a future problem that Strossen does *not* seem able to satisfactorily address in advance, concentrating as she does *only* on principle and *only* on law. The fundamental question remains: why and whence the stubborn persistence of antipornography sentiment, despite defeats and the strength of countervailing arguments?

Several explanations come to mind. For one, as already surmised, the conservative tenor of the times leads to a growing number of supporters joining the MacKinnon/Dworkin side, not necessarily for profeminist reasons. A second answer involves playing devil's advocate with my own argument: for perhaps Strossen *does* provide a response in *Defending Pornography*. One could say, as Strossen concludes on the final page of her book, that pornography is an easy target, an easy answer: the belief that sexism can be resolved through a single issue, a piece of legislation, gives people hope and makes their involvement with feminist movement politics a more focused and potentially gratifying endeavor than a fight conducted against an abstract and amorphous "patriarchy" much more haltingly.[23] After all, the procensorship stance suggests something *to do* while the anticensorship position argues for *not doing* something. Indeed, each of these points has some validity, but together they do not suffice to explain the phenomenon. In the first place, many women and men have been swayed by arguments made by the MacKinnon/Dworkin antipornography side who have no leanings toward conservatism themselves and who would disagree with Dan Quayle's "family values" brand of imposed traditionalism. Second, it makes little sense to infer that the appeal of antipornography legislation is *entirely* a function of single-issue politics' attractions. Rather, certainly for some and perhaps for many, the continuing appeal of procensorship and anti-sex "MacDworkinite" politics may result in addition or exclusively from the belief that there is indeed something objectionable about pornography as we know it, and from the perception that challenging pornography comes *closer* to challenging still male-dominated institutions and structures than seems politically possible from within the pro-sex side.[24]

Furthermore, unless this last explanation is taken seriously, we may be left with an appeal to various forms of feminist "false consciousness": that is, women believe pornography is objectionable but this is because the issue is believed to proffer a quick fix, a distraction or displacement from more authentic considerations; women *think* pornography is "bad" for them, and against their interests, but it really isn't; women may object to, or feel uncomfortable with, pornography, but this is really only because they may be sexually repressed. With this, though, it would be Strossen's argument that would threaten to turn on its head, and to undercut itself rather self-defeatingly. For this is precisely what Strossen does *not* want to say about women on the pro-sex side of the issue's fence. For good reason, she does *not* want women who enjoy pornography or work in the sex industry to be told—condescendingly, as MacKinnon and Dworkin have stated or implied—that they don't know what they "really" feel or do while moving through life in unwitting collaboration with patriarchy. But, then, consistency should also demand that the reactions of those women who do feel suspicious toward, or affronted by, pornography not be belittled, dismissed, or too simplistically explained away. To so react would threaten to reproduce aspects of the MacKinnon/Dworkin stance toward the world, just as that stance had itself become ironically linked with the attitudes of its apparent adversaries.

Rather than seeing them as unwitting, then, it is preferable to acknowledge that women on the other side of this issue perceive something of value in the antipornography position, something that resonates with their own experiences. And, consequently, there may be dangers for feminism not only in restricting pornography but in altogether discarding the feelings behind the prorestriction position: what Strossen calls the "MacDworkinite" stance will not simply go away if only out-argued. Once we accept that the antipornography position ought not be thrown out altogether, we are ready to examine precisely what about it continues to resonate for many women.

THE RESONANCE OF MACKINNON AND DWORKIN'S
ARGUMENTS: AN ANTITHESIS

In her book *Speaking of Sex* (1997), legal scholar Deborah Rhode writes, "Most males first learn about sex through pornography, and the messages it sends are not exactly calculated to encourage relationships of mutual respect, caring and intimacy. Selections like 'Cheerleader Gang Bang,' 'Black Bitch,' 'Teen Twits and Twats,' and 'Jap Sadists' Virgin Slave,' link sexual pleasure with female degradation and racial domination." [25] Rhode suggests that even if intelligent arguments can be made against restricting pornography, their force is weakened if they presuppose that such images have no power.

In this regard, turning to Sartre may again be helpful. At one level, the existential assertion of "nothingnesses" that intervene between causes and effects remains accurate and potentially liberatory: social forces do not have the ability to be fully *determinative*, however hugely and remarkably influential they may be.[26] However, to take this assertion to its furthest extreme—namely, that images influence *nothing* (or *nothing significantly*)—would be a proposition just as absurd and potentially restrictive as a belief in total determinism. Here, once more, either/or formulations threaten to obscure rather than clarify our analysis and vision. Many theorists have instead emphasized complexity, including Emile Durkheim, mapping the sociological scope and varieties of social facts; Sartre himself, laboring in later philosophical works to show even "nothingness" becoming straitjacketed within structured limitations (consciousness itself hedged in, sometimes hopelessly, by circumstances);[27] and Stuart Hall, exploring in interdisciplinary work the weight and resiliency of culture: it would be ludicrous to deny the simultaneously ideological and material sway of images and representations.

Indeed, the recent growth of cultural studies as a body of work and a force in the academy, burgeoning at the same time that "backlash" and antifeminist forces have also gained momentum, has been founded on the explicit recognition of mass imagery's powers. Why bother analyzing, dissecting, deconstructing the representational displays and arrays of popular culture—projects engaged in by many feminists and scholars who would position themselves far from MacKinnon and Dworkin's side—if not for an intuitive understanding that cultural imagery matters? Moreover, as Hall—himself a major figure in the development of cultural studies—has noted, the ideological sway of imagined representations is most effective when brought about by persuasion to social consensus rather than by force or state-imposed restrictions. He explains this notion of *hegemony,* itself culled from Gramsci:

> That notion of dominance which meant the direct imposition of one frame-
> work, by overt force or ideological compulsion, on a subordinate class, was
> not sophisticated enough to match the real complexities of the case. One
> also had to see that dominance was accomplished at the unconscious as well
> as the conscious level: to see it as a property of the system of relations in-
> volved, rather than as the overt and intentional biases of individuals; and
> to recognize its play in the very activity of regulation and exclusion which
> functioned through language and discourse before an adequate conception
> of dominance could be theoretically secured. . . . Hegemony implied that the
> dominance of certain formations was secured, not by ideological compul-
> sion, but by cultural leadership.[28]

Such an analysis is clearly relevant to this examination of pornography. For it follows from Hall's explanation of hegemony that rather
than being mutually exclusive, at least two dimensions frequently can
and do coexist with regard to the operation of cultural imagery: such
images may circulate quite consensually and lawfully while *at one and
the same time* being intimately bound up with the reproduction of dom-
inant/subordinate relations within inequitably structured societies. In
the specific case of pornography, Strossen's already-cited arguments
make a strong case that these images and representations *ought* and
need to circulate consensually and legally even under such inequitable
circumstances: there are particular benefits to pornography's relative
lack of restrictions, and severe problems that attend its present or future
censorship.

But advocating its legality does not logically require believing that
current pornography's forms, contents, and conditions of production
are *entirely* unobjectionable or nondiscriminatory; one need not conclude from an anticensorship position that pornography ought to remain immune to, and unencumbered by, political challenges or gender-
related protests. Rather, like most of the popular examples already
mentioned—from Hollywood filmmaking to Madison Avenue magazine production, from rock to rap, from MTV to cyberspace—pornography is part and parcel of, and tangled within, cultural webs linked to
male-dominated attitudes and institutions still badly in need of feminist
transformation. Consequently, it ought be possible to adopt an anticensorship position that does not deny the existence of *connections* between images and effects, ideas and materiality, representations and
structures—between, finally, pornography and patriarchy. These con-

nections, of course, need not be causal. Thus, if we can get beyond the limitations of a too-strictly polarized logic, a feminist position ought be possible that permits pornography to be *both* defended *and* criticized and that avoids its becoming *either* unhappily repressed *or* mindlessly glorified.

Yet so far this analysis still begs the very question that it posed: is there indeed an ideologically problematic content to much of pornography that partly explains the ongoing objections and discomfiture of many women and men? Here Gramsci's concept of hegemony again can be useful in making sense of the continuing debates surrounding pornography and its relationship with feminism. Surely, particular pornographic images—from film to film, say, or magazine to magazine— vary greatly. However, even taking into account such internal differentiation, there still exists something that could be called a dominant or *hegemonic pornography*. By this, I mean that as long as a given society remains largely controlled by men in terms of who hold a preponderance of economic, political, and technical power, certain sexual representations are likely to become ideologically predominant over others.[29] It is likely that accordingly, the forms and contents of the narratives presented in pornography will differentially cater to male desires and fantasies (though again, such influence is not deterministic).

Thus, hegemonic pornography, as I am calling it, is characterized by repetitive themes often interwoven in formulaic fashion through individual examples of this particular mainstream and commercially profitable cultural genre. For instance, it is not at all difficult to discern such ideological threads linking together separate titles like "Cheerleader Gang Bang," "Jap Sadists' Virgin Slave," and "Teen Twits and Twats"; recurrent themes are also easily noticed by anyone glancing at the pornography sections of most video stores, or looking at the posters on a street where a number of porn flicks are playing. Pornography thus manifests a rather remarkable and somewhat ironic homogeneity amid its apparently rich and ultracommodified diversity.

Therefore, not *only* are "real" erotic pleasures aroused in many people in and through much of hegemonic pornography (the so-called sex side of the debate) but *also* just as "real" is a texture of domination and subordination in much of what is depicted (the so-called sexism side of the debate). As we have seen, pornography's representational domains continue to be under the sway of a national and international sex industry that is both hugely profitable and still largely run and controlled by men.[30] But unless that industry becomes much more equally owned, operated, produced, imagined, and shared by women (as well as by men who are now excluded from power)—and not by only *some* women, but by women ranging across further complicating divides of class, race, ethnicity, and sexual orientation—why *would* we expect pornography to reveal a wider gamut of sexual images and possibilities, or find its homogeneity "remarkable"? Clearly, women lack equal social powers from which to imagine sexuality; it remains difficult to find equal confidence in giving and demanding pleasure, in desiring and being desired, from positions of social, political, economic, and cultural strength that have not yet become collectively comparable with men's. How or why, then, should the world enacted and then represented within pornography look any less asymmetric, less skewed, than the world outside?

Within what I am suggesting is a dominant or hegemonic pornography, women are indeed recurrently depicted as enacting men's fantasies. Even when reversals of this tendency seem to occur (as in lesbian sex scenes, for instance, often formulaically figured into dominant narratives), they may only further confirm—through the use of titillating variations and temporarily exciting role reversals[31]—the more usually patriarchal, generally heterosexual pattern of men's desire taking precedence and priority over women's. Moreover, within hegemonic pornography, it is usually only some body types and shapes that are favored—usually young rather than old, thin rather than heavy. Here, too, variations are commonly introduced (not only in body types but also across such other social categories such as race, ethnicity, or class) but again primarily for titillating diversion; divergences generally serve to reinforce rather than to genuinely diversify the conventional range of patriarchal preferences being asserted, enacted, imagined, and fantasized in and through pornography.

This is not the place to provide a qualitative or quantitative empirical account of a "hegemonic pornography" that I am describing, for the moment, in mostly conceptual and theoretical terms. But this brief analytic characterization may have helped clarify *why* the MacKinnon/ Dworkin procensorship side persists. We now can easily imagine many women feeling alienated both by their lack of control over the *production* of pornography and by their sense of being somehow left out from the promised pleasures of its *consumption*. For some women, though certainly not all, their own experiences, sexual needs, feelings, frustrations, and desires do not seem to be tapped or depicted in that hegemonically pornographic movie, magazine, or book. For many, an uneasy sense—and how, after all, could such a sense be deemed *altogether* unfounded or inappropriate?—remains that somehow pornography, like patriarchy itself, is indeed not *fully* in their/our/women's interests.

A CONCLUDING SYNTHESIS

And so it seems reasonable to conclude that, at least in our present social context, still dominated by gender bias, contemporary pornography is not altogether unobjectionable (though perhaps, in a more feminist future, it might yet evolve toward providing pleasures and satisfactions distributed more democratically). But what I am *not* willing to concede is that anything in the "antithesis" section negates the arguments of the "thesis." Perhaps the patriarchal character of present-day pornography ought to convince feminists not to jump on a bandwagon of censoring or restricting its proliferation but to do precisely the reverse. Concentrating on one issue abstracted from others all others, as Dworkin and MacKinnon have urged in the case of pornography, paradoxically tends to *de-radicalize* feminism rather than contributing to its growth or to its ability to realize its earlier and more wide-ranging vision.

Quite possibly, we need to do two things at once. On the one hand, using vague definitions to censor pornography also restricts those who do find enjoyment in and through it; even if hegemonic pornography commonly reflects the dominant/subordinate character of most relations between men and women, many can still find pleasures in niches, in cracks, through reimaginations. A rigidly prorestriction position is not only judgmental and potentially repressive but may *take away* from some women explicit or implicit imagined vehicles for bodily happiness sometimes experienced *in the present,* without offering a substitute. Clearly, the anticensorship side espoused by Strossen advocates this first protective measure and makes an important case for not perpetuating sexual repressiveness.

But on the other hand, nothing about an anticensorship position prevents us from raising a second question that, following the first imperative becomes that much more critical *if* feminists are to stop short of restricting pornography: How can future transformations of sexuality *simultaneously* be assured of being worked toward? How can we ensure that pornography in its present incarnations does not remain unchallenged, accepted with resignation as though its underlying relations are unchangeable? On this side of things, Strossen seems to have less to suggest from her feminist perspective; in fact, none of the changes she broaches at the end of *Defending Pornography* address issues of changes in sexual power per se, though these are extremely important for ensuring that pornography evolves in a more democratic direction in the future.

MacKinnon and Dworkin at first appear to have more to offer on this point. For there can be no doubt that both these feminists fully recognize the depth of interaction between images and effects: "Social inequality," MacKinnon writes in *Only Words* (1993), "is substantially created and enforced—that is, *done*—through words and images. Social hierarchy cannot and does not exist without being embodied in meanings and expressed in communications. . . . Social supremacy is made, inside and between people, through making meanings." [32] They fully realize that gender-biased assumptions pervade society throughout a mind-boggling range of psychic, social, cultural, and fantasized manifestations. But why does that realization lead to the far too limiting and ultimately de-radicalizing conclusion—thereby ultimately thwarting MacKinnon's and Dworkin's ambitious intentions—that campaigns to legally restrict pornography are the best way to confront the still-leviathan-like weight of male-dominated societies?

If we focus instead on the particular cultural manifestation that I have labeled hegemonic pornography, a broader answer comes to mind, one far less confining than antipornography legislation per se. Most important, this approach suggest the need for a *multifaceted radical feminist movement* in which the issue of pornography would figure as one large question among others, without taking on a decontextualized *over*significance. Lacking such perspective, we are unlikely to make much progress on pornography in the future, and at that second longer-term and more radical level. For people create images, and come to shape desires and experience sexuality, in specific ways, in part because of their socialization regarding gender within nuclear families. Thus, psychoanalytically oriented examinations and critiques of dominant family structures eventually can affect—though perhaps such influence may seem unlikely—the particular form and contents of pornography. Similarly, women's decisions about working in the sex industry, or how or if sexual freedoms are experienced, also must be understood broadly, as largely influenced by questions of economic power and powerlessness; in other words, questions of political economy are involved. Thus activism on issues related to class—such as the effects of 1990s welfare restructuring on women abruptly cut off from social supports—

is indirectly but definitely connected to questions of sexual freedom and pornography's persistence in mostly hegemonic forms. And why should MacKinnon and Dworkin have limited their protests against the sexist content of media to pornography? One can eschew censorship but not hesitate to call attention, in the larger context, to women's still-limited collective access to controlling cultural production overall.

To their credit, MacKinnon and Dworkin have continued, even in the conservative decades of the 1980s and 1990s, to call attention to the persistence of male-dominated structures of power. In the process, they have become associated with radical feminism, a connection that brings them not merely authority and power (as one sometimes senses from Strossen's account) but also a good deal of excessive and disproportionate demonization. But it is wrong to see Dworkin and MacKinnon as representing the sole remaining vestiges of earlier radical feminism, for the movement of the 1960s and 1970s was insistently multi-issued and multidimensional. As MacKinnon came to concentrate so much energy solely on legal resolutions and outcomes, radical feminism itself became too closely associated with the pornography issue, which has too severely limited it. Ironically enough, the turn to law—with its own tendency to espouse either/or positions—may have affected both Strossen and MacKinnon, as their respective positions each show a disconcerting tendency to flip to the other because of their exclusive emphasis on one side of the censorship debate, whether pro- or anti-.

Yet if feminism is to move beyond the divisions of those debates, which at once arose internally and were exaggerated by outside observers, thinking outside the limitations of either/or divides is crucial; it is the first step in resuscitating a movement now splintered and defensive. Sexual pleasure needs to be protected *and* sexism to be challenged. When *both* dimensions are simultaneously engaged, women of all ages, colors, and classes—including the teenager I was as well as the wonderful young women I now have the privilege of teaching a generation later—will once more be able to participate in the radical dismantling of gender bias and sexual inequities, the continuing project that all feminists ought to be proud to have begun.

The Beauty Context

Looks, Social Theory, and Feminism

Is it possible for most women today to live unhampered by judgments about our appearance? Are we free of looks-ism? Decidedly not, not yet, neither in the United States nor in most places around the world where rewards to beauty still collude with sexist injustices. "One is not born, but rather becomes a woman," Simone de Beauvoir bravely declared as she tied the development of femininity to bodily objectification.[1] Central to that process was the creation in women of heightened concerns about approval from gazing male others. Will he love me if I look this way or that? Could I contentedly look on myself? What emphasizes my better features, or best hides my haunting inadequacies? How can I avoid losing my attractiveness as I face inevitable aging, decay, death?

The Second Sex was published in 1949, over a decade before second-wave feminism confronted America in the 1960s and 1970s, and long before gender bias was widely acknowledged. But, in the interim, has much really changed? Have we really "come a long way, baby," as the woman in the Virginia Slims ad absurdly intones? Or, perhaps, matters have shifted in the opposite direction. Alongside the emergence of feminism and feminisms, women's studies, men's studies, gender sections of bookstores, discourses about discourses on sex, postmodernism, and embodiment—when it comes to looks, our situation may have worsened right in front of our eyes. This chapter's purpose is to explore how such an ironic predicament itself became possible, and why.

LOOKS-ISM: AN OVERVIEW

I do not employ the word *looks-ism* devoid of irony, but rather with some skepticism about the infinite multiplication of "isms" conceivable amid human interaction. So many isms have been generated that one wonders whether oppression itself, its most common contours and general motivations, has been banished as a focal point for intellectual scrutiny. No, I mean to highlight something else by referring to looks-ism as a phenomenon discriminatory insofar as it sets up categorical divisions, placing far greater importance for one sex than the other on the cultivation and maintenance of particular bodily appearances to gain love, status, and recognition. The term compels recognition that beauty expectations are systemic; it insists that they are anything but arbitrary or merely idiosyncratic. Instead, such expectations conform to Emile Durkheim's simple yet far-reaching definition of a "social fact." These are aspects of the world that exist above and beyond the ability of individuals to control; their existence is verified even more when one attempts to defy than to accommodate oneself within them. As social facts, then, beauty expectations exist prior to us, thick and weighty though by no means unalterable.[2]

Of course, in an excessively individualistic culture permeated by the commodification of just about everything, the counterargument can be made that appearance-based exhortations and rewards routinely affect *everyone,* and not just women.[3] In this regard, too, the term *looks-ism* allows for flexibility, insofar as women (and other men) often judge men as well by looks-based criteria. Furthermore, in a lawyerlike defense it could be added that among beauty's by-products are to be found playful pleasures as authentic as painful tyrannies. But despite the democratic potential of looks-ism—and even its increasingly universal application—its force remains extraordinarily gender-specific. As such, it would be foolish, and suspiciously so, to contend that appearance-based exhortations and rewards do not still carry differential meaning, effects, and consequences for women. For women, the evaluation of looks has been systematically bound to the asymmetries of gender as a whole. Whether a woman is "lovely" or "homely" has affected prospects of marriage and heterosexual companionship, states that themselves have been differently touted to women than to men. It is hard to underestimate the pervasive influences of this cultural divergence on both women and men's day-to-day feelings and experiences. For instance, it remains immensely more likely that a sixty-year-old heterosexual woman who for whatever reason finds herself alone—perhaps divorced, widowed, or simply as a result of life choices—will worry, and have reasons to worry, about her chances of finding sexual and emotional companionship than will a man of the same age. He, in general, still sees his options as relatively open and fluid; she fears being seen as ridiculous or sexually undesirable.

Thus, looks-based assessments are commonly linked to our ability to achieve the kind of emotional happiness that all human beings commonly seek. Simultaneously, the possible shapes of such satisfaction have been constricted both by sex and by presuppositions about heterosexuality that grew up alongside sexism.[4] For looks have been unequally connected to women's very sense of themselves, to traditional expectations and to the force of tradition, to whether we believe ourselves to be attractive or unattractive human beings in general. Though in many situations these existential realities affect men, they usually do not determine men's lives.[5] This structured and constructed social fact appears in all societies where male domination prevails, and is thus found almost everywhere. Consequently, whether we refer to expectations about appearance in material or ideological terms—whether we prefer to speak of an institutionalized "fashion-beauty" complex or an enculturated "beauty myth" (the terms favored by feminist authors Sandra Bartky and Naomi Wolf, respectively)—looks-ism poses special problems for women, though by no means only for women nor for all women identically.[6] The problem of looks-ism is especially applicable to heterosexual women, though the rigid expectations we will see that it creates—about youth, about race, about some body types rather than others—may be felt in a variety of ways potentially detrimental to all women, and indeed to all human beings.

Keeping this usage in mind, we can proceed to investigate the claim that women's situation in terms of looks-ism has gotten worse. Indeed, evidence from many sources suggests that women's concern about looks has intensified in recent years. Confirmation can be gleaned both from without and within, by stepping back to survey the wider social landscape or by turning inward to examine personal experience. In *Unbearable Weight* (1993), feminist philosopher Susan Bordo describes an eightfold increase in the number of inquiries received by the

New York Center for the Study of Anorexia and Bulimia between 1980 and 1984, after experts on eating disorders in the 1970s had proclaimed anorexia to be rare. Other statistics that Bordo cites are equally disturbing: 1 of every 200 to 250 women between the ages of thirteen and twenty-two suffers from anorexia; 12 to 33 percent of female college students struggle with induced vomiting, diuretics, and laxatives. Strikingly, too, 90 percent of anorectics are women, as are 80 percent of those who have their intestines partially removed to help control their weight.[7]

Nor is anorexia confined mostly to a narrowly defined group, as was for many decades too casually presumed. Recent research shows that eating disorders reach across categories.[8] According to sociologist Rebecca Thompson, both overeating and undereating affect women of differing races, classes, and sexual orientations. This goes against the medical establishment's conventional wisdom about anorexia, historically believed to predominate only among white and middle- to upper-class teenagers. However, Thompson's interviews show not only that a much more varied group of women experience eating problems but that they attribute these problems' genesis to complex sources: to a range of biases and frustrations broader than feelings about their looks alone. The reasons they offer include, and sometimes center on, traumatizing experiences of discriminations related to race, class, or both. Still, Thompson's research confirms that eating disorders continue to manifest themselves in largely gender-skewed forms. Thus whether racism, poverty, childhood sexual abuse, or looks-ism per se is felt to have been its major stimulus, anorexia still disproportionately affects and threatens the health of women.[9]

There are also signs that anorexia is affecting girls at younger and younger ages; it is no longer rare for eight-, nine-, or ten-year-olds to fret about their weight.[10] Such worries bear little relation to medical well-being, fitness, or even conventional standards of good looks. For instance, in a 1984 *Glamour* poll of 33,000 adult women, 75 percent stated that they were too "fat," although 30 percent were under their medically thought-to-be-optimal weight (and only 25 percent were above).[11] Other sources also suggest that such self-critical attitudes are frequently—and, indeed, *more* frequently of late—to be found among adolescent girls as well. Take another recent popular cultural indicator, a 1995 best-seller titled *Reviving Ophelia;* this book's commercial success is in itself revealing. The author, clinical psychologist Mary Pipher, emphasizes that social pressures are creating more severe depression, suicidal feelings, and anorexic tendencies in this generation of young girls than in prior generations. Despite the changes since the 1960s, and the "lip service paid to equality," discrimination remains a reality and the cultural changes of the last decade have made adolescence even more difficult. High on the list of the pressures cited by Pipher is the desire to be beautiful, which she found commonly expressed as appearance has grown increasingly important:

> In the last two decades, we have developed a national cult of thinness. What is considered beautiful has become slimmer and slimmer. For example, in 1950 the White Rock mineral water girl was 5 feet 4 thin inches tall and weighed 140 pounds. Today she is 5 feet 10 inches and weights 110 pounds.
> Girls compare their own bodies to our cultural ideals and find them wanting. . . . The social desirability research in psychology documents our prejudices against the unattractive, particularly the obese, who are the social lepers of our culture. A recent study found that 11 percent of Americans would abort a fetus if they were told it had a tendency to obesity. By age five, children select pictures of thin people when asked to identify good-looking others. . . .
>
> Girls are terrified of being fat, as well they should be. Being fat means being left out, scorned and vilified. . . . Almost all adolescent girls feel fat, worry about their weight, diet and feel guilty when they eat. . . .
>
> Particularly in the 1980s and 1990s, there's been an explosion of girls with eating disorders. When I speak at high schools, girls surround me with confessions about their eating disorders. When I speak at colleges, I ask if any of the students have friends with eating disorders. Everyone's hand goes up. Studies report than on any given day in America, half our teenage girls are dieting and that one in five young women has an eating disorder.[12]

Pipher's concerns have also been confirmed by academic researchers. In a 1990 study of *Seventeen* magazine, Kate Peirce concluded that the feminist movement may have influenced editorial content in the late 1960s and early 1970s. By 1985, however, 60 percent of the editorial copy that year was devoted to beauty, fashion, cooking, and decorating.[13] One finds this situation confirmed anecdotally as well, through the stories and lives of friends or associates who have young daughters concerned about their weight, noses, or hair, often at even earlier ages than mothers in their thirties or forties recall themselves worrying. For instance, when I mentioned the subject to a former professor who lives with a well-known feminist writer and activist, he urged me to please send him a copy of whatever I wrote on this topic. Even though their ten-year-old daughter is by conventional standards considered "very pretty," she is already cautious about her weight and sharply criticizes her mother's nose as allegedly much too large. Another colleague, who has herself suffered lifelong discrimination because of her weight, suggested that I interview her four-year-old niece for this essay. Not only did this small child continually mock her aunt's "fatness," but during several visits to restaurants she modestly ordered for herself only a "diet Coke and garden salad."

Even as worries about looks commence in young women ever earlier, these anxieties also seem to be enduring longer at the other end of the life cycle, accentuating concerns as women age. Cosmetic surgery is the most obvious case in point. There is currently a boom in this field, both in the United States and Europe. In *Backlash* (1991), Susan Faludi notes that cosmetic surgery is the fastest-growing subspecialty in American medicine; in *The Beauty Myth,* Wolf estimates that operations doubled every five years in the United States before tripling between 1984 and 1986 (the rate has doubled every decade in Britain).[14] In Germany, over 100,000 cosmetic surgery operations are annually performed; in the Netherlands, between 10,000 and 20,000. Back in the United States, more than two million procedures were undertaken in 1988, a figure even more striking in that it registers an increase from 590,550 in 1986.[15] According to Kathy Davis, using 1987 data, 90 percent of the operations are performed on women: virtually all breast corrections, 91 percent of face-lifts, 86 percent of eyelid reconstructions, and 61 percent of all nose surgery. In all, women are undertaking nine times more operations than are men.[16]

A study by Eugenia Kaw yields similar results, concluding that 20 percent of all cosmetic surgery patients in the United States in 1990 were African American, Latino, or Asian American; over 60 percent of this group were women.[17] As Thompson's interviews suggested, racism can play a crucial role; Naomi Murakawa has pointed out that many Asian American women turn to blepharoplasty, or double eyelid surgery, for reasons that have at least as much to do with race as with gender. According to Murakawa, the imposition of racialized standards often generates the feeling that unless Asian women live up to white Western ideals of beauty, they will not feel valued or accepted.[18]

This development can be seen just as clearly by examining the data of everyday experiences, anecdotal evidence, the testimony of inner feelings. One only has to casually regard the walls of New York City's subway cars, or skim through the pages of the *Village Voice, New York* magazine, or the *LA Weekly,* to find more advertisements for free plastic surgery consultations than would have been seen just a decade ago. Whether self-identified as feminists or not, women more often than men are finding the will, time, and money to surgically alter their bodies. The perception that such desires are becoming increasingly common figured prominently among the inspirations of Kathy Davis's excellent interview-based study on women's reasons for undertaking cosmetic surgery in the Netherlands, perhaps the only society in the world to have included this surgery among its national health insurance benefits.[19] As Davis recounts, she decided to write a book after conversing with a friend who was

> an attractive, self-confident, successful professional woman. She was also a feminist. To my surprise, she told me over coffee that she was about to have her breasts enlarged. I must have looked fairly flabbergasted, as she immediately began defending herself. She said that she was tired of putting up with being flat-chested. She had tried everything (psychoanalysis, feminism, talks with friends), but no matter what she did, she simply could not accept it. She saw no other solution but to do something about it. Finally, she said, she was going to "take her life in her own hands."[20]

Nor is it difficult to find such stories closer to one's own life, to one's own mind-and-body. Expressing feelings reminiscent of those described by Davis's interviewees, a dear friend of mine who is single and in her late fifties told me how she felt much better—ten years younger, able to see herself again as a sexualized being, not ashamed to meet men—after her face-lift and having the skin tightened beneath her chin. These elective medical technologies, which when first developed were usually available only to the upper class, have recently become accessible to persons on a fairly tight budget like my friend's, going down in relative price over time just like VCRs or computer software. To be sure, in her case much saving was required, and the cost of such operations is still not even close to being comfortable for many single women, given their average incomes and the enormous disparities of class in the United States.[21]

Nevertheless, it would be a gross exaggeration to imply that more women than not wish to technologically remold their/our bodies. Greater numbers do so now than in previous decades, but for most people an operation is often frightening, unaffordable, deemed unnecessary, or just plain unwanted. For both sexes cosmetic surgery remains an exception, albeit a growing one, to the rule.[22] Not so misleading is the same statement, however, when applied to cosmetics alone. When it comes to the popularity of beauty aids of all sizes, kinds, and prices, most women partake of their advertised magic, hoping to produce at least temporarily beautifying effects. Signs of expansion, not diminution or even stabilization, are to be found here. The cosmetics industry has been remarkably profitable, managing to grow and thrive steadily through the fitful stops and starts of late-twentieth-century capitalism. In *Labeling Women Deviant* (1984), sociologist Edwin Schur estimates 1979 expenditures on cosmetics and personal hygiene products as follows: cosmetics, nearly $3 billion; women's hair products, nearly $2 billion; women's fragrances, close to $2 billion; skin preparations, approximately $1.5 billion; and diet aids, close to $400 million.[23] Compare this with figures a little over a decade later when Wolf estimates the diet industry in 1990 to be a vast $33 billion business, the cosmetics industry to gross $20 billion annually, and cosmetic surgery to gross $300 million.[24]

By this point, perhaps I can rest my case, or at least the part of my case that frames my larger concern: the still asymmetric problem posed by beauty expectations—by "looks-ism"—for many women, and therefore for contemporary feminism. This ongoing dilemma seems to have worsened in certain ways; at minimum, the situation has not altered. Based on this social knowledge, then, what ought to or can be done? Before considering that question, a good deal of analytic ground must first be covered. Thus the next section takes up a whole complex of reasons for so much interest continuing to be placed, and investments made, in beauty as we know it. This segment explores a number of theoretical possibilities, ranging from biology to the social, cultural, economic, and back again. Why, and whence, these hugely common concerns about dieting, and dieting ever younger? Why, and whence, the determination to look younger, and to keep doing so at older and older ages? What alternative explanations can be credibly entertained, gender-related and not?

At the same time, "Why Looks-ism?" addresses another question that I may seem to have foreclosed prematurely, assuming rather than demonstrating a negative, doomsaying view. How do the statistics and anecdotes above justify my contention that things have "worsened"? Clearly, I am making a value judgment, stubbornly and unfashionably, though in this era the epistemological validity and power of ethical claims have themselves been jeopardized, and those making them thrown on the defensive. Some might argue that perhaps our beauty system, our present situation, *isn't* so bad after all. Yet, as we will see, not only do our society's obsession with and overvaluation of looks create gender-skewed damages, but beauty expectations for everyone are illusory in the extreme. Above all, paradoxically and by no means obviously, *looks-ism is not what it appears.*

Society has conflated *beauty* and *attraction,* enmeshing them so closely together that we become utterly alienated from our full experiencing of the latter because of the supposed power of the former. In the process, the concept of "beauty" too has become contaminated and oversimplified to the point where it must be totally rethought. Thus throughout this chapter, I argue for both the desirability and necessity of a *different understanding of attraction.* Though some people will find this revision of greater relevance than others, in principle, its application is not limited to people of only some social backgrounds and sexual orientations. Rather, dominant ideas and illusory notions are likely to restrict the cultural imagination available to all members of a particular society.

For our ongoing elevation of looks to a disproportionately privileged position does not accurately capture what are people's actually far more diverse, complicated, and multidimensional experiences of intense attraction to one another. We are frequently stimulated by someone's energy and movements in thought and body, by subtle responses evoked through an interplay of emotional, intellectual, physical, spiritual, and psychological factors. Moreover, such stimulations occur on levels at once social, cultural, and symbolic, so that the attraction is rarely to beauty per se even *initially,* the moment at which even those sympathetic to my contention might be dubious. But initial attractions may be *already* richly symbolic: the way a given woman, a given man, moves and sets off diverse associations in one's mind as well as body can explain even "love" or "lust" at first sight.

In what follows, by no means do I intend to posit a merely utopian critique, but I mean to render our notions of beauty and attraction more complex and indeed realistic. For there is little point in recommending an alternative vision impossible to be lived in the world as we know it. Instead, I will investigate the fascinating question of how looks-ism succeeds so brilliantly at maintaining what strikes me as a quite remarkable sham, a rather amazing mass deceit. Although in its tremendous oversimplifications it does not come close to matching our experience, it is nevertheless sustained from without and frequently reproduced from within. How and why does looks-ism manage to stay so central to our *beliefs and experiences about attraction* in spite of contravening evidence of a much more complex day-to-day reality—that is, of love, eroticism, desire including but also *regularly* and *already* transcending reactions to conventional "looks"?

Nothing in the following sections should be taken to mindlessly deny the relevance to this discussion of fitness and bodily well-being, of considerations about health. Without doubt, at certain levels of under- or overweight, the quality and even continuance of life itself can be put at risk. Likewise, it would be silly to overlook the enormous pleasures to be found in various forms of exercise, in bodily control and discipline, in athletic and musical exertions that link mental and bodily dynamics and practices. Becoming attracted to a "fit" person may incorporate mental as well as bodily dimensions even if we do not explicitly admit that we are drawn to a characterological manifestation, to a symbolic representation in bodily form of our own projected yearnings for *control and discipline*. But, as Susan Bordo has also noted, more than meets the eye is culturally operative here as well. Clearly, looks-ism goes well beyond *mere* considerations of health. Those who are "obese" in the United States know only too poignantly that the social attitudes they encounter commonly do not reflect kind and disinterested medical concerns but disdain, repugnance, and sometimes even hate. The intensity of such reactions cannot be explained on the grounds of health or fitness alone. Similarly, current interest in fitness, and women's (sometimes men's) growing interest in cosmetic surgery, frequently transcends simple considerations of health, even turning into just the opposite—to behaviors that gravely and often obsessively *endanger* health and even survival. Such efforts may become symbolic rituals to find, through looks, forms of love and attention originally frustrated or denied elsewhere.

Such caveats apply not only to "Why Looks-ism?" but to the following section, "Why Looks-ism *Now?*" Here, too, a range of interlocking theses explore precisely why the situation may have intensified in the United States in the 1980s and 1990s. It is certainly possible that in other societies, analogous cultural and socioeconomic developments may be fostering comparable anxieties about bodily appearances; I will leave it to readers to assess whether this analysis applies elsewhere. Since beauty expectations continue to be mostly aimed at women, in whom they produce varying consequences, the final section ("Beauty— For Women and Feminists") examines complicated divisions that come into being along overlapping social axes, from the good woman/bad woman dichotomy on through class, race or ethnicity, and age. Such an analysis is necessary so that we can circle back to explore our opening

dilemma in the chapter's concluding section: "What Has Been and Can
Be Done?"

One last cautionary note before continuing: with regard to beauty,
our historical context is a highly contradictory one. On the one hand,
the very existence of feminism has made women ostensibly *more* aware
of and sensitized to potential damages wrought by sexism and gender-
biased looks-ism. After all, *The Beauty Myth* and *Backlash* resonated
with contemporary readers, quickly becoming best-sellers in the early
1990s and bringing both Wolf and Faludi commercial name recognition. This response attests both to how much remains to be done and
to feminism's immense and ongoing accomplishments, to the historic
changes that have gradually been taking hold. Yet on the other hand,
we just as surely know that the Virginia Slims ad lies: we haven't come
anywhere near far enough (except in margins, niches) to overcoming
not only beauty expectations but also many other vestiges of sexism as
they affect all women, poor and well-to-do, across race and ethnicity
and sexual orientations. But then what are we to do amid such insuffi-
cient and incomplete changes—how to survive, how nonetheless to enjoy those pleasures available to us? Understandably, many women may
pragmatically conclude that looks-ism is simply something we have to
live with into the foreseeable future; in any case, maybe it has some
benefits, if only for some of us and some of the time. Maybe it's not so
bad after all . . . maybe we can devise feminist reinterpretations, feminist reappropriations . . . ?

Yet even more important to emphasize is a thought-provoking resemblance between contemporary debates about beauty and the other "sex
debates" and "sex wars" that have likewise occupied feminists since the
late 1970s and early 1980s.[25] These could more specifically be dubbed
sex versus sexism debates, since the "sides" have repeatedly broken
down along the following similar lines. On one side are generally found
those feminists who underscore women's needs and rights to pleasure
(emotionally, bodily, sexually) *at the moment,* even as and if the larger
male-dominated society that surrounds us remains violent or inequitable, showing class and racial as well as gender bias overall. On the other
side are those who emphasize the need to transform male-dominated
social structures, to consistently indict patriarchy, even if in the process
less attention is paid to encouraging whatever personal pleasures
women can find and take *now.*

Thus experiencing pleasures in the present has been set against ob-
jecting to inequities still lingering from the past. And it is a theme, a

split, that over the last decades has shaped the discussion of a succession of substantive issues: whether pornography should remain uncensored, or not; whether sadomasochistic sexuality should be practiced, or not; whether prostitution ought be legitimized as "sex work" or remain illegal; whether violence against women in American society has been paid too much attention, or not nearly enough.[26] The current feminist debate over our present subject, beauty, is therefore by no means exceptional in its structure. Is the quest for beauty really such a severe problem or not? Moreover, this debate seems to be intensifying. In other words, feminist disagreement over what beauty means for women seems to be heightening *in a way that parallels the very phenomenon examined*— that is, the way in which looks-ism continues to survive and even to grow as a hugely ambivalent source of pains and pleasures for women in general. As we will see in "Beauty—For Women and Feminists," this may redound to the benefit of the "beauty myth," leaving the basic *idea* of beauty still unexamined and waiting to be born.

Three examples vividly illustrate the current deepening of feminist debate about beauty. First, the emergence of a so-called Madonna phenomenon in the 1980s and 1990s had to do with many things, but a debate over looks was close to its core. When teaching during the academic year 1990–91, I was shown three senior theses whose central focus was whether or not Madonna could properly be called a feminist. Following the publication of Madonna's own book *Sex* (1992), moreover, a group of academics contributed essays to a 1993 volume titled *The Madonna Connection*. It presents a range of opinions on the extent to which Madonna helps, or harms, the broader gendered problem I have been dubbing "looks-ism." Thus, for instance, Cathy Schwichtenberg writes admiringly of Madonna: "Through strategies of simulation, she transforms the 'truth' of gender into drag, a dialectical fragmentation between two terms, and then fissures this destabilized sex identity further by means of splitting and displacement to advance a prodigious sexual plurality. In more general terms, her disingenuous figuration says much about the political promise of postmodern strategies."[27]

Susan Bordo disagrees, calling attention instead to the *illusion* that Madonna can indefinitely remake herself. For Bordo, Madonna may be a "postmodern heroine" but not necessarily an admirable one, nor a good role model for young women already confronting sexist biases. In watching Madonna, one forgets the huge amount of work that was required to discipline her body and maintain the image of "Madonna";

instead, Bordo stresses the material limits within which even a Madonna has no choice but to operate, pointing out her eventual subordination to conventional beauty norms and cults of thinness:

> Madonna has been normalized; more precisely, she has self-normalized. Her "wanna-bes" are following suit. Studies suggest that as many as 80% of nine-year-old suburban girls (the majority of whom are far from overweight) are making rigorous dieting and exercise the organizing discipline of their lives. They don't require Madonna's example, of course, to believe that they must be thin to be acceptable. But Madonna clearly no longer provides a model of resistance or "difference" for them. . . .
>
> Indeed, the video's (Open Your Heart) postmodern conceits, I would suggest, facilitate rather than deconstruct the presentation of Madonna's body as an object on display. . . . On this level, any parodic or de-stabilizing element appears as utterly, cynically, mechanically tacked on, in bad faith, a way of claiming trendy status for what is really just cheesecake—or, perhaps, pornography.[28]

Bordo's final words are even more decisive:

> Turning to Madonna and the liberating postmodern subjectivity that McClary and others claim she is offering: the notion that one can play a porno house by night and regain one's androgynous innocence by day does not seem to me to be a refusal of essentialist categories about gender, but rather a new inscription of mind/body dualism. . . . This abstract, unsituated, disembodied freedom, I have argued in this chapter, celebrates itself only through the effacement of the material praxis of people's lives, the normalizing power of cultural images, and the sadly continuing realities of domination and subordination.[29]

We can take a second, more recent, example. In *Reshaping the Female Body* (1995), Kathy Davis also places her book within a particular feminist debate over beauty—this time concerning her specific focus, cosmetic surgery. She found that when she appeared on panels to present her research conclusions—that given the lack of change in attitudes, a state of affairs that many women are quick to comprehend, cosmetic surgery can be "empowering"—audiences reacted critically. She notes that they approved Kathryn Morgan's view on cosmetic surgery as the more properly feminist one.[30] In the tradition of other "sex debates," Morgan takes a far more censorious attitude toward cosmetic surgery and Davis's perspective, stressing the patriarchal attitudes that are reinforced every time a particular woman undertakes surgical changes to her body.

The third group of examples bring us to the time of my writing these pages, the summer of 1996; coincidentally, interest in the subject of beauty was itself highly visible. Many journalists were asking why cosmetic surgery is gaining in popularity and noting the huge amounts of money being spent to alter supposedly imperfect bodies.[31] Others hailed the emergence of a new beauty ideal in the "body custom-built for athletics," a look that allows women both to sport muscles and to be attractive.[32] Around the same time, Nancy Friday's *Power of Beauty* also appeared, a 552-page text that could hardly be further from Naomi Wolf's earlier observations in *The Beauty Myth* or give better evidence of growing debate. For Friday argues that the "old feminist" attitudes toward sex and beauty have alienated many potential feminists over the last twenty years:

> Why did a book like Naomi Wolf's *The Beauty Myth* rally women from college campuses across the country? It offered the standard panacea for all of women's ills: Big Bad Men made me pursue beauty, starve my body. As much media coverage as the book received, it didn't detract women from the heated pursuit of beauty that had started up again in the mid-eighties. Nor did it deter the author from fondly including men in her next book, who turn out to be beloved, wanted, needed.
>
> Beauty/sex/men will be that route by which we exit the old feminism. It is a good road; well argued, written about, and practiced, it is already taking us into a more modern feminism. Writers like Camille Paglia, Katie Roiphe, Christina Hoff Sommers, and Nadine Strossen, to name a few, have already put their published voices on the line; puff-balls of smoke from the old feminist headquarters label them "pseudo" feminists, post-feminists, "faux" feminists, silly girlish names that betray the weaknesses of the old guard.

Thus, Friday argues, Gloria Steinem "excommunicates" Paglia "from 'her' feminism" because the critic has the temerity to disagree with her and to be "much in favor of beauty, power and sex." [33]

While Friday's book hardly offers a full-fledged theory, its ideas certainly capture the flavor of a historical moment in which assumptions about beauty are not changing. What appears to be a more coherent ideology surfaced in *Newsweek*'s cover story of 3 June 1996: "The Biology of Beauty: What Science Has Discovered about Sex Appeal." Quoting several anthropologists and psychologists, Geoffrey Cowley states: "when it comes to raw sex appeal, a nice chin is no match for a perfectly sculpted torso—especially from a man's perspective. Studies from around the world have found that while both sexes value appearance, men place more stock in it than women. And if there are social reasons for that imbalance, there are also biological ones. . . . The new beauty research does have troubling implications. First, it suggests that we're designed to care about looks, even though looks aren't earned and reveal nothing about character."[34]

Thus, not only is there growing debate within feminism about beauty but the topic seems at the same time to have become linked to a wider 1990s willingness to rediscover and revalidate sociobiological perspectives. This tendency, which appears cyclically, is usually attached to politically conservative impulses. In the 1990s biological analyses have been applied to a wide range of issues from crime to welfare—witness the reception of Richard Herrnstein and Charles Murray's *Bell Curve* (1994)—before this more recent application to beauty.

In the case of feminism, however, I sense that arguments over beauty have been unwittingly shaped by the either/or conceptual framework that has characterized sex debates over the course of the 1980s and the 1990s.[35] In beauty, like the other issues dividing feminists, is symbolized a need to move beyond such intellectual and political polarization. For, of course, Madonna can and may indeed still believe in feminist goals; of course, women can feel empowered, and still be feminists, when turning to cosmetic surgery because they fear loss of social value in day-to-day life. Simultaneously, it is *also* true that Madonna is likely to have a hard time not being affected by the problems she parodies while aging herself: can and will there be a "Madonna" when she is sixty-five?

So, too, considerations of biological health *and* socially constructed sexism are simultaneously enmeshed within the phenomenon I have been calling looks-ism. There is truth in *both*—all—of these statements. But so what? Such dichotomous perspectives can lead us to concentrate on the wrong questions—"wrong" insofar as such either/or oppositions generate inadvertently depoliticizing effects. For once this has been said and done, *then what*—where do we go from here? Instead of asking "Is Madonna a feminist?" we can concentrate more productively on the social conditions that give rise to this dilemma in the first place. Rather than raise a divisive and guilt-engendering question, "Can the woman who undertakes cosmetic surgery be a feminist?" it is much more useful to focus on ensuring that women have every reason to feel, in our society, *that it is possible to still be viewed as attractive when aging without such surgery.* Unless we insist that the problem be posed in such a way that we focus our criticism and calls for change on *collective* practices and representations, and not simply on *individual* decisions, we risk perpetuating an unacceptable state of affairs. We risk maintaining the status quo simply by asking too much of those individuals and too little of that still highly discriminatory society.

In the end, then, we have to come back to the issue of what is to
be done. How can we create a future that no longer engenders beauty
expectations in a way that harms both sexes, one more than the other
(affecting women and men through other social distinctions, too, notably race and class, which frequently overlap)? How can expectations
about appearance be transformed beyond recognition, a change that
potentially benefits all human beings? For even if not consciously or
explicitly recognized, a paradox is there, lurking in our social uncon-
sciousness: as looks-ism begins to die, only then can erotic attraction
start fully and democratically to thrive.

WHY LOOKS-ISM?

When broaching the topic of beauty expectations in a recent undergraduate class, I told my students about a conversation with a close friend.
This man, who is very sympathetic to feminism, had asked me some
months earlier if I knew Naomi Wolf personally. If so, he would be
grateful for an introduction since he believed he had fallen in love.
"How could you have fallen in love," I inquired only half-jokingly,
"when you have never even met this person?" "But I have just seen her
picture on the back cover of *The Beauty Myth*," my friend replied. The
combination of that glimpse of a very attractive woman with long
brown hair and the feminist intelligence demonstrated in the book had
sealed his infatuation.

I believe my friend allowed me to tell this tale in a classroom, as he
agreed to its retelling here, because we both realized the irony of his
yearning for the author of *The Beauty Myth* on the basis of her looks.
And yet, as we both also understood, it was not *just* her looks at all.
My friend is unconventional and progressive in most of his views, and
many women think him "cool": a leftist, political, with fond memories
of the 1960s, thoughtful, articulate; certainly, he would not have become infatuated with simply anyone—not with a Phyllis Schlafly nor
Margaret Thatcher, no matter how beautiful they might or might not
have been. Rather, the fact that Wolf wrote *The Beauty Myth* and was
a feminist made the idea of being attracted to her that much more ap-
pealing. It was not a politically incorrect attraction; it potentially as-
suaged inklings of guilt in someone who intellectually understands, and
sincerely agrees with, most feminist indictments of sexism and its ills.

Yet from the standpoint not only of this generally pro-feminist male
but also of our present inquiry into what this implies for American

culture generally, infatuation with Naomi Wolf is significant for *allowing the question of beauty to appear to be in question* (as it may indeed be—but only in theory, not necessarily in our practices). Moreover, where does this dilemma leave Wolf herself—what if this particular female author had not been conventionally attractive? Could she still have written *The Beauty Myth*, and would the book have been marketed to mass audiences? One could argue that if Wolf had been by conventional criteria unattractive, her perspective would have been vulnerable to the accusation that she was simply crassly self-interested in her protests against biases related to looks.

My point is twofold. First, feminists find ourselves in a contradictory bind, in a potentially no-win situation not of our own creation. Ironically, Wolf's looking attractive can reinforce rather than subvert the beauty myth she intends to attack. On the other hand, if she weren't considered good-looking, could she have defied the problem her own book so astutely depicts? [36] If Wolf were not at least reasonably attractive by conventional criteria, no one might have ever heard of her or her indictment in the first place. Second, such seemingly "personal" data are an important part of the phenomenon at hand, both—to put it in academicized terms—methodologically and theoretically. This point is worth reiterating, since our subject is neither abstract nor impersonal, involving feelings and thoughts we experience as well as analyze. In and beyond ourselves, both, we are deeply implicated in our opening query about why evaluations of beauty still permeate the lives of women, seeping into our self-conceptions and the conceptions of others.

One possible explanation for looks-ism can be culled from the above story, and from others like it. I have often discussed the genesis of attractiveness, not only with my Naomi Wolf–infatuated friend but also with other male colleagues and intimates, family members and friends, since the subject matter fascinates me as an academic and, over the course of a lifetime, as a woman. There is usually agreement that looks are high, if not uppermost, on the list of what is initially and crucially attractive to men about women. One could characterize this as frequently a necessary if not a sufficient precondition for being perceived as a potential sexual and intimate partner. While women often respond similarly to men, feminist analyses of gender from de Beauvoir onward anticipate a different tendency that is often experientially confirmed. For women, looks are often one of a number of factors that allow men to be perceived as attractive, including—and these are sometimes *more* important, singly or in combination—the possession of power, intellect, and prestige. In other words, looks are not rigidly fixed, not nearly so much a sine qua non of male attractiveness to women. This becomes even clearer with age: men forty and over do not generally suffer loss of heterosexual appeal to the same extent as still, too often, do women their age.

Given this little-changed social context, it is not surprising at all that women are turning more and more often to cosmetic surgery. Their action could be interpreted as a *rational* strategy to maintain or improve their ability to continue feeling valued, loved, and attended to in a world still inequitably divided by gender. Paul Willis has described British youth's accurate "penetration" of the dismal situation that confronts them at school and in a class-sundered society (an interesting choice of words in our present context);[37] women's realization that expectations surrounding beauty have not changed, which leads to their pragmatic accommodation to a still discriminatory status quo, seems likewise perceptive.

Moreover, if men are pushed further on the question of why certain kinds of women's looks are consistently deemed attractive, or what this means, or how it comes to be, I have noticed that often their answers become vague, peculiarly unintellectual, almost mystical. Sometimes men I have spoken with become uncharacteristically silent or inarticulate. Others become defensive, petulant, annoyed, even angry, as though I were inquiring into something that ought be taken for granted by and clear-cut to both of us. These responses often contrast sharply with the surplus rationality and logical thinking that are supposed to be the main by-products of socialized masculinity (and masculinities).[38] "I don't know why I feel this way but there isn't anything that can be done about it. . . . This is just how I am, and I'm going to be this way for the rest of my life" is one such less than perfectly cogent response from a person who would otherwise enthusiastically engage with me in academic debunking of rigid, essentializing categories. Another male colleague, a Marxist-influenced sociologist, offered, "She's just beautiful—I don't know why, she just is," an emotional, impatient answer that cuts off explanation (as though it were a self-evident Althusserian determination "in the last instance"). In an extremely poignant example, a husband, much to his dismay and terrible anguish, found that he could no longer feel aroused by a beloved spouse of many years who had lost one "beautiful" breast to a mastectomy. It was cruel for him to be left with lifelong guilt, as it must have been even more excruciatingly cruel for his wife, yet certainly his sexual feelings were not—how could they be?—simply alterable at will. His body seemed as though separate from him, as though possessed of customary habits or a mind of its own.

Implicit in these answers is the belief that feminine beauty *just is,* mysterious and irrational, justified in itself like the mountains or the skies or the trees. It seems to exist in a realm of transparency, which one is foolish—possibly inspiring anger—to doubt or malign. Beauty, by this interpretation, is a cult. But this is hardly a satisfying explanation; instead, such beliefs obscure precisely what they purport to illuminate. For if the appeal of beauty really were so naturally inexplicable— if it were simply like the moon or the trees—how is it possible that only some homogenized standards of beauty (in the contemporary United States these include thinness, youth, whiteness) become culturally favored over others for reasons we know to be quite sociologically explicable in terms of dominant cultural biases?

Then, too, how and why is it that criteria of feminine beauty and fashion shift noticeably from historical era to era (from the 1950s to the 1990s, for instance) or from society to society (from Japan to France to Iran), or both, like variations on the common theme of discriminatory beauty standards themselves? How could this occur if the phenomenon of beauty were merely "natural" rather than socially created and sustained, and therefore no more simply *im*mutable than changeable simply at will?[39] And it seems silly to think that the body could "choose" independently of the mind when we know the two to be profoundly interrelated. Rebelling against the long insistence within Western civilization on dualisms, on separating mind from body in a hierarchical fashion that alleges the superiority of mind *over* body, mind *over* matter, social theories of "the body" have become exceedingly hot topics in the late 1990s.[40] We are rightly, and radically, interested in "bringing the body back in." It is equally important, however, that we do so in a way that does not in reaction tend to veer to the opposite extreme, making it fashionable to privilege body *over* mind or to force mind *under* body so that we are unwittingly involved in reinventing the wheel. Unless we explicitly recognize a dialectical interconnectedness between the two—how our minds constantly affect our bodies and vice versa, each dimension related, but not reducible to a mere effect of the other—it may *look* as though we are changing more than we are, or as though this question of appearance is wholly intractable.

I suspect there is an explanation-behind-the-explanation that provides our first rationale for looks-ism's persistence. Hidden beneath claims that attraction to women's beauty "just is" may be hard-to-admit beliefs that something about this particular phenomenon is *biologically anchored*. Could it be that large numbers of men, and also women (why would we necessarily be different in this regard, steeped as we all are in the same overlapping cultural influences?), secretly harbor suspicions that something about attraction, about beauty, is indeed natural or biological, stubborn and maybe even eternally fixed? If there is the slightest ring of truth in such a suggestion, it would be stronger than the "just is" thesis formulated above. For if we believe looks-ism to be natural and unchangeable, we should not be particularly surprised that it has become so—and in such a way as to render predictable, not at all anomalous, any finding that "beauty myths" keep repeating themselves cyclically through history, time and time again. The belief itself would have the power to create "tradition," achieving its own self-fulfilling prophecies.

It is interesting to speculate about whether this argument may be difficult to "prove" empirically—a difficulty that becomes quite predictable—*because* of its validity. For who these days wants to admit to being driven by biological thinking, especially among persons who agree on logical grounds alone that looks-ism remains sexist and problematical in its social ramifications? Rather, a subtle biologism may continue to constitute looks-ism's best-kept, because potentially most embarrassing, secret. Otherwise, looks-ism would have to be acknowledged as one of the last holdouts of an ideology of the "natural" in a universe increasingly committed to just the opposite: to socially moldable and plastic possibilities; to rapid scientific and technological innovations; to social theories that tend to celebrate de- and reconstructions; to beliefs in the possibility of uprooting other discriminatory isms, including racism and sexism as amply manifested in contexts other than this one, because they have rested on similar specious ideologies. Many feminist ideas obviously have now gained more legitimacy than ever precisely because we no longer respond to claims of biological determinism nor rely on assumptions making it likely that such claims will become self-fulfilling.

Thus, it may be especially difficult to openly discuss—whether in public, political life, in philosophically and theoretically oriented circles, or even in private conversations—any subject matter that is *felt* or suspected, whether rightly or wrongly, to contain "biological" or "natural" dimensions. Such reluctance may become itself a problem, even if in other ways it has quite justifiable origins; there has been excellent reason to fear that "sociobiological" discussions, past and present, only provide ammunition for ex post facto justifications of beliefs that were actually based a priori on race- or gender-related biases. But still, what if feelings that beauty's appeals are biologically based and somehow natural nonetheless exist, politically correct or not—feelings that cannot be easily acknowledged or admitted to? That very denial might drive such feelings underground and thus render impossible any internal and dialectical transformation, making the cult of beauty even *more* powerfully alive for having to remain quiet, unarticulated, and inadmissible. In addition, the kind of furtive biologism and defensiveness that now burden the topic may also be reflected in the trouble encountered by any messenger annoying enough to broach it: to wit, the uncharacteristically impatient reactions of male friends to questions about beauty, and perhaps the reactions to reading this. We may find ourselves surprisingly angered and even scandalized by efforts to penetrate beauty's "mystery," reactions that suggest investments more deeply seated than we consciously know.

But *why* would beauty be sensed to have a biologically based or natural component? Let me supply a devil's advocate who assumes there *is* a biological/natural basis for differentially valuing certain sorts of women's looks. What would that biological/natural basis be? "Instinct, species survival, vestiges of a primordial and utterly animalistic drive," I hear my imaginary champion responding. "Women are biologically capable of bearing children in only the first half of their lives. Name me one society you know in which women become sexier as they age, where social attitudes and images eroticize those who are older as much as or more than women who are young," he or she continues, becoming more animated. "Name me one place anywhere around the world where women's breasts are valued and eroticized more when sagging than when they are relatively upright, rounder, and pointier. Isn't that because it is only with a younger woman that it is possible to reproduce—and thus this is the appearance that excites men for good, justifiable, life-affirming, and species-protecting reasons?" (This presumes, as does my devil's advocate, that heterosexuality too is self-evidently natural.)

To which I would respond, as would a number of other feminists, that it ought by now to be plain that sexuality and reproduction are only *sometimes* related. Technological developments have been rendering even *that* connection no longer necessary. Once seemingly inevitable ties between reproduction and *heterosexuality* have been breaking down as well; it is now common for women who are lesbians to have babies through artificial insemination or adoption; advocates of gay marriage are challenging older definitions of family. Moreover, even if species survival were once an issue, human beings have long been in no danger of becoming extinct worldwide: today, more likely sources of concern are overpopulation and immigration. Yet societies without population shortages have not moved away from looks-ism, gradually diminishing the value they previously accorded feminine beauty.

Overall, instead, the trend in advanced industrial societies has been to sever ancient bonds between sexuality and reproduction. Sexuality has become associated with far more varied joys than simply reproductive ones: with the liberation of diverse erotic practices, with the assertion of legitimacy and freedom for gay and bisexual as well as "straight" men and women. Now, of course, millions of people turn to sex far more frequently in search of pleasure than procreation. How, then, could a drive toward reproduction explain persistent cultural preferences for younger rather than older female bodies? And how, therefore, can my devil's advocate continue to justify his or her preference for breasts that do not "sag" (a clearly pejorative term that has lost none of its negative value, even though the tie between sex and reproduction has been loosened)? On the contrary, if looks-ism originally came into being because of reproductive imperatives, we ought to be finding that it is now withering away—not thriving. The evolution of culture and society itself ought to be rendering a biological need for set standards of beauty increasingly obsolete.

Moreover, in terms of *sexual potency and pleasure*, it is well known that male sexuality tends to peak around the late teenage years, whereas female sexuality tends to peak much later, well into a woman's late thirties and early forties. So how and why did it transpire that our cultural representations and values do not reflect these facts? By such physiological criteria, as society has steadily moved in the direction of valuing sexual pleasure and not simply reproductive functions, the *older woman's* body (if anyone's) should be eroticized rather than the younger adolescent girl's; our social norms ought to approve of matches between older women and younger men, rather than the double standard of approving only the opposite pairing. But in spite of such physiological (literally biological) evidence, contemporary societies are still much more likely to value young women's bodies, indicating that *the problem may indeed have little to do with biology, or biology alone:* rather, it is likely that power plays a crucial role. For it may be well-to-do men—those possessing cultural, economic, and political capital—who hold greater power to put forth their own *social constructions of biology.* If many men *believe* that it is with younger women that greater physiological pleasures are possible, then that social construction itself can begin to create self-fulfilling effects in the minds and bodies of those very same men, as well as in others'. And yet this "biologically based" belief itself remains overwhelmingly cultural in its formation.

The devil's advocate position presumes that explicit overvaluation of certain kinds and shapes of youthful bodies through the promulgation of social and cultural norms is necessary to ensure species survival. Yet why wouldn't the opposite proposition even more convincingly demonstrate the presence of ongoing biological imperatives, if indeed they existed? If such attraction is really natural and instinctive, and assuredly known to be such, then it would not be necessary to prize any one set of appearance characteristics more than others. If we were so sure it was natural, like the sun and the moon, why *not* then thoroughly democratize our images of women's (and, for that matter, men's) looks? The best proof of the biological argument would be to build a society in which it had become quite commonplace to see in movies and on magazine stands images of men and women of various shapes and sizes staring back at us, old and middle-aged and young, blessed with skin in wonderfully varied hues, interestingly and heterogeneously represented as though valuable and valued (as advertising aims to make us feel). For what possible harm could ensue from so transforming our imagery if we knew looks-ism to be securely anchored in biology anyway? Men would flock en masse to younger women no matter what we did, and then only to women with the exact same looks that are now held up to us as worthy of emulation. My devil's advocate should be rushing to bring about such changes, I would insist: only then would he or she be able to *prove* beyond debate that a biological thesis is correct, that looks-ism is natural and beauty "just is."

But, as far as I know, not many people who share the opinions of my devil's advocate are rushing to advocate such experimentation in social science. Rather, as we have seen, few people these days call for changing the social fact that only certain kinds of bodily images and representations dominate our cultural landscape—which means that perhaps my devil's advocate *isn't* really so sure that looks-ism is natural, after all.

And thus one of the best possible responses is that contemporary looks-ism would not be so visible, so ostentatious, if biology alone could explain its persistence. That which is social is so symbiotically intermeshed with the biological that the two are virtually indistinguishable. They have become overdetermined in such a way that even the possibility of separating biology from culture can be asserted or defended only with great difficulty.

I suspect that my devil's advocate somehow secretly knows this and thus may hold onto his (or her) biological claims for dear life. For if it is impossible to extricate the social and cultural from the biological even if we wished to, then change *is* possible. If these two levels—social/biological, biological/social—constantly and unavoidably interact with one other in dialectical fashion, then we can conceive and re-create the world in the most humane fashion possible. There is every reason to expect, not simply to hope, that in the long run conscious intentions will affect unconscious thought processes, slowly seeping into our psychic, bodily, and sexual associations. One would only cling stubbornly to a predominantly *biological* argument if there were vested interests and powerful habits that one wished to keep in place and to protect. Many men (and some women) could then go on asserting that beauty "just is," even though this does not have to be the case.

Thus, when we try to understand our interrelated topics of looks-ism and beauty, it is key to examine how biological arguments are *used* self-fulfillingly, effectively ensuring that gendered power remains in place. Biology *is* not destiny, à la Freud, but certainly *becomes* destiny when that is how it is defined. Remember again, as I would remind my devil's advocate, that biological arguments were once used to maintain the impossibility of ever changing gender asymmetries. Stephen Goldberg wrote of the supposed inevitability of patriarchy; not so long ago, Norman Mailer attacked Kate Millett's *Sexual Politics* (1970) not only on the grounds of its author's looks but because she dared to ignore her biologically ordained role.[41] And not much earlier, people held that biology prevented women from doing so-called men's work. By now such beliefs have been dislodged, revealed as having been both false and ideologically self-serving. However, while it is commonplace to accept that gender inequality itself is not biologically based, has the debate shifted, focusing instead on beauty—clearly a last bastion of sexist distinctions and discriminations?

Some readers may be disappointed to find a sociologist entertaining and then immediately squelching considerations related to biology. Re-admitting biology is arguably a refreshing change from the kind of radical social constructionism that predictably represses from sight any bodily, physiological, or material considerations that do not neatly accord with the worldview of the constructionist in question. To those readers, and to my devil's advocate who perhaps is still not convinced that biology can be ruled out as a major explanation for looks-ism's stubborn perpetuation, I point out that *the particular case made in favor of a biological explanation was relatively weak, even on the grounds of biology itself.*

For someone who continued to insist that heterosexual attraction is natural and based on ongoing needs for species reproduction and survival would still have to account for our basic question: *why looks-ism?* All that follows from this view of naturalness is that heterosexual attraction itself is presumed to have a biological basis; it implies no particular requirement about the *form* heterosexual attraction needs to adopt. Indeed, there is nothing about changing the cultural favoritism shown, say, thinness over obesity, or bigger breasts as opposed to smaller ones, that has anything whatsoever to do with reproductive necessity. People can, and do, reproduce themselves perfectly well across a huge range of divergent looks. In fact, biology suggests that a cultural obsession with thinness ought even to be discouraged, since at anorexic levels menstruation has been known to diminish or stop, which hinders reproduction. To be sure, biological considerations of species survival do suggest that men would be attracted to women prior to menopause, when reproduction is still possible. But since such concerns have diminished markedly in modern society (and since changes in technology and culture have enabled those who are neither heterosexual nor all that young to biologically reproduce or to adopt offspring), perhaps ongoing attraction to youth is based on an altogether *different* biological reality.

Perhaps, then, our devil's advocate may be barking up the wrong biological tree *even when* he or she falls back upon arguments about "nature"; to the extent that any biological basis for looks-ism continues to exist, it may have less to do with reproduction than we first presumed. Rather, insofar as looks-ism manifests itself in the form of attraction to youth, this may reflect human beings' still very immense *fear of death*, a fear related to biology that, unlike concerns about reproductive survival, there is no reason to think has or will become less well-founded in the foreseeable future.

If fear of death is indeed operative, then the theoretical picture changes in exceedingly important ways. For in that case, looks-ism's eventual obsolescence would also entail having to confront the attitudes that keep us oriented toward habitually avoiding, rather than accepting, reminders of our mortality. Moreover, this shift in emphasis forces us to recall that looks-ism is not in itself essentially *gender-specific*. It has only *become* so because of previously existing structures of power: in particular, patriarchal modes of social organization to which looks-ism by now is firmly affixed. Yet there is nothing gender-specific about the fear of death. Had women ever held similarly unequal and differential powers, perhaps we too would have much more frequently evinced attraction to younger men, younger women, on the basis of this similarly human appeal. (In numerous individual cases, of course, women can and do make this choice at present, preferring younger men or younger women.)[42] For by associating with youth, any human being may feel less fearful of intimacy because supposedly more shielded from loss, relatively protected from the reminders of existential uncertainty that mark our bodies—no matter how illusory or ineffective such feelings of protection might be.

And therefore, we are also reminded of the need to return to much more explicitly *social* explanations of looks-ism, but now in such a way that we do not have to repress considerations of a "natural" dimension of life altogether so that they are not conflated with commonplace biases related to sex, heterosexuality, and race. Reconsiderations of biology need not categorically be denied. However, as we are about to see, no longer is a biological theory *required*, strictly speaking. Thus, for now, the best way to proceed may be to retrace our steps, bracketing considerations of nature and the biological at least for the time being (as we did with references to looks-ism itself) while we return to the social, the cultural, the sociological. And a good place to recommence may be to consider how huge numbers of little boys and little girls growing up in contemporary societies are likely to imbibe looks-ist propensities simply by looking around.

We can go back again to de Beauvoir, to the enormous power and impressive pulls of social processes that traditionally urge us to "become" gendered women or men. And we can add to de Beauvoir's insights other, specifically anthropological observations about the development of Western science. As Emily Martin points out in the edited volume *Body/Politics: Women and the Discourses of Science* (1990):

Historically in the West, vision has been a primary route to scientific knowledge. We speak of "knowledge as illumination, knowing as seeing, truth as
light"; throughout Western thought, the illumination that vision gives has
been associated with the highest faculty of mental reasoning. Recently, however, the role of vision has come to seem problematic. Some have singled out
reliance on vision as a key culprit in the scrutiny, surveillance, domination,
control, and exertion of authority over the body, particularly over the bodies
of women.[43]

All that little boy and little girl have to do, after all, is to stare up at any
or most billboards, to turn on the television and watch commercials, to
surf the visual kaleidoscope presented by cable or the Internet. They
could simply go to the movies, on the way surveying the magazines in
any bookstore or newsstand. Or, when older, they could gaze upon and
become understandably influenced/aroused by those body types which
are more likely than others to be featured in the bulk of dominant pornography, or which are regularly to be seen pornographically posed in
a range of other forms of mass media.[44]

When yet a child, she or he, he and she, could continue strolling
down the street and could watch men watching women's bodies, sensing which kinds were ranked higher as they passed by or what kind
of clothes were most likely to increase or decrease the likelihood of
commentary (and perhaps wondering why such commentary was offered so often by males in public and in groups). A child might psychically incorporate such incidents, noticing how frequently in everyday
life one can see a man looking at a woman, eyeing her up and down,
more or less surreptitiously, in an elevator or a restaurant. Though how
come, the child might wonder, *she* isn't doing that anywhere near as
much—why doesn't everyone get to be sexual when they feel like it?
How come it's okay for *him* to do this so often when she hardly does it
ever at all? Or these children may notice how football games watched
every Sunday by their dads do not involve women as central to their
action, only as parties who must look "pretty" when rooting on the
side.

Then there are the sorts of influences traceable back to political economy, to the "fashion-beauty complex" as Sandra Bartky has creatively
described it.[45] In addition to the influence of media and culture on gender, another quite plausible explanation for looks-ism's perpetuation is
social, revolving around not patriarchy alone (thus far analyzed too
often in isolation) but also capitalism and *its* systemic drives. For beauty
clearly is big business: there are deep-seated economic, in addition to

psychic, investments in looks-ism as we know it. Think back to the figures cited above, to what Wolf approximated to be a $33 *billion*-a-year diet industry, a $20 *billion*-a-year cosmetics industry, a $300 *million*-a-year cosmetic surgery industry, and a $7 *billion*-a-year pornography industry. By now the last estimate ought be revised upward closer to $10 *billion*.[46] Once established as businesses profitable on these mind-bogglingly massive scales, how could corporate entities *not* become driven by their own sociocultural aims and motives, to the point that questions of biological or natural origins become indeterminable or irrelevant?

If Marx was onto something, or if we even just heed John Kenneth Galbraith noting capitalism's brilliance at creating not just new commodities but freshly perceived needs,[47] then we can safely anticipate that looks-ism will not be withering away any time soon. There would be too many reinvestments involved (again, of a purely economic kind) for beauty to transform into anything other than an achievement sworn to be made possible through the faithful application of dazzlingly new invented products, technological procedures, or cosmetic advances. This may help explain, in part, why the fashion-beauty complex has also begun to spread its tentacles toward men, more than at other times in capitalism's gendered past. As we have seen, this complex has not so far managed to draw in men in anything approaching the numbers of female consumers; the extent of future efforts and the degree of their success remain to be seen. When it comes to beauty, the question of whether to honor traditional gender ideologies or to dismiss them as impediments to maximizing profits may strike corporate managers as still unresolved and confusing. At present, though, it seems clear that companies like Clinique continue to gear the lion's share of their advertising attentions toward women even as managers and executives market Clinique for Men.

If Jonathan Swift were alive and could be commissioned to satirize this issue, what vision might he have invented to illustrate this social explanation of contemporary looks-ism's persistence—to illuminate the political economy of beauty? Perhaps he would encourage us to think of a fictionally outrageous but telling situation, in which suddenly everyone decided to see how the universe looked if we stopped buying and using all diet aids, cosmetics, cosmetic surgery, and pornography (following, for argument's sake, the order of Wolf's listing). Suppose we could get everyone to agree to do this on a global basis, for approximately two years. My point is not that such a boycott can, or ought to, happen; I am no reborn Luddite, sadly and hopelessly trying to stave off contemporary developments as workers once tried to halt the Industrial Revolution, nor have I forgotten about the question of playful pleasures activated by appearances—the fun many people, women and men, can and do sometimes experience in dressing up, wearing makeup, and looking and being looked at. Rather, it serves to emphasize the profundity of these social influences by imagining life abruptly stripped of them. For what indeed would happen as a result of our modest proposal? How *would* the world now appear?

At first glance, the ramifications of this proposition seem analogous to those of dismantling, or greatly diminishing the budgets of, our military-industrial complexes. In both cases, many jobs would be lost. However, whereas cutting back a military-industrial complex could free public funds for job creation or other kinds of economic redistribution, the business of beauty is private. Thus, there might not be much effort to find new jobs for the great number of people displaced if there were no longer any beauty-related business to be done, when billions of dollars had changed hands before. Think too of the research and development that goes into creating additional lines and products and of the implications for advertising and advertisers. Think of the huge numbers of experts who would find themselves out of work because their livelihoods revolved around Foucaultian "regimes" of diet, hair, makeup, or sexiness.[48]

This would all take place in a globalizing economy that thrives and increasingly depends on service- and information-oriented industries. Looks-ism's demise, even if only temporary, would depress these businesses. Their bad fortune would only add to the anxieties already circulating as the next century approaches, its arrival anticipated with not only hopes but trepidation: fears of unemployment, and of jobless futures,[49] would likely be that much more aggravated; we might feel more strongly that science and technology not only routinely bring astounding wizardry but also cause human economic obsolescence. With this, our modest proposal seems already on the verge of metamorphosing from a dream into a nightmare from which we would be only too glad to awaken. Already, we might be ready to welcome back our intense desires to appear beautiful.

But I suspect that we have only scratched the surface of what might be revealed if the fashion-beauty complex disappeared for even a short time. For this line of reasoning may have taken us toward a too-limited social theoretical framework, one that unwittingly brings functionalist and Marxist strands of thought into perverse coalition. We may therefore be overlooking insights offered by later developments in contemporary social theory rather than incorporating them into our survey. The most important of these is the understanding that large, external structures *and* the relative freedom of an individual's personal choices (or "agency") *both* matter; both must be considered. Once again, beauty demands attention not only to external effects but to our inner feelings about looks.

For a given advertising firm owned by a multinational corporation cannot force people to buy the particular beauty products it touts. All advertisers can do is attempt, sometimes successfully and sometimes not, to influence an unpredictable process that is highly risky for entrepreneurs precisely because individual agency exists and matters. After all, it was in the interests of its own survival that capitalism developed the admirable resiliency for which it has so often been complimented (including, perhaps most notably, in the prescient writings of Marx himself). Thus, with regard to beauty, perhaps advertisers would have already gone further toward changing a looks-ist status quo if they were convinced that such change was profitable, necessary, and desired by their clients. Clearly, some smaller-scale variant of our Swiftian boycott *could* have taken place long ago, when the beauty industry was less entrenched; just as clearly, it did not. Analyzing the beauty system seems to leave us no choice but to look at the matter both ways, dialectically— from the outside in as well as from the inside out. Looks-ism is indeed a social fact foisted upon us from without, but at least to some degree we also re-create it in turn. Our next question, then, ought to be *why* we might wish to reinvent looks-ism *ourselves* in the aftermath of its slipping away. It is possible that we would experience nostalgic longings for the present beauty system quite apart from the economic anxieties suggested by our Swiftian speculations—even if, for example, forms of guaranteed income existed or lost jobs were sure to be replaced. Would we indeed miss the beauty system? If so, why might we want it back? Our investigation here must likewise turn back, but now to a focus on the *pleasures* possibly constructed by our current beauty system, not merely its pains.

Let's return, then, to the social explanation of socialization itself. Consider how accustomed that little boy and little girl have become to gazing at advertisements on billboards, on cable TV, or in magazines, to internalizing what has long been familiar in the outside world. The Swiftian boycott threatens to strip the world of certain stimulations, not just of certain problems. To those who have been acculturated in a commodified society, things may seem lacking in color, in sights and sounds, in sensuality and sexuality; the world may look repressed and repressive, downright prudish, lacking in accustomed visual joys. We may find ourselves free-associating, and not very enthusiastically, to pre-1980s images of Communism with a capital C—to the People's Republic of China under Mao, or to the Soviet Union before and even after its breakup—seen in shades of gray, economically deprived, bored and boring, insistent on a massive sameness. Then, too, would we have as much to laugh about, to show or share with girlfriends or boyfriends, about how we have done or redone our hair, our eyes, our outfits? What about shopping, in city boutiques or suburban malls? These activities can be viewed in not merely economic but also social/psychic terms as modern occasions for establishing or demonstrating intimacy, whether with friends, family members, or any small group on which one relies for day-to-day comfort and feelings of belonging.

But simply considering even these feelings about relative sensual and sexual deprivation that might result from looks-ism's disappearance does not take us far enough into the social analyses capable of explaining *from within* our subject's persistence. For perhaps an additional and even more important possibility is that without looks-ism, an important means of making social distinctions among ourselves would be lost.[50] Without looks-ism, we find ourselves shorn of an entire classification system—the system of beauty, ancient and by now indeed profoundly familiar to us—*through which we are used to gaining, maintaining, or losing a sense of class.* "Class" is a concept that can benefit greatly from being construed in a sense much wider than the purely economic, as the case of beauty makes abundantly clear. It sometimes refers to money, of course, but not exclusively or even primarily. As exemplified through the beauty system, this idea of class needs a significant revision and extension even beyond what Max Weber suggested. Weber expanded the idea of class to include how much one stands to lose or gain in terms of possessing other social "goods" that relate to status and recognition, but he devoted little attention to thinking about pleasures related to procuring bodily happiness and—most critically of all—love, as a form of class.[51]

With this line of thought, an earlier one now also becomes clearer, namely, the provocative idea that looks-ism may not be what it appears. For the beauty system as we know it may have far less to do with the *physical* characteristics around which it is *supposed* to center (i.e., the given shape of a nose or a breast, the presence or absence of wrinkles or weight) than with the much broader cultural meanings that looks succeed in symbolizing. Regularly, and repeatedly, looks-ism is attached to something *else,* to something *other;* it points beyond its own parameters, amounting in the process to much more than only what appears. So reinterpreted, looks-ism emerges as paradoxical indeed, distinctively talented at distracting us through its surface glitter, making us less likely to glimpse a whole complex of feelings, desires, and thoughts to which this classification system nonetheless alludes.

For instance, say a young working-class male is going to a party with a "beautiful" or "gorgeous" young woman he has met, someone he knows his friends are likely to call among themselves a "babe." To him, she resembles a movie star or pop culture icon—perhaps Cindy Crawford or Whitney Houston. But is it really his date's actual physiognomy, her "look," that is making this young man feel so good, excited, proud, even in love as he dresses and scents himself to go out on a date? It would seem difficult to argue that it could be *only* this, for that would require a predictably clear-cut, one-on-one correlation between specific socially valued physical characteristics and our very individual experiences of sexual, emotional, and mental connection and satisfaction. For all we know, when taking into account these multifaceted criteria, our working-class man might find himself far more compatible, or even much more pleased on what strike him as "purely" physiological grounds alone, with someone who is considered quite plain. Here, then, is one of looks-ism's interesting sleights of hand. Despite its ties to a classification system that facilitates making restrictive and exclusionary distinctions, the beauty system nevertheless manages to convey the impression that it promotes a culture broadly conducive to sexual and erotic stimulations, seeming genuinely to encourage the possibilities of fulfillment *in general.*

Perhaps it is indeed the panoply of meanings to which his date's "gorgeous" looks have become attached that account for much of this young man's pleasure as he prepares for his date? Or is he excited by both the physical and social aspects of attraction, which once more have become so enmeshed that it is no longer evident to him—nor to us— which is which? At the very least, as we have seen, it is safe to conclude that social influences cannot be ruled out in societies in which looks-ism provides powerful criteria for routinely categorizing and assessing women's worth. Thus we should not be at all surprised if some of his pleasure stems from expectations that the artificial value of her "gorgeousness" in the outside world might become psychically self-fulfilling as it slowly becomes attached, and accruing, to him. Perhaps he is happy because he anticipates his friends' approval, or because she reminds him of a star (and thus of the larger world's often positive valuations); perhaps it is the very *idea* of her long, lovely hair, or the particular way she dresses, that makes him think, "Yes, this is my type, the type of woman with whom I would like to be seen." In this instance, analyzing looks-ism may point us not only toward gender but also back in the direction of distinctions made on the traditional economic grounds of class. It is in the context of loss of value experienced *elsewhere* that this particular young man may be especially eager to keep beauty alive, and to re-create a sense of worth otherwise unavailable to him.[52]

Of course, it would be foolish to surmise that only young working-class males are affected by such richly significant symbolism. Images of beautiful young women—on the arm of a wealthy older gentleman, or sitting in a three-star restaurant next to a captain of industry, or emerging from a car with a man who heads an organized crime operation—are by now so familiar as to constitute their own sort of Hollywood-promoted cliché. But clichés are rarely total fabrications. It is still easy to find younger women in the roles of sexual and intimate companions, perhaps mistresses or wives, of well-to-do older men. And, as already suggested, it remains *less* common—though certainly also not unusual or scandalously aberrant, particularly in societies now sensitized by feminism—to encounter similar associations between younger men and well-to-do older women that reverse the more conventional gendered pattern.[53]

For we are still in a world in which one of the rewards, and outward visual manifestations, of masculine power once achieved involves money, prestige, and influence reliably converting into sexual access to "beautiful" women's bodies. But here again we are faced with the same question implicitly posed by the young man's desires. Is it a particular body per se to which that older man, that captain of industry or organized crime head, finds himself so drawn, and which he surveys with a much-cultivated appreciation? Or is it the very social fact of certain bodies having come to be viewed, throughout a given culture, as something prizable, so that perhaps there is a challenge in assessing and "winning" such bodies, a game which is not altogether dissimilar to sport? For, indeed, the sort of body viewed as the epitome of value is likely to be just the sort a powerful man in that culture begins to think he wants, he deserves—he now desires to "have."

But, as has been insightfully observed in the work of R. W. Connell,[54] this prerogative of masculinity is not available to all. Rather, it usually presumes even further and added forms of social differentiation being made *between men* (as analogously exist between women): in contemporary societies, most commonly these relate to race, economic class, and sexual orientation. Thus, access to women's bodies is a reward especially to be expected for those possessing what Connell dubs "hegemonic masculinity." By this term, which helps fine-tune our theoretical understanding of gender's complexities, he means the particular form of masculinity that becomes most highly valued in a given culture, time, and place. In many societies, certainly including our own, hegemonic masculinity is associated not only with "handsomeness" (a point that, because of looks-ism, I would downplay in importance more than did Connell) but far more significantly with privileges that result from possessing money, power, or whiteness. Thus, hegemonic masculinity *by definition* embraces precisely what we have been discussing: the anticipated ability of this form of masculinity to facilitate intimate association with women whose looks are considered most valuable in particular (sub)cultural or society-wide settings.

To illustrate this symbolic facet of looks-ism in relation to masculinities, one could point to the importance of public appearances themselves, of *being seen* with a "beautiful" woman—walking along a grand avenue, or sitting in a restaurant, or getting out of a car. These are all simultaneously moments of public display, of being seen and in particular being seen *by other men*. Of course, such public displays produce their own sense of enjoyment, no matter how much they may differ from what is being experienced existentially, in private. For whatever separates the life experiences of an organized crime chief from those of a Fortune 500 corporation's chief executive officer, both are likely to know the sense of importance that follows noticing, from the corner of one's eye, other men noticing—and not just underlings, but coequals too—the stunning woman who is accompanying them in public one night.

Here, then, is a second sleight of hand, a second symbolic allusion that resonates well beneath the surface of beauty expectations. On its face, looks-ism seems to be about distinctions between women: what a particular woman is wearing, how she is wearing her hair, how nice may or may not seem her breasts, how thin or fat she is. *But such assessments of women's looks are even more fundamentally driven by the character and symbolic meaning of relations between men,* relations that are differentiated along lines of class as well as race (although such distinctions are relatively ignored and underanalyzed, since *theoretical* attentions often follow the direction of the surrounding culture—i.e., toward women).[55] In its most sexist incarnations, then, looks-ism becomes tautological: it involves the power to make precisely the sort of distinctions between masculinities that its own classification system enables. So with regard to our Swiftian scenario and the question of why we might re-create looks-ism if deprived of it, at least one facet of a response now becomes clearer. The loss of looks-ism could place masculinity itself at a loss, removing a criterion by which its internal processes of definition and differentiation historically became possible. Without it, a person attempting to be masculine might suddenly feel disoriented, revealing the extent to which looks-ism is bound up with our usual perceptions, feelings, and thoughts about gender.

And it would likewise be foolish to presume that these constructs have symbolic meaning only to men. For how could all of this not apply equally to the social creation of femininity and femininities? To women, too, a given look can represent many things that include but go far beyond whether a particular man is handsome or "cute." A given woman, too, may like the *idea* of a particular look. If she is heterosexual, perhaps his earring in one ear makes him look '60s-ish and free and she likes that, or his longish hair or wire-rimmed glasses evoke left/liberal or intellectual associations that she appreciates (and she, too, thinks to herself, "This is my type"). Another woman may be drawn to a man's conservative, clean-shaven appearance or the neat-looking cut of his suits. However, precisely because of the unequal and asymmetric ways in which gender has grown, many women are likely to perceive such symbolic meanings at once similarly and quite differently. Many women will realize that the social worth currently figured into hegemonic masculinity accords relatively less value strictly to looks and relatively more to economic or political power; position and prestige; allegedly to whiteness (in still largely racist social contexts, like our own); and perhaps to those statuses which rise with possession of scientific, technological, or other forms of intellectual know-how.

By extension, looks-ism per se may not be nearly as much in the interest of *women's* vicarious symbolic pleasures as it is seems to be in *men's.* If increased importance is to accrue to women because of their

association with a particular male partner, it is less likely to occur on
the basis of his handsome masculine looks alone.[56] Thus women may
be more likely than men to already realize that "looks" are not entirely
or even predominantly *about* physical appearance. Yet even if appearances thus become relatively less important *to* women, they need not
be perceived as any less important *for* women. Clearly, many women
understand that this remains a large part of what men across divergent
classes, races, and statuses differentially value. In societies still permeated by gender, *attraction* itself—to men as well as women, with the
differences observed above—becomes not only mysterious but often
predictably and sociologically skewed. We now are better-equipped theoretically to understand our empirical observations about gender and
attractiveness. However, much more needs to be said about looks-ism's
ramifications for and between women, a central question in the context
of gendered asymmetries and other complex social distinctions.

Yet first we must make one more round of inquiry into symbolic
distinctions. For our project of investigating looks-ism's persistence has
now moved from one kind of social theoretical explanation capable of
encompassing many levels (including that of "political economy") toward another. From the notion of economic class as promulgated by
Marx, we have moved into the territory of more complex formulations
related to capital such as those proposed a century later in the work of
Pierre Bourdieu. Bourdieu is well known for showing that modern capital is a multifaceted phenomenon, far more complex than can be discerned from the predominantly economic concept of class that characterized earlier Marxist theory. Thus, capital can assume many forms,
from investing in machinery to investing in ourselves. Moreover, such
self-investment can itself take different forms, depending on whether
individuals are attempting to accumulate academic credentials by using
their minds or to realize value by disciplining their bodies (in this latter
instance, developing "bodily capital").[57] With this, not much of a leap
is required to see that a social classification system could easily begin to
surround looks when viewed as a phenomenon that becomes valuable
in three overlapping ways: as a commodity, as Marx describes it; as a
form of capital, as Bourdieu depicts; and as both, at once commodified
and capitalized on.

Indeed, looks falls into each of these three categories simultaneously.
In the first sense, looks can be taken to signify a valued possession; it *is*
a commodity, a characteristic or "thing" that one either personally does
or does not "have," according to a given society's criteria of value. This

is a sociological restatement of the thesis that beauty "just is": it is what my friend believes, despite the seeming contradiction with his feminist sympathies, Naomi Wolf to "own"; or what that working-class young man, in common with the corporate and crime bosses, believes his date (and, by extension, himself) to "possess." Thus understood, looks can be categorized among those traits Talcott Parsons deemed "ascribed" by and at birth, for it is something we cannot merit but find ourselves simply *to be*. [58] This account helps explain a given person's guilty hesitance to admit he or she is a looks-ist: enlightened societies are supposed to favor achievement over ascription, the latter being associated with feudalism and certainly not with modernity or postmodernity. One may be able to alter the cultural assessments by which a given trait is treasured, but not the trait itself. In other words, I can change whether I live in a racist culture, but not my present skin color; I could conceivably alter age discrimination, but not my actual age; I could affect some hypothetical culture that happened to favor small noses (for whatever historical or idiosyncratic reasons) but not very easily my own nose size.

But the second sense, cultural capital, also is highly relevant—clearly capital of the bodily kind, which is most relevant to beauty and looks, can be increasingly *worked at* and *worked for:* looks are not merely ascribed but more and more frequently *achieved.* Here, we are firmly on contemporary soil as we enter the rapidly changing world of "technoscience." For one can, after all, change one's nose to some extent through surgery; indeed, given the growing sophistication of technology that Davis and Wolf describe, one can alter a wide gamut of other bodily features as well. Under some (and only some) circumstances, one can work to look younger or to try to "pass" as whiter. The present-day popularity of health clubs, fitness, and exercise relates not only to staying well but of course to consciously remolding—sometimes to the point of obsession—looks and bodily appearances. I may be especially motivated to achieve a certain look: perhaps if I work out four times a week, I can make myself thinner (and often, to a gratifying extent, I succeed); if I use this machine or that every other day, perhaps I can tone my arms or widen my chest or flatten my stomach (and to some extent, this too is often true—I can). Alternatively, if I use a certain beauty procedure, maybe I can straighten my hair in the way most valued by a society in which looks-ist and racist standards have coalesced. And what is cosmetic surgery if not the embodiment of technology's remarkable new abilities to approximate our bodies more closely to dominant cultural specifications of attractiveness, of femininities, of age? Such specifications certainly also apply to race, as one particular surgery currently demonstrates: "correcting" the eyelids of Asian American women, an operation increasingly found where Caucasian eye shapes are held to be "better."[59]

Clearly, then, looks and beauty are part of a system of cultural capital, not simply a priori possessions but things that many individuals seek to accumulate. Yet beauty as we know it is even more complicated. On many occasions, it involves *both* that which is ascribed *and* achieved, *both* that which is commodified *as well as* that which is capitalized on. This leads to a quite mad, because self-contradictory, relationship between these two aspects of social valuation. When it comes to beauty, I sometimes try to appear *as if* I *were* a thing: I may be working to achieve a look that would have been most desirable if simply ascribed *by nature* (think how frequently hairdressers receive requests from their clients to make their hair "look natural"). Translating this into social theoretical terminology, one could say in Parsonian language that looks-ism often demands that an illusion of ascription be achieved; in Bourdieu's vocabulary, that cultural capital is enlisted in the service of trying to appear a (commodified) thing. Thus, I may energetically try to transform myself from an active agent into a relatively inert look, or passive appearance; I may vigorously work at masquerading in the costume, or guises, of an image. If I am a model, I may put on makeup in order to pose for hours in front of a camera for a static photo or even, since we are in a sophisticated and health-conscious age, to give the appearance of vigorous activity (though from within a visual form that is by its very structure still-like).

From this perspective, too, looks-ism is not what it appears. In a philosophical sense, its views are backward: the specific kinds of social distinctions it makes are opposite to those one would propose on the grounds of maximizing human happiness alone. Looks-ism tends to favor the achievement of passivity over the activities of achievement; it favors essences over existences. In so doing, looks-ism effects a third sleight of hand, an especially clever one insofar as it is extraordinarily subtle. For contrary to all expectations, looks-ism tends also to prefer *death over life,* according higher social valuation to images of stasis than to existing faces of change. The paradox is striking, for looks-ism purports to prefer youth precisely to avoid death and associations with deathliness.

Yet in a culture that values the ascribed appearances of youth or the sense conveyed by thinness of limitless control over one's body, no one can win. No matter how one tries to play cards of science and technology in the service of looks-related goals, the house eventually prevails. Because the rules insist on seeming to defy death or to gain limitless control, human players invariably lose. Thus, what appears to be the triumphs of science and technology, our society's highest exemplars of objective rationality, may amount to just the opposite: the victory of a quite extraordinary irrationalism. The ongoing maintenance of looks-ism therefore demands a strategy of indefinite postponement rather than the exposure of social and cultural expectations that are themselves maddeningly impossible.

Via this argument, looks-ism emerges as not particularly in anyone's human interest, at the same time the world is not likely to look this way at all. However collectively short-sighted we deduce contemporary looks-ism to be, its maintenance also continues to be experienced to be in some people's immediate self-interest if not in others': in that of men more than women, no doubt; in that of people whose color is white more than those not white; in that of some men more than others, when class and race are both figured in, as well as some women much more than others (as we will soon analyze more specifically); and, certainly, in that of the youthful rather than the elderly. Yet even the ability to feel valued throughout the whole of one's life, as death's inevitability is becoming more and more apparent on the body's surfaces, eventually manifests latent social power. It is a power that the man going on sixty, especially if rich and white, is likely to realize with far greater ease than can many women or less well-to-do men, who by contrast sense their general life prospects slipping away rapidly with age.[60] If, for instance, I am a forty-five-year-old actress who can afford it, I may feel impelled to go through five, six, or seven face-lifts over the remainder of my lifetime, hoping to resuscitate my looks and to seem eternally youthful and lively, only to find in the process that my face begins to look strained and strangely masklike anyway.[61] In this case, I have been condemned to deny death in a way that amounts quite fundamentally to a cruel denial of life: for the only way to stay forever young is either to be a thing or to die early.

But this is getting ahead of ourselves, straying from an issue that now can and needs to be reconceived: how both the pleasures and pains of beauty ought at this point be more intelligible as we experience them *from within*. For the beauty system provides a powerful raison d'être for many persons, a seductive representational system through which myriad social distinctions—masculinities, femininities, classes, races, sexual orientations—can be melted down to common currency, as though a brand of money. Looks-ism is thereby the occasion of particular drives and the cause of certain motivations. For some, we saw that it provides a source of value that one can or does *have;* for others, it constitutes a mode of calling, something one can work hard *for* or *at.*

Therefore, delving into distinctions as a social explanation of looks-ism's persistence is akin to seeking what continues to fuel the tenacious perseverance of *class* itself, understanding "class" in the wide-ranging and multifaceted sense already discussed. And so the theme of looks-ism pointing past its own boundaries emerges yet again. But this time, it is the subject of beauty itself that becomes *theoretically symbolic,* hinting at a psychic and social problem that *also* remains little understood, whether in the works of Marx, the writings of later Marxists, and even the significant reworkings of Bourdieu: *why, and whence, our ongoing drives and desires to sustain inequitable social distinctions in the first place?*

For until we have better comprehended *this* question—the dilemma of oppression itself, far too complicated to more than tease out here—there may indeed be reason for concern that we would reinvent something like beauty outside ourselves, when or if we were to find it missing inside ourselves. Our topic thus offers a fascinating instance of a dialectical process. Looks-ism as a social fact exerts weighty influences a priori; as unavoidably existential "agents," we continually re-create it in turn. *Indeed, we have no choice but to perpetually re-create something;* this point about performativity partly explains the keen interest in Judith Butler's 1990 work of feminist theory, *Gender Trouble.*[62] According to a dialectical analysis, things cannot possibly stay still; history most definitely does recur in one sense and in another most definitely cannot recur. Nor can looks-ism continue without some sort of participation by *both* women *and* men, in roles that regularly change and transform.

What I have been calling looks-ism's sleights of hand can now, and for a fourth time, be again apprehended. For perhaps this is its most brilliant performance of all: *looks-ism repeats itself by appearing not to repeat itself.* Change does happen, as particular looks do transform over time: one minute we like the round voluptuousness of a Sophia Loren, at another the androgynous childlike look of a Kate Moss; advertisers may slowly begin to discriminate less against women of color (as long as a given women reflects, at least to some degree, generally accepted and white-influenced norms of beauty). Women may seem to have more autonomy: Madonna inserts more feminist allusions into her performances than ever did, or could, a 1950s figure like Marilyn Monroe, to whom in the 1990s she consciously alludes. But the earlier question remains: will Madonna be able to remake herself until she is seventy, or eighty? Will any woman be able to conquer the deeper problems of looks-ism that subsist beneath the surface, and the structural limitations it imposes?

Therefore, in common with other classificatory systems, beauty regularly bequeaths and relies on *both* pains *and* pleasures; it routinely sustains both "winners" and "losers." Within these systemic terms, someone always seems to come out all right; because of social changes, the identity of that "someone" may even alter to some degree. But despite this apparent similarity, the closely symbiotic relationship in U.S. culture between looks and age discrimination means that, again, no one is entirely immune. If sexiness, if attractiveness, if vibrancy of life itself becomes associated mostly or only with the bodies of younger people in a given society, then "winners" in this case eventually all become "losers." In this sense, analyzing looks-ism is distinctive insofar as it points social theory closer toward glimpsing a possible connection between attitudes of denial toward death and our investments in rigid "class" systems per se. For a privileged person may tell himself, for example, that he can hold onto his money forever, or that his (white) racial coloring will indefinitely accord him benefits. And of course, to a good extent, this has been the case in class- and race-stratified societies. But it is also the case that even if money helps greatly in keeping death at bay, an unavoidable and quite material limit to this immunity is nevertheless built in to the supposedly immune person's life.

For now, however, this limit faced by all human beings is not likely to be perceived. Most people are much more accustomed to focusing on how the removal of our current schema of looks would take away a popularly agreed-upon basis for social distinctions, one that is especially comforting because it is so familiar and ancient. And it would do this at a historical moment when human beings particularly need and desire such familiar distinctions, even if we have little sense of why. Practically speaking, then, the woman whom looks-ism deems ugly might be happy if we were to do away with such discriminations, but what about the person generally agreed in a given time and place to be beautiful? Those who are older might be delighted by reduced age discrimination, but what about those who feel subtle surges of power from delighting in the knowledge that they are still young (a form of relative security that may be especially cherished, given that youth is often such a terribly *in*secure state)? What about the person who has spent much of her life working to look a certain way, devoted to dieting? Might she feel that her efforts were meaningless, that she now had no calling, under newly democratized circumstances? Would the woman who saved for cosmetic surgery relax, now that standards had themselves become relaxed, or would she feel surprised at her own disappointment when the apparent justification for her efforts was gone? And what of the man who feels that his value is bolstered by his looks, or his muscles, however speciously; or who has become accustomed, amid the prejudices of racism, to having exaggerated sexual prowess attributed to him. Might he, too, feel contradictory pulls if looks-ism seemed to be withering away? And then, of course, the man who feels proud to have that beautiful woman on his arm—would he, too, experience inklings of loss, now uncertain of what drives him, when he thought he knew so surely before?

Such reactions are all possible—perhaps they are likely to occur. Thus when we consider each of these social, psychic, and cultural reasons, whether alone or especially together, it becomes crystal clear why looks-ism might indeed linger from past until present, long after it had lost any bioevolutionary justification. Indeed, it would be surprising if looks-ism were *not* persistent, if second-wave feminism had found soon after its arrival on the American scene that the beauty system was easy to transform, offering no resistance to change. This would have been astounding regardless of which explanation(s) we find most credible— whether we attribute looks-ism's longevity to the depth of gender socialization as it affects psychic perceptions (including, of course, perceptions about that which is or is not biologically determined); or we seek a powerful cause in capitalism's politics and economies, in drives toward profit simultaneously affected by gender and class; or whether we accord greatest analytic significance to beauty's symbolic meanings, both social and psychic, as it facilitates complicated and customary distinctions all around us. At this point in our argument, the Swiftian vision of a beauty-free world seems most preposterous, not our present social arrangements. The former recedes back toward where we found it, in the realm of that which was, after all, only imagined.

We have covered a good deal of ground in considering why looks-ism *in general* would be extremely difficult to uproot. Yet by no means have we gone analytically far enough: at least two critical and thorny issues have barely been touched. Even though it is clearer at this juncture why looks-ism hasn't changed *much*, the initial observation about its *worsening* remains nearly as puzzling as when we began. Consequently, a different question ought next to be formulated: in the concrete social context of 1980s and 1990s America, not so much why looks-ism at all, but "why looks-ism *now*"?

This again raises the question of feminism's own complex influence, kept bracketed thus far in the discussion. But both feminist movements *and* beauty have remained very much alive in the United States over the last few decades, since the second wave was born amid the other social movements of the 1960s. As we noted when we began with Naomi Wolf, beauty thrives even in the mode of seeming to have changed. At the same time, the need to *appear* transformed itself suggests that to simply dismiss feminist influences would be as extreme and inaccurate as to see these influences as having been entirely successful. Thus, a second unexplored issue now ought to be considered: for although we have shown the difficulties incumbent on altering a social fact, such "facts" are by no means unalterable. An analysis is necessary to assess what has or has not been attempted, and what remains yet to be tried. Thus, we will return to feminism, to its important contributions and remaining tasks, not only because of beauty biases' enormous ramifications for women and for all human beings but because feminism has a key part to play in the desired change.

WHY LOOKS-ISM *NOW*?

There are three possible answers to the question this section poses, the first following logically from the preceding discussion of looks-ism as a symbolic classification system. We will again start from Naomi Wolf's arguments in *The Beauty Myth*, but now also bringing in the organizing concept of Susan Faludi's *Backlash*. The success of both books in part reflected feminism's burgeoning mainstream legitimacy. Published only a year apart (in 1991 and 1992, respectively), they suggested similar responses to why looks-ism might be worsening at precisely this historical moment rather than another.

Wolf and Faludi argued that by 1990, second-wave feminism was suffering from the by-products of its successes even more than its possible failures. Far from being passé, feminism was all too relevant. It was being punished for uncovering social truths and accurately predicting trends much more than for its "errors," of which it was also accused in the conservative years inaugurated along with Ronald Reagan in 1980. Precisely because feminism's call for change resonated profoundly with many women, it also generated impulses to protect the traditional and the familiar. It is therefore not surprising to find vigorous social reactions against feminism beginning to unfold. A number of social movements rose in the 1980s and 1990s with the express purpose of opposing feminist gains, not only the Right to Life movement but also Republican organizing that defined itself against feminism in shaping its "defense" of "family values."

In the United States of the 1980s and 1990s, then, not only the notions of feminism but those of antifeminism have filled the air. Faludi vividly depicted an onslaught of backlashes, a sense of reaction that unified an otherwise diverse range of cultural, political, and economic developments and events. For Wolf the "beauty myth" epitomized backlash at its most insidious. It was by no stretch of the imagination coincidental, Wolf argued, that this beauty myth was being trotted out, resuscitated, and given new injections of life just as feminism, too, was taking cultural hold. Wolf agreed with the observation above that looks-ism is much more than it appears; it is being used to hinder women's social progress. Her very thesis was an explicitly historical one. Recall *The Beauty Myth*'s powerful opening pages:

> It is no accident that so many potentially powerful women feel this way. We are in the midst of a violent backlash against feminism that uses images of female beauty as a political weapon against women's advancement: the beauty myth. . . . The contemporary backlash is so violent because the ideology of beauty is the last one remaining of the old feminine ideologies that still has the power to control those women whom second wave feminism would have otherwise made relatively uncontrollable: It has grown stronger to take over the work of social coercion that myths about motherhood, domesticity, chastity, and passivity no longer can manage. It is seeking right now to undo psychologically and covertly all the good things that feminism did for women materially and overtly.[63]

Thus, whether we call it a beauty myth or looks-ism, the effort to maintain and now advance expectations about women's appearance was anything but accidental. Rather, those expectations were contributing to keeping women in their/our conventional places just when they/ we were moving out of them. Women might then circle around rather than move ahead, held back by deep-seated ambivalences: perhaps if we become too powerful, we will not be loved. And, although all human beings crave love and recognition, this very need is of course itself already gender-skewed, so that women are likely to feel its potential loss as *especially* punitive and depressing. Better then, as Wolf suggests society was implicitly warning, either *be* pretty and attractive by conventional standards or work very hard at *becoming* and *staying* that way—even if the standards themselves are biased, impossible to meet, or both.

But Wolf's and Faludi's interrelated explanations are also capable of illuminating the other side of our coin; if useful, they ought apply correspondingly to men. And, indeed, backlash does suggest why looksism would swell with new symbolic meanings *both* for men and women. Men, too, might find themselves acting more "looks conscious," now that the appeal of assessing women's looks was even more overdetermined. Adding to the beauty myth's older seductions were new desires to maintain power by asserting compensatory comforts.

By criteria both symbolic and material, by the 1990s women as a group had certainly begun to accumulate more cultural capital than ever before in U.S. history. This does not mean that opportunities were not, as they continue to be, hugely discrepant *among* women as a group, immensely different depending on whether a particular woman is poor or well-to-do, or faces overlapping prejudices, including those of race and homophobia as well as gender. Nor have the gains come close to erasing earlier gaps: when viewed as a group, women still earn only seventy cents to every dollar earned by men.[64] Yet, despite such ongoing collective inequality, for many men the very idea of feminism—and the relative inroads that they quite correctly perceived women making—had started to pose a novel threat. With women entering, and excelling in, spheres previously open only to men, older turfs of masculinities were being disturbed; prerogatives of power were being dislodged, whether many men liked it or not. A man could no longer rely on the certainty of defining himself as at least *relatively* secure vis-à-vis women, no matter what his race or class.

At such a moment, it makes a great deal of sense that the comforts of the familiar become even *more* alluring than before. For at least looks-ism offered a way to retain gender-differentiated power and control somewhere, in a traditional, familiar form indeed. To be sure, women might now be firefighters, police and corrections officers, lawyers, doctors, dentists. But this did not mean they were necessarily considered pretty or attractive, nor that men would find such defiers of tradition sexually and emotionally desirable. It was, in other words,

still possible for men to make distinctions between women on the basis
of looks, whether consciously or unconsciously. Through looks-ism,
men could still exact this compensatory symbolic price. In exchange for
the relative removal of social barriers that had thwarted women in *public,* women ought at least to look the way they had before; otherwise,
they would find themselves thwarted in *private.* They should at least
match the traditional expectations of appearance in the personal realms
of emotionality, intimacy, sexuality, and love. Women would have to
compensate to make up for the forms of relative value and recognition
taken away from men by continuing to worry, and likely with more
anxiety than usually beleaguers men in the late 1990s, "How do I
look?"

Thus proceeds one interpretation of why looks-ism has worsened
now, and a quite plausible one at that. But as indebted to Wolf and
Faludi for these ideas as feminists ought be, their explanation offers
only one important component of a fuller response. The backlash thesis
proffers a necessary, though not sufficient, explanation of looks-ism as
a problem still very much alive in the contemporary United States at
this historical moment. Perhaps a better interpretation has to be *multifaceted,* as is the society from which it springs; it must be able to account for other complex and inequitable discriminations, too, ones to
which gender cannot be reduced any more than these other forms of
discrimination can be reduced to gender. Indeed, if Wolf and Faludi
are right about their backlash thesis, then any intelligent redress likely
requires significant attention paid *both* to gender as an autonomous
form of social power *and* to other social discriminations that create
other good reasons why men and women would look to gender for
compensatory comforts and recognitions. Even though beauty is usually
thought of as being an exclusively feminist issue,[65] a now past-Wolf line
of reasoning suggests that it both includes and goes beyond *distinctions
of gendered "class" per se.* The sources of maintaining looks discrimination must be sought both in and beyond sexism, in the numerous
wellsprings of energy that continue to fuel it.

The limitation of powerful arguments like that of *The Beauty Myth*
is the extent to which feminism is envisioned as stuck in a zero-sum
game of narrowed socioeconomic proportions; the same zero-sum
thinking has also begun to cripple liberal feminist thinking, rendering
its insights inadequate, though often accurate as far as they extend. For
this structure creates the following dilemma. *Either* men agree to or are
coerced into giving up forms of economic and political power they held

before, allowing women in, so that women can gain but only at the price of men having to lose; *or* women remain within the old system that demeans them, so that men can enjoy their present power, at the price of women continuing to lose badly.[66] But clearly the parameters of such an argument need to be challenged and enlarged: rather than staying within a conceptual straitjacket, the horizon of social value, legitimacy, and mutual recognition must itself be expanded,[67] and in ways which demonstrate that eliminating one form of discrimination can and need not be purchased at the price of perpetuating others.

Thus, nothing about *widening* a Wolf/Faludi thesis need imply that feminists ought once more to subordinate women's interests to men's. Such a move would of course be preposterous, besides being historically blind.[68] Second-wave feminism initially emerged out of this very problem: the habit within other 1960s social movements of prioritizing just about any other cause before women's. I am suggesting instead that implicit within feminism's own analyses is an argument to continue practicing a lesson we have already begun to imbibe: the need to think, feel, and act in several ways and on several fronts *simultaneously.*[69]

These considerations bring us to a second reason why looks-ism may be worsening now, which should be *added* to the first. Wolf and Faludi persuasively pinpoint the role of reactions to feminist gains, but they pay little attention to the socioeconomic context of the 1980s and 1990s, which aggravated such reactionary impulses. Yet it is not surprising that looks-ism is worsening at a time when economic insecurities are also increasing—at a moment when globalizing capitalism is leaving huge numbers of people, across varied social strata and circumstances, commonly anxious about their livelihoods. There are many different indicators of this fear.[70] President Clinton found in 1992 that, despite economic reports showing slight improvements, an overwhelmingly Republican Congress was nevertheless returned in the midterm election; in 1995 John Sweeney was elected as a new AFL-CIO president amid perceptions that change was badly needed, and in France workers rebelled against government-imposed austerity; in 1996 Pat Buchanan unexpectedly threw the Republicans into confusion, winning primaries soon after he began to emphasize the importance of class. Through all these events, a latent sense of doubt was manifested, a feeling that all is not well with the globalizing capitalist political economy. "How can I survive such rapid and bewildering socioeconomic transformations? Will I?" it is hard not to wonder. "Will I be able to maintain my job? Will there be new ones to be found? What if no 'safety net' is there to reassure me if all else fails?"

Although at first glance someone might wonder what any of these apparently public events have to do with seemingly private assessments of beauty, I would urge that person to look again. For as psychologists of various stripes concur, in times of crisis, people turn for comfort to that which is most habitual. We try to maintain, sustain, to use in the present whatever social distinctions may have helped us to gain recognition, security, attention, and acknowledgment in the past. We may clutch at straws, even straws that fill us with ambivalence, that we somehow suspect or know can only provide temporary relief anyway—even straws that may have been, or may eventually become, partly destructive of us as well. So why would it be surprising that young women in the late 1990s clutch at looks as though at straws? However tradition-based and potentially sexist, at least recognition for looks can yield an immediate sense of gratification, of self-importance, in a world in which other axes of acknowledged worth can by no means be counted on to stand still, to stop shifting. If anything, as young people have every reason to perceive and to fear, the average person's chance of finding self-worth acknowledged in *economic* terms has *also worsened* over the same decades during which looks-ism, too, has intensified.

It thus becomes that much more ludicrous to "judge" women who are undertaking cosmetic surgery in ever-increasing numbers. The importance of augmenting or reducing one's breasts, or one's nose, or lifting one's face, or seeking eyelid surgery, is that it indeed represents a *socially symbolic* effort. Those taking such actions hope to maintain, or to improve, their socially assessed worth in both their own eyes and those of a world that seems intent on whittling away traditional (and even long-standing sexist) sources of value. Similarly, this second point makes useless and socially insensitive any judgment of a young woman who works assiduously to maintain her good looks because she suspects they are all she has to outweigh the disadvantages related to bias against her class or race, or a young man who works hard at maintaining his muscles, attending carefully to his body because he uses it for his living, perhaps as an athlete or as an actor in a pornographic film. As Connell observes, not of hegemonic but now of such *marginalized* masculinities, some men learn to keep their bodies youthful and in superlative shape because this may seem (or be) the best or sole avenue available for advancement—maybe even for survival. In this regard, the sorts of race and class disadvantages frequently associated with marginalized masculinities position *some* men similarly to *many* women. Opportunities to develop socially valued skills of the mind are rendered relatively inaccessible to men who have thus been marginalized; they are more likely to be valued for skills centered visibly only on the body.[71]

But, in an equally important respect, the person who becomes marginalized in his masculinity is still structurally positioned so that he may have, or take, gender-specific "privileges." Now we can view a given marginalized man from the other side, not so much from a position of relative powerlessness (which can also render men *looked at,* their bodies assessed), but also from a common male prerogative of relative power, that of *looking.* A particular working-class man, or a man who experiences terrible discrimination because of his race and class, may engage in annoyingly sexist comments centered on women's looks. Like an upper-class man in this respect, except that dispossession has put him in possession of a compounded motivation for doing so, he may engage in objectifying or even violently sexist practices, with or without his friends. Thus, the powerlessness of marginalized masculinity may be transformed into its opposite—power through the marginalization of another, of a particular woman or of women generally—creating sexist wrongs that cannot be rationalized away by subsequent explanations, no matter how overdetermined their cause.

Yet though they are not justifiable, we cannot analyze these sexist wrongs if we wholly ignore the class- and race-related pains that their perpetrators are often simultaneously experiencing—their widespread sense of devaluation and lack of recognition. Such acts must be situated within a historical context; it is hardly astonishing if gendered injustices and compensatory sexism have increased in tandem with other social insecurities. In response, feminists may find it necessary to do two things at once, both in theory and in political practice. On the one hand, it is absolutely necessary—a categorical imperative—to condemn terrible and inexcusable acts of sexism; on the other, the existence of men's pain, as well as women's, and the need for redressing such pain's complex sources in and beyond the structures of gender should not be blithely *ignored.*

Our promised return to an earlier theoretical revision with regard to biology, again not completely forgetting or repressing this dimension of our problem, brings us to the third interrelated explanation for looks-ism's intensification *now*. For it is possible that the complexity of looks-ism's historical accentuation also involves *increasing fears of death, fears whose intensity we have no reason to believe have diminished or even merely remained the same*. Indeed, out-of-control socioeconomic anxieties make us literally as well as figuratively fearful for our lives, apprehensive about our ability to sustain even an outward appearance of *liveliness*. At such times, we are more likely to take pleasure in the exercising of *control*. In *Unbearable Weight* (1993), Susan Bordo cites "control" as one of three theoretical axes helpful in illuminating the obsession with weight characteristic of U.S. culture. Such practices as dieting or exercising enable one to feel that some control can be exerted over one's body even if not over the world outside.[72] Thus, it is quite explicable why *particular* criteria of valued feminine beauty—in our case, youth relative to age, thinness relative to weight—are the preferred looks at this historical place and time, the United States of the 1980s and 1990s. These particular looks accord pleasure because we have come to associate them with control; through them, it may feel as though we can defy even the basic facts of life and, by extension, of death.

But again, the impression created by these looks is only illusory. Science and technology have not managed to eradicate contingency, even as they often convey an *appearance* of unlimited possibilities. And such appearances bear very high costs. A person may find her- or himself noticing that one move aimed at heading off some bodily deterioration requires yet another defensive move, and another. The male athlete trying to stave off the effects of aging may well discover that he has to work harder and harder to maintain a litheness that in any case will never match that of youth. A woman who has one face-lift may discover a few years later that she needs to have one more, and then one more. We may meet the new social standards of thinness, only to find that the new beauty myth requires that we weigh not 120 pounds but 115, and then not 115 but 110.

Thus, looks-ism takes us to the heart of what may indeed be a hugely contradictory historical moment. As we enter a new century, we are enjoying unpredecented technological advances; but at the same time, such changes bring equally unprecedented miseries and uncertainties for and about our lives. We need now to become even more specific about these contradictory tendencies as they affect *women* most particularly.

BEAUTY—FOR WOMEN AND FEMINISTS

As we turn from looks-ism's historical persistence to its specific ramifications for women, a reader might wonder where "I" fit into this picture. Given my earlier insistence that there are both theoretical and methodological advantages in examining the topic from within as well as from without, to thereafter exclude myself completely would be a strange omission indeed. Rather, it ought be perfectly relevant to inquire why I felt compelled to analyze the ongoing importance socially accorded to physical appearance in general, and to women's appearance in particular. Was it a mostly psychic pull, originating in strong personal/political feminist commitments, or was it mostly self-interest (because of being conventionally unattractive, perhaps)? Or maybe motivation is a more detached, intellectual matter, so that any "private" relevance is best treated parenthetically (and certainly not required, as a mandatory confession) by any writer who hopes to systematically approach social scientific subject matters. Another possibility is that motivation has many dimensions coexisting in constant play, but in such a way that their relevance varies: recognition of the explicitly personal thus becomes necessary only when its influence in such multiple levels rises most poignantly to the fore.

Leaving myself out of the discussion would be especially unfortunate in the case of beauty, as we have seen that looks-ism refers beyond itself to constitute a form of class. Thus, in this instance quite obviously, the observer upon reflection has little choice but to admit that she or he is part of and influenced by what is being observed. Like any system that compels classification into one socially constructed box as opposed to others (into categories of race, for instance, or gender, or wealth), and whether we like it or not, looks-ism has unavoidable consequences *of some sort* for any person born and immediately labeled—in this case "female."[73] And while one need not dogmatically insist that therefore all studies of stratified systems require the observers to reveal their "place" within it, I am convinced that opening my own position to scrutiny *here* opens the door to a fuller investigation than would otherwise be possible. In the case of beauty, with its distinctive capacity to link questions of mind with the questioning of bodies, we are in the presence of a phenomenon that places everyone in simultaneous positions of student and studied. When it comes to looks, we are all potential participant-observers.

Thus, what more reasonable place to start than with my own heterosexual experiences pertaining to looks-ism, as it produces consequences both systematic and asymmetrical for women? My concern with the topic grows out of a long-standing intuition of the beauty system's potential divisiveness. As far back as I can remember, my own relationship to the beauty system has been what I would characterize as two-sided. From my perspective, the social reality of beauty as a classification system has been easy to glimpse; it has also been a standpoint from which the perception that all women are somehow affected would be difficult to deny.[74] As a white, lower-middle-class child in an urban elementary and junior high school, I was chubby and often called a "butterball"; by no means was I one of the little girls the boys would develop crushes on, or value as one of the "prettiest" in the class. After puberty, this altered as I became thinner, and by high school and college I was sometimes seen by "boys" as "good-looking." I could eventually understand the seductive appeals of, and heady emotions raised by, on occasion being told, "You're beautiful."

These experiences meant that by college, I was already well aware that being chubby *or* pretty resulted in different consequences. A set of social distinctions were already being promulgated, already alluding beyond themselves. When I was younger, the beauty system had definitely operated to produce deleterious effects in me, a "fat" little girl; it generated self-doubts and worries about whether and how I would get boys to like me, how I would ever be assured of humanly needed emotional and bodily recognition, of attention, of love. A few years later, I suddenly found myself—as though gratefully inheriting a bundle of money—enjoying just the opposite sensations and impressions. Now I was all right: I was sufficiently attractive; I could get dates, find men who would be glad to sleep with me; maybe one day I could have a long-term boyfriend and eventually a husband after all. Now I was "well enough off" within the terms of the beauty system, and did not have nearly as much reason to fret about its possible perniciousness or my uncertain position. Did I?

For, in other respects, even after high school and college I never lost the sense of the system's duplicitous potential to take away what it bestowed (or vice versa). I had already imbibed how it felt to be seen first as "unattractive," then as "attractive." But I was also learning the different meanings that could accompany going back and forth between these two states, during any one period of my lifetime: sometimes looking "good" but sometimes not good-looking at all; sometimes dressed up, sometimes not; sometimes trying, sometimes not; my looks sometimes working, sometimes not. In other words, I was gaining a sense of *fluctuating back and forth between both states,* almost experiencing both at once: appearing relatively endowed by looks at one moment, feeling relatively poorer at the next. And each state brought its own pleasures, but also its pains.

In high school and then sometimes later in college, I would put on makeup and short dresses to look sexy when I went to local dances. I enjoyed being looked at; it felt good to be even an object of appreciative attentions. But there were disadvantages, too. I wondered, for instance, whether my youthfully sexualized persona was betraying the intellectual parts of my being. Then, too, what about the other young women who were still considered "chubby" or were coarsely labeled by young men, called "dogs" or worse? Was I making them feel bad by looking sexy myself, even though I knew just what they felt like? What about my mother, or other older women in my family? Did they feel jealous of me or subtly resentful (feelings that are likely to exist in many women because of the social facts of contemporary looks-ism)? If so, were these emotions directly or indirectly expressed, and was I becoming saddled with awful and lasting guilts from which it might take many years to extricate myself, if indeed I ever could?

And then there was the problem, already mentioned in chapter 3, of trying to have a serious and forceful intellectual conversation when in .that "being looked-at" mode of femininity. Can many young women manage it now? Certainly, I was not able to manage it then. The best I could do was generate another persona who looked different (to the point of being unrecognizable, I was sometimes told) when editing the high school paper and then when I started another newspaper in college. With my long hair tightly wrapped into a bun and heavy glasses donned, I would become "worse looking" but also ready to argue aggressively and actively, even furiously, now that I did not look sexy to most men at all. For it felt difficult to exist in both modes at once, incorporating rather than splitting the sexual from the intellectual in one and the same person. At that time, I couldn't have imagined how a woman could become like the great male thinkers whose works we were reading in college courses on Western civilization (a list of thinkers from which, of course, women were and still are often noticeably absent). I could not envision a woman having that sort of confidence and power if she felt gazed-at more than able to gaze assuredly at the world herself.

But such disadvantages also operated in reverse. Just as it was a

problem to feel intellectual when acting sexual, so I perceived it a problem to feel sexual when acting intellectual.[75] At such times, the situation
would somersault. I found myself envious of the young woman who
could be sexy (even though I knew, on some level, she was also me). For
my intellectual persona did not feel particularly heterosexually attractive, as I sensed that if I projected too much confidence or power, I
might not be desirable—except, perhaps, by someone rare and hard to
find: a dreamed-of person, someone who had managed to deduce that
looks-ism was not necessarily what it appeared. This person would view
things in a way that gave greater value to another person's activity over
her apparent passivity, so that she became "sexi*est*" when most the ar-
chitect of her own destiny. But, in general, if that female newspaper
editor was too smart, or too trenchant, perhaps no one would want to
caress her; she would be perceived as possibly threatening, as not capable of bestowing on a male companion the kind of competitive edge and
comparative superiority by which he had become used to feeling most
"a man."

I have personally encountered three dualisms. The first was my experience of feeling ugly and then prettier. The second was what I have
just described, this rapid alternation between two points on a looks-ist
continuum. Now a college professor, I no longer find it so difficult to
meld a sense of "looking good" with feeling intelligent. But now I am
facing a third duality that revolves around age. For I can still pass fairly
well: some days, going out of my way to work at looks, I can be mistaken for one of my students, possessing the knowledge that I seem (or
so I am told) very young, that my looks haven't changed in ten years.
But on other days, I will feel that I don't particularly care, wishing instead to dress down and to rebel. When I thus move out of (rather than
into) a state of relative attractiveness, I have a sense of liberation at no
longer having to bear so much of the burdens of looks expectations; I
experience the freedom of knowing I must then define myself by other
means. At the same time, there is the worry: Will I still be able to be
heterosexually attractive as I age, to find the bodily and not only mental
recognitions that, like most people, I have come to cherish? At such
moments, I feel utterly able to understand the women interviewed by
Kathy Davis who undertook cosmetic surgery. For there is no point in
bothering to resuscitate fading looks, I fret, noting a new line here or a
new physical change there.

But here the personal, the political, and the intellectual all intersect in this interpretation of looks-ism. For what I have sensed all along, up until and including the present, is that *the various situations and positions in which women find themselves vis-à-vis looks are, and are by definition, co-related.* Obviously, as has long been observed, the very existence of something called "masculinity" depends on an opposite pole, "femininity," for its survival, and vice versa; similarly, the existence of "hegemonic masculinity" depends in its turn on subordinated or marginalized versions of manliness. But this is also true of femininities, including their partial definition by and through looks. The existence of the "chubby" woman is always set against the figure of the thinner one, one devalued and the other overvalued in terms of comparable looks-ist worth. My sexualized and less intellectual persona was closely related to her opposite, the split-off intellectual who had difficulty believing herself sexy. And, of course, the greater sexual attractiveness accorded the bodies of younger women tends to accompany (certainly in the contemporary United States) the older woman's body becoming *de*-eroticized in most mainstream cultural representations. Thus what I am describing is not simply a schizoid set of experiences of a solitary individual. Instead, looks-ism is a social fact that rests on the splitting of women: it could be said to be based upon a schizophrenic social psychology.

Every woman is connected with other women via the beauty system regardless of whether she wishes to be, just as in language a signifier cannot simply be divorced from other signifiers even though on its face it seems unique and wholly individual. The referential system in this case, though, classifies real people as well as words; it alludes simultaneously to minds and bodies, to materialities as well as ideas. Nor can we simply remove ourselves from this interrelationship, even if we try to set ourselves outside it, by judging others' looks negatively or by detaching ourselves from predicaments that seem only to affect *them*. These multiply positioned personae are all in a sense disconcertingly copresent, even if not immediately apparent. In this regard, any effort I make to dissociate from "them" is also effectively a dissociation from "me": eventually, I am likely to find that my distancing was illusory. I may glory in my thinness now, but my being can be transformed into its demeaned opposite at any moment—perhaps when I become depressed by the circumstances of my life for a while, or lose my sense of being in control. And if being socially, politically, economically, and intellectual powerful is felt by some women to require becoming desexualized, then sexualization for many heterosexual women will also tend to become

associated with social, political, economic, and intellectual power-
lessness.

In this regard, the last dualism becomes most striking. For how can
I afford to ignore the relationship between looks-ism and age discrimination, between preferences for women's younger bodies and social disdain for women's older ones? As we noted earlier, the house invariably
wins, and not even the technological brilliance of our time has yet come
close to changing that outcome. As a young woman I will eventually
become the old woman constructed as my opposite; to the extent I de-
lude myself otherwise, my opposite is likely to stay haunted by images
of me.

Thus to be the beauty system's beneficiary on one side of the coin
(and at one moment in time) is always to risk becoming dispossessed
on its reverse (and at another); the advantages of one "class" position
is at once separable, but also utterly inseparable, from the disadvantages of others. Consequently, the interdependent character of classification systems comes best into relief when one person's situation is
viewed *relationally,* placed in the context of the beauty system as a
whole. It was to underscore this relativity—a motive that for me seems
necessarily both personal and political, both interested and disinterested, not only abstract and intellectual but also passionate and emotional—that I felt justified in commencing with myself.

But beginning this section with myself is one thing—ending here
would be quite another. The distinctions that I have described merit
consideration in general as well as in particular, for our subject is indeed
a social fact that influences all women, even as the degree of influence
varies greatly. In the following I take one analytic step back, classifying
this set of divisions between women more systematically.

DISTINCTIONS BASED ON (HETEROSEXUAL) LOOKS
AND COMPULSORY HETEROSEXUALITY

Because of gender discrimination and what Adrienne Rich has called
"compulsory heterosexuality," it seems impossible that someone who is
born female can entirely escape the imposed character of the beauty
system.[76] From the time she is a young girl and then as judgment can
change through various life stages,[77] women find themselves having to
assess personal value *in relation to* a given culture's dominant expectations and representations of heterosexual looks. Of course, women can
always rebel against these expectations, in which case force and energy

must be put into the task of reacting *against* the potential problem. Short of overt rebellion, though, various "classes" are likely to come into being along this first axis of gender differentiation.

It may be that one has been born beautiful or extremely good-looking by present social and historical standards, or that one becomes viewed as beautiful at some point in one's life. By this particular measure, that individual is relatively well-to-do, as though a member of an upper middle class. Another woman may find that by contemporary criteria, she is not considered pretty at all, so that her worth will have to be proven otherwise: perhaps through her overall personality, her sense of humor, her intelligence, her competence, or any of a number of other traits by which she tries to distinguish herself quite apart from her looks. This person, relatively class-less if only on the ground of beauty, is likely to experience the looks-ist system as not in her interest at all. But her lack of investment in the system is in some ways an advantage. Unlike the very pretty or beautiful woman, who may feel that she has much to lose in attention and social value, the person considered plain when young may find it less painful to grow older. For she has much less at risk in changing, of anything thereafter being taken away; she has long been used to seeking recognition elsewhere. What was once a detriment thus gradually transforms into a bonus.

Then there will be those who find that they are neither richly endowed nor very deprived in a looks-ist system. Such a woman is caught in between, in a kind of middle class, and that position forces her to make certain decisions. She must ask herself, "Should I work at improving my beauty position—staying thin or trying to do my hair and makeup as best as I possibly can? Or should I concentrate on developing other aspects of myself, since I am not beautiful but still 'well enough off' without having to devote all that much time to my looks?"

The above analysis tends to limit our discussion insofar as, to be judged, one must be affected by the authority and opinions of the party who judges. For a stratification system based on beauty to operate effectively, it must function within a larger power structure that renders this or any other such classification structure meaningful. Of course, within patriarchal societies it is men who as a group still possess precisely such disproportionate influence and authority (even though this authority varies depending both on a given man's personality and also on added social factors such as his sexual orientation, race, and class). What then of women who do not care much about how men judge their physical traits? Women across sexual orientations may value other women's judgments more than men's. In particular, for many women who are lesbians, the approval of another woman or women is far more important, desired, and sought after. How then will looks-ism appear or disappear? Clearly, looks-ism does not *only* affect heterosexual women. Such a limitation is far too simplistic and inaccurate, failing to encompass how the rewarding of certain looks as "feminine" leads to a dualism, to other looks becoming demeaned as "not feminine" by contrast. For the looks associated with the straight woman—her hair, her skirts, her fashion styles—are those most likely to meet with approving male attention in a power structure dominated by heterosexuality. Such dualism encourages a potentially huge divide between women, not only between heterosexual women on their continuum of looks class, discussed above, but also between a woman who is straight and her sister who is not. As Rich so brilliantly noted, this tends to enforce compulsory heterosexuality indeed since now the straight woman—whether judged by men as good-looking or plain—may find that she defines herself in contrast with the look of the lesbian "other." And, in this divisive process, looks-ism can serve as quite an effective mechanism, whether deliberately or not. A friend's sixteen-year-old daughter, who is both straight and very pretty by conventional criteria, often discusses shopping and dressing in terms of not wanting to look "like a dyke" if she wears a certain hairstyle or mode of dress. This young woman seeks not just to win approval of her appearance but simultaneously *to avoid disapproval.* My friend's daughter also operates on the basis of an often extremely mistaken stereotype, assuming that a woman who is lesbian necessarily does not wear makeup or dress in the style she associates with heterosexuality; this may or may not be the case.

Thus, looks-ism acts in the service of patriarchal and heterosexual dictates. In so doing, it tends to increase the amount of discrimination in both the sexist and the heterosexist world in which a woman who loves other women knows that she too must live. Still, this does not yet address how a woman who is lesbian, or bisexual, reacts *herself* to the social fact of looks-ism. Here I suspect that the relationship between sexual orientation and looks-ism becomes complicated indeed; one must be wary not to veer into essentialist assumptions or overgeneralizations. This is an important layer of our subject matter, though I treat it only briefly; others can and have explored it better and more thoroughly.[78]

A woman who is lesbian, or bisexual, may well respond to heterosexual looks-ism by giving obvious notice to the world—and especially to

other women, whose perceptions and opinions matter most to her—
that she neither conforms nor wishes to conform to a heterosexually
"sexy" appearance. Perhaps, like many lesbians, she does not use
makeup, nor does she wear clothes or hairstyles generally associated
with a heterosexually imposed "beauty myth." Other women who are
lesbian may find annoying any generalization that does not recognize
one's freedom to dress in ways supposedly associated only with heterosexual women's looks and tastes. In either case, many lesbian and bisexual women who find looks-ism quite dreadful may take special pleasure
in being able to by-pass certain oppressively sexist and heterosexist realities, among which looks-ism figures prominently. It is possible that
women in this situation also suffer less from the alliance between age-
ism and looks-ism, which can cause so much damage and loneliness
over the course of many heterosexual women's lives.

But here we are beginning to slide into a possible utopianism. One
whose sexual orientation is lesbian or bisexual is not automatically unaffected by looks-ism, nor can we assume that she does not place great
emphasis on looks as a basis for attraction. Even though her specific
experiences (including experiences of discrimination) are likely to be
different than those of a woman who is straight, a particular lesbian
may still place inordinate importance on other women's appearances as
a basis of attraction, whether or not the "looks" that appeal to her
reflect dominant heterosexual criteria. Or, on the other hand, women
may develop alternative criteria, whether individually or communally,
that are creative and relatively independent of the dominant criteria.

Still, these comments sketch only gender- and sex-related distinctions
between women as facilitated by looks-ism. I began with divisions between straight and lesbian women, and those among heterosexual
women themselves. But the divide is fundamental to the workings of
looks-ism, apt to reappear *within* and to further complicate the categories that follow.

DISTINCTIONS PREMISED ON HETEROSEXUALITY: THE LOOKS OF THE "GOOD WOMAN" VERSUS THE "BAD WOMAN"

This distinction is kindred to, but not identical with, my youthful experiencing of a split between intellectual and sexual facets of being. But in
this context it is more exactly described as a distinguishing of "madonnas" from "whores," or of "virgins" from "tramps," part of the long
history of heterosexual double standards imposed on women. In addi-

tion, this is a split that, unlike the multiple masculinities so usefully identified by Connell, has not been generated with anywhere close to an analogous rigidity for men as for women. Precisely because of the close historical ties between male-dominated societies and sexual double standards, it sounds almost comical to make a distinction between virginal "good" men and men who are nymphomaniacally "bad."

Yet it is well-known that precisely such overtly manifested sexual symbolism is often applied to women, according to whether one tends to look and act like a woman who is "good" or a woman who is "bad." The "bad woman" is, of course, the one who appears to be sexually available (whether she herself has made that choice or not). She is the embodiment of unfettered male fantasy.[79] Introducing this alleged-to-be "bad" persona requires that our analysis become one level more re-fined. For now, even female persons born relatively well-to-do on the basis of looks become divided among themselves, as a lesser class within their class is created. For the "bad woman" is likely to be attractive, too (a scandalous member of the same family). In this, she definitely has something in common with her quite differently constructed "good" sister.

Still, it should be remembered that this division between bad and good women comes into being only relationally itself, and indeed in relationship to *male fantasy.* From the standpoint of many men, what is most characteristic of the attractive "whore," and what makes the prospect of sex with her so steamy, is her being counted upon to "want it"; sex may actually be built mostly around pleasing *him,* but in a mode in which it seems to be just as hotly craved by *her* (maybe even more so).[80] Quite possibly, male clients of sex workers—of "call girls" and prostitutes—would be horrified to discover what several ethnographic accounts have revealed in this regard. Women often say what they know their customers want to hear, having become skilled at feigning sexual performances, a skill in which they sometimes themselves take compli-cated pleasures.[81] Moreover, these accounts complicate this bad girl/good girl distinction so typically imposed on heterosexual women even further. For not infrequently a given prostitute or call girl is even feigning her apparently heterosexual orientation. Here, too, many a male customer is being fooled far more skillfully than he may realize.

In other words, men might be shocked to discover that the situation was not as it appeared—or perhaps many male clients secretly know? In the latter case, perhaps the man finds it is this very performativity

that makes sex with the "bad woman" so damned good. One does not
have to worry about the other; because she is "bad," mutual recognition and reciprocity are not, so strictly speaking, required. On the other
hand—and again the contrast is by definition—he may find sex with a
"good woman" relatively bad (and even if she, too, is good-looking). It
is more constrained, not steamy, because it needs to acknowledge the
other person's actual likes and dislikes; but it also has the relative advantages of being mutually considerate and respectful and friendly. Of
course, each woman's look is likely to correspond to these divided male
projections and desires, these unequally empowered fantasies (themselves acquired and enculturated through a long history of systematic
and structured gender inequities). Traditionally, the "bad woman"
looks sultry, slutty, sexy; the looks of the "good woman" seem more
elegant, her clothing tailored, her behavior and manners much more
ladylike.

Further complexities arise in this account. This "class" distinction
between good and bad within the category of "attractive women" may
occur in the same economic class, or it may involve the superimposition
of one or more added forms of social differentiation (e.g., economic
class and race). Thus the figures of the "wife" and the "mistress," vari-
ants of this good woman/bad woman dichotomy, may in a given case
involve two women whose social circles are close or overlapping; perhaps the two women had been accustomed to socialize as parts of cou-
ples, or perhaps they were even friends. Or it may be that a well-to-do
man is "keeping" someone, but a woman who he has assured himself
is several cuts above a professional sex worker, someone he consciously
chooses because she is relatively classy (say, an expensive mistress as
opposed to a woman who works the streets).

Another possibility is that a middle- to upper-class man wishes to
maintain simultaneously class *and* sexual distinctions between himself
and the attractive "bad woman" he nevertheless desires. He may spo-
radically, but purposely, visit prostitutes who are almost certainly working class and undoubtedly poorer than himself. In this instance, it may
be that her relatively lower class status combines with what he perceives
as excess sexuality to make this woman even *more* exciting, that much
more refreshing than would seem a "bad woman" of a class closer to
his own. A panoply of complicated emotions may be involved. Perhaps
he feels guilt about his own richer life, so that visiting her is a sexualized
sort of "going native," reflecting the fascination with an exotic other
that he otherwise represses from daily consciousness; such repressed

feelings are now able to be expressed under these controllable circumstances and in small doses. Or he may take certain pleasures of condescension in the hierarchical situation that, in combination with other feelings, produce psychic and bodily surges of desire. To be sure, such class differences are not alone in these effects. They can be joined to or even replaced by the next set of distinctions.

DISTINCTIONS BASED ON CLASS AND RACE

As we saw above, obviously some distinctions among the beauty "class" positions have directly to do with economic class: the man who keeps a relatively more elite mistress may enjoy seeing her in expensive Christian Dior black lace lingerie, as opposed to the cheaper and more garish-looking apparel he would be likely to find in an inner-city house of prostitution. Nor are such class divisions limited to bad woman/good woman divisions between women; the two axes of distinction may or may not overlap.

For class in the economic sense is quite capable, all by itself, of creating chasms between women in and through the medium of looks. Examples are so easy to conceive, and plentiful, as to necessitate only the briefest evocation here.[82] The upper-middle-class woman from the Upper West or East Sides of Manhattan often does not want to be caught looking anything like the working-class woman who shops for her clothes at the Macy's basement in Brooklyn, or even like the lower-middle-class woman who looks for sales at Mandies. Hardly would she order anything from a Sears catalogue, or find herself buying clothes items at J. C. Penney or Wal-Mart. It is much more likely that she would shop in Lord & Taylors, Saks, Bloomingdale's, maybe Talbot's: her tastes may range from Donna Karan designer labels, to a little less expensive but still acceptably recognizable brand-names like Ann Taylor, Ellen Tracy, Jones New York, or Ann Klein. She may be drawn to Bruno Magli, Ferragamo, or Ecco shoes, more concerned (and able to pay for the cost of) these labels than the working-class woman who looks for her shoes at Fayva's or maybe at Coward's. It is most likely a working-class young woman who still teases her hair and wears hair spray, while the upper-middle-class woman is far more likely to want a sleek cut that nevertheless exudes that look of "naturalness." And these examples could be applied to other cultural contexts: the exact names of stores, places, brands might change at the same time a looks-ist class continuum persisted.

In relation to looks-ism, then, class matters enormously. But so do a set of distinctions among women that relate distinctively to race. Racially marked divisions, which overlap with these categories of looks and class, at the time same create a social hierarchy all its own; race has been constructed throughout American history in such a way that it intersects with, yet certainly cannot be reduced to, a mere function of other discriminations. In Western racist societies, it is whiteness that has often been purported to be "good" and other skin colors alleged to be "bad"; like gender bias, racialized thinking splits the world asunder for its own self-interested purposes, manufacturing relative superiority and inferiority. As a number of scholars have carefully noted, U.S. history clearly exemplifies the insidious results of combining two processes of splitting: one good woman/bad woman dichotomy (based on race) becomes enmeshed with another (based on sexuality).[83] Thus African American slaves were subjected to now familiar blaming-the-victim ideologies in cases of rape.[84] It was not unusual in the least for white slaveowners to justify violence against female slaves on the basis of racist mythologies concerning sexuality. Nor, as bell hooks has described, was it unusual for white women reformers of the time to incorporate such rationalizations and shiftings of blame into their own worldviews; hooks recounts how white women called for blacks to be sent back to Africa so that white men would not be seduced by "temptresses"— those imaginary beings created by the projections of the powerful themselves.[85]

In contemporary settings racism continues to operate, but of course much more subtly, working on a number of levels. On one, race creates hierarchically structured criteria for rating female beauty in American society, constituting its own stratified system that sets whiteness at its top. Sometimes a woman of color may become especially sexually desirable *within this hierarchy,* though perhaps only temporarily, and then at moments that involve exoticizing race. In other words, race-based sexual mythologies persist. Look at a sample of personal ads in the 1990s from cities throughout the United States. It is easy to find men advertising for female sex partners who are Asian or African or Latina Americans, the advertiser being essentially (and in the grips of essentialism) convinced that skin color and racialized difference indicate greater sensuality, or specialized sexual prowesses.

But, as was also true of class, the relationship between race and looks-ism does not depend solely on a bad woman/good woman dichotomy; once again, analyzing looks-ism demands added layers of theoretical refinement. Since sexism clearly repeats itself across races and ethnicities, anyone who happens to be born a woman *and* a person of color may find herself categorized within her own racial/ethnic group's hierarchy on the basis of looks (relying on our first set of distinctions, which tends to apply *across* classes and races). Like a white woman, she too will probably find herself classified as relatively richer or poorer in terms of looks "class." But her situation only *partly* resembles that of a Caucasian female's; in other respects, it is clearly quite different. For one thing, perhaps a woman of color encounters standards of looks in her subgroup that do not match those dominant in a hegemonically white culture. For instance, as students have told me repeatedly over the years, many African American men do not want women to look at all like such white models as Twiggy or, more recently, Kate Moss. It is not unusual for an African American woman who is much more well-rounded—not "fat" but with an ample behind—to be seen as more beautiful than a white woman whose entire body is "skinny." This point could be elaborated in far greater detail, well beyond what there is room or need to belabor here. For chances are that tastes and standards in beauty may vary between the African American and, for instance, the Afro-Caribbean, with further differentiation depending on which country in the Caribbean is in question, or even which of several cultural subgroups within *that* particular nation. And the same could certainly be same about other racial and ethnic groups regarding their specific standards of beauty.

Yet what happens to these cultural differences in beauty standards for women among different ethnic, racial, immigrant, and transnational groups in the face of a dominant U.S. (beauty) ideal? How does this potential clash affect a woman of color who may feel vulnerable to judgment according to several standards of beauty and to a complex interaction transacted between them? The beauty situation becomes that much more complicated, and overdetermined, in its ramifications for her. Along with the gendered beauty standards themselves, it is likely that distinctions arising from economic stratification apply to her too. (And how could economic stratification, like beauty, *not* affect all women in some way, since by definition it ranks all members of a given society?) In other words, this particular woman will of course in some way encounter "class" in terms both of looks and of economics (i.e., as traditionally conceived). But now it appears that a woman whose race subjects her to additional discriminations experiences yet another variety of "class." Now there is one additional level, a whole new set of complications introduced by the relationship between looks-ism and race. The woman of color must contend not only with the bad woman/ good woman dichotomy, which itself historically was at once racialized and gendered, but also with the maddeningly mixed cultural messages regarding what constitutes beauty, anyway, for a woman who is not white.

How do we then make sense of variations within a larger culture that supposedly values pluralistic diversity? What we have been describing is a society that tends to subordinate reality—diverse and heterogeneous human looks—to paradoxically homogenized artificial standards, whether that valued standard is thinness, youth, upper-class ideals, or whiteness. Yet in the United States, men of other ethnicities, not only African American men, may tend to agree that Kate Moss would not be *their* ideal of beauty, either. Anyone familiar with Philip Roth's novels has encountered the Yiddish word *zaftig* to indicate a preference within Eastern European cultures for a woman who looks soft, well-cushioned—who has a little "meat on her bones." Moreover, the devaluation of the older woman's body may not be nearly so rigid or cruelly isolating within the overall aesthetic context of other societies; some women who arrive here from other nations are surprised at the degree to which a cult of youth is everywhere fostered. The newcomer may sense subtle cultural differences and sensibly conclude that women are made to feel even more worthless and valueless as they age in this country than in her nation of origin (though other women from yet other societies may find traditional strictures of gender much easier to challenge here).

Many other examples of variations from the uniform standards exist; however, the vast majority of these examples are united insofar as *some* kind of overall beauty standard is valued more in women than in men. Variations are real and significant, but so is the common theme that bridges the differences. To generalize for a moment: yes, a given WASP may like the Kate Moss type, placing his tastes at odds with those of a given Italian or Jewish or African American man who favors a version of the more *zaftig* type. Some men prefer large breasts, others small. And, yes, perhaps women in other societies find the cultural costs of aging less painful. But it is still just as important—and just as true— that most cultures accord differential emphasis to *some* kind of feminine beauty being achieved as a cultural ideal, even if the particular look that is idealized varies from place to place or from time to time.

Such specific subcultural preferences are still similar in that *some* looks have become routinely overvalued for women in contrast with the relative demeaning of others, and that looks in general have been routinely overvalued for women relative to men.

But we have by no means exhausted the ramifications of systemic complications introduced by race in relation to looks-ism. For even if, say, a particular man of color knows that his own standards of beauty may be different than dominant ideals, it can be difficult to resist the assault and hugely influential intrusions of commodified U.S. culture. In this sense, looks-ism becomes not only sexist but imperialist in its imposition of white-defined standards. For instance, as recounted in *The Autobiography of Malcolm X* (1964) or Eldridge Cleaver's *Soul on Ice* (1968), and then critically retold in Michele Wallace's *Black Macho and the Myth of the Superwoman* (1979),[86] black men in the United States commonly undergo complex struggles with internalized beauty standards. How does one resist starting to lust after the (attractive) white woman at least as much as the (attractive) black woman? This is a painful problem that may strike many men who have faced racist discrimination as at least, and probably more, troublesome on the grounds of race than gender. For what appears to be more normal, by general agreement across classes and cultures and races and ethnicities, than to desire a "beautiful" woman? The problem here is *which* beautiful woman one comes to want and why, bracketing for the moment the possibly discriminatory ramifications of desiring a beautiful woman per se. It is how looks-ism *becomes specifically racialized,* a phenomenon that a particular man may come to resent and be suspicious of, that may make him feel alienated from himself. Does he desire a particular woman because of her positive individual traits, or because of her whiteness—or has the virulence of racism made it impossible for him to assess which is which? He, or any other man who has also faced discrimination in the United States on account of his race, may feel that *this* is the dilemma of beauty—racism—not so much, or at all, looks-ism itself. Thus, the coexistence of racial and gendered discriminations subtly helps render looks-ism apparently harmless, obscuring the latter's *additionally* distinctive harms *across* race on the basis of sex. Looks-ism's deep connection with sexual discrimination may, in this particular instance, become easier to obscure or to rationalize away.

We have now returned yet again to the symbolic meanings of looks-ism as it so often tends to point beyond itself. But now the spotlight is on how looks-ism's symbolic and vicarious meanings could be expected to unfold *in relation to race*. For is it really the white woman's particular skin color, her hair, her look, that a given man who has faced racism desires when and if he finds himself desiring her at all? (Earlier, we asked a similar question on the basis of class: was it a particular physiognomy that made the working-class young man so happy in preparing to go out with his "gorgeous" date?) Or is it the way that a person of particular race and gender (say, a white woman) comes to symbolize access to a whole world of recognitions, privileges, and attentions from which many minority men have been forcibly excluded throughout U.S. history? If so, the white woman ironically may take on her own exoticism, that of a woman who is part of a dominant rather than subordinated group. Here again it would be surprising if feelings toward her were simple rather than complicated, if they were *not* tinged with symbolic wants and possibly symbolic resentments as well.

Still, and again, where does this leave a particular woman of color in relation to all of this? She is likely to know only too well how American looks-ism, which we are slowly beginning to conceive as incorporating gender, class, *and* race in its systematizing effects, potentially places her in quite a bind indeed. As a woman, she has in common with all women being differentially valued on the basis of looks, on the basis of beauty. But beauty by whose standards? By the standards of her own community (which may tell her one thing) or by the standards imposed upon that community from outside (which may tell her another), or by *both* as she tries to make sense of their complex interaction? If she deeply understands racism, she may find herself hurt, bitter, enraged, when a man of her own race is more attracted to a white woman. We might recall a particularly effective scene in Spike Lee's *Jungle Fever* (1992), in which a group of women of color (whose own skins are a range of hues) engage in a lively round-robin discussion about gendered and racist beauty norms; their conversation occurs soon after the husband of one of the characters has left her for a white woman.

Not only, then, may a (heterosexual) woman who faces discrimination on the grounds of race as well as gender find that she frets about her looks—about whether she will be able to find humanly needed love, recognition, emotional and bodily attentions—but she also faces the dilemma of how to respond to the demands of *white* looks-ism. In such a potentially alienating situation, faced with this now multiply overdetermined social fact, how should she react? How should she look? If

she is black, for instance, will she, ought she to, spend large chunks of
time trying to achieve not just beauty but beauty as defined in white-
dominated and racist terms? Should she wear her hair naturally, for
example, or straighten it (and, if the latter, will guilt be added to the
annoyance of having to worry about looks at all)? Should she worry
about whether she is thin enough, or not? Clearly, as the films of Spike
Lee evidence, there is reason for concern about black men's internaliza-
tion of white-dominated assessments of beauty. His female characters
are usually not only beautiful but endowed with looks that reflect
white-influenced standards of hair and of weight; Lee has expended less
effort to present a critical analysis of sexist than of racist biases experienced by African Americans and other women of color.

But for a woman who is susceptible to both racial and gender discriminations, the ramifications of looks-ism are potentially damaging
indeed. In addition to being divisive on the basis of gender, looks-ism
also brings into play racially sexualized dichotomies (as these intersect
with common patriarchal splits between bad women and good), class
as traditionally conceived, and certainly the racial hierarchies that differentiate "whites" from "others." Only a new designation—looks
"class" rather than class?—can do justice to this complex layered situation, which depends for its perpetuation on the demeaning of other
colors to elevate the symbolic significance of whiteness. Here, again,
looks-ism manages to link the predicament of all women, even if such
interconnectedness becomes a cause for serious concern and action only
to some. But there is yet another distinction that eventually affects all
women in the United States.

DISTINCTIONS BASED ON AGE

Enough attention has already been paid to this distinction that only a
few points merit addition here. Age discrimination, too, can occur both
across and within the categories just mentioned. The degree to which
looks-ist distinctions based on age trouble women and create painful
divides varies tremendously depending on a number of other social factors, including class, country of origin, and cultural attitudes within
ethnic/racial groups. Even within the same class or race or ethnicity,
other psychic, educational, and cultural differences regularly shape the
attitudes of individual women, differentiating the reactions of one
younger person from the next, one particular daughter from another,

one relationship between an elder and younger women from the next.[87]
This gamut of attitudes reflects varying feelings about sexism and gender that affect how women experience processes of aging.

Yet, as we saw in the example of race, such actual diversity does
not override the simultaneous existence of homogenizing social forces,
which frequently operate to obscure these differences. Reality is subordinated to visual ideals, flaunted and manifested everywhere: in the contemporary United States, the ideals favor thinness, whiteness, and also,
of course, youth. The very person who personifies such beauty ideals in
the pages of magazines, in newspaper ads, in movies, and on television—the "model"—is usually unable to maintain her career into her
forties, fifties, and sixties, *seemingly of necessity or as though by definition*. So, too, it is a notorious fact of Hollywood that the average forty-
or fifty-year-old actress has a far more difficult time finding interesting
parts, or parts at all, than a male actor of similar age.[88] And one more
well-known example: the looks of the television news anchor are likely
to encounter greater scrutiny as she ages than those of her male counterpart (despite occasional exceptions to this rule).

But perhaps some will immediately object that things are very different now, after feminism, that older women are much more likely to be
featured in mass media cultural representations: think of Jane Fonda,
Susan Sarandon, Elizabeth Taylor, Meryl Streep. And, to some extent,
these critics would be right; there are surely some signs of change; Hollywood is beginning to catch up with this well-founded feminist protest.
But, unfortunately, this beginning is not nearly enough; even such exceptions still generally operate for the most part to confirm, rather than
fundamentally to challenge or to deny, looks-ist expectations about
women's looks. For how much painstaking effort must Jane Fonda or
Elizabeth Taylor put into maintaining the sort of beauty associated with
being in fact many years younger? Then too, since these actresses would
have been considered exceedingly attractive even when they were
young, offering them as examplars of aging may not hold much comfort
for huge numbers of "average looking" women as they grow old.

Moreover, holding up these women to exemplify social change sends
a decidedly mixed message. For the implication is that women are now
able to exude sexuality when old—but only so long as they continue to
look young. Once again, the transformation of looks-ism occurs on the
surface only, in relation to its outward form rather than its underlying
contents; little actually alters in the guise of seeming as though a good
deal has. To a woman who acts, the results must be ironic and infuriat-

ing. Many major male actors, and certainly white male actors, are just "average" looking; whether one calls to mind the admittedly unsexy Woody Allen or envisions Jack Nicholson, James Wood, Robert Duvall, Dustin Hoffman, John Turturro, or Gerard Depardieu, none of these men would be a likely candidate to win a beauty contest judged by criteria of classic male handsomeness. Rather, their ability to win roles is likely to be based on contacts, skill, on the interesting characters they won in earlier films, and on their force of personality, which can compensate for their only mediocre appearances. To be sure, there are many handsome actors. What about Robert Redford and Paul Newman, now also turned directors? What about actors Mel Gibson or Kevin Costner, both of whom would be judged by many women to be "gorgeous"? Yet, even taking many such exceptions into account, clearly a far greater *range* of men's appearances end up becoming cinematically representable at all ages than one finds in the case of women; it is far more likely that women must be young and beautiful looking if they are to become "starlets" and remain successful female stars.

When considering these looks-ist distinctions based on age, we need to examine most closely their potentially divisive ramifications when it comes to questions of *generation*. Happily, many women enjoy a wonderful sense of intergenerational solidarity, feelings only strengthened after the advent of feminism. Of late, and at an explicitly political level, there is reason to hope that such linkages are being affirmed even more than in the past, when age discrimination was sometimes complained of *within* the feminist movement.[89] For other women though, perhaps not touched by feminism, feelings of competitiveness may continue to do battle, until a time comes when there is no longer a social basis by which such feelings can easily be explained. The problem at present is that looks in relation to age become a matter of the luck of the draw. Whether or not one is born into a household where women love each other across generations, and in defiance of sexism, is a matter of individual chance rather than the outcome of sociological transformation. For this reason, it would be thoughtless to view the phenomenon being described in *only* individualistic or psychoanalytic terms, as though separable from the world of systemically structured gendered distinctions we have been surveying throughout. Psychology and psychoanalysis themselves must deal with the troubling ramifications of socially structured sexism, of looks-ism, as it comes to affect and split the psyches of individuals.

Feminism may be progressively lessening these generational strains.

Yet it is still not uncommon to discover particular women who, when youthful daughters, felt a sense of jealousy being communicated to them by their mothers; and, once again, this observation may resonate across the categories of social distinctions we have been exploring. Many women can identify with descriptions of a mother who has conveyed a sense of guilt as her psychic legacy, even if quite unintended; indeed, this mother might be horrified if confronted by the discovery of the effects she unwittingly contributed to generating in her own daughter. For perhaps most relevant here is that society has certainly not transformed yet to the point where a large enough proportion of women, of mothers, feel sufficiently fulfilled by their own life circumstances. The immediate cause of dissatisfaction may be sexism alone, or more often sexism in conjunction with a vast array of additional factors that continue to affect men as well, from inadequate education to lack of economic opportunities. When a particular woman, a particular mother, *does* feel confident that her own life has been fulfilling and secure, the dynamic I describe may not occur at all; instead, the mother may feel recognized through other forms of value, other sources of self-worth, that have little or nothing to do with looks.

In many other cases, however, a mother may indeed have felt herself valued for much of her life on the basis of her looks, her sexual attractiveness, her femininity. But just at the time when she enters middle age and begins to feel increasingly uncertain about that attractiveness—a feeling that, because of gender asymmetries, is *more* likely to affect her than her daughter's also-aging father, who may be living in the same house—her daughter is blooming, blossoming, entering her "prime." It is the younger woman who garners attentions that earlier might have been hers, who is looked at with desire, becoming relatively valued by the world just as the older woman is becoming relatively devalued. Perhaps she notices her husband or her boyfriend noticing her daughter, gazing more at this attractive younger woman in the household, whereas before he was far more likely to gaze at her. Or perhaps, as in other variations on this structurally age-discriminatory theme, the daughter turns out to be plainer than her mother, who was always the "beauty" in the house. Even in this case, age-ism may eventually take its toll. A friend recently recounted to me her own poignant experience of noticing that somewhere along the way—when her mother turned fifty-three, or maybe fifty-four—men started to respond to the middle-"class"-looking but younger daughter rather than the formerly "rich" but now aging older beauty. In each of these instances, then, looks-ism creates a material sociological basis on which to *anticipate* in at least some cases that a given mother may find herself both loving and secretly resenting her daughter, feeling both great affection and a certain amount of jealousy.

And why would she *not* feel both? For in writing this, I decidedly intend to blame institutionalized sexism, not to fault individual mothers. Of course, we ought not to omit, either, the theoretical importance of believing in degrees of personal responsibility and in the possibility of exerting individual agency. But in the context of looks-ism's continuation at present, society sets up mothers in such a way that we expect them to politely accept—if they are not to be viewed as unpleasant and unhappy individuals, suffering a judgmentalness that only aggravates an already painful loss of recognition—the social facts of age and gender discrimination all around them. But why ought social happiness to depend on or require the heroic efforts of individuals, thus limiting such happiness only to a few? Until there are wider social changes, there is more reason to *expect* a mother would feel sad and pangs of jealousy toward a younger woman than there is reason to expect from her the opposite.

By logical extension, looks-ism thus also creates a basis for its own ideological reproduction; one could call this a variant on the theme of what Nancy Chodorow has called "the reproduction of mothering."[90] Viewed now from the standpoint of the younger woman, the daughter understandably enjoys the privileges of youth, even as these advantages may at the same time be saddling her with long-lasting psychic burdens. The daughter may begin to internalize her mother's devalued status in unconscious ways. A number of psychoanalytically oriented feminists have noted this tendency, including Jessica Benjamin as well as Chodorow. Both stress social causes of the daughter's desire to separate from her mother. As the daughter begins to define herself heterosexually (an assumption that limits Chodorow's theory by overlooking the equally important question of daughters who do not), she tends to do so in favor of identifying with the superiorized father *against* the inferiorized mother (all the while remaining unconsciously tied to the figure of her female parent as well).[91] But in such a scenario, often applicable at least to a daughter developing a heterosexual orientation, the daughter may find herself at once flattered and embarrassed by the glances of her father or other older men, somehow realizing that they represent a world of looks and gendered power in which her mother competes only at a disadvantage. And, to the extent that her sense of self has become bolstered, that her sense of value gradually grows and comes to depend upon the differential reinforcement and attentions her budding youthful looks now inspire—how will that younger woman begin to feel as eventually she ages in her turn?

It is certainly possible that the daughter too will later feel in danger of losing the cherished recognitions to which she herself has now become accustomed. Ironically, she may be at risk of turning into her mother, the very person against whom she had defined herself negatively (sensing earlier that only in so doing could she find her own happiness). But as she grows older, she too may find herself beginning to worry about her body, her weight, even if she had never done so before. Now she finds herself wondering, am I sufficiently content with the shape of my breasts and my nose, with my weight? How do my looks compare with younger women's when I look into the mirror to find myself looking not nearly so fresh now as they do—might I need some form of cosmetic surgery indeed?

Amid such stresses, she may start to convey, and again perhaps quite inadvertently, a socially explicable set of resentments similar to those once conveyed to her. And so we find ourselves faced with yet another theory about why and how looks-ism can come to repeat itself over time, in cycles of specifically intergenerational repetition. This theory now encompasses psychic *feelings,* including those which Freud far too unsociologically and uncritically deemed simply "oedipal" and which, like Chodorow, he failed to adequately investigate in relation to people who are gay and lesbian as well as heterosexual. For just as we have seen that sexism and expectations of appearance are closely intertwined, so now we have found that the "reproduction of gender" and the "reproduction of looks-ism" are also closely related, tied to one another through intrafamilial processes that bring them very much into contact with one another in the process of women's sexual—and, in particular, often their heterosexual—development.

Such intergenerational repetition is likely to have an even more striking effect—and again, in particular, on heterosexual women. Through looks-ism, women's energies become habitually channeled *much more into comparative evaluations of one another than into challenges aimed at transforming the looks-ist system overall.* Again, looks-ism's tendency is to set up women, encouraging each of us to ask, "Which woman is more or less fortunate than myself within the particular 'class' terms of looks-ism as we know it?" Distinctions of looks in relation to age therefore reflect the recurrent problem this section has been treating all along. It may be an older woman who worries about her looks-ist worth in comparison with the younger woman and considers how she might be able to look "better" vis-à-vis this other who is receiving more attention. Or perhaps the relatively poorer woman yearns to buy clothes that could make her look classier, or the "bad" woman sometimes feels pangs of envy toward the "good," just as the "good" may have moments when she feels jealous of the "bad." In all of these cases, the dominant emotion many women feel becomes a dissatisfied unhappiness with *themselves* rather than a sense of anger targeted *outside* at systemic causes of these predictable divisions. In other words, there is indeed a general problem that weaves together all of the cases I have cited by way of elucidating this argument. In each of the examples, women face authentically different predicaments *at the same time* looks-ism has created a basis for each to feel some amount of common cause with her relatives (and correlatives): both dimensions contain some truth; *both* make sense and need to be acted upon. Therefore we can finally conclude our consideration of distinctions with an overarching category.

DISTINCTIONS BASED ON LOOKS-ISM

Coming back now full circle to a point made by way of introduction, we observe that the feminist thinking about beauty seems at present to be characterized by a growth of debate *about looks-ism itself.* This, too, superimposes yet another level of divisions upon those already delineated. In addition to splits between women of differing sexual orientations, between so-called good women and bad, one class and another, or one race and another, there may also have developed through the 1980s and 1990s a tendency to oppose relatively "good" feminists against those who are relatively "bad."

When stepping step back to look at this recent history with analytic distance, we should also again be careful to note that feminist debates have not involved absolute differences so much as disagreements over relative emphases. Still, the latter have sometimes become intense and divisive, providing another example of damaging comparisons made predominantly between women; in this case, some feminists have been judged "better" or the more "authentic" on a range of substantive issues. Resentment about such distinctions in the early 1980s was precisely what led to the feminist "sex debates" examined in chapter 3; and, like the issue of beauty, these too have not yet withered away.

Arguments still persist about whether liking pornography or sadomasochism (chapters 4 and 5), or thinking prostitution ought to be decriminalized (chapter 6), makes one a better or worse feminist. Am I a truer
feminist if I believe that women who turn to cosmetic surgery can be
better off (the position attributed to Kathy Davis), that cosmetic surgery
is intrinsically alienating because of its origins in male-dominated societies (Kathryn Morgan's position), or both (as my own reading of Davis
takes her book to have sensibly concluded)? Last but not least in this
context, how does a given woman's attitude about whether beauty in
general is a good and important thing affect her standing as a feminist?
Might that position divide her from others with whom she would otherwise share major, collective feminist concerns?

Initially, by way of introduction, I argued that the question itself can
become unproductive insofar as it distracts attention from the still male-
dominated context in which debate itself emerged and reemerges. Now
that we have considered that context, we can return to this earlier question. Thus this last of our analyzed divides between women related to
looks-ism has the potential of being the most important one of all, for
it bears most directly on the question of what can or cannot be done
about looks-ism as *at once a social and a political fact*. After all, it is
feminists who have been, and remain, the most likely to protest this
ongoing human problem, which is faced most of all by women but also
by men (for the latter, a problem often similar but also often different).

Moreover, nothing about these observations about the potential
traps of divisiveness negates the fact that there *already exists* a rich
theoretical literature produced by second-wave feminism on this subject, about beauty and its *systemic* rather than merely *individual* manifestations. By way of concluding this investigation, then, we will return
to that literature; without its massive contributions, this entire discussion would have been inconceivable. Exactly what, then, have feminists
already said concerning what can or should be done about beauty? Can
anything from this history help us discover whether and how we might
move beyond our present impasse with regard to looks-ism?

WHAT HAS BEEN AND CAN BE DONE?

In surveying the history of second-wave feminism, it strikes me that
three stages of treating beauty can be identified. In an early *protest*

stage, beauty was viewed as indeed part and parcel of women's general subordination. Feminists knew that looks, that objectification, comprised a key part of discrimination against women, but critiques were at first understandably negative in character; an alternative theory of attraction did not come into being. By the late 1980s and early 1990s, a number of important feminist writings considered the topic in greater depth. While these were highly significant and bold in their visions, in this *beauty myth* stage most writing about beauty sought to democratize and fundamentally reform—but not necessarily replace—the notion altogether. The disproportionate importance attached to beauty for women was better documented than ever before, as were looks-ism's damaging repercussions along lines of gender, race, and class. The beauty myth was called on to open its gates, so that persons possessing diverse bodies, colors, sizes, and weights could also win approval and recognition under its aegis. Thus, in this stage beauty itself was still discussed as though the concept could be taken for granted and rendered transparent: the idea of beauty tended to be accepted even as its present form was deemed unacceptable.

At present we are in what can be characterized as a *beauty debate* stage; feminists and other social critics now go back and forth between whether we are "for" or "against" this notion, still virtually unaffected by history. This chapter itself began with typical questions: Are we for or against Madonna or cosmetic surgery? Do we prefer Wolf's *Beauty Myth* or Friday's *Power of Beauty*? And while my own viewpoint ought by now to be clear—that a democratized beauty system is preferable to the discriminatory status quo—I also wonder whether looks-ism would finally fade, rather than simply becoming increasingly embroiled in controversy, if we no longer believed in the concept of beauty as we presently think and feel about it. The possible success of a fourth stage yet to come therefore rests on an explicit recognition of just how complex most attraction is, involving far more than simple appearance. Before we can sketch the general outline of such a fourth stage, that of *attraction's revitalization* beyond the too-confining limits of beauty, we need to retrace the tracks of earlier feminists. Unless looks-ism is placed in historical perspective and significant early contributions acknowledged, we risk having to reinvent the wheel by forgetting significant contributions that came before.

Perhaps the first and certainly the most famous early confrontation with beauty was a demonstration, held outside a convention center in

Atlantic City, New Jersey, against the Miss America pageant in September 1968. As Suzanna Danuta Walters chronicles in *Material Girls* (1995), second-wave feminism was connected from its beginnings with efforts to focus media attention on the problem of beauty.[92] In August 1968 "No More Miss America!" was written and distributed to publicize the theory behind the planned protest. Note how its participants conceived of the demonstration:

> We will protest the image of Miss America, an image that oppresses women in every area in which it purports to represent us. There will be: Picket Lines; Guerrilla Theater; Leafleting; Lobbying Visits to the contestants urging our sisters to reject the Pageant Farce and join us; a huge Freedom Trash Can (into which we will throw bras, girdles, curlers, false eyelashes, wigs, and representative issues of *Cosmopolitan, Ladies' Home Journal, Family Circle,* etc.—bring any such woman-garbage you have around the house); we will also announce a Boycott of all those commercial products related to the Pageant, and the day will end with a Women's Liberation Rally at midnight when Miss America is crowned on television.[93]

When placed in this feminist historical context, the immodest Swiftian boycott imagined earlier may no longer seem quite so utopian. Now the idea of that boycott emerges as strange because conceived from the vantage point of the late 1990s. In the late 1960s, too, certainly the notion was radical, striking those in the media as quite preposterous, even though reporters quickly were intrigued. But to feminists then it obviously did *not* seem nearly so preposterous a symbolic gesture or idea as a similar political protest would strike feminists now.

To be sure, we should not idealize this history. In the 1960s, too, small radical feminist groups—the Redstockings, the Feminists—disagreed among themselves about whether it was okay to wear makeup or not, and about how to live by feminist principles.[94] But there was a critical difference: August–September 1968 was still a moment when all parties could easily agree that the larger society, its symbolic ritualized institutions and dominant representations of social "reality," needed to be protested, confronted, and materially changed. In other words, whether or not it was okay to wear makeup, something had to be done about the social facts that had given rise to this divisive dilemma.

September 1968 was a significant historical moment in another respect as well. "No More Miss America!" addressed itself to a wide range of women: "Women's Liberation Groups, black women, high-school and college women, women's peace groups, women's welfare and social-work groups, women's job-equality groups, pro-birth control and pro-abortion groups—women of every political persuasion—all are invited to join us in a day-long boardwalk-theater event, starting at 1:00 p.m. on the Boardwalk in front of Atlantic City's Convention Hall." Moreover, the second of the ten points protested explicitly took up the question of close connections between discrimination on the basis of looks and of race: "2. *Racism with Roses*. Since its inception in 1921, the Pageant has not had one Black finalist, and this has not been for a lack of test-case contestants. There has never been a Puerto Rican, Alaskan, Hawaiian, or Mexican-American winner. Nor has there ever been a *true* Miss America—an American Indian." Other points included protests against "The Unbeatable Madonna-Whore Combination" (i.e., the good woman/bad woman dichotomy discussed above) and "Miss America as Big Sister Watching You" (i.e., the divisions between women on the basis of looks already analyzed).[95]

Clearly, then, early radical feminists were cognizant of existing divisions between women of class, race, age, sexuality, and generations. They also knew well the role played by beauty expectations in maintaining these divisions and displacing political attentions from society to other women. Therefore, this protest stage against beauty was characterized by their belief that looks-ism simultaneously operated *across* other complex and equally valid social distinctions to create a broad-based commonality between women at least on this basis. Consequently, to employ the category "woman" was quite analytically and politically precise. Radical feminists did not experience nearly the epistemological self-doubt, the fear of essentialism, that has now begun to accompany and undermine feminists' political usages of the term; on the contrary, placed in historical context, that usage was felt to be necessary.[96]

Still, we need to consider how beauty was treated in the feminist writings that accompanied and followed these actions in the protest stage. Several distinctive categories of beauty can be discerned within this evolving feminist literature, the unfolding beauty field.

EARLY OBSERVATIONS ABOUT BEAUTY IN MAJOR TEXTS OF FEMINIST THEORY

Early radical feminist writings predated and helped fuel the early political protests just described. Again, beginning with Simone de Beauvoir's *Second Sex* and then later in works including Kate Millett's *Sexual*

Politics, Shulamith Firestone's *Dialectic of Sex,* and Ti-Grace Atkinson's *Amazon Odyssey,* [97] one finds beauty treated not as an independent topic but as inseparable from a *broader feminist worldview.* One surmises that de Beauvoir deliberately chose not to devote a separate chapter of *The Second Sex* to "beauty" and "looks." Rather, what we have been calling looks-ism is intricately woven into the fabric of her analysis, in accordance with her general phenomenological views regarding objectified relations and the enculturated demand that women develop a passive "femininity." Similarly, Millett, Firestone, Atkinson, and other theorists showed little interest in analyzing beauty as an isolated issue. Once more, beauty was seen as specifically manifesting the objectification of women broadly conceived; it involved *particular* psychic and social practices through which women's freedom became limited.

DETAILED STUDIES OF SPECIFIC ASPECTS OF THE BEAUTY QUESTION

Beginning in the 1970s, however, we also find an explosion of attention being paid to different types of beauty expectations. This includes a literature on thinness, for example, from the work of Kim Chernin on through Susan Bordo's more recent and superlative essays, "Reading the Slender Body" and "Anorexia Nervosa." [98] Writers on obesity have ranged from Susie Ohrbach and Marcia Millman to, more recently, Becky Thompson, who treats overeating as well as undereating as signs of the social demands that affect women; interest and concern about the question of cosmetic surgery also continue to grow, as we have seen. [99]

Thus, by the late 1990s, a much wider range of writers were paying close attention to the overlapping effects of beauty and looks-ism. At the same time, the development of subtopics within this larger subject may also be related to a historical shift in the social circumstances in which such writings were and are being penned. In general, the earlier feminist writers mentioned above were not academics; in general, the more recent writers are (an academic tendency, of course, from which by no means could or would I exempt myself). This difference in standpoint correlates to a difference in relative emphases. Writings in the first group focus primarily on *the larger political goals of a feminist movement,* and then on the question of beauty within this; writings in the second group tend to investigate *narrowed specific subsets of the beauty system,* and then consider the larger goals of feminist political and social movement issues within these.

A SHIFT FROM IMAGES OF WOMEN TO WOMAN AS IMAGE

As Walters observes in *Material Girls*,[100] a European-influenced explosion of feminist cultural theory in the 1980s and after slowly shifted feminists away from the "images of woman" approach that had characterized earlier and less sophisticated feminist interpretations of various media. Rather than content analysis, "woman as image" came to dominate both film criticism and analyses of other popular culture genres (sitcoms, soap operas, MTV). Among the best-known feminist writers who adopted this newer approach to film theory were Laura Mulvey, Teresa de Lauretis, and Tania Modleski.[101] Their writings were greatly influenced by a range of European theory, from Lacanian psychoanalysis and Derridean deconstruction through the writings of Michel Foucault, Jean-François Lyotard, and Jean Baudrillard.

This shift has been extremely significant with regard to how looks-ism, too, would be studied and newly conceived. For, of course, examining "the look," "the gaze," was virtually emblematic of the new approach. Whereas feminist writers' main interest had previously been *what* was being produced, now they concentrated on *how*. Now the germane questions included how images are constructed and what spectator positions are presumed by cultural producers who thereby aid in looks-ism's reproduction both consciously and unconsciously. Narrative theory examined how particular plot lines serve to produce and reproduce sexist presumptions—where, if at all, are resistances or cracks in visually based domination to be found?[102] Yet this academically oriented feminist approach to beauty has tended to stress *analyzing* and *deconstructing* rather than *actually transforming* dominant and admittedly sexist images. By extension, it is not surprising that these writers paid less attention to protesting and altering *power* relations and relations of production inside the film and other media industries. As a result of this change in emphasis, it may be harder for us to maintain our sense of looks-ism's capacity to regenerate itself in ways that unavoidably involve both material conditions of images' production and the representational content of images themselves.

Walters describes this shift as taking us away from a notion of *ideology* (which had been at least partly material in its intellectual orientations) toward a far more abstract and disembodied notion of *discourse*.[103] At the same time, relatively speaking, these recent feminist cultural analyses of looks have turned away from the simultaneously theoretical and political motivations that had fueled the writings and commitments of earlier feminists. "The philosophers have only *inter-preted* the world in various ways," said Marx in an oft-quoted if hard-to-live-by declaration, "the point is to *change* it." [104] If so, then an earlier concept of feminist praxis may have become subtly distilled in and through this third category of attitudes toward beauty. Nevertheless, the much more sophisticated set of cultural analytic tools associated with this shift also contributed to the steady growth of feminist theory through the 1980s and the 1990s.

CONTEMPORARY REAPPROPRIATIONS OF BEAUTY

It would be tremendously misleading to portray the above three categories as encompassing *all* significant texts produced in the three decades that separate the 1968 "No More Miss America!" from the present. Particularly from the mid-1980s through the 1990s, we can find numerous writings about beauty that depict the issue in a wide context of revolving, evolving, and newly developing feminism*s*. For instance, beauty appears in *Black Feminist Thought* (1990) amid sociologist Patricia Hill Collins's concern about the effects of overlapping forms of discrimination on women of color. In one chapter Collins examines media presumptions that continue to typecast African American women on the basis of looks, recycling "bad woman" and "good woman" myths that rest on gendered as well as racial biases.[105] Sandra Bartky's references to a "fashion-beauty complex" assume a socialist feminist weltanschauung, within which beauty and narcissism are seen as critical to understanding how both gender and class sustain themselves.[106]

Particularly significant are three other overtly political works, also penned after Ronald Reagan's election in 1980 inaugurated a long era of social conservatism. Because they express a clear-cut commitment to transforming what I have been calling looks-ism through feminist political intervention, they avoid the problems of other more academic critics. In order of publication, they are Robin Lakoff and Raquel Scherr's *Face Value: The Politics of Beauty* (1984); Wendy Chapkis's *Beauty Secrets: Women and the Politics of Appearance* (1986); and a work already discussed several times in this chapter, Naomi Wolf's *Beauty Myth: How Images of Beauty Are Used against Women* (1991).[107] Each title announces that some sort of power relationship is being analyzed within the book's covers; in each, a desire for change is clear, and each is written to address an audience outside an academic context alone. Note, too, the mixed professional affiliations of these authors:

Wolf is not a professor but a professional writer; Chapkis does not identify herself on her book jacket as an academic, though she presently
teaches; and Lakoff and Scherr were teaching at the time. Moreover,
Face Value was written by one woman whose background is part
Chicana and one woman who is white; more than *The Beauty Myth*,
their book is careful to treat looks-ism in terms of both race and
gender.

Yet, despite these decided advantages, one cannot help but wonder
whether these contemporary texts made a significant dent in the worsening aspects of looks-ism that we examined as the beginning of this
chapter. By the time the writings of Lakoff and Scherr, Chapkis, and
Wolf appeared, feminism had already come under a barrage of attack
from conservatives. In the 1960s and 1970s, writings by feminist figures
like Firestone, Koedt, Morgan, and Atkinson could still be perceived as
interconnected, as part of a movement: individual theoretical contributions were rendered doubly powerful for being tied to feminism and its
collective political efforts. Later feminist movement activity became
much more oriented toward defense, and thus it may have become *relatively* more difficult for later writings to produce a collective impact
analogous to that of the early works. It was more likely that such writings would be instead perceived as the achievements of *individuals,* regardless of an individual author's intentions. I am by no means implying
that these later works had no impact at all. Rather, my point is that
shorn of a confident social movement that insists on some type of feminist praxis, it is hardly astonishing that two developments coincided.
On the one hand, the publication of political works about beauty was
occurring, and calling for significant changes to take place. On the
other, and around the same time, looks-ism was worsening in many
respects as it actually affected and affects women's lives. Less was
changing than it appeared.

It is indeed ironic that only two years after the extraordinarily political and astute *The Beauty Myth* was published, Naomi Wolf's next
book was *Fire with Fire* (1993), a work that puts forth a very different
perspective. From its first chapters, one would barely know that "the
beauty myth" was still alive, let alone arguably becoming more powerful. Instead, Wolf now contends that we ought to stop thinking of ourselves as "victims": the times, she concludes, have been changing. My
friend who had spotted a small photo of Wolf on the back jacket of *The
Beauty Myth*—the image that had propelled him to fall "in love"—
might be amused to notice that the paperback edition of *Fire with Fire*

prominently displays an even larger picture of this undoubtedly attractive author, now on its front cover. The relevance of "seeing" Wolf had clearly not diminished, or even stayed the same; rather, her good looks had somehow become *more* important. More precisely, perhaps, any contradiction with the perspective of *The Beauty Myth* had become easier to ignore. Wolf herself seems to believe that things have improved. She proposes that we begin to think in terms of "power feminism" versus "victim feminism," a move which presumes that women indeed now have sufficient power to be asserted (a presumption that may apply to some women some of the time, but not to many others).[108]

Consequently, if looks-ism is to become politicized yet again, it is critical first to insist that beauty expectations be altered from *without,* not only from *within.* We may draw the opposite of Wolf's conclusion in *Fire with Fire:* feminism needs to become *more* rather than *less* collectively politicized, *more* rather than *less* concerned about how to draw on the strength of interlocking theory and social movement activism to revive itself. Of course, we must also remember that Wolf's conclusions are her own; they give us no indication of whether the other authors of the works I have mentioned would agree. Indeed, my reading of *Face Value* and *The Politics of Beauty* suggests that Lakoff, Scherr, and Chapkis would probably disagree strongly with the post–*Beauty Myth* direction of Wolf's thinking. For there is no reason why individual works could not add up to more than the sum of their parts once again, when and if conceived anew within the framework of a revitalized social movement. Moreover, as Walters suggests with regard to media criticism, new approaches may be needed that combine the sophistication of contemporary cultural theory with a commitment to actually changing—not *only* deconstructing—the form and content of ubiquitous cultural imagery.

However, both this chapter and the feminist history of second-wave treatments of beauty have demonstrated a second point: we *also* need to reconsider the situation from within the movement, not only in terms of changes required in the external world. The burgeoning feminist social movement provided internal forums where women could talk about, air, and share feelings about the ways that "looks-ism" somehow affected us all. Among the subjects considered by consciousness-raising groups were the problems bequeathed by looks-ism of feeling obsolescent, of having diminished self-esteem. Now, aided by more sophisticated theories of gender and the growth of interest in men's studies, we see more clearly the enormous relevance across gender of such personal/political opportunities, for the ramifications of beauty expectations damage *both* sexes, even if in different ways. Men need such forums as much, if not more, than women.

The third point is the most important to emphasize, because it has received the least attention in this history of feminist writings up through and including the strongly assertive works of Lakoff and Scherr, Chapkis, and Wolf in the 1980s and 1990s: *looks-ism is not what it appears.* For in most writings, as even the conclusions of the more recent works show,[109] the hoped-for outcome is not the overcoming of looks-ism but its democratization—still on the basis of *looks*. Looks become not unimportant but more inclusive, allowing new images, new sizes, different colors, ages, shapes, sizes, and genders to be favored. The authors wish to *reform* the concept; not so clear is that it is being altered fundamentally.

And while it should by now be obvious that I certainly agree with this need for democratization—I called for it earlier and I now call for it again—nevertheless, something more is needed. I fear that many reading this long chapter, sometimes or often agreeing with it on logical, rational, even principled grounds, will nevertheless forget about looks-ism soon after turning the last page, feeling as though it makes little difference in the end. "After all is said and done, beauty just *is*," I can still envision such a person concluding, "I strongly doubt that any of this can change *me*." But there may be a missing element in the analyses of beauty that, if reasserted, could help diffuse looks-ism by revealing its multiple and complex *sleights of hand*. This theoretical revision ought to make it harder for looks to stay immune from criticisms of looks-ism, for the status quo to remain. I hope that it will encourage a new understanding of *attraction*—one that can no longer be equated with, nor reduced far too simplistically to, a mere function of "beauty."

For despite beauty's far too symbiotic associations with attraction and with sexism, which would seem to require that the concept be replaced altogether, democratizing it has generally been the main focus of feminist writers. This is true even of two wonderfully interesting and more recent works about beauty, Sara Halprin's *"Look at My Ugly Face!"* (1995) and Ellen Zetzel Lambert's *Face of Love* (1995), both of which strongly criticize the term's traditional contents but not so much the term itself.[110] That beauty is thereby subtly saved, even while being criticized, may result both from a different intention and also perhaps from an unwitting and extremely understandable reluctance on the part of these authors to be perceived as so outlandish that their writings would never be taken seriously. After all, to challenge a social fact as deeply and profoundly accepted as beauty can and will strike many as quite absurd. To call for replacing the beauty system as we know it is indeed risky, as anyone carrying such a message may provoke great annoyance directed back at the messenger. One who keeps at least the predominant *idea* of beauty intact may not seem so implausibly radical, so "out there" as to be oddly disinterested or antagonistic toward the obvious joys of visual pleasures, somehow against the erotic joys of seeing. For who, after all, is against the beauties of beauty—even if this is a tautological proposition that takes the concept of beauty itself for granted?

But what is this alternative interpretation at which I have been hinting right from the start, which might alter beauty's content as well as its form? In the end, it strikes me as crucial to emphasize that attraction and eroticism are not nearly so based on mere static, physical looks as we are accustomed to—and by now extraordinarily invested in—believing. Rather, attraction frequently has far more to do with a changing interrelationship, a constant interplay between that which exists within and without us, a movement from our minds to our bodies as well as from our bodies to our minds. Most of all, it involves an unbreakable, constant connection between socially created desires and the incarnation of those desires in particular bodily shapes and forms.

In this fourth stage, attraction's revitalization, we need a concept that is *dynamic* and *relational*, highlighting and incorporating—rather than obscuring and denying—the constant connection between appearances and contexts. As we have seen, looks-ism's greatest success and its most insidious danger is in hiding this interrelationship so beautifully, which encourages many people to believe fervently that it is *beauty* one wants, because beauty itself allegedly bestows pleasure—not what beauty has come to *mean* as a contemporary form of class. Thus, as we bring to bear the insights of theorists from Durkheim to Marx (applied originally to quite different contexts), we recognize that beauty in contemporary society has become totemic, worshiped as if all-powerful even as the social process of its own creation (and re-creation) is quite cleverly mystified. For the more beauty is accepted at face value, the more people will be inclined to pursue "it" instead of exploring the far more complicated *feelings* of which looks are ultimately only *representative*.

And thus if looks-ism itself is to be overturned, we must turn on its head the very concept of beauty. In and of itself, a physical trait is ironically disembodied, lifeless, and mute—not particularly or necessarily exciting at all. To be sure, it would be overly simplistic to assert that *any* recognition of physicality, any acknowledgment that biological factors sometimes have an autonomous influence, must be alien to this new concept of attraction. Clearly, the biological fact that extreme overweight is dangerous for health and life will not be affected by a theoretical reconsideration (though one can hope that the pervasive, socially motivated contempt and disgust toward those who are obese will disappear). Nor will a given person cease to discover that sometimes her or his body "fits," or does not "fit," better with another's purely on the basis of physical or sexual criteria. But we need to recognize that questions of attraction are much too complex to be reduced—as at present—to an overreliance on the belief in beauty alone. Biological factors have already been shown incapable of explaining the extreme homogenization of looks and the attendant discriminations that have remained so characteristic and common in modern societies. They cannot explain why, in the late 1990s, beauty expectations have become *more* restrictive and harmful for women at the same time that concerns about looks are also intensifying in men.

But if beauty is not fundamentally a question of the superiority of one physical trait over another, what *is* it about? Here, our earlier discussion of class and classification proves extremely useful. Like drives toward wealth and power, deep and ongoing beliefs in beauty may mask even deeper psychic and social hopes that—via our association with certain "looks," whether in ourselves or through others—perhaps we will be able to satisfy needs for legitimacy and recognition that are otherwise not being satisfied in our lives.

And perhaps it is such *complex but common pleasures of recognition*—not mainly or even predominantly any essence of "beauty"—that people often seek when acting out their desires in relation to looks. When I feel better with a "beautiful" woman or a "handsome" man— or when I feel good that I look "beautiful" or "handsome" myself—at the heart of such pleasure is a sense of security that now, finally, I can or will feel loved and lovable. Now I can be recognized through intimacy and through the multifaceted pleasures of a caress. It is not, then, the shape or size of a given nose or lips, or the exact form of her or his body, that matters most, even though I may fervently tell myself otherwise. Similarly, it is not a given woman's actual "thinness" that so satisfies the corporate executive accompanying her when recognized by other men; not necessarily a man's actual muscles to which another woman or man is drawn and which provides that companion with satisfaction when they are together; not the blondness or redness of a woman's hair per se that perhaps renders her so sexy to another woman. Indeed, such associations often come *later,* only after a certain bodily shape or form or sound has already become culturally invested with the power to bestow these recognitions, these legitimations. (In the most American of novels, F. Scott Fitzgerald seems to provide a similar insight when he has Gatsby think, at a moment when his obsessive love for and attraction to Daisy became clearest to him, that her voice was "full of money.") Yet I may *believe* it is the physical shape or trait, not the hopes and dreams previously cathected into that given form, which brings me pleasure.

Thus, the transformation of looks-ism points beyond *democratizing looks* to a need for *democratizing social recognition.* Looks-ism appears to be only one of the most common manifestations of this basic human hunger. If so, then the project of challenging looks-ism is indeed profoundly democratic, involving the need for social legitimacy itself to be redistributed—across races, classes, genders, and sexualities, as these frequently come to overlap with "looks"—if greater human happiness and fulfillment are to result. The more we sanely acknowledge the needs of human beings to be recognized in general, and not to be arbitrarily demeaned, the more looks-ism stands a chance of itself being redressed.

For if we assume that this interpretation provides even the germ of a new conception (albeit one left for others to expand), then it also follows that *attraction is best viewed dynamically rather than statically,* as having far more to do with *energy* than is often consciously acknowledged. Dynamic drives may become linked to and cathected with particular persons toward whom we are drawn precisely because they are perceived as better able than others to provide pleasurable feelings of the diverse forms of recognition we seek. Of course, seeking recognition and approval is basic to most people's interactions; in and of itself, it is not problematic but rather a satisfying and probably unavoidable part of life. Problems result only when ongoing quests for recognition become artificially restricted by the limits and biases—biases that can be quite destructive to others and ourselves—of our own social imaginations. The difficulty with looks-ism is not that it involves at once mental and bodily pleasures of recognition, but that it has been constructed around spurious and discriminatory demands—that it makes it appear *as though* only certain people's looks (certain genders, races, classes and not others) have the capacity to make us feel joy and pleasure.

Our new concept of attraction will have to incorporate the self-recognition that results when, for instance, a young man finds himself aroused and excited by someone who is "gorgeous": even then it is likely that physical traits of beauty or handsomeness per se do not primarily explain that person's immediate and continuing appeal. Faced with such a realization, the young man may attempt to change the conditions that are denying him recognition elsewhere. For if attraction is understood largely in terms of energy and complicated drives to achieve pleasurable recognition from others, then indeed all along it has not been "beauty" but a relationship between looks and complex social meanings that is at the center of erotic desire. Yet, without a new concept of beauty, it may be difficult to recognize *explicitly* what is nevertheless *implicit* in the situation—that I want a given person not so much because of her or his looks but because of the socially constructed associations with which I have learned to connect that look. With explicit recognition, however, it then may become possible to make or unmake, change or not change, the totem of beauty in which we are invested.

Also through such explicit realization, statements like "thinness *is* beautiful" or "overweight *is* ugly" may increasingly strike us as disingenuous. It is no longer so credible to assert that younger women *are* sexier than women in their sixties, or that whiteness *is* a better look to possess, *because we have called into question the taken-for-granted presuppositions on which such statements are based*. Though this process, the taken-for-granted character of a concept like "gender" itself may be called into question. This is because in the very process of developing a different theory of attraction, we channel attention *toward* rather than *away* from understanding our own creative relationship not only to looks and looks-ism in particular but to our cultural constructs in general. It becomes easier to perceive that current social interpretations tend by "idealizing" to impoverish the reality: a much richer and more diverse world of sensual and existential possibilities for social interaction.

We still need to consider just how this change could come about. Certainly, as we have seen, one way is to return to earlier feminist emphases on *transforming* media images, not just analyzing or deconstructing them. It is important that feminists exert power to produce changes in representation; little boys and little girls still generally grow up believing that "beauty" *is* only the homogenized looks that continue to dominate contemporary imagery in the United States and elsewhere around the globe. And thus once again we circle back to a point made much earlier: to transform looks-ism will involve, at least in part, altering how the world looks *from without*.

But it also will involve altering how we think and feel about the world *from within*. I am by no means proposing that people never again use the word "beauty" or experience the pleasures with which that term has long been associated. Rather, I hope that we will begin to use this and other related words *very differently;* I would wish for the world to be even more "beautiful" than before, and for pleasures to be freed rather than cruelly circumscribed. At the same time, we must beware of the word taking on new automatic usages, promoting new forms of rigidity and unwittingly recycling an old tired notion, thereby perpetuating a looks-ism that brings potential misery to all human beings—especially to women.

Thus if looks constantly point past themselves, as I have argued, then our attraction to one another *already* includes something more, something other, than what appears. Looks are not what they seem, but obscuring or revealing of *much more*. For attraction comes not only from the glint or smile or expression of an eye, or the movement of a leg or someone's whole body as it becomes energized and activated in space, in time; not only, or merely, from the pleasure of watching someone dance, or the sensuality of mind and body alive in the surfaces of a finger as it evocatively traces, sometimes slowly or other times more rapidly, its way along the physical contours of another. It is more than this, too, reaching out to encompass the way in which that other personality, outside and in, seems to intermesh with one's own; the mutual understandings that make people feel intimate with one another; the way she or he may remind me of someone else, in ways conscious and unconscious, evocative of history and of culture; and the whole universe of symbolic social meanings that attract me to a given sex, a class, a certain ethnicity, for reasons I may or may not apprehend. It works at multiple levels when one wishes so badly, so desperately, not only with one's body but with one's mind, heart, and perhaps even soul, to make love to another person, him to her (or her to him), or her to her (or him to him), wishing to communicate multifaceted sensations of love.

What I have contended throughout, however stubborn or unfashionable to do so will seem in the end, is that *looks-ism has it all wrong*. Because it isn't what it appears, anyway, so that in a sense there is no choice but to invent a new way of defining and perceiving the inner and outer wonders, indeed the renewed beauties, all around us. A new conception could allow for different shapes and different sizes; it could even allow signs of death to become visible on the surfaces of our bodies as we aged because no longer would such changes be seen as *reducing* sensual pleasures but as *extending* their reach. Thus, I am proposing not a negative conception but a positive alternative, not to take away visual and sexual joys but to add to the scope of how we perceive pleasure and its depths.

Now we can finally jettison the inelegant term "looks-ism" with which we began in favor of this alternative notion, one that gives renewed meaning to attraction, to love, and to the erotic facets of human existence. Whether we wish to call this new concept simply eroticism, or dynamic attraction, or energism matters less than our recognition that a new name must be sought. Our present vision is far too static, too inert, too prone to favor passivity over activity, essences over existences. Most of all, our present conception is *inaccurate,* failing to acknowledge the complexities and diversities of the real world in which we exist.

Most ironic, perhaps, is that many people may intuit the grave inadequacies of our present conception. Men and women both may find themselves disappointed when in bed with the beautiful other about whose body they previously dreamed. Many people already have sensed, long before they read any arguments about or analyses of the subject, looks-ism's symbolic allusions well past its surface appearances. And many others already experience that the mysterious character of love, of falling in love, often has little to do in the end (and did it have much to do even in the beginning?) with looks. Then why do we persist in homogenizing illusions? Why not admit explicitly and welcome what we know to be the case in any event, after all is said and done?

The reason cannot be fear of lost pleasures, for I hope by now to have made a fuller case for my initial submission that looks-ism's obsolescence would free, not impede, erotic possibilities, which now are coercively and prematurely foreclosed. Perhaps we are afraid that if we do away with looks-ism in favor of something more like dynamism, we will lose our ability to believe in class, in the comforts of our habitual classification systems? Perhaps we paradoxically fear pleasures and freedom? But just as looks-ism itself had to be invented and reinvented in order to become customary, so too could a more dynamic and less damaging vision become gradually familiar in its place. For to have questioned discrimination on the basis of looks, to have seen such discrimination as intimately connected with sexism, to have closely examined a world where much more of importance is occurring than simply what appears—all this was a project well worth beginning by feminists and well worth continuing in the maturing and innovative works that have since been produced as feminist and social theories have developed. The point now, though, is not only to reinterpret what is beyond the apparent. The goal, and the hope, of philosophy, of sociology, is *also* to change the world, not only *what* but *how* we see that which is there, right in front of our eyes. From such alteration may result the withering, not the worsening, of those discriminations on the basis of looks that have limited our individual and collective sense of vision.

CHAPTER FIVE

Prostitution and Feminist Theory

Notes from
the Sociological Underground

Consider the following situation: A feminist sociologist has just completed her Ph.D. thesis, an insightful and well-documented ethnography
of prostitution. The work is based on participant observation, an approach richly developed in urban sociology of the Chicago School as
well as cultural anthropology à la Franz Boas. In terms of locale, the
study contains an interesting comparative dimension, having been conducted both in the Netherlands and in New York City. However, participation for the dissertation research took place only in Amsterdam,
where prostitution has for some time been decriminalized: this was done
to avoid the methodological complication of engaging in activity illegal
in the American context. There, the sociologist was supported by a
Dutch fellowship and donated whatever small moneys she earned to an
international organization dedicated to the rights and health care of
prostitutes. At her New York site, the study was conducted equally in-
tensively. Here, though, time was spent hanging out with sex workers,
observing and sharing in a majority of activities exclusive of waged labor. The sociologist was already somewhat acquainted with the sex industry in New York; as a college freshman, she had worked part-time as
a topless dancer in Manhattan in order to earn money for her education.

It may not surprise a skeptical reader to learn that the described
study doesn't, to my knowledge, exist. But what if it did? And what if
this feminist scholar was about to present her findings at an American
Sociological Association annual meeting as part of a committed effort

to find a good teaching and research-oriented academic job, preferably
at a well-respected college or university? Would she face more obstacles
than anyone else—if so, why would she? Should she? Clearly there are
many precedents of sociologists being respected, or at least not
shunned, as a result of choosing to engage in various forms of participant observation of groups belittled by mainstream society (recent examples include Judith Rollins, who worked herself as a domestic to
better perceive the experiences of this group of workers; Terry Williams,
studying "cocaine kids" and users of crack; Martin Jankowski, living
with gangs, who were familiar from his own youthful experience; and
Loic Wacquant, entering the ring to deepen his understanding of boxers).[1] Such researchers may sometimes even be seen, and experience the
feeling of being perceived, as "cool," kind of hip, possessors of special
ties to worlds most of us do not similarly know or that we are inclined
to avoid. In such cases, to its credit, sociology has the potential for
conferring legitimacy upon chronicles and chroniclers of the illegitimate
and illegitimized. On the other hand, why is it so difficult to imagine
this hypothetical feminist sociologist of prostitution encountering analogous recognition? It seems much more likely that she would meet with
discouragement, repeated jokes,[2] humiliation, discrimination overt or
covert—if she wasn't too hesitant to come forward at all; if she ever
even conducted the study, for she might fear being perceived as a martyr
or a freak or she might heed advisers' cautions about potential harm to
her professional career.

The skeptic might also protest that research on prostitution is *not*
comparable to studying people who enter gangs, or work as domestics
or boxers. For a sociologist to participate in prostitution, I can hear
someone arguing, means doing something that is *illegal,* something potentially destructive to and of the body. I anticipated the first objection
by having the hypothetical researcher limit her participation to a liberal
and legal setting. As for the second point, the same concerns could extend to the cited researcher on gangs who finds himself engaged in dangerous fights as part of his study, or the student of boxing who perhaps
is punched to the point of severe physical injury. Would their methodol-
ogies be seen as similarly problematic, maybe verging on the masochistic, or viewed more positively as part of a process of simultaneous self/
other exploration and therefore as cause for fascination? To this, a critic
might again counter, still, prostitution is *different:* it involves added
dangers for women, danger of rape and other forms of attack specifi-

cally affected by gender. However, one can imagine other kinds of participant observation, also exposing women to ongoing danger and the possibility of assault by men, that would probably *not* produce the same disapproving objections as prostitution: undercover police or government work, say; or work done with violent felons on parole or probation; a cross-class study of batterers; or, returning to gangs, women studying or living with mostly male members of organized urban groups who have been known to gang rape. Such proposals might well evoke appropriate concern—but stigmatization? Likely not.

But perhaps the point is made even more vividly if we construe the feminist as having decided not to study prostitution after all. Imagine that she decides not to leave the United States; noticing that research on the following topics is also needed, she debated with her advisers about making her doctoral thesis either (a) a participant observation of topless dancers (going back to her earlier experience so as to treat it sociologically) or (b) a participant observation of women who appear in pornographic films. She eventually chose to do a study of women who posed for pornographic magazines. In these cases, nothing illegal will have transpired. Yet when the time came for job hunting at the ASA convention, would the outcome be so different than if she had elected to study prostitution? If fear of social and sociological disapproval would again be so enormous as to render these other studies possibly undoable as well, then whatever is occurring likely involves more than just issues of law, "method," or safety. There must be something about openly participating in studies of *sex*—especially (though not exclusively) if the study is conducted by a woman, especially (though not exclusively) if the study is about sex for sale, that is, plain, blatantly commercial sex—which situates prostitution along a wider continuum of activities that produce awkward and loaded reactions, in and outside of sociology, in other women as well as in men.

Something must be going on because, all in all, relatively little serious study has been done on the subject of American prostitution—including (and most surprisingly) in the area of feminist theory. This is particularly striking when one thinks of the immensity of current interest in women's studies, and the sheer number of sociology, anthropology, and criminology departments scattered across the United States. I suspect that the relative paucity of consideration is neither accidental nor insignificant. On the contrary, prostitution (and its study) ventures into waters that we unconsciously find threatening: it remains marginal and comparatively untheorized precisely *because* something about it is so central and meaningful. To analyze prostitution unavoidably raises *both* the ongoing specter of gendered oppression in patriarchal societies and our often schizophrenic—partly acknowledged, partly tabooed—passions about sex: the combination evokes highly conflicted and disconcerting reactions. The resulting ambivalence may be so strong that it has affected even sociologists, feminists, and feminist sociologists—groups that one would expect to be open and sympathetic toward the subject for reasons at least intellectual, if not also political. But whatever motivating factors may be operative, I propose that our failure to take prostitution seriously, as a practice extraordinarily common across as well as over the history of male-dominated societies, impoverishes the abilities of both feminist theory and sociology to understand sexual, psychic, and socioeconomic phenomena in all their complexity.

Before we turn to how and why prostitution poses important problems for feminist theory, the issue of ambivalence deserves further exploration.

DOCUMENTING AMBIVALENCE:
AN ACADEMIC OVERVIEW

Has the study of prostitution really been so conflictual as I claim? Looking more closely at the content of existing writings provides one form of response. Based on a literature review conducted for this chapter, I classified books and articles on prostitution in the United States as generally falling into one of the following four categories.[3]

Historical Studies   In this area can be placed outstanding works about English prostitution and Victorian society (by Judith Walkowitz), a number of books on prostitution and the progressive reform era in America (by Ruth Rosen, Anne Butler, and Barbara Hobson), and Alain Corbin's study of prostitution in France after 1850.[4] I refer to the British and French studies because of their influence on American scholarship (Rosen, for example, in her study of American prostitutes in the early twentieth century draws heavily on Walkowitz's work on Victorian England). If we were to exclude them, though, we are left with a quite small number of specifically American historical accounts.

Writings by and about Prostitutes   Connected with the rise of a prostitutes' rights movement in California, a 1970s development in which the group COYOTE (Call Off Your Old Tired Ethics) played a leading role, several collected volumes of working women's own writings have appeared (see, in particular, *Good Girls/Bad Girls: Feminists and Sex Trade Workers Face to Face* [1987], *Sex Work: Writings by Women in the Sex Industry* [1987], and *A Vindication of the Rights of Whores* [1989]).[5] Much of this literature aims at enabling prostitutes to describe and redefine "sex work" for themselves. Some of the included essays advocate recasting prostitution as a form of legitimate work that should not be so stigmatized; a large number of sex workers' writings argue in favor of decriminalization. Unlike the historical studies, these works of self-description have been written and published in contexts outside academia.

Studies of Outsiders' Attitudes toward Prostitutes and Prostitution
Here we find writings, usually academic articles, that treat "pros" and "cons" of prostitution from the myriad perspectives of external observers. Studies in this category testify to tremendous ambivalence toward prostitution in American society at large; unintentionally, they also provide an illuminating backdrop to the picture of stigmatization painted by sex workers themselves. This literature includes not only works debating prostitution's continued illegal status, but also the philosophical and political questioning of whether feminists in particular *ought* be supportive or opposed (for the latter view, see especially Kathleen Barry's well-known book, *Female Sexual Slavery* [1979]).[6] Some articles take up the actual attitudes held by groups like feminists and college students;[7] others study reaction to recent prostitutes' rights organizations within a social movements framework. Of these last, efforts to overcome stereotypical images of prostitution have been portrayed in a fairly positive light, although the feminist movement has been relatively unsuccessful in this effort; Lena Dominelli's interesting analysis of an organization named Programme for the Reform of the Law on Soliciting stresses both the contributions and limitations of this British group's actions.[8]

Contemporary Studies of the Relationship between Prostitution and Society   This subdivision includes the work of anthropologists, sociologists, and feminist theorists (who may or may not be academics). One influential essay of socialist feminist theory, written from the perspective of structuralist anthropology, places prostitution in a much larger context. In "The Traffic in Women: Notes on the 'Political Economy' of

Sex" (1975), Gayle Rubin traces the commodification of female sexuality in capitalist societies to the traditional exchanges by men of women as objects of trade.[9] By virtue of this analysis, one is able to understand the roots not only of prostitution but of marriage, too, as two sides of a thoroughly patriarchal coin. Both prostitution and marriage originated from this trafficking—a common heritage that sharply diverges, nonetheless, as in the process madonna status is bestowed only on the married woman, while those more overtly prostituted are labeled as whores. Rubin's point is certainly very much in keeping with other well-known tracts of feminist theory. From Friedrich Engels to Simone de Beauvoir, numerous writers have tried to characterize marriage as a glorified form of prostitution, thereby hoping to remove the grounds for discriminating between the two. And, of course, Rubin's perspective is one with which radical feminists of the American second wave, from Kate Millett to Shulamith Firestone and Ti-Grace Atkinson, would concur. Nevertheless, Rubin's anthropological work and that of other feminist theorists do not constitute major studies of prostitution per se. They are highly significant in positing a particular relationship between prostitution and patriarchal societies; at the same time, however, the authors discuss prostitution itself quite abstractly, seeming to shy away from detailed examination of its actual workings and the various parties involved.

Within sociology, numerous more specific studies of prostitution have in fact been done. Charles Winick and Paul Kinsie's *Lively Commerce: Prostitution in the United States* (1971) has the virtue of completeness, investigating prostitution from a variety of angles and containing chapters on madams, pimps, johns, the law, the military, and international finance. Less virtuous is its tendency to use outdated terms, thereby making rather unsociological statements from an atheoretical and unwittingly masculine standpoint: for example, the question of prostitutes' possible "frigidity" is raised; and the authors also note, "Contrary to the way they are usually represented in mass media, prostitutes tend to be physically unattractive, and some have fairly flagrant defects."[10] On the other hand, Barbara Heyl's *Madam as Entrepreneur* (1979) is useful in taking almost the reverse approach, trying to shed light on the institution of prostitution as a whole by focusing in depth on the life history of one prostitute.[11]

More current sociological work on prostitution includes Eleanor Miller's *Street Woman* (1986), a sympathetic study of female street hustlers in Milwaukee that is influenced both by feminist criminology and by the University of Chicago's stress on urban ethnography. Miller was especially interested in discovering how different racial backgrounds influenced recruitment into what she calls "deviant street networks." Yet, for purposes of this overview, note that Miller's focus on *hustlers* again differentiates *Street Woman* from an explicit examination of prostitution per se. Miller defines hustling as "simply 'illegal work' that underclass people often engage in . . . to make ends meet." This category, much broader than prostitution, also includes persons charged with larceny, embezzlement, or robbery. Consequently, prostitutes enter her sample not as the study's sole focus but because some women arrested for felonies—Miller's one criterion for inclusion—had also been brought in at least once on the less "serious" misdemeanor offense of soliciting.[12]

But I think two of the best contemporary studies of prostitution on its own terms have been conducted outside the bounds of American sociology. The first, *Working Women: The Subterranean World of Street Prostitution* (1985), comes close to being a long-term participation study, though it did not involve any actual engagement in sex work.[13] Ironically, the book was written not by sociologists but by a social worker and minister, Arlene Carmen and Howard Moody. Both associated with the Judson Memorial Church in New York City, they aimed to influence a general audience by describing eight years of direct work and interaction with prostitutes. Their research began after no one came out to a clinic the church initiated to meet the health care needs of prostitutes (several of whom had reported ongoing abusive treatment, including economic and sexual harassment, by Manhattan physicians). When Carmen and another woman then visited Times Square massage parlors and street corners to publicize the clinic, they discovered and began to document the immense sense of fear, intimidation, and neglect that "working women" regularly experienced.

What is most extraordinary about this account is its lack of any judgmental tone and the sincere effort it demonstrates to avoid treating prostitutes as demeaned "objects" of study. Disclaiming any pretense to objectivity, Carmen and Moody instead are purposely "partisan and 'empathetic' to those 'working women' whose lives are made more miserable by their being forced into the illicit subculture of criminal activity."[14] Simultaneously, the authors attempt to dispel popular myths they see as fueling antiprostitute prejudices, such as the notion of contact with prostitutes spreading venereal disease more rapidly than sex outside prostitution. They cite Winick and Kinsie's statement that VD attributable to prostitutes accounted for only 3 to 5 percent of total occurrence, and another study's finding that 25 percent of high school teenagers tested positive for the disease compared to less than 5 percent of prostitutes.[15] Updating these 1970s figures to reflect their own experience, the authors go on to report that not one of the twenty patients who gradually did begin to visit the health clinic designated especially for prostitutes showed evidence of VD. In contrast, out of a similar number of clients who used the church's regular clinic, infections regularly appeared. Carmen and Moody were told that "almost all working women used rubbers with *every* customer, no matter what sexual act was performed, and their faith that it protects them against VD was borne out. . . . Thus the myth about prostitutes as carriers of venereal disease was the first we were able to lay to rest."[16]

Backstreets: Prostitution, Money, and Love (1986) shares *Working Women*'s admirable preference for investigation over judgment.[17] Written by two Norwegian criminologists and now available in translation, *Backstreets* is the finest work focusing on prostitution alone that I discovered among the specifically academic writings in this category. However, it hardly counts toward exemplifying a good study of U.S. prostitution. (We should note that numerous other anthropological studies of prostitution have, and are, being conducted *outside* the United States) Cecilie Hoigard and Liv Finstad, who followed twenty-six prostitutes in Oslo, Norway, open *Backstreets* with in-depth material about the day-to-day routines of their Scandinavian interviewees' lives. These beginning ethnographic observations, and the detailed description that follows, are skillfully linked to the book's conclusions rather than to any preconceived notions that the authors themselves might have held.

Like Carmen and Moody, Hoigard and Finstad are supportive of prostitutes and concerned about improving the daily conditions of working women's lives. On the other hand, unlike the authors of *Working Women*, they are opposed to decriminalizing prostitution and pessimistic about the possibility that it might be reformed into a profession that need not be intrinsically alienating. From their findings, Hoigard and Finstad conclude that prostitution is inseparable from sexism, from a patriarchal context of control that precludes women's access to real economic powers and choice. Each of their interviewees cited money as a primary motivation for starting to turn tricks; the women also recounted having to develop psychological defense mechanisms to avoid the alienated feelings that their labor indeed provoked.

Perhaps even more impressive than its well-argued case for opposing prostitution while supporting prostitutes is the relative complexity of the book's methodological approach. *Backstreets* treats prostitution as tied to the political and sexual economy of "mainstream" society, enmeshed in it most obviously by the frequency of its use. Its authors construct the practice of prostitution multidimensionally, carefully considering the perspectives and characteristics of customers as well as pimps. Hoigard and Finstad thereby touch on an issue relevant to all studies of prostitution, though not expressly taken up in most. Unlike *Backstreets,* many works on this subject suffer from the tendency to erroneously equate studies of prostitu*tes* with studies of prostitu*tion*. Consider the works discussed above: *The Madam as Entrepreneur, Street Woman,* or even the highly "empathetic" *Working Women.*[18] As their titles indicate, the latter works have studied not prostitution but prostitutes, at present an overwhelmingly female workforce that services an overwhelmingly male clientele. (Male prostitutes, by most accounts a minority of all prostitutes, also work for predominantly male customers.)

But for a given study to focus mainly on female prostitutes—the male customers managing to vanish as though by magic from the social and sociological picture—runs the risk of reproducing, in print, the same gender bias that surrounds the treatment of prostitution in practice. Prostitution as far as I know is a unique offense in that it is systematic practice to arrest, blame, and hold responsible only one of two parties who have undoubtedly committed this "crime." Although the john's activity is illegal as well, only the prostitute is arrested and penalized— through fines, varying periods of incarceration, or both—in the overwhelming majority of cases. This remarkable fact is true in the United States as well as in other countries where prostitution is illegal. Yet, clearly, prostitution is only possible if defined relationally, as an interaction that takes place between *two* parties.[19] The sexual demands (and economic resources) of a primarily male clientele could even be said to be more important to the system than prostitutes entering this profession on the side of supply: men's desire precedes, and functions as a necessary condition for sustaining, prostitution's existence. Moreover, numerous historical and anthropological accounts (recall Rubin's argument) depict prostitution as originating coercively, in social groups already patriarchally organized: it was probably not initially women's idea.

From this analysis, one might conclude that accurate studies of prostitut*ion* should be designed to focus *at least* 50 percent of the researcher's attention on men. Similarly, to be complete, literature in this area should not be limited to writings about prostitution and prostitutes, but should also encompass studies that exclusively investigate this male customer and his traits. Interestingly, I could not find one such study, an omission particularly revealing in a time of growing interest in the subfield of "men's studies" by those wishing better to understand the totality of gendered subordination.[20] Nor does it seem sufficiently plausible to attribute this literary *solely* to methodological difficulties connected with trying to contact male informants. One-on-one interviews that ensured men's anonymity could conceivably produce snowball samples for a sufficiently determined researcher; at minimum, it would not be difficult for books to routinely include sections that acknowledged this difficulty, reflecting on how it might be overcome. And, in some cases, the pitfall has already *been* overcome: *The Lively Commerce* and *Backstreets* demonstrate that it must be possible to study customers, since they are exceptions to the rule that male clients are entirely absent from studies of prostitution.

The rarity of attention to male clients suggests instead a quiet symmetry between attitudes toward prostitution in society at large and attitudes that inform the starting point of most sociological research. This observation brings us back to issues of conscious or unconscious bias. Several points now emerge in response to the initial question of whether the scarcity or distribution of the extant literature implies deeply embedded and ambivalent attitudes toward prostitution.

First, numerically, there are simply not that many studies of prostitution in the United States. Second, these four categories in a survey of the field—historical studies, writings by prostitutes themselves, studies of attitudes toward prostitution, and contemporary studies of the relationship between prostitution and society—attest to a distinct separation between studies undertaken *by* and those undertaken *about* prostitutes or prostitution. A distance seems to be maintained between subject and object so that often those who study prostitut*ion* holistically do so from afar—historical projects, studies undertaken outside the United States, or works by feminists dealing with crucial but abstract theoretical matters. On the other hand, works about prostitut*es* have been written either by sex workers themselves or by academics who conduct attitudinal surveys and analyze prostitutes' self-organizing from the relatively removed perspective of a social movement. Where sociologists have undertaken ethnographic research (which has occurred with prostitution in numerous instances), a wider picture may be eschewed in favor of a narrower focus on prostitutes. Additionally, the benefits of participant observation—whether that entails participation in waged sex work or simply intensive observation of other women's work—are seldom brought to bear.

This divorce of subject and object is both symptomatic and reproducing of sociological ambivalence: it results in a self-fulfilling circularity. For a crucial advantage inhering to participant study of the kind already undertaken in sociology with persons who sell drugs, or enter gangs, or work as domestics or boxers is that it makes us see the world from the vantage point of supposed "others." Ideally, our perceptual habit of seeing other women and men as entirely separable from ourselves is broken down, altered, inverted, or subverted. In studies of sex workers, even those that are sympathetic or empathetic, these boundaries are rarely broken down; on the contrary, a sense of otherness is maintained and perpetuated.

Thus we come to a third point, one not terribly surprising given the previous two. A related manifestation of ambivalence is that within sociology as a discipline, research on prostitutes and prostitution routinely falls under the rubric of "deviance" or "criminology." In a particular department, books and articles on the topic—if covered at all—are more likely to be assigned in classes with titles like "Deviant Behavior and Social Control" rather than "Urban Sociology," "Intro," or courses devoted to gender, race, or class inequality. I admit to this tendency myself: my unthinking, immediate impulse would be to place texts about prostitution on a "Gender and Deviance" syllabus rather than make them part of a "Social Problems" bibliography. At the same time, books about drug dealers and crack users, gangs and boxers (to use those examples already selected) find their way with greater ease into a fuller range of course offerings. Furthermore, prostitution may even be treated as deviant within deviance itself, that is, within the interrelated subfields of deviance and criminology. For instance, at the American Society of Criminology conference held in New Orleans in November 1992, I found only two panels on prostitutes or prostitution out of a total of more than two hundred sessions. And, within the literature referred to above, Eleanor Miller, while generally nonjudgmental in *Street Woman* about her informants, nonetheless makes numerous and now quite debatable references to a female "underclass" later recruited into "deviant networks."

By now, we have a suggestive case for the *existence* of sociological ambivalence toward prostitution as a subject, as an object of study. But why this ambivalence—how else can it be explained?

AMBIVALENT ATTITUDES: THE FEMINIST AND THE PROSTITUTE

As we have seen, few sociological studies of prostitutes in the United States have been done that rely on any type of participant observation, and none that marries the academic and the prostitute in the same person. (See this chapter's afterword, however, regarding changes now taking place that affect this conclusion.) But since we are making a foray into feminist and social theory (by design as well as necessity), returning to our hypothetical scenario may help discern what underlies the absence we have noted in the actual literature. Our imagined Ph.D. student either actually engaged in sex work (in Amsterdam) or only hung out with sex workers (in New York City); let's assume for a while that her participant observation research did *not* include waged labor. The sociologist has decided to confine herself to the restricted U.S. example, both to avoid illegality and out of concern for her own safety. Now, her work is similar to the intensive research done by Carmen and Moody, except that she has decided to include a more stratified range of women in the study (from "working women" to highly paid call girls). Given this added detail, what conditions might have prevented her in theory from undertaking even this delimited—though still unusual—project in fact?

One issue has already been mentioned: namely, the factor of reception. Fear of disdain or ridicule in a professional context, of being in effect contaminated by the deviance ascribed to the prostitutes themselves,[21] might have inhibited the study even before its inception, in a field that remains male-dominated at its uppermost echelons. But our hypothetical sociologist might also have worried about the work's reception among other women, raising a second significant question as to whether—given that I have further presumed "her" to be both female and feminist[22] —she ever would have found the topic compelling. Say she did overcome the concerns already mentioned about physical danger; perhaps she is willing to take risks (as women have certainly shown themselves in other forms of field work), or she has prior experience with sex work. And say she is willing to confront, and try to overcome, the likely problems of reception. Still, even then, as a feminist, she may not feel that research in this area is particularly worthwhile or socially useful. Here we have a new possible source of ambivalence: that is, feminists' own internally divided attitudes about prostitutes and prostitution. Laurie Shrage's article "Should Feminists Oppose Prostitution?" (1989) exemplifies one pole along a continuum of feminist thought on this subject and is therefore worth quoting at length. Shrage notes that "most feminists find the prostitute's work morally and politically objectionable. In their view women who provide sexual services for a fee submit to sexual domination by men, and suffer degradation by being treated as sexual commodities." She continues:

> Our society's tolerance for commercially available sex, legal or not, implies general acceptance of principles which perpetuate women's social subordination. Moreover . . . the actions of the prostitute and her clients imply that they accept a set of values and beliefs which assign women to marginal social roles in all our cultural institutions, including marriage and waged employment. *Just as an Uncle Tom exploits noxious beliefs about blacks for personal gain, and implies through his actions that blacks can benefit from a system of white supremacy, the prostitute and her clients imply that women can profit economically from patriarchy.* Though we should not blame the workers in the sex industry for the social degradation they suffer, as theorists and critics of our society, we should question the existence of such businesses and the social principles implicit in our tolerance for them.[23]

While on one level Shrage does not wish to "blame the workers in the sex industry," on another, her analogy invoking "an Uncle Tom" belies her own stated goal. Clearly, to some extent, Shrage does hold women who become prostitutes personally responsible. Not only do they themselves profit from patriarchy, but they "imply" that others can as well: thus they are ideologically complicit. She clearly believes that prostitutes collude with patriarchy in a way inimical for feminists and feminism.

Certainly Shrage's view represents only one feminist position, and not necessarily the predominant view within feminism as a whole. Other feminists, as demonstrated by the contributors to Gail Pheterson's already-mentioned collection, *A Vindication of the Rights of Whores*, have come to reject "antiprostitution" stances that treat prostitutes as either actively antifeminist or by definition not feminist. And at the other pole of the feminist continuum on this issue, many favor decriminalizing prostitution and according greater legitimacy to "sex work," a more neutral social construction. Nonetheless, the attitudes expressed in Shrage's essay are influential and noteworthy, for they are enmeshed with other ongoing "sexuality debates" that have split feminist theory and the feminist movement since the 1970s (particularly its radical feminist branch). A feminist's belief that prostitutes' work is "morally and politically objectionable" is probably connected with her belief that pornography should be legally restricted (as Catharine MacKinnon has proposed),[24] or that sadomasochistic sex should be condemned. On the other hand, feminists opposed to censorship and censure hold these positions to be themselves antiquated and antisexual, potentially repressive rather than automatically liberating in their ramifications for women. Since these debates continue to provoke controversy (sharing prostitution's own propensity to invoke simultaneous connotations of both sexism and sex), it would hardly be surprising if many feminists ended up feeling ambivalent—or even hostile—toward prostitutes. One likely result would be to shy away from research into prostitution, avoidance winning out among the contradictory feminist reactions—disapproval, tolerance, indifference—to the topic.

Thus, an empirically observable gap between subject and object in studies of prostitution is in theory comprehensible indeed. For a good argument can be made that prostitutes are the most isolated and stigmatized of any group of women within patriarchal societies. Not only are they demeaned by society as a whole, sometimes particularly by police, johns, and pimps, but even feminists—an appellation that generally connotes concern for overcoming the oppression of *all* women—waver about the legitimacy of prostitutes' status within and beyond the politics of feminism. One sign of the thoroughness of her marginalization is that of all women, it is the prostitute who can be expected to have the most difficulty bringing well-founded charges of rape, domestic violence, or sexual harassment.[25] Because she is the "vamp" personified, the prototypical opposite of the virgin,[26] victim-blaming myths about women's consent to rape and other forms of sexual assault are so easy to apply that many prosecutors are dismissive—literally and figuratively—of her charges. Given the difficulties that any woman faces in rape cases,[27] particularly those involving date rape, how much more trouble will a prostitute encounter in making anyone believe, or become concerned about, her alleged attack? How can she hope for any recourse against sexual harassment she may experience on the job, when even the possibility itself may sound self-contradictory to sexist "common sense," as though patently inapplicable to anyone in the prostitute's profession(s)? Evidently, not many people are interested in taking up her cause, or coming to her defense, even at a time when increasing awareness about violence against women has surfaced within the media and cultural discourse more generally. Even a feminist would be hard-pressed to recall any organized or well-publicized feminist demonstrations, for instance, on behalf of a prostitute who has been raped or otherwise assaulted.

We should keep in mind, though, that prostitutes are not the *only* group of women toward whom feminists have manifested divided loyalties. Lesbians, of course, have also suffered from the biases of other women, not just the power of the state: one could cite Adrienne Rich's well-known objection to the invisibility of lesbian existence even within major feminist texts in "Compulsory Heterosexuality and Lesbian Existence" (1980),[28] or point to the early history of the National Organization for Women (NOW) in New York City, marked by a fierce dispute over whether or not to support lesbian rights. On the other hand, feminists across a wide range of theoretical leanings—from liberal to radical, Marxist to socialist, psychoanalytically oriented to postmodernist—agree that state-sponsored discrimination against lesbians should itself be outlawed. Most would concur that virtually by definition, any non- or postpatriarchal society would have to oppose antigay practices and beliefs: it is hoped not that lesbianism might "wither away" with a patriarchal state but, on the contrary, that it will be freed from shackles that have previously repressed its free expression. For Rich's contention is now well-accepted within feminist theory generally: she argued that preventing women from loving one another is a central feature of social controls exerted in male-dominated societies like our own.

However, as Shrage's remarks demonstrate, no such theoretical consensus can be presumed about the hoped-for fate of prostitutes and prostitution in some idyllic postpatriarchal society of the future. Quite the opposite is true: the question of what most feminists believe the future of prostitution should be—whether it ought to be somehow reformed or encouraged to wither away over time—is a much more complex and hotly debated question. To be sure, the contrast between the two issues is to some extent false. Sex workers' own writings, as well as the ethnographic studies cited, document that women often belong to both groups—stigmatized both as prostitutes and lesbians, at risk of being subjected to violence in one or both categories. Nevertheless, since the distinction does apply to many women's actual experience, and is often perceived and maintained by outsiders, it has some analytic utility.

That feminists are much more ambivalent about prostitutes' than gay persons' rights also seems to have affected support for social movements centered on these respective issues. Ronald Weitzer has compared the relative success of the gay and abortion rights movements with the less effective prostitute rights movements in gaining national attention during the 1970s and 1980s. He concludes that resource mobilization theories, which hold "ideological and moral factors as secondary to material and organizational variables," best explain the latter organizations' weakness and relatively lower profiles.[29] But in separating "ideological" from "material" factors somewhat artificially, Weitzer may understate the importance of a divided feminist movement in explaining the absence of interrelated support for prostitutes' rights groups. Unlike the gay liberation or women's movements, the cause of prostitutes' "liberation" is not firmly approved of, nor theoretically justified, in many feminists' minds. It does not fit as readily, therefore, into a characteristically liberal and American framework of "rights." Thus, lack of ideological support by feminists may have played a larger role than allowed both in Weitzer's study *and* in our subject at hand—that is, why prostitution also has not gained much attention as a legitimate focus of gender-oriented research in American social science.

Feminists, then, are extremely split on the subject of prostitution as object of study. This is a factor that, when combined with other factors, may have contributed to the paucity of research in this area. However, the question remains as to what position *does* make most sense for feminist sociologists in general—and our hypothetical sociologist in particular—to adopt toward prostitutes and prostitution. Are there obvious points on which feminist theory of most types could agree? Can the splits detected between subject and object, feminists and prostitutes, be overcome—and, if so, how?

TOWARD A SOCIOLOGICAL FEMINIST THEORY OF PROSTITUTES AND PROSTITUTION

If we step back to an overview of the relationship of prostitutes and prostitution to feminism as a whole, an even more basic split comes quickly to mind: the so-called good woman/bad woman or madonna/whore dichotomy, so frequently observed to characterize patriarchal societies that it has become a truism of feminist perspectives. Although resting on a fairly simple concept, the distinction is nonetheless central to exploring the social construction of prostitutes and prostitution, as perceived both by other women and by men as a dominant group.

Various ideas have been proposed about why a good woman/bad woman divide recurs wherever different gender privileges are also systematic. Whether one believes it arises from the character of men's sexual fantasies en masse (a notion that itself demands further explanation) or prefers Engels's interpretation vis-à-vis the origins of private property, the fact remains that labeling women as madonnas or whores exerts controlling pressure on *all* women. Whether the split is intentional or not, it creates a "nice girl" persona (the mother, the wife, the girlfriend) perpetually shadowed by the specter of the "bad" (the prostitute, the mistress, the "other woman"). A sense of security and attractiveness may chronically elude the nice girls, who know that there are always women construed as more sexualized, "sexier," toward whom men can and do turn with regularity. Simultaneously, they know that moving beyond or testing the borders of that role (even, perhaps, by becoming assertively feminist) may bring recrimination or slur, symbolic of the withdrawal of male approval. A rebellious woman may not be seen as femininely gendered at all: she becomes a "dyke," a lesbian, off the chart of heterosexuality altogether; or, within straight boundaries, a "tramp," a "slut," a "whore." The prostitute, then, is the heterosexual bad girl epitomized. Interestingly enough, almost every patriarchal culture uses terms of opprobrium like "whore," *putain,* or *puta* not only literally but figuratively to chastise women's disapproved-of behavior, sexual and otherwise.

On the other hand, the woman in the position of this *putain,* the mistress, the "other," is well aware of her double, too. She senses that any power derived through sexiness is borne only at the price of other types of powerlessness, that is, her own insecurity compared with the relatively desexualized but socially acceptable mother, wife, or girlfriend. A woman who is a sex worker, say, may be ashamed or afraid to acknowledge her occupation in legitimated public contexts (our ASA example being just one possible case in point); thereby her behavior has been affected and to some degree controlled. Like the nice girl who is her opposite, she can feel intimidated because of the existence of an other side. Thus, as Naomi Wolf has suggested about beauty standards keeping all women in a state of self-doubt (see also chapter 4, above),[30] so separating madonnas from whores perpetuates a chasm among women as wide and sure as any that splits workers from one another under capitalistic conditions, or prevents members of an oppressed racial minority from uniting around a mutual cause. It deflects attention from those aspects of gender-based subordination that are *commonly* experienced onto only those that are different for these two groups of women.

Additionally, it is intriguing to ponder whether the logic of this good woman/bad woman split illuminates *why* only prostitutes are habitually arrested for prostitution, as mentioned earlier. Look at the problem from a slightly altered vantage point now—from the standpoint of *men* as unequal possessors of power. If prostitution were to be decriminalized across the United States, then prostitutes would escape the bad girl's outlaw(ed) status to some degree. However, there might be disadvantages to this change. Perhaps the seductive appeals of the forbidden, part of the bad girl's sexiness to and for her mostly male desirers, would diminish with legalization. Yet there is no particular reason why bad girls can't be re-created, or maintained, even if prostitution is decriminalized. But a second disadvantage is less easily dispelled. Since decriminalization openly admits that men wish prostitution to exist, the efficacy of bifurcating women into bad girls and good might be compromised. If bad girls were no longer clearly recognizable (and sanctionable), what advantages would those enjoy who conform and are good? In fact, the historical studies of Walkowitz and Rosen suggest that not only men but mothers, wives, and girlfriends also would likely protest such a change. During eras of Victorian and Progressive reform, organizations dedicated to curbing and prohibiting prostitution were often led by "nice" women; more recently, as documented by Carmen and Moody, sex workers around Times Square perceived women demonstrators from Women Against Pornography (WAP) as anachronistic, as if somehow earlier reformers had managed to be born again in their midst.[31]

Viewing the opposite position through patriarchal lenses shows it to be just as problematic, however. If prostitution were to remain *illegal* across the United States, unchanged except that both prostitutes *and* johns were arrested consistently whenever the crime occurred, then prostitution's popularity would be apparent anyway. Here, though, the benefits of power are what risk being compromised: if new laws were vigorously enforced, resultant arrests of men would likely be so widespread (across class and race) that decriminalization might well rapidly ensue for this reason alone.[32] *Therefore, an outcome predictable from the good woman/bad woman dichotomy of feminist theory is exactly what exists:* prostitution continues to be illegal, but, for the most part, only prostitutes are charged with criminal activity.[33] In this way, the procedural status quo in criminal justice protects a fundamentally sexist division with which it is connected. It is declared in public (and to, and sometimes by, nice women) that prostitutes are bad, offenders: at the same time, the fact that prostitution is a practice equally involving both parties is obscured, because it is punished for only one sex while permitted to the other. A decidedly contradictory set of attitudes thus underlies the institution as presently structured. Prostitution is desired by men but, under gender-biased conditions, no responsibility is taken for desiring it.

Of course, prostitution is not everywhere illegal, nor does it manifest itself in the same way uniformly. As already stated, it has been decriminalized in the Netherlands; in the United States, in 1923 Nevada became the only state with a legalization statute, still on the books although it restricts prostitution to brothels and permits it only in counties with population under 400,000. Still, it seems fair to say that these are exceptions to the usual rule throughout the United States and many other societies, in which attitudes toward sexuality often display a schizophrenic character. In general, the practice of arresting only prostitutes, and the good woman/bad woman split that practice expresses and maintains with almost perverse accuracy, is ensconced within a system insecure and divisive for women *as a whole*. Therefore, it is not only prostitutes but all women who are affected. From the perspective of the good woman who may be suspiciously or ambivalently disposed toward her other, however, a collective oppressiveness may be difficult to intuit.

But this analysis does not sufficiently clarify the issue of how feminists themselves should view prostitutes and prostitution. If anything, an argument for the intrinsically alienating character of institutionalized prostitution may appear to have been reinforced, in accord with Shrage's theoretical essay or Hoigard and Finstad's empirically based conclusions. So far, prostitution emerges as an oppressive phenomenon much more in need of uprooting than reform. Dissected a little more carefully, though, prostitution can be seen to contain two potentially separable elements. It comprises (a) a set of desires, beliefs, and practices that, under patriarchy, have been gender-biased, extremely discriminatory to and of women, *and* (b) an exchange relationship in which sex is offered for sale—prostitution's sex-economic dimension. These two dimensions can be disentangled, at least in theory. For while feminists would obviously insist that the gender-skewed aspects of prostitution must change in any postpatriarchal situation, it is less clear that sex for sale is itself necessarily problematic. Are sex-economic exchanges indicative only of past and continuing patriarchal relations, or do they also correlate with capitalism or the much-heralded tendencies of contemporary postmodern cultures? Could we conceive of a revisited prostitution (whether called by that name or another) which was not by definition sexist?

Of course, quite massive changes would have to take place for the pervasiveness of bias within prostitution, as we now know it, to dissolve. As sex workers have themselves suggested, one goal would be for prostitution to become a kind of sex therapy, professionalized and no longer stigmatized. But the larger social, economic, and cultural context in which prostitution occurs would have to alter, too, for its sexist character to disintegrate: this would require not just decriminalization and the provision of safe employment conditions, but a greater equality in the numbers of male and female sex workers; customers would also need to be both sexes, so that the term "john" would become as obsolete as "policeman" or "fireman"; heterosexuality could not be privileged as a matter of course; ideally, a range of ages and body types would be able to be employed. Not exactly a small proposal.

Perhaps the requisite changes would be so radical that, were they to occur, the outcome would no longer be recognizable as prostitution. Since underlying attitudes about sex and the general position of women would have had to alter concurrently, perhaps a freer society would result, one in which sex-economic exchanges were no longer sought. However, what if they were still desired by some, which is at least a strong likelihood? Then the interesting question arises as to whether a reconstructed context of sex for sale ought be problematic from a specifically *feminist* standpoint. For many, maybe most, there is good reason to hope that evolution away from the gendered troubles of patriarchy will lead to new mergings of bodily and emotional experience, blendings of intimate tenderness with lust. But isn't it possible that others (and, again, we should assume that women as well as men could be among their number) might wish to retain the separation, whether occasionally or on a more ongoing basis, out of a truer sense of choice rather than compulsion? If so, is this necessarily objectionable? If objectionable, why? And why for all persons? Perhaps such objections themselves mask biased assumptions not particularly liberating for women, especially in our imagined future when current symbiotic connections between sex and sexism are slowly to begin breaking down.

On another level, as we continue to seek a feminist synthesis, we need not rest a case on the intricacies of futuristic speculation: sex for sale has a much more concrete meaning now. As virtually all the referenced writings of and about prostitutes reiterate (past and present), most women initially undertake sex work *for money*. Shrage's point about ideological collusion is out of touch with the reality that for many women, becoming a prostitute is similar to becoming a drug dealer or a gang member: the decision is often quite rationally, in the sense of economically, motivated. Though most sociological studies of teenage illicit activity have focused differentially on young men, prostitutes also exemplify Merton's innovator category as much or little as do such other, traditionally masculine, strategies for "getting paid." [34] As noted, few well-known recent studies have focused on prostitutes and the specific characteristics of their lives in the United States. But we do know that high-level drug dealing opportunities or gang membership will scarcely be offered to women. [35] Rather, what Pierre Bourdieu has called "bodily capital"—or, better, sexual capital, the latter term describing the gendered sex worker's case more exactly—may be the major, or only, resource available to a particular person who is female. She may be supporting a child, boyfriend, or other family members. Or she may have been poor most of her life and long to feel a greater sense of control over the conditions and circumstances surrounding her; she may yearn to buy "nice" things—a car, clothes, whatever. A given individual may realize that sex work can easily yield better and quicker money than is otherwise available. In this respect, she is acting much like the youths Williams depicted in *Cocaine Kids,* who also seek more lucrative and controllable employment than is available at minimum wage fast-food and unskilled jobs.

Similarly, in contrast with a low-paying clerical job, for example, some women describe a sense of adventure, excitement, and most of all power in turning tricks. For some sex workers, narcissistic enjoyment can spring from seeing desire in someone's eyes, knowing the dependency admitted by this attentiveness (however transient and fleeting), making him pay and in fact "getting paid"; gratification can arise from a sense of controlling the interaction as well as from giving him, and at moments oneself, pleasure. And Hoigard and Finstad record these women expressing feelings of superiority that are comparable to those reported by Rollins in her study of women domestics, *Between Women.* The structural standpoint of the subordinate often makes possible a more accurate, holistic comprehension of a dominant/subordinate, employer/employee relationship than does the position of the apparent superordinate. Like the domestic worker who consciously feigns behaviors desired by her employer, so sex workers interviewed in *Backstreets* were often the only ones aware they were faking pleasure.[36] As Hoigard and Finstad recount, johns often seemed quite foolish, aroused and persuaded by moans, groans, and ritualized statements that they (ironically) paid to hear. They may not have had a clue about what was actually taking place in the individual woman's mind and body. The sex worker, though, has the advantage of a fuller insight into both their positions, the power of secretly knowing that what to him appeared authentic may have been to her actually ridiculous and revolting.

None of this should be a cause for extreme romanticizing, on the one hand, or scandal, on the other. Prostitutes' experiences, situations, and circumstances differ greatly over the gamut of this highly class-stratified occupation. Some women work in conditions that are overtly oppressive and leave little room for exerting control; they may be exposed to dangerous conditions on and off the streets, subjected to the arbitrary power of boyfriends and pimps, cops as well as customers. For others, the job may be relatively "cushier," their lives closer to being independently entrepreneurial, with greater potential for sometimes being interesting, varied, or enjoyable.

But wherever a particular working woman exists along such a continuum, one analytic point is applicable across the board. To negatively judge *any* prostitute who undertakes sex work, sex for sale, is exactly as foolish as it would (or would not) be to hastily condemn young males like Terry Williams's cocaine kids, or members of gangs studied by Martin Jankowski or Mercer Sullivan, for their techniques of survival.[37] And this would be foolish indeed. It is as silly to compare the prostitute to an "Uncle Tom," and to blame her Uncle Tomming for reinforcing a patriarchal system, as to accuse other underground economic workers of collusive capitalism. In each of the cases, rather, many persons have turned to illegal opportunity structures—the turns themselves shaped by and permeated with gender—to get from American society (at once patriarchal and capitalistic) some of the legitimacy, recognition, and attentiveness it failed to actually provide. Similarly, all can be interpreted as rebellions against blocked life chances correctly "penetrated," or comprehended, a term and action related to what Paul Willis calls "resistance" in his study of British working-class "lads," *Learning to Labour* (1977).[38] Even if the final result is generally "accommodation"—people ending up reabsorbed or sometimes beaten down inside social structures essentially unchallenged by their stratagems—it seems senseless to criticize such logical defensive reactions.

Oddly enough, though, I suspect it may be easier for many sociologists to relate to the drug dealer's or gang member's predicament than to the prostitute's. For one thing, as we have seen, he has been studied more regularly than she, with greater respect tending to be accorded both him and his professional observer; works based on ethnographic and participant methods have come closer to overcoming subject/object divides for him than for her. Then, again, there is that matter of sex. Even if sociologists are just as liberally disposed toward understanding the prostitute's sex-economic exchanges as the gang member's more well-known and distinctly economic ones, the former is doubly vulnerable simply because she sells her body and arouses sexual and sexist reactions. Moreover, as the prostitute invokes the good woman/bad woman split by her relationship to sexual capital (a patriarchal social fact tending to set her apart from, and pit her against, other women), specifically *feminist* identification with her may be that much more difficult to achieve. Like the nice woman, the sociological feminist may react in ways mixed with, and structured by, ambivalence.

Yet, it strikes me as most suspect of all to blame prostitutes—however subtly or unconsciously—for a system of patriarchal prostitution that is clearly not of their or our creation. The reasons for this being so problematic are multidimensional. First, in terms of feminist theory, to be ambivalent or antagonistic toward the alleged other, the bad woman, plays right into the deeply embedded assumptions that split women from one another. Gendered powerlessness and insecurity are thereby reproduced. Second, in terms of class, to somehow differentiate sex-economic from other economic strategies for finding work is again prejudicial toward the prostitute. It holds her responsible for one form of sale-of-self when most of us transact other such sales on a routine basis: like "whore," the phrase "to prostitute oneself" is also used figuratively in everyday parlance but with a negative connotation, as if something out of the ordinary had occurred. Moreover, such bias perpetuates old and ongoing habits in the fields of deviance and criminology of building sociological generalizations mostly on young *males'* class experiences. Third, in terms of gender, can we really criticize some women for taking pleasure in the power of temporarily sexy and salable bodies, unless others are faulted consistently as well? Hollywood actresses celebrated for beauty, for example, or models, singers, Madonna (her "good girl" name revealing in this context) and her followers, women who spend billions on cosmetics and surgical procedures struggling to prolong such sexiness . . . How is it possible to justify using a term like "Uncle Tom" to describe the prostitute unless we indict them, ourselves, or both simultaneously? Unless we indict an entire system in which sex and sexism are continually conjoined?

No, for all these reasons, it strikes me that a feminist approach to this topic should rigorously *avoid* blaming or reproaching *prostitutes* for how they cope within gender-skewed conditions. At the same time, and just as important, it need not therefore allow *prostitution* to escape forceful criticism. A synthetic stance would be best if two-pronged, at once immediately pragmatic and with some vision of the longer run. For whether or not sex for sale could be freely chosen in some foreseeable utopia, right now it is often the only option available to women for surviving a sexist present. Thus, the policy implications of observers like Carmen and Moody should be taken quite seriously when they depict how miserable many street women's lives are made by constant threats of incarceration, onerous fines, lack of medical care, and physical fear of police in addition to johns. As they suggest, decriminalization would be likely to help ameliorate these effects, these by-products of an illegality that now is blatantly discriminatory against women. A focus on faulting prostitution rather than prostitutes underlines the need for broader improvements as well, particularly guaranteed jobs and income supports for all women (including health and child care, and family allowances where applicable). Under such conditions, women would never *have* to become sex workers out of necessity rather than interest. And, just as Williams's research asserts the importance of designing work for inner-city youth to meet more than subsistence needs alone, so alternative jobs to sex work ought to try to provide a modicum of variety, opportunity, and control. There is a self-interested reason, moreover, for this changed feminist approach: decreasingly ambivalent attitudes toward prostitutes might redirect attention to issues about which feminists are not ambivalent at all, ones nonetheless germane to our topic. We might more profitably concentrate on altering our ongoing cultural assumptions—working toward the democratization of bodily images, for example; or increasing women's share in social ownership of wealth, including but not limited to the sex (and media) industries that provide sex work. Or we might consider how to make sex itself a less threatening and loaded aspect of life than at present, so that schizophrenic cultural attitudes toward it are not expressed at women's expense.

In the end, where does this leave the hypothetical feminist sociologist with whom we opened? If my suspicions are merited, then a newly synthesized view of prostitutes and prostitution would gradually affect the context in which her work could make its debut. No longer split in our conceptions of prostitutes' legitimacy, we might find—as sociologists or feminists, as persons affected by ingrained habits of separating bad girls from good—the subject/object divide to which I refer in theory less formidable in practice. It is important to be able to perceive, and overcome, any unwitting sociological tendency to mirror common social biases like that of sex workers being treated ambivalently, at once sought as objects of desire and as subjects cursorily dismissed. For unless we can envision a scenario in which a feminist sociologist *could* have done that participant observation thesis *if* she had wanted to, without fear of ridicule or scorn, then we can be sure that sex and sexism remain firmly allied in our midst. On the other hand, if this chapter stirs respectful consideration of the project's potential validity, it will have moved a little closer toward actualizing its own possibility. Maybe she'll make that ASA presentation one of these days after all, landing a well-regarded job at UCLA, Chicago, Smith, or, closer to where she began her study, at New York University or City University.

AFTERWORD

Since I completed the "Prostitution and Feminist Theory" in the winter of 1994, several developments have led me to write this afterword. First, immediately following the essay's publication, three colleagues with whom I am only casually acquainted asked the same question, inadvertently providing supporting "data." All three commented that the essay seemed interesting, and then each proceeded to inquire, confidentially, whether I myself had been a prostitute: otherwise, one of these colleagues speculated, why else would you be so interested in this subject matter? These comments suggest that something about sex work is distinctive, and perhaps distinctively jarring, exposing the researcher to potential vulnerability above and beyond the dangers entailed in the researched activity itself. Would an ethnographer of drugs be similarly questioned about whether he or she had been an addict (otherwise why would she or he study drug taking)? Or the student of poverty questioned as to whether he or she had personally been impoverished (because otherwise why study poverty)? Rather, the legitimacy of studying these topics closer to hand—in these examples, drugs or poverty—is taken for granted far more unthinkingly than is the significance of closely studying sex. Yet sexuality permeates a wide range of social strata; it refers to a dimension of life with which nearly everyone engages at times, with others or alone, in act or in fantasy. And sexuality is distinctive because it evokes conscious as well as unconscious responses, involving no less the body than the mind, and our capacity to feel as well as to reason. Ironically, perhaps this capacity to break down usually split dimensions of experience is at the root of the discomfiture that results when the subject of sexuality is raised. The listener senses that he or she may not be able to contain a defensive laugh, a nervous titter, a sexualized comment that escapes his or her lips after an allusion to sex is made. Why doesn't this special trait—this ability of discussing sex to produce an immediate echo of the phenomenon itself—make sexuality worthy of study rather than likely to be demeaned? The reason may be that unless its significance is consciously accepted, the strongly visceral character of studying sex continues to produce schizophrenic reactions: on the one hand, often, titillation and attraction; on the other, a desire for control and therefore for distance.

The second development relates to the first. After the prostitution essay had been in print for close to a year, I contacted, or was contacted by, nearly ten feminist scholars around the country who study sex work in the United States. Several of these scholars are graduate students in sociology, though not all: some women are studying prostitution; one person has studied phone sex workers; still another has written about lap dancing. This development suggests that amid the vitality of feminist scholarship and interest in feminist theory, serious attention to sex work may be increasing. The more this occurs and the more that supportive networks among feminists as scholars and activists can be maintained, the less likely it becomes that sex work research can continue to be demeaned. A number of these scholars, though again not all, have engaged in participant observation research: one graduate student plans to write her dissertation as a participant observation study of exactly the supposedly "hypothetical" situation with which this essay begins and ends. Some related work has already been published. For instance, Wendy Chapkis bases her fascinating study *Live Sex Acts: Women Performing Erotic Labor* (1997) not only on a set of interviews with sex workers but on knowledge gained as a certified massage practitioner in California and Amsterdam; Chapkis mentions that while she only engaged in limited participant observation, she did sell sex one afternoon to women clients in Amsterdam.[39]

Yet, along with this variation, almost all of the women I spoke with (I am not aware of a male sociologist at present who is studying sex workers, male or female) concurred that peculiar reactions were frequently forthcoming from men in professional contexts after they heard that a particular feminist scholar was studying sex work. Some women were afraid to openly acknowledge the work they were doing; others had encountered initial discouragement at their choice of dissertation topic, and the concerns of advisers about whether graduate students would later have difficulty finding jobs. Sexual innuendos were frequently forthcoming, and several women told me that sexual advances were made on the basis of presumed connections between sex work and the scholars' own supposedly generalized desires. Thus, the sociological study of sex tends to evoke a sociological study of sociology: as is theoretically intriguing indeed, a "meta" level of analysis is created that shifts attention from sex to sexual reactions to its study.

Still, the fact remains that Chapkis is an employed professor and that women are building networks to support growing interest in studying sexuality as part of feminist and sociological theory. Whether this results in altered attitudes outside the academy as well, where political divides between sex and sexism can leave some feminists suspicious of sex workers and others suspicious of those feminists, remains to be seen. What we do know is that the lives of sex workers, as of women much more generally, encompasses far greater complexity than relative emphases placed on either considering "pleasure" or "subordination" suggests. Both sides are intimately enmeshed with one another, as Chapkis knows when she dedicates her study, one no longer hypothetical at all, to "the differences among us and the solidarity between us." [40]

CHAPTER SIX

Feminism and Sadomasochism

*Regarding Sadomasochism
in Everyday Life*

"In 1974, It was Free Sex. In 1984, It was Safe Sex. In 1994, It's Mean Sex: S&M Culture Goes Mainstream." So pronounced in one undifferentiated breath a glittery cover of *New York* magazine on 28 November 1994, followed by an article that just as unambiguously asserted sadomasochism's popularity in contemporary American culture. The story proceeded to describe both women and men as part of an S/M "boom" that doubled the membership of support groups like the Eulenspiegel society in five years since 1989, increased the number of advertisements concerning sadomasochistic practices in *Screw* magazine, and led to psychology's *Diagnostic and Statistical Manual* removing sadomasochistic sex from its list of behaviors stigmatized as "pathologies" (a list that has its own troubled history).

To bolster this theme of sadomasochism's greater symbolic popularity in 1994 compared with twenty years earlier, an array of mainstream cultural examples were cited: advertisements (from Gianni Versace through Chanel and Betsey Johnson); television show plot lines (on *Melrose Place, Beverly Hills 90210,* and *One Life to Live*); and contemporary films with S/M overtones (*Eating Raoul, After Hours,* and *Basic Instinct,* among a longer list). The article also quoted Madonna's mass-marketed book *Sex* as a "post-feminist statement of control projected through images of dominance and submission." Even brief allusions to philosophy and politics were brought in, buttressing the point with back-to-back sentences that first mentioned Michel Foucault and the then–Speaker of the House, Republican Newt Gingrich. First Foucault is described as a "wildly influential" thinker whose ideas about sadomasochism as an "operative metaphor for all social relations" resonate in the academy, then the author questions whether it could be coincidental that "Newt Gingrich, the most authoritarian figure on the American political scene in years, was just given a mandate to whip the country into shape." [1]

And I wonder whether any of this can be coincidental indeed. For I open with this popular cultural example, which may be unwittingly revealing about the very phenomenon it describes, in order to typify a contradiction that poses ongoing dilemmas for feminism and other social movements interested in bringing about multilevel changes in society. A split often seems to separate perceptions of sadomasochism as a personal practice from perceptions of sadomasochism as socially or politically generated. Here, the contradiction was suggested by the same article's seeming at once to anoint sadomasochism's apparent ascendancy while voicing suspicion about an authoritarian setting in which that ascendancy seems to have occurred. But perhaps even more to the point, the journalistic treatment above exemplifies the taking for granted of a particular connotation of the term "sadomasochism." Obviously, the article presumes a commonly accepted definition of "S&M" as constituting *only* a sexual practice; sadomasochism is conceived to concern nothing beyond sexuality.

Yet a broader interpretation is also possible. Indeed, a different tradition of thinking about sadomasochism can be identified in social theories that span a period from the Frankfurt School writings of Erich Fromm in the early 1940s through the work of Jessica Benjamin in the late 1980s and beyond.[2] According to this view, sexuality is an extraordinarily important but by no means unique incarnation of general ontological desires for domination and subordination, which are more widely rooted. The usual cultural linkage with sex is thus seen to focus our attentions too restrictively, channeling our customary gaze toward an individualized object and away from structural critiques.

But what if instead both levels are entailed whenever we deal with this particular phenomenon? Sadomasochism may involve a dynamic lived at the level of an individual's psyche, including of course sexuality, *at the same time* that it also relates to the organization of quite imperious and seemingly impervious social structures. Perhaps, then, sadomasochism is best described as *both* sometimes a legitimate form of consensual sexuality *and* a practice that is often rendered especially at-

tractive, maybe even predictably seductive, precisely because of its resonance with common experiences of our everyday lives.

This conceivably dual character of sadomasochism—its simultaneous relation to questions of individuals and the social, to agents as well
as structures, to the sexual in addition to other arenas in which our
energies are routinely expended—may frequently remain unrecognized
in common cultural discourse precisely because of the ambiguity it suggests. It creates a sense of uncertainty as to how and if such two-
sidedness can at once be considered and acted on. In a popular cultural
medium, one side only tends to be featured: articles that pronounce "In
1994, It's Mean Sex" stress the predominantly sexual definition of a
consensual S/M as explored by individuals, as the phrase resonates with
the pleasurably kinky and the sexy. In this presentation, it is possible to
envision sadomasochistic sex as liberating, exciting, when taking place
within consensual contexts shorn of repression. All this quite legiti-
mately reflects one of sadomasochism's experiential manifestations. On
the other hand, when a different web of associations is entertained in
cultural consciousness, almost the opposite sense of sadomasochism can
rise to the surface, stressing not what is freely chosen at all but the
oppressing or oppressive. Here, what comes to mind are painful aspects
of control exerted, and not always consensually, outside as well as
within the realm of sexuality. And in other social contexts and situations, all this may have experiential validity as well.

Therein lies a source of thought-provoking complexity and of what
I again suggest may be a two-sided paradox central to sadomasochism
as a phenomenon both psychic and social, at the present moment. Because sadomasochism simultaneously encompasses both sides of any
dichotomy that is made between the sexual *or* nonsexual, social *or* individual, it ought not be all that surprising to find Michel Foucault and
Newt Gingrich so blithely and unquestioningly conjoined. In fact, it
may be a quite logical outcome, virtually to be anticipated. An alternative explanation is that aligning two such opposite figures with sadomasochism is symptomatic of American media's proclivity toward brev-
ity, toward the oversimplified and sensationalistic. Another possibility
is that postmodern sensibilities are more tolerant of the use of paradox;
indeed, its appearance in writing has gradually become the norm rather
than an anomaly.

But I think it just as likely that the paradox marking *New York* magazine's otherwise quite simplistic presentation stems from exactly the
kind of individual/sexual versus social/political polarization of sado-

masochism one could anticipate finding in our particular historical context. Foucault appears as representative of a rebellious or potentially subversive side to individuals' S/M sex at a time when sadomasochistic forms of surveillance are sensed to be everywhere; on the other hand, the reference to Gingrich brings back awareness of sadomasochism's compulsory and more troubling sociopolitical side, a punitive undercurrent (say, here, a willingness to cut programs for the poor) that extends far beyond the realm of the sexual per se.

The two facets exist side by side: at one level, this contradictory presentation of sadomasochism's character smacks of the fashionably postmodern; at another, it would be problematic to simply divorce sexual sadomasochism from sadomasochistic politics (making the latter seem as a consequence maddeningly unchanged or unchangeable). For, to return to the article's question, can it be coincidental indeed that "S&M" is sensed as gaining new acceptability during the Republican-dominated years of the 1980s and 1990s, a time when social anxieties are rising to worrisome heights?[3] Or that, by contrast, "free sex" was the well-known motto in the 1960s? The difference seems to be connected with the different contexts. When conservative social controls are being exerted, whether by favoring "family values" or stigmatizing certain social groups (those on welfare, for example, a form of stigmatization increasingly characteristic of the mid-1990s),[4] perhaps sadomasochism becomes a very apt symbolic metaphor.

Moreover, as we turn to feminism, it can be argued that the ongoing history of a split over sadomasochism in contemporary American second-wave feminist debates reflects an analogous problem. How, on the one hand, to endorse the freedom to explore S/M consensually and erotically (if people so desire) *without,* on the other, leaving untouched the coercive societal or patriarchal institutions within which gendered sexual desires have incubated?

These assumptions and complications about sadomasochism found in one magazine article merely provide a take-off point for the two related concerns of this chapter. One is to explore how sadomasochism and contemporary feminist concerns relate *in particular;* the other is to investigate the question of interpreting sadomasochism *in general.* To these ends, I have organized this essay into three sections. The first broaches how a possibly characteristic splitting of sexuality from the social links the issue of sadomasochism with others like it within contemporary feminism. In the second section, I summarize arguments made in an earlier work in order to develop a possible framework through which sadomasochism can be defined in and beyond the sexual.[5] In service of this widened definition, the section provides criteria for analyzing sadomasochism in a broader sense, testing them against examples from the worlds of work and everyday gendered relations. This dynamic, and its frequent and patterned recurrence in myriad spheres of "everyday life," demonstrates that sadomasochism appears to be a phenomenon commonplace rather than rare. It therefore makes little sense to think of sadomasochistic desires (including but not only sexual desires) as "deviant," for they seem to be far more generally distributed than we are accustomed to admitting, woven into the texture and fabric of everyday social relations. Moreover, it makes little sense to think of sadomasochism predominantly in terms of an "anti-" versus "pro-" debate. The last section, then, briefly considers the implications of this analysis for reframing the sex/sexism split that is the overarching theme of this book. By then the theoretical and political problem of splitting sex and sexism with regard to sadomasochism should appear less onerous, or inevitable, than it may have seemed initially.

Before proceeding, however, I must insert one last prefatory note. Many may believe sadomasochism to be far more *intrinsically* paradoxical than the sociologically driven and externally influenced phenomenon—the particular form of interaction—I have begun to highlight. By this interpretation, ambiguity necessarily attends a situation, thought to be unavoidably sadomasochistic, in which we all find ourselves, most of the time—a situation fundamentally related to strivings toward power or powerlessness that may be played out in fantasy or in history. In this case, those shifting back-and-forth transformations between sadists and masochists—sometimes one in the role of subject and the other as object, often changing positions with their opposites again and again—appear as existential givens. Such movement may be rooted in human conditions of dependency and the desire to escape it, in struggles ultimately over and about death. Insofar as this interpretation holds true, we ought to be concerned not so much with changing as with accepting the dynamic, sadomasochism being likely to recur under most or any conceivable social arrangements. Or perhaps we would conclude that the very act of acknowledging sadomasochistic desires and experiences, rather than denying them, is an important change in and of itself.

My perspective here is not altogether in disagreement, but it does emphasize the importance of a different point. Because even if sadomasochism can be traced in part to dimensions of human existence that concern mortality and dependency, to aspects of life changed not easily if at all, we cannot separate out its eternal versus historical entanglement so long as the social world can itself be shown to be organized punitively and in many respects undemocratically, being coercive in various avoidable ways (for example, with regard to relations of class, gender, or perhaps race, with their socially created restrictiveness). Or, put another way, we may never be able to intelligently distinguish one set of influences from another as long as the following statement rings true: if sadomasochistic desires and compulsions did *not* exist in us somewhat primordially, the social demands of systems structured (for example) capitalistically in the economic sphere or patriarchally in terms of gender relations could surely themselves have created such desires and compulsions. And the political ramifications of such an analysis, if valid, are extremely significant indeed. For if we believe that sadomasochism has *only* to do with the individual and the psychic, we may have less confidence and determination in attempting to transform the external universe that channels our internal needs and feelings so that they conform to the demands of oppressive social situations (thereafter leaving those socially created situations basically unchanged). On the other hand, if we concentrate only on external change, we may be in danger of repressing self-exploration and sexual freedom, of deceiving ourselves again and again about the psychic wants and feelings—for example, rage against powerlessness or attractions toward it—that do exist in individuals and that are not very easily affected unless openly admitted.

Consequently, an important challenge for both feminism and other social movements involves finding ways (on the one hand) to preserve and act on transformative visions of imagined possibility while (on the other) not thereby repressing, or denying, the psychic or sexual needs and feelings of individuals in the existential moment. How can these two dimensions, the need both for improved futures and for pleasurable presents, be encompassed—at once, or perhaps in a more dialectical back-and-forth movement between the individual and social, the social and individuals—so that neither side is denied, forgotten, or rationalized away? In the specific context of the United States, where feminism and other social movements are surrounded by a cultural ethos of individualism, the question seems particularly germane. We may tend to deny or underrate the influence and changeability of the social, even when we give lip service to an interconnection between the two dimensions. But we will closely consider sadomasochistic dynamics only after first returning to feminism and a set of "sexuality debates" that are also part of this contemporary context.

SADOMASOCHISM AND FEMINISM: REFRAMING THE ISSUE

Just as a contradiction between individual practices and the social roots of sadomasochism can be exemplified in a popular cultural treatment like *New York* magazine's, so two analogous interpretations emerged in feminist reactions over the course of second-wave American feminism in and after the 1960s. On the one hand, many early feminists were suspicious of what could be dubbed *social sadomasochism*. They defined sadism and masochism in such a way that both were associated with the specific historical traits of patriarchy, and therefore with a male-dominated form of social organization highly damaging to women.

But this interpretation was joined in the 1980s and 1990s by concerns about freedom to explore S/M as a sexual practice. For, on the other hand, many women began to object that even feminists were now mandating permissible behaviors in a realm as unpredictable and complex as sexuality. They saw such restrictions as yet another layer of internal censorship imposed on women and argued instead for emphasizing women's simultaneous needs for and rights to bodily freedom and sexual exploration. And consequently, if only in some feminists' writings, a different interpretation developed that focused on *sexual sadomasochism*.[6] In other words, sadistic and masochistic behaviors enacted in "real-life" situations that involved actual coercion were taken to be extremely different from consented-to sexual situations involving play. For instance, although in real-life encounters a masochist often experiences a lack of control, S/M often entails role reversals and mutually agreed-upon exploration that accords the "bottom" at least equal power to that possessed by the "top."[7]

Thus, two contrasting conceptions can be traced from the beginnings of the second wave until the present: the first strand views sadomasochism and its relationship to feminism in mostly negative and problematic terms; the second treats S/M not so much with suspicion, or as fundamentally incompatible with women's equality, but as a personal practice of women and men to further their own purposes and pleasures. Certainly, what I am describing is to some extent a matter of *relative* emphasis; many feminists' viewpoints have not, and do not necessarily now, split so easily into one of these categories *or* the other. Yet such emphases had created tensions by the early 1980s between those feminists who were more concerned about calling attention to social sadomasochism (and its problematic aspects) and those who emphasized sexual sadomasochism (and its potentially liberatory aspects). This debate began to produce not only different relative emphases but animosities, as different feminist activists and writers became associated with each position (for instance, Andrea Dworkin and Ti-Grace Atkinson with the first, Gayle Rubin and Pat Califia with the second).[8] It also took place in print; well-known texts include *Against Sadomasochism* (1982), a volume of essays written after the ninth Barnard College Scholar and the Feminist Conference brought the sadomasochism debate to explicit feminist notice, and, associated with the second position, *Coming to Power* (1981) and *Powers of Desire* (1983).[9]

These two interpretations of sadomasochism within feminism became publicly visible in the context of a controversy that surfaced at and after an academic conference, "Towards a Politics of Sexuality," held at Barnard College in April 1982. Sadomasochism became a key issue when Barnard College administrators censored a preconference brochure that contained the image of a razor blade placed between the spread-eagled legs of a woman. But the core of the dispute was the claim of a West Coast lesbian group called Samois (named after the dominatrix in Pauline Réage's classic 1965 work on sexual sadomasochism, *The Story of O*) that Samois, like any other feminist participants, was entitled to representation on conference panels. Members of this particular group of feminists openly proclaimed the legitimacy of sadomasochism as a sexual practice in which they had every right to engage.

The outcome was that the planners of the Barnard conference defended Samois's right to participate, citing sexual libertarian grounds. Alice Echols, Carol Vance, and Ellen Willis were among the feminists who at and through this conference questioned the previously unexamined dominance that "cultural feminist" attitudes had assumed within the women's movement as a whole. Echols and others contended that cultural feminists, including women involved with the group Women Against Pornography (WAP), often tended to associate women's sexuality with a pure and idealized vision, imagining an idealized "erotica" from which disconcerting and misogynistic images of power and powerlessness would be carefully omitted. But what if, as Echols and Willis persuasively argued, this view of women's sexuality had also resulted in setting up, in effect, a feminist superego of "politically correct" sexual practices? What if it tended to intimidate those women whose experiences did not neatly correspond to this vision, which struck them as unnecessarily sanitized and condescending? Women might come to fear acknowledging pleasure they find in heterosexuality, in pornography, or in sadomasochistically oriented sexual practices, whether politically correct or not. By repressing the truth of some women's psychic realities, these feminists argued, feminism risked reproducing yet another version of sexual repressiveness, a central component of the oppression of women against which feminists had rebelled in the first place.

This was the position, the "side" of the issue's multifaceted complexity, that feminists interpreting sadomasochism in predominantly sexual terms tended to emphasize. But what about those feminists who continued to object to this interpretation, so strongly in disagreement that they published *Against Sadomasochism* in response to the importance of the Barnard conference? What were the reasons for the ongoing suspicions of those whose positions inclined, and again relatively speaking, toward the social sadomasochism side?

Three overlapping considerations, which predated the surfacing of the debates at the 1982 Barnard conference, lay behind this wariness. First, patriarchy, as the term was defined in early radical feminist writings, placed women in relatively masochistic positions simply by virtue of its "normal" processes of gender socialization. Sometimes in the history of feminist thought this perspective has been implicit, sometimes argued overtly.[10] The theoretical characteristics of patriarchy itself may be taken as implicitly related to sadomasochism as follows. By definition, in a patriarchal society—a society that follows "the law of the father"—men consistently hold dominant positions of power. The scope of male dominance extends across the board, as Kate Millett wrote, from apparatuses of state control, like the military and the police, to the realms of economic, political, technological, and scientific knowledge.[11] As feminist theorists have by now elaborated with extreme thoroughness, this system of social organization has traditionally confined women to the family and associated them with the private worlds of nature, domesticity, and emotionality because of their reproductive functions and their apparently closer contact with biological processes. It has thus followed that under patriarchy, the powerful, male public sphere has been considered superior and more valuable than the female private sphere. According to a well-known argument by anthropologist Sherry Ortner, this differential has been rationalized by the perception of nature itself as threatening and out of control: since women are associated with the world of biology, they, like nature, need taming and domination.[12] A host of secondary hierarchies ensues, rooted in the primary one promulgated along these lines of sexual politics: women come to be seen as the "second sex" of Simone de Beauvoir's description, as passive rather than active, secondary rather than primary, and inessential rather than essential.

It is not difficult to segue back to sadomasochism from this condensed yet evocative feminist analysis. Patriarchy creates a tendency for women to be situated in a relatively powerless position even as men enjoy a greater sense of power in comparison: thus, women can be seen as situated masochistically insofar as masochism tends to *deny* one's own sense of power and ability to be relatively independent in the world. A more than average dependency on a male other is built into a socially constructed feminine role as women seek *human* recognition inside a patriarchal system that in effect sadomasochistically denies even the possibility of such recognition. At the same time, deference to the other's power and ability to affect one's life may become the only means to forge a vicarious, if estranged, relationship to self. To undergo self-subordination may become habitual. Thus, a proclivity in women to assume a self-denying (and, in this sense, masochistic) role more regularly than do men strikes me as a rather predictable, logical, and ultimately self-protective outcome of any society organized patriarchally, of any situation that sunders human characteristics by gender, bestowing unequal worth on its divided parts.

Of course, the relationship of sadism to a socially conditioned masculinity can be similarly explained. Just as women confront relative powerlessness vis-à-vis men, so men become habituated to relative power and privilege vis-à-vis women. If theorists of patriarchy are correct, men come to believe in the inferiority of that feminine sphere which came to be constructed as linked to the world of nature and feelings. Men could be seen to be placed by this form of social structure in a position relatively sadistic (again, as a sociopsychological correlate to patriarchal imperatives), insofar as it encourages here not a denial of one's sense of relative independence in the world but a denial of one's sense of relative *dependence*. Socialized masculinity may create a sense that one's power is not contingent and limited, so that underlying feelings of dependence may become expressed through the exertion of controls that can be said to take sadistic forms.

Thus, the first reason for feminist wariness toward sadomasochism is that masochism (as a denial of self, which impedes feelings of relative independence) and sadism (as a sense of one's self as having unlimited power, which impedes the ability to acknowledge relative dependence on others) were both seen as stemming from divisions basic to societies organized around patriarchal principles. For both men and women, a foundation for potentially sadomasochistic dynamics is set when persons cast on either side of this gendered divide, constrained within masculine and feminine personalities, later attempt to clutch, cling, grasp, seize, or merge with the other. Perhaps they obsessively, compulsively, reach to repossess that part of themselves that has been coercively alienated. In reaching for a male other, women may be reaching for a vicarious sense of self-confidence and independence to deal with the world in a matter-of-fact and instrumental way. Men may yearn to possess vicariously the ability to be expressive, intimate, vulnerable, and psychologically introspective about feelings conscious or unconscious, to tolerate uncertain and uncontrollable parts of life to which we are all subject.

But this "problem" with sadomasochism—its being seen as associated with, and indeed inseparable from, the characteristics of patriarchy as a system that radical feminists were only beginning to analyze in the 1960s and 1970s—points to a second and related source of distrust. For if patriarchy itself tends to produce masochism and sadism (these thereafter becoming incarnated through gendered divisions constructed along the lines of socialized "femininity" and an opposing socialized "masculinity"), we should not be surprised that the term "sadistic" can be applied to behavior both in and outside the realm of the sexual. Someone would be sadistic in a heterosexual relationship if he (as is statistically more often the case) beat or used physical coercion against a person with whom he was involved; his actions might also be called sadistic if he exerted dominance and controls not so much bodily but emotionally, psychologically, or economically. This radical feminist usage is illustrated by Dworkin's analysis (whether one agrees with or finds too simplistic her interpretation) of Heathcliff's feelings of desire and anger toward women in Emily Brontë's *Wuthering Heights* (1848), an urge to control that included but went beyond a narrow conception of sexuality:

> His radical cruelty, based on class hate, reminds one, however unwillingly, of the more attractive virtues of those born to dominance: an indifferent or even gracious or affable condescension; a security in power and identity that can moderate or sublimate exercises in social sadism. Heathcliff's is a radi-

cal, violent revolution incarnated in a socially constructed sadism that appears to have the force of nature: it levels everything before it. Brontë's feminist genius was to show how this sadism was made; how and why.[13]

Given this linkage of sadism with oppression in the actual exercising of patriarchal controls generally, it is not surprising that a conflict arose at the Barnard conference over the interpretation of the term. The older view of someone as sadistic who genuinely controls (whether physically or psychologically) someone else in a compulsory manner was quite at odds in emphasis with the later stress on sexual freedom and exploration. In the second interpretation, someone might be "sadistic" (or the "top") in a mutually consenting relationship meant not to enact but to *mimic* or reproduce (as though an enacted representation of) a situation of actual coercion. Although the difference between actual and mimicked sadomasochism was critical for those feminists who believed sexual sadomasochism to be potentially liberatory or found it experientially pleasurable, those holding to a framework that stressed social sadomasochism (as Dworkin in her literary analysis) were more likely to minimize or erase the distinction altogether.

But there is a third important historical reason that helps explain the sexism/sex split within feminism over the issue of sadomasochism, relating to the common usages and connotations of the term "masochism." If patriarchal society tends to socialize men differentially into a relatively sadistic position, certainly this situation is not women's "fault" in any way. Yet the concept of masochism has its own distinct history of being defined as the "taking of pleasure in pain." Within the psychoanalytic tradition, for instance, Freud himself was guilty of speaking about masochism as a biologically given trait of women. In *Three Essays on the Theory of Sexuality,* he envisioned sadism as a primordial vestige of male aggressivity, and in both that work and "The Economic Problem of Masochism," he took for granted the existence of a feminine masochism that he called the most "easily observable" of three types of masochism he wished to identify.[14]

This theme was reiterated and supposedly clarified by analyst Helene Deutsch in her massive *Psychology of Women* (1944–45).[15] In Deutsch's treatment, masochism is not a defense against an intolerable social and psychological environment but a biological mechanism of human adaptation. Only the biological life of the human female contains the painful experiences of menstruation and childbirth. According to Deutsch, women would be unwilling to bear these strains unless they also took pleasure in their pain. And, since reproduction is clearly not a luxury the race can afford to eschew, female masochism is necessary to human survival. It is not to be changed, nor is it changeable. Neither Freud nor Deutsch—representative of theorists whose legacy included a belief in the inevitability of sadomasochism's gendered shapes—seriously considered the possibility that the association they observed between women and masochism stemmed largely from social and cultural factors rather than from any innate predisposition.

Thus when we consider recent feminist debates, we again should not be surprised that the idea of masochism—or women adopting masochistic positions, even in sexual play—stirred controversy, given this history of associating masochism with "pleasure in pain." Once more, feminists thinking in terms of social sadomasochism tend to place relatively greater emphasis on the *actual* circumstances that gave rise to women's masochistic positioning in comparison to mimicking and reinterpreting that position in sexual play. Conversely, feminists interpreting sadomasochism through the lens of possible sexual pleasure, freedom, and mutual exploration are more likely to stress the importance of play itself rather than insisting on the need to transform the social structure of "patriarchy." Moreover, they view the masochist in S/M sex not as necessarily powerless but as someone who has just as much power as the top by virtue of her or his ability to stop sexual activity that is no longer desired. Compare the sense of sadomasochism in the Dworkin quote above with Pat Califia's affirming view:

> [Sadomasochism] is surrounded by a lot of fear and distortion. Relationships in which one partner physically abuses the other or dominates her emotionally are often described as sadomasochistic. The newspapers routinely refer to sex murderers or rapists as sadists. Armchair psychologists are fond of labeling friends who frequently get involved in situations that cause them distress of threaten their survival as masochists. Unhealthy relationships, violent crimes with a genital or sexual component, and self-destructive behavior do exist. But in this section a distinction is made between coercive or suicidal activities and sexual sadomasochism. Sadomasochism is defined here as an erotic ritual that involves acting out fantasies in which one partner is sexually dominant and the other partner is sexually submissive. This ritual is preceded by a negotiation process that enables participants to select their roles, state their limits, and specify some of the activities which will take place. The basic dynamic of sexual sadomasochism is an eroticized, consensual exchange of power—not violence or pain.[16]

Califia vigorously denies that masochism is a biological position of innate powerlessness:

The bottom need not be self-destructive, nor is she genuinely helpless. She is likely to be very aware of her own sexual fantasies and preferences and exceptionally good at getting what she wants. The power she loans to her sexual partner is not permanently lost, nor does it inhibit her ability to maneuver and succeed in the rest of her life. Both partners benefit from an S/M exchange because both of them obtain sexual pleasure from it.[17]

Where does this sexism/sex split, these two potentially conflicting emphases within recent feminist debates, lead? What are the implications of these two seemingly opposed interpretations of sadomasochism, each drawn from feminist theory? Is it possible *both* to be critical and even judgmental of a social structure such as patriarchy (which seems indeed to be organized sadomasochistically), *and* at the same time to avoid reinforcing the repression of sexual pleasures and diversity, including those which may take consensual shape through the exploration of the sadomasochistic desires that we find all around us? It was in part because of my interest in the feminist debate just outlined, and because of the lengthy conversations it inspired, that I tried to reframe the debate somewhat through my dissertation, later revised and published as *Sadomasochism in Everyday Life* (1992). I will now ask the reader's patience as I summarize the argument of that book as a way of suggesting a third position.

For I argue that there may well be a *sadomasochistic dynamic* that corresponds at a social psychological level to the coercive structures of patriarchy, as well as those common to capitalism, all around us. Indeed, this sadomasochistic dynamic enacts itself quite coercively in a number of realms, including but not limited to the sexual (where, of course, it may take coercive forms as well): the examples taken from everyday gendered relations and work illustrate a commonly sadomasochistic texture often experienced in both arenas, frequently quite apart from sexual interactions. This argument suggests that our social stress on sadomasochism as only or primarily sexual may distract and displace attention from the much deeper structural roots of coercive dominance/subordination relationships in society. Moreover, we see that it is critical to indict sadomasochistic social structures *and* absurd to indict individuals for an often sadomasochistic shape psyches and sexualities are quite *likely* to assume. We therefore need to do two things at once: to keep our eyes on the *social structures* that are coercive in our lives (and focus on how to alter them) while vigorously defending the right and importance of *individual agents* to find sexual pleasures and enjoy sexual self-determination and free actions to which they mutually consent in the present.

SADOMASOCHISM IN EVERYDAY LIFE: A POSSIBLE ALTERNATIVE THEORY

To sum up thus far, my argument about sadomasochism is built around two related premises. First, we have tended to view sadomasochism as an extreme rather than more typical form of behavior, as an individual and predominantly sexual phenomenon that can easily be "deviantized" or "stigmatized" as unusual. Second, not only are sadomasochistic dynamics more ordinary than extreme, but sadomasochism may be the social psychology one would be most *likely* to find in all contemporary societies that are structured like our own. It is the social psychology that correlates more precisely to the characteristics of class-divided (and, therefore, capitalistic) and male-dominated (and, therefore, patriarchal) modes of social organization. But this argument—via a route that will eventually bring us back full circle to a connection with feminist "sexuality debates"—may enable us to see the two interpretations, *social sadomasochism* and *sexual sadomasochism,* as not necessarily mutually exclusive. Both positions have some validity; moreover, if we are to ensure sexual freedom and to challenge a restrictive set of social structures, aspects of each need to be acknowledged.

However, we are at the moment far from reaching these conclusions; first we must consider the definition of "sadomasochistic dynamics." Why use this concept, anyway, rather than some less controversial labels (say, victims and victimizers, or the relatively powerful and powerless) to describe relationships of dominance and subordination? One advantage of sadomasochism stems, somewhat paradoxically, from its narrowly sexual common meaning. When we refer to power relations as "sadomasochistic," we apply the same concept to a gamut of social interactions ranging from sexuality (our most "private" contact between self and other) through the workplace and street interactions (our most "public" places of contact with the outside world). In this way, the feminist insistence on how power dynamics occur not only in the public, seemingly "political" sphere but also in allegedly "personal" arenas (like a bedroom or kitchen) makes the two clearly and theoretically connected. Precisely *because* of sadomasochism's strong association with sexuality, it becomes hard to disconnect the term from its potential applicability across a wide continuum of social relationships.

In addition, sadomasochism refers to an *internally transformable* dynamic. As numerous theorists have described, sadomasochism is an evocative concept indeed insofar as sadists always have the potential to transform into their opposites, and vice versa. Freud describes this phenomenon in his *Three Essays on Sexuality:* "A sadist is always at the same time a masochist, although the active or the passive aspects of the perversion may be the more strongly developed in him and represent his predominant sexual activity." [18] Although Freud, too, clearly associated sadomasochism almost exclusively with its sexual manifestations, the idea of internal transformability has immense possibilities, as we will soon see, when sadomasochism is applied to the not necessarily sexual situations of everyday life.

There is a further advantage, somewhat separate but related to the ones mentioned above: the concept of sadomasochism is not essentialistic. In no way is it determined by class or race or gender: for instance, women are usually socialized into more masochistic positions of powerlessness, but they also have the potential for sadism; men, often encouraged into more sadistic postures, have a similar capacity for masochistic turnabouts under certain circumstances. Referring to power relations through the medium of a sadomasochistic dynamic, then, differs from other descriptions of victim/victimizer, dominant/subordinate relationships in explicitly acknowledging, and encompassing, how the victim of one interaction can be the victimizer of another, and vice versa. To take one of innumerable examples that could be cited, a woman perhaps masochistically situated in relation to her husband may become sadistically abusive toward her child; the man who is masochistically powerless at his job may act quite sadistically at home where he has relatively greater power. Thus, sadomasochism has the potential to capture more accurately the character of power relationships that are much more complex than has usually been recognized or than many people may wish to admit.

A final advantage is that while the traditional notion of masochism has often been used to blame women for their own victimization, the very act of maintaining the concepts of sadism and masochism necessarily allows for change. For perhaps the only thing intrinsic to the dynamic I am describing is that it constantly shifts. Thus, one cannot *by nature* be a masochist or sadist, even if one acts *as though* such an identity were etched in stone: instead, one tends to become inclined one way or the other through the pressures, constraints, and socializing influences of particular situations. Change, then, becomes an ever-present possibility, and sadomasochistic dynamics themselves need not be inescapable when oppressive or rigid in their operations.

This addresses the benefits of using the term "sadomasochism" rather than another more static—and *less* specifically known to be internally transformable—description of relations based on power and powerlessness. But we have not yet touched on the problem of *what* this dynamic is, of what we should take it here to entail: more specifically, then, what are the characteristics of sadomasochistic dynamics as I have been referring to them? In *Sadomasochism in Everyday Life,* I argue that there are a set of basic traits through which one can identify sadomasochistic dynamics at both an individual and on a more collective level. This set of characteristics was initially culled from an examination of five novels, some of which are seen as "classic" literary expositions of sadomasochism (such as Pauline Réage's *Story of O* and Leopold von Sacher-Masoch's *Venus in Furs*).[19] In addition, I drew there on three sets of concepts based in different academic traditions of thought—existentialism, psychoanalysis, and symbolic interactionism (sociologically influenced)—in order to explore these traits' validity. By exploring three different theoretical languages (and arguing that one can translate between them), I became persuaded that each was saying basically the same thing. Consequently, I became more confident in generalizing about how sadomasochistic dynamics tend to operate.

A first characteristic of a classically "sadomasochistic dynamic," then, is that it is based on a hierarchical relationship between two unequal parties, one dominant and the other subordinate. Initially, this appears to be a dyadic relation, though we will see that it extends from the level of a pair of persons outward into other social relationships within the world. In other words, if one starts, as I do, from a virtually axiomatic premise of sadomasochism—that every masochist implies a sadist, every sadist a masochist—then sadomasochism has the potential for necessarily expanding beyond isolated dyadic pairs.

Yet, within any one particular couple, between any one particular sadist and masochist, certain tendencies unfold; there are usually a set of evaluations that the dominant party feels important enough to bestow upon the subordinated one. Again, virtually by definition, the dominating sadist is the one who asserts that he or she is somehow "better," while the subordinate masochist must seem relatively "secondary" or "inessential."[20] Still, while necessary, the existence of hierarchy is by no means a sufficient condition for the presence of a sadomasochistic dynamic as I am defining it. Not all hierarchical relationships are sadomasochistic: clearly not, since many teacher/student, boss/worker, parent/child relationships involve differential power but will not in any other way fit the remainder of the definition. Therefore, there is a second key trait—probably the most important criterion of all—for determining whether or not a particular dynamic is sadomasochistic.

This second characteristic is that the party in the more subordinate, or masochistic, position cannot just break away at will: some sort of punishment or reprisal will predictably ensue. Fundamentally, then, sadomasochism comes into being when or if it becomes impossible for a subordinate party to question or in any way challenge her or his relation to a "superordinate" without knowing that punitive consequences are likely to follow. Obviously, S/M sex, as Gayle Rubin, Pat Califia, or the Eulenspiegel society would describe it, does not meet this criterion: the rules of the game of this form of sexual exploration explicitly involve consent, precisely in order to differentiate it from the dynamic on which I am now focusing. But one knows that the seeds of sadomasochism are present if, for example, a teacher punishes the student who raises a question or challenge. Or, to cite another example, if any attempt to start a union or exert some influence in one's company is met by immediate dismissal or intimidating threats that one's livelihood could be lost. Or perhaps a parent becomes physically or emotionally abusive should his or her child express anger or dissatisfaction, even sometimes simply as a result of starting to grow and become separate. Consequently, sadomasochistic dynamics are most recognizable by the sense of threat—sometimes manifest, always latent—that underlies them, a reprisal often revealed most surely just at moments when the party situated masochistically becomes emboldened enough to challenge the sadist by breaking away and whether the attempt succeeds or not.

Third, the sadomasochistic dynamic is characterized by a situation of symbiotic dependence that bonds both a particular sadist to a particular masochist and a particular masochist to a particular sadist. On each side of the coin—from whichever perspective we view the relationship—both parties share a sense of interdependence on the other. They are linked by a common perception that neither can survive, physically or psychically, without the other. Nevertheless, although both know through experience what it is to be extraordinarily and symbiotically dependent on another, the *forms* of that dependence greatly differ for a sadist and a masochist.

For the sadist, his or her dependence is unknown or unconscious; the vulnerability it implies is his or her best-kept secret from self and others. On the surface, the sadist appears to be the more independent one, the one in control; but his or her willingness to punish the masochist for rebelling from their interaction testifies to the extremity of this dependency. The masochist, on the other hand, has no choice but to acknowledge dependency; her or his structural position within the dynamic makes it clear how much the sadist is needed. Because the sadist cannot acknowledge dependence while the masochist can (and even though it is clear to us, looking on from outside, that *both* are symbiotically bound up with each other), a fascinating paradox comes into being. The apparently independent and "in control" sadist appears to be an actually *weaker* and probably *more* dependent party than the seemingly so dependent masochist because *only* the latter can admit to her or his vulnerability. Thus, the psychic and social realities experienced internally by sadist and masochist could be said to be virtually the *opposite* of what surface appearances would indicate.

The fourth characteristic of a sadomasochistic dynamic has already been mentioned: this form of relation between power and powerlessness is constantly changing. Its only permanent feature is to be forever shifting, perpetually in flux. This point, too, has quite radical ramifications. For once the sadist has a masochist in a hierarchical position of control and subordination, as is allegedly the goal of their interaction, then what? How does the dynamic move on in time—how can the sadist continue to get pleasure once the masochist has come to be controlled? Indeed, the only way for the dynamic to continue over time is if the masochist in some way rebels so that control can be exerted again and again. This may happen spontaneously; or perhaps the sadist will find him- or herself trying to bring about the masochist's mutiny. How strange and interesting, if so, because this is just the opposite of what the sadist is *supposed* to want—unlimited control and obedience!

Two analogous paradoxes follow from this. On the one hand, the sadist comes to need an uppity masochist, one who rebels against his or her power but only slightly, only within the rules of the sadomasochistic game I have begun to describe. The sadist has thereby begun to desire something paradoxical indeed, to wish for a highly ironic disapproval in the mode of approval: just the opposite of what he, or she, on the surface seems to desire. On the other hand, the masochist, who apparently seems to desire only that she or he be controlled, finds her- or himself becoming surprisingly uncontrollable. The masochist may discover that she or he possesses unexpectedly great power; just the fact that the sadist wants continued rebellion tends to reveal the superior's ironic dependency and relative *powerlessness*. For, just as the sadist cannot entirely escape evidence of his or her actual dependence on the masochist, the masochist begins to realize that she or he cannot entirely be controlled—the masochist can never completely wipe out evidence of her or his actual *independence*. (I think of the 1986 film *Kiss of the Spider Woman* here: though he is jailed, and entirely powerless, the masochistically situated prisoner still has the mental power of imagination, and thus possesses a certain undeniable freedom even in conditions of utter captivity.) The masochist finds that she or he does not want only disapproval from the sadist—again, on the surface, the masochist supposedly only wishes to be controlled—he or she also (and again paradoxically) wishes desperately for approval. Thus, the correlate of the sadist's paradoxical desire for disapproval within the mode of approval inside the sadomasochistic dynamic is the masochist's desire for approval from the sadist within the mode of disapproval.

Each, then, sadist and masochist, can be shown through this analysis to long for something other than their apparent aims: the sadist is much more dependent, the masochist much more independent; each desires precisely the opposite—the sadist craving rebellion and the masochist approval—of what the dynamic taken at face value would suggest. Perhaps most unconsciously, most unwittingly of all, each may secretly desire that the dynamic be eschewed altogether. For a fifth and final characteristic of the dynamic is its eventually becoming unstable, unsustainable, and even irrational within its own terms. Sadomasochistic dynamics exemplify perhaps the ultimate "push/pull" form of an interactive relationship: unable to stay still, always on the verge of crisis, and thus tending toward its own self-compelled destruction. Thus a classic sadomasochistic dynamic points toward its own dissolution over time. Again, this is of course only a *tendency,* not an axiomatic law: the sadomasochistic dynamic is resilient and creative; perhaps it can go on indefinitely. But it is shot through with paradoxes, and so it will often be in that push/pull state: insecure and crisis ridden.

Such extreme instability is the result of sadomasochistic dynamics splitting apart what are two *simultaneous* human needs. If a dynamic can be imagined that is *not* sadomasochistic, by way of contrast, it would have to be one in which "mutual recognition" had become possible: two parties would both be able to recognize that each is at once dependent on, and to some degree also independent of, the other.[21] But sadomasochism slices these two sides of ourselves asunder so that the sadist tends to act *as though* highly independent (denying and repressing the dependent and vulnerable side of his or her needs); the masochist tends to act *as though* highly dependent (thereby denying and repressing the independent side of her- or himself, the side that desires power rather than powerlessness). Sadomasochism, therefore, by definition rests on the impossibility of mutual recognition to keep it going, for it to thrive. By definition, it cannot allow both sides of our human needs— needs for simultaneous dependence on and independence of others—to be acknowledged.

But who cares about this sadomasochistic dynamic, anyway? What does it matter? Before concluding by returning from sadomasochism as it is now being explored *in general* to the issue of feminism and sadomasochism *in particular,* we ought first examine what, if anything, this interpretation can (or cannot) explain about the social world around us. What reason is there to believe that such dynamics are common, that they affect day-to-day relationships not only in but also outside experiences that are specifically sexual?

We will consider two "everyday life" examples by way of illustration: the mundane worlds of work and gendered relations, respectively, to show how sadomasochistic dynamics may indeed be quite frequent rather than rare. Simultaneously, these examples support two claims with which we began: namely, that sadomasochism is much more accurately characterized as normal than exceptional, and that sadomasochistic social psychology correlates with the way we have structured many of our most basic institutions.

WORK

Let's start with employer/employee relations and a supposedly extreme example. If one envisions the day-to-day social relations in organized crime, commonly known to exist though allegedly only at the margins of society, it is not difficult to see how this mode of illegal social organization exemplifies the dynamic defined above. Certainly organized crime's structure is hierarchical; its sadomasochistic iconography is unmistakable. The second critically defining trait of sadomasochism is also present: organized crime depends on ominous silence, on shared understandings that any attempt to break away will be met by severe punishment. One cannot be a middle-level organized crime member, decide midlife that one wishes to change careers, and have one's superior okay this decision casually and supportively. Rather, for a person situated masochistically to break away may involve literally placing one's life at risk.

But is the situation so different for the average worker? Take sexual harassment, one of many examples that could be drawn from the world of work: the implication is that the victim could lose his or her job or possible promotion unless consenting to provide sexual favors. This, too, suggests the potential presence of a sadomasochistic dynamic. But I would argue more broadly, and theoretically, that capitalism itself is based on *conditional psychology* and that workers quite routinely— and, at certain historical moments like our own, to more extreme de- grees—experience extreme fears about losing their jobs. To the extent one fears being unable to survive—literally or figuratively, emotionally or bodily—if workplace authority is challenged, then everyday relation- ships at work may also possess a sadomasochistic character. These rela- tions could themselves be said to be sadomasochistic by this definition. Fear for one's life, then, may be the stick lurking behind the carrot, beneath the surface, making the production of a certain level of sado- masochistic anxiety far more a normal than a deviant aspect of the mundane workings of capitalism. Workers routinely generally fear the consequences of forming unions, especially in times of immense eco- nomic anxiety about job loss and global restructuring. Antiunion poli- cies from the Reagan administration onward, combined with such fears, make it hardly accidental that union membership has been at its lowest rate since the 1930s, down from 25 percent of the workforce at its highest point to only 16 percent now. Moreover, as sociologist Arlie Russell Hochschild wrote in *The Managed Heart* (1983), more and more jobs are in the service sector, requiring what she calls "emotional labor." One is expected not only to use one's body to perform jobs but also to meet emotional requirements: perhaps the repression of anger and the availability of a smile, whether or not one feels like smiling (say, if one happens to be a flight attendant, one of the examples Hochschild herself cites).[22] Or emotional labor may be required if one works as a waitress or public relations executive, each of whom may be expected to act constantly cheerful regardless of true feelings, even in the face of mistreatment by customers or clients. One's emotional affect also has to be controlled properly to avoid the threat of possible loss of liveli- hood—and the sense of social legitimacy and belonging to a community that often come along with it.

In his writings about capitalism, Marx was not much concerned about exploring this particular problem: the kind of social psychology that accords with the structured socioeconomic system he was describing. Obviously, I am arguing that the dominant social psychology that corresponds to and is produced with capitalism is inclined to become *sadomasochistically structured.* Marx's theory itself tended to deal with "objective" relations much more than "subjective" ones, an imbalance that itself probably reflects gender-biased assumptions called into question by contemporary feminist theories: it is precisely a personal versus political dichotomy that I am here challenging. Moreover, there are also ways in which the sadomasochistic dynamic described here illuminates interactions common in any class-divided system. Of course, sadomasochistic dynamics have existed not only in capitalist societies but in communist societies as well. Within the latter, yet another recycling of the dynamic often took place, so that parties situated masochistically and sadistically tended to reverse places rather than ceasing to exist as sadists and masochists: this illustrates applying the dynamic to a group, not only to an individual's situation.

But the sadomasochistic dynamic can illuminate the world of work even further. Take precisely that characteristic of transformability, which exists at the heart of sadomasochism. In a large corporate law firm where I worked some fifteen years ago, legal secretaries who were subordinately placed (or masochistically situated) relative to the partners (their bosses) might take on the role of the boss when dealing with a Xerox operator or mail clerk over whom that secretary had greater power. Or the young associate, meek in relation to a senior partner, might suddenly transform into a short-tempered and imperious party when dealing with his or her own secretary. In a different work setting is the domestic worker, studied by sociologist Judith Rollins, who published her research in *Between Women* (1985). As Rollins, an African American woman who posed as a domestic in order to conduct her study through participant observation, describes, a white woman employer might act rather sadistically (by the definition given above) toward a black domestic employee. Yet both knew that the white male husband, absent during the day, was the real boss in the home; relative to him, the white woman employer was powerless, though relative to the black domestic employee, she possessed power.[23] As is typical when sadomasochistic dynamics are applied to social situations that (like most) are *not* merely dyadic, people frequently find that they are in both a potentially masochistic and potentially sadistic position *at once.* It would seem, then, that an important advantage of conceiving sadomasochism in an internally transformable dynamic is the insight it provides into how power relationships in society are produced and reproduced. Because social situations may be structured in layers, sadomasochistically, we may be encouraged to channel anger at the powerlessness we experience onto others below us rather than express it toward those above us who actually have greater control over our lives. Such redirection of anger may serve to compensate for this powerlessness, enabling its continuation over time by making ongoing sadomasochistic relations much easier to bear. Thus, the white woman employer who expresses displaced anger at her employee may therefore be less likely to target the proper recipient, her husband.

But we should consider if yet another sadomasochistic characteristic is applicable. Do relationships of work give evidence of the sadist indeed desiring an "uppity masochist," of his or her wanting the masochist to rebel so that disapproval within the mode of approval may secretly, and paradoxically, be desired? In contemporary "management training" literature, many accounts can be found of the ideal worker whom bosses seek when hiring employees. As the sadomasochistic dynamic would anticipate, these characteristics often combined features like "competence," "reliability," and "dependability" with calls for "independence" and "initiative." Ideally, the boss does not desire someone who is mindlessly controlled but a person who questions and takes initiative—within the rules of the game, not threatening the dominant party's power to an intolerable degree.[24]

Examples attesting to the sort of common social psychology being described can be found in daily business and professional life. In his best-selling account of life as a management trainee at Salomon Brothers, Michael Lewis depicts the sort of person least and most sought out by the partners. At a training session, a young woman asked the partner about his "secret for success."[25] By thereby admitting his power and her powerlessness, she earned not the partner's respect but his scorn. Much more desirable were the young trainees who were sharp and challenging, but again within limits, not so aggressive as to disturb the rules of the game altogether. Or think of the graduate student who manages to win the famous professor's attention and favor. Is it likely to be the one who repeats slavishly what she or he is told, or the one who is something of a challenge to that professor's authority—although of course never failing to acknowledge the professor's power? Or consider the editor at a big publishing house—why does this person choose one novel out of a thousand submissions? Again, the editor will probably choose something that seems "different" but not radically so; moreover, once chosen, a given author, or graduate student for that matter, may become a hot property by virtue of having been given one offer, thereby gaining a certain desirable independence relative to the editor (or to a senior professor).

These examples strongly suggest that workplace relationships share a common social psychological texture; they are structured in a way that suspiciously resembles the sadomasochistic dynamic with which we began. Like the sadist and the masochist, boss and workers under capitalistic conditions have a relationship that by its very structure discourages mutual recognition. Bosses, as individuals or collectively, cannot easily acknowledge the depth of their dependence on the worker(s) and therefore the latter's value. Simultaneously, people who work—that broad and shifting group, ranging from lower-level organized crime members to an associate at a law firm or a flight attendant or a domestic employee—are unable to acknowledge the extent of their own power. Like sadomasochistic relationships more generally, those at the workplace split dependence and independence. Structured around this split, these relationships may be shifting, unstable, and often in a state of flux.

GENDER RELATIONS

Here again, let's start with an apparently extreme case, then move to social relationships that are more mundane and everyday. Perhaps the two, the seemingly extreme and the clearly quotidian, are interrelated like distant relatives who nevertheless are part of the same family; perhaps the two exist as separate points that are nevertheless connected on a single continuum. Thus we will begin with relationships of battering and domestic violence. It is not hard to see how these fit within the definition of a sadomasochistic dynamic: again not simply hierarchical, the relationship depends on threatening or threatened exertions of force; once more, too, a sadomasochistic iconography is unmistakable. Our definition predicts that the sadomasochistic underpinnings of the relationship will be most clearly revealed when and if the person being battered, who has a very high statistical probability of being a woman, threatens to leave. At that moment, the extreme and symbiotic dependency that was always present becomes disclosed because the batterer, who has a very high statistical probability of being a man, becomes angrier and more violent. This is an empirical fact with which workers at social service agencies and psychologists who deal with domestic violence are all too familiar. In some cases, the batterer may become temporarily romantic and repentant for a while, before punishment tends to begin again. But whatever happens at a given moment, there is little doubt that the relationship is one in which the batterer's apparent "power" and control hide the depth of dependence actually felt.

As with the examples from the workplace, however, a sadomasochistic texture may also pervade intimate gendered relationships even when no force or extreme violence is present. In such cases, the presence of a sadomasochistic dynamic is subtler and harder to trace. Yet the formats of gothic romances and soap operas still regularly feature gendered relations that are decidedly push/pull in character, sometimes including (albeit in a much softened and usually nonviolent form) some of the now-familiar characteristics of this dynamic. Similarly, there are numerous commercials, like the Calvin Klein Guess jeans series, that feature a subtle or not-so-subtle sadomasochistic edge: think of the popular cultural examples cited within the *New York* magazine whose cover declared, "In 1994, It's Mean Sex: S&M Culture Goes Mainstream." Moreover, when visiting local bookstores, one may discover that sections devoted to "intimate relationships" have not only recently grown but regularly feature literatures concerned with "codependent" gendered relationships: only a few years ago, titles like *Women Who Love Too Much, The Pleasers,* and *Is It Love or Is It Addiction?* were common.[26] Some books on codependency became or are becoming best-sellers; their titles indicate that relationships of extreme dependency are about to be described, and a seven- or twelve-point process probably will be *pre*scribed as to how the problem might be overcome. When we look even more closely into this literature, we find that its authors are generally therapists who take a mostly individual approach to the recurrent circumstances their books depict.[27] At the same time that this therapeutic literature frames the problem as though treatable only at the level of individuals—rather than insisting that it also requires social structural changes far more collective in scope—the books' best-selling status belie the authors' individualistic orientation: why would the books become best-sellers unless they reflected some more general theme, resonating in large numbers of people in a given society at around the same time?

Indeed, the gendered relationships described in this popular literature bear a striking resemblance to aspects of the sadomasochistic dynamic we have been examining. For instance, there is often a push/pull character to the relationships being described. The how-to, *Women Who Love Too Much* texts are likely to suggest, as a matter of course, that an overly needy or "clingy" woman will certainly "turn off" men. By extension, it would appear that being much more distant—but not so distant that a relationship becomes impossible—creates a more desirable female persona. Moreover, consider that in most male-dominated patriarchal societies like our own, the well-known "madonna/whore," "good woman/bad woman" division is a stock feature of patriarchal fantasies. Men often take comfort in security, and yet they seek uncertainty, novelty, and experiences of mystery through "affairs." But why are these dichotomies of wives versus mistresses, good women versus bad, themselves so common? I see their pervasiveness as an outgrowth of the tendency of these societies to set up men in a relatively sadistic and more powerful position, women in a relatively more masochistic and less powerful position. But just as the sadist can never get full recognition and satisfaction from an absolutely controlled masochist (but secretly looks for rebellion, secretly craves challenges to his or her authority), so the man who has taken away the freedom of a woman, of an other, may find himself paradoxically dissatisfied as well. He turns to a relatively freer and uncontrolled mistress, with whom he can give fuller play to the more dependent side of himself. And so, on the other hand (and just as we would anticipate, given the sadomasochistic dynamic's tendency to internally transform), a woman who may be relatively powerless elsewhere may find herself endowed with relative power in her role as mistress—at least, we should add, temporarily.

Moreover, just as Marxist theory helped illuminate *why* workplace relationships so commonly contain a sadomasochistic texture, so feminist theory makes it easier to understand push/pull gendered relationships. Returning now to Simone de Beauvoir's classic *The Second Sex* (1949), we are reminded that many second-wave feminists have described the deeply rooted socialization processes that accustom men to differential possession of power, women to feeling relatively powerless. From this analysis, it is not very difficult to see once again how patriarchy—as a form of social organization in which men are the dominant party, women the subordinate—also does not allow for mutual recognition. Rather than seeing two people in a relationship as mutually interdependent—each being vulnerable to the other, but also partly autonomous—patriarchy, like capitalism, splits one side of ourselves from another. The man is the "macho" one, apparently independent and strutting through the world with immense confidence; as de Beauvoir recounted so well, he has been told from early childhood that he must not let on to feelings of dependency. On the other hand, women are socialized to acknowledge their dependence on and "need" for others, especially the man; for women, power and independence are much more difficult to assert for fear of the rejection that might follow such assertiveness. Thus men may grow up feeling angry toward women for the dependency they feel but must suppress; conversely, women may end up exerting power and expressing their own anger in ways that may often be indirect. Together, their mutual relationship may indeed result in characteristically push/pull patterns, frequently rather than infrequently, because of a fundamentally sadomasochistic division at patriarchy's—like capitalism's—very heart.

RETURNING FULL CIRCLE TO FEMINISM

But what does all of this bode for the particular form of split with which we began, not so much between dependence and independence but between feminists who interpret this phenomenon in such a way that they stress *social sadomasochism* as "opposed" to those who emphasize *sexual sadomasochism?* The argument just presented demonstrated that a sadomasochistically shaped dynamic seems indeed to characterize a range of social situations; it may be a form of social psychology that is not deviant at all, but rather one that tends to become normalized. If so, social sadomasochism and sexual sadomasochism are perforce intimately related, while at the very same time they are far from being identical.

For the feminist divide that has characterized these relatively different interpretations of sadomasochism springs from a false either/or conception. Instead, two things apparently apply to sadomasochism *at once;* several interpretations need to be interwoven if feminism is to be strengthened by a vision of long- as well as short-term value. We have seen that sadomasochism as defined above accurately describes coercive social relations between dominant and subordinate encountered in a wide range of situations, in a variety of institutions and settings. Not only do sadomasochistic dynamics unfold within extreme situations, as in the contexts of organized crime and domestic violence, but under circumstances of everyday life that are not necessarily overtly coercive: an underlying sadomasochistic texture links our experiences of gendered problems with class-related insecurities, with other problems that in some respects have become aggravated rather than ameliorated by the conservativism still predominant today. At the same time, we have every reason to expect that sadomasochistic sexual desires will also be common in our fantasies or practices, that sometimes we will seek to express them both through our bodies and our minds. Rather than being shocking or surprising, such desires are understandable and predictable; it makes no sense to repress their exploration in consensual sexual practices, or to judge individuals who as feminists quite correctly stress that personal sexual freedoms are *also* intimately connected with this social movement's liberatory dreams.

Neither of these positions is itself problematic. Neither merits pitting feminists against each other in such a way that we end up arguing over what might otherwise have amounted to two easily agreed-upon points: women need to be freed *from* sexist structures and freed *to* enjoy sexual agency. Yet in second-wave feminist debates over sadomasochism there appeared a disastrous splitting of these legitimate considerations, confronting feminist politics with the following dilemma: *either* feminists must indict the coercively sadomasochistic and gendered dynamics produced by the organization of contemporary societies *or* feminists must defend the rights of individuals to free sexual exploration and expression (encompassing, not surprisingly, desires for S/M sex). But why can't we do *both?*

For unless we manage in some mutually satisfactory way to link the two interpretations with one another, the glib superficiality of a *New York* magazine treatment may indeed remain the dominant approach in our society. Yes, perhaps sadomasochistic sexuality has attained greater cultural visibility in the 1990s than in the past, as that article cheerfully announced. And, to the extent that this is symptomatic of increasing acceptability of sexual diversity in American society, this *is* something to be cheered. But to the extent that sadomasochistic dynamics are still being generated by the structure of the society as a whole, how do we ensure that such a celebration of freer sexuality is not bought at a price of socialized compulsions? How can we guarantee that the occasion for celebration will not obscure the persistent existence of sadomasochism *outside* consensual situations, as subtle social processes encourage us to artificially narrow our focus and limit our analysis to sex while ignoring sadomasochism's much more far-reaching cultural influences? Only a feminist movement that goes beyond false dichotomies may be able to provide alternative understandings and experiences of feminism and sadomasochism as they touch each other in everyday life.

CHAPTER SEVEN

Victim Feminism
or No Feminism?

The Case of Rape

The controversy sparked by Katie Roiphe's 1993 book, *The Morning After*—along with an outpouring of media interest, intensified after Antioch College announced soon afterward that it was instituting codes of sexual behavior—is symbolic of a larger problem that continues to divide the feminist movement over issues of sex versus sexism. Roiphe's major concern in *The Morning After* is whether the feminist movement has overstated the problem of violence against women in American society. Subtitled "Sex, Fear, and Feminism on Campus," her book asserts that feminist concerns about date rape have slowly but surely become exaggerated. Moreover, according to Roiphe, anyone—even someone aligned with the feminist movement—who states this publicly risks being labeled "politically incorrect."

Roiphe suggests that a dogmatic feminism, insistent on conceiving women primarily in terms of victimization, predominates in the feminist movement. But this perspective does not accord with the experiences of many women, according to Roiphe, who do not feel constantly threatened or victimized by men. In her opinion, the vision promulgated by such victim-oriented feminists is repressive, sanitized, desexualized, and desexualizing. She recalls

> sitting through a workshop on date rape freshman year, thinking, This is not me, this has nothing to do with me. The naive female victim in the film being shown was worlds away. Her fifties-style dates were not the kind of dates my older sisters went on. She was passive and innocent, and overly impressed by

229

the boy's intelligence. She didn't drink. It might as well have been a documentary about the mating habits of the fruit fly. The thing I didn't know then was that the mating rituals of a rape-sensitive community, and the attitudes that went along with them, would be a part of feminism as I would experience it from then on.[1]

The publication of *The Morning After* thus seemed to manifest a new division within feminism, another incarnation of a pattern familiar from feminist "sex debates" of the decade before. As the media quickly grasped, now there was an easy way to denigrate dominant tendencies in older feminism: the concept of "victim feminism" was used to put down feminist insistence on the pervasiveness of sexism. To the extent victim feminism existed, its referent was to a strand of radical feminist theory about violence against women traceable to Susan Brownmiller's well-known work *Against Our Will: Men, Women, and Rape* (1975). Claiming that a structured relationship links rape with patriarchal societies, Brownmiller argues that rape is a form of social control intimidating to all women. It does not matter if a particular woman has been raped herself: just the knowledge that violence can be encountered at any time serves to keep all women in a state of fear.[2] It is this viewpoint with which Roiphe so vigorously disagrees, and from which she feels alienated.

But it is not only Roiphe who has voiced this feeling. Interestingly enough, in her second book, written after *The Beauty Myth* (1991), Naomi Wolf develops a related theme and provides more evidence of a new either/or divide emerging once again. In *Fire with Fire* (1993), she too refers to the "rise of a set of beliefs that cast women as beleaguered, fragile, intuitive angels: victim feminism." "Victim feminism," according to Wolf, "is when a woman seeks power through an identity of powerlessness."[3] In making this point, however, Wolf explicitly dissociates herself from Roiphe's views:

> Right now, critics of feminism such as Katie Roiphe in *The Morning After*, and Camille Paglia just about anywhere, are doing something slick and dangerous with the notion of victimization. They are taking the occasional excesses of the rape crisis movement and using them to ridicule the entire push to raise consciousness about sexual violence. Roiphe, for instance, paints an impressionistic picture of hysterical "date rape" victims who have made it all up, but she never looks squarely at the epidemic of sex crimes that has been all too indelibly documented by the Justice Department and the FBI.[4]

And yet, while clearly wishing to separate her perspective from Roiphe's (especially from Roiphe's underestimation of the extent of violence against women in the United States), Wolf unintentionally aligns herself with Roiphe by differentiating "power feminism" from "victim feminism." Wolf even titles part 3 of her book "Power Feminism versus Victim Feminism." Power feminism concerns matters of individual agency, Wolf explains. It is about self-determination, about a woman not "merging her voice in a collective identity"; it "is unapologetically sexual" and "understands that good pleasures make good politics"; it "hates sexism without hating men." Roiphe in all likelihood would agree with all this, as she would with Wolf's characterization of victim feminism. As the opposite of power feminism, victim feminism, in Wolf's words, involves being "judgmental of other women's sexuality and appearance," "even antisexual"; it "projects aggression, competitiveness, and violence onto 'men' or 'patriarchy,' while its devotees are blind to those qualities in themselves." Victim feminism implies that "real feminists must renounce power and pleasure because of the ideological requirements of a collective identity." Finally, even though Wolf takes issue with Roiphe, she too refers to a "tendency toward rigidity" leading to a "too literal translation of influential theories," such as those of Brownmiller. The interpretation of Brownmiller as implying that "all men are rapists," Wolf contends, "has helped close down discussion between men and women, clouded feminist thinking about men and sexuality, and done men as a whole a grave injustice."[5]

All of this sounds strikingly familiar. The victim versus power feminism dichotomy, aligning Roiphe and Wolf (despite their disagreements) *against* "victim feminists," brings to mind the "sex debates" of the late 1970s. Again, on one "side" are feminists associated with a collectively oriented analysis, with indicting patriarchy as a form of social organization premised on male domination. And again, this side is portrayed as distinctively uninterested in questions of individual pleasure and as relatively asexual in its concerns. (By 1993, when Wolf's and Roiphe's texts appeared, their characterization of victim feminism evoked the stance associated with Catharine MacKinnon and Andrea Dworkin in earlier debates about pornography; by now, a historical trajectory of recurring associations had already been established.) Just as before, on the other side are feminists (now dubbed "power feminists") who are more explicitly interested in issues involving sexual choice, exploration, and freedom.

But let me concentrate specifically on Roiphe and *The Morning After,* since this work crystallized the application to the subject of violence against women of a similar debate already dividing feminists in patterned ways about other issues. First, what is the larger context in which Roiphe wrote *The Morning After?* Second, if we take Roiphe's book to be symbolic, of what is it symbolic specifically? My concern is to assess whether and why *The Morning After* might be part of a backlash against feminism, rather than merely a constructively intended feminist critique.[6] Yet are some of Roiphe's ideas worth taking seriously despite an outpouring of intense criticism by other feminists that also followed the book's publication? And, if so, is there a way to incorporate some of Roiphe's insights without reinforcing a perspective that may feed into the backlash against feminism at a time when this movement particularly needs revitalization?

THE HISTORICAL CONTEXT OF ROIPHE'S *MORNING AFTER*

Despite the controversy that surrounded the publication of Roiphe's book, her perspective is not particularly new when viewed within the longer history of the so-called sex debates. The larger symbolic significance of *The Morning After* may be illuminated if we look at second-wave American feminism developmentally, tracing a Hegelian movement of thesis/antithesis/synthesis, from second-wave feminism through Roiphe and back again.

Thesis   Without second-wave radical feminism, Roiphe would not have had a set of ideas from which to rebel. For, first and foremost, the context of Roiphe's book is second-wave American feminism in the late 1960s and early 1970s, when it was on the offense and exploding with debate. This was a movement that, to quote Alice Echols, "dared to be bad,"[7] insofar as radical feminists were defining sexuality as political and calling for the breakdown of boundaries between public and private forms of behavior. Most of all, theoretical writings in this period portrayed a wide variety of issues—from violence against women to limitations on women's reproductive freedom, on through homophobia and the problems of rigidly traditional nuclear families—as interrelated insofar as each manifested the discriminatory consequences of gendered power. So strongly resonant was the radical feminist critique that it slowly spawned other feminisms—adding variations and complications of class, race, psychoanalytic orientation, and postmodernist leanings.

Antithesis   And it was precisely because of the strength of early radical feminist ideas that a reaction against feminist theses set in. Indeed, the forcefulness of the backlash that emerged in the Reagan-Bush era of the 1980s and early 1990s was an ironic tribute to the significance of the feminist challenge. Reworking Susan Faludi's well-known discussion, I see "backlash" as definable through two major criteria: first, the undermining of and attempt to reverse feminist gains across a gamut of interrelated areas as mentioned above; and, second, a proclivity toward blaming feminism for a host of social problems it could not reasonably have caused. As feminism was blamed, the effects of the feminist critique of society were put in danger of being diluted and co-opted beyond recognition, while hopes of augured future changes seemed to recede.

Synthesis   What happens when in a short period of time feminists actively challenge American society, only to be met by a backlash so enormous that it verifies the pervasiveness of the original obstacle? I believe that one can expect confusion: a time of theoretical and political disarray, when it is not certain where the original movement forward ends and backlash begins. How, then, should feminists react? How can we distinguish between the internalized effects of that backlash itself and the normal processes of theoretical/political self-criticism and refinement that characterize any growing social movement?

It is in this light that I believe Roiphe's book merits examination. For, again, *The Morning After* does not move past the structure versus agency dichotomy that has been dividing feminists for decades but merely applies it to the particular issue of rape and to general concerns about violence against women. This reiteration may explain much of the media's interest: the framework of debate was already familiar; it was easy to fill in the blank with Roiphe's name and rehash a story at once novel and routine. But, based on this observation of a pattern, am I justified in classifying *The Morning After* as part of a Faludi-esque backlash rather than simply as a disagreement within feminism?

ROIPHE AND BACKLASH

Regrettably, *The Morning After* is filled with theoretical and methodological inconsistencies that undermine the stronger points of Roiphe's own argument. Let us return to my criteria for defining whether backlash is present in a particular response to influence exerted by a growing social movement like feminism.

My first criterion asks whether a given cultural phenomenon, here
Roiphe's perspective in *The Morning After,* tends to undermine feminist
gains. Insofar as the book cites as examples of feminist weaknesses actions that are arguably—even from Roiphe's own perspective—exertions of collectively accrued political strength, the answer must be affirmative. A self-contradiction is evident when, for instance, Roiphe
argues that Take Back the Night demonstrations cause women to become powerless and victimized. At the same time she presumes that
"rape-crisis" feminists are a powerful political presence, or why would
she be writing about their formidable influence? If victim feminism were
simply disempowering for women, how did rape-crisis feminists become a social force to be reckoned with by the younger generation for
whom Roiphe believes herself to speak? Of course, Roiphe's very ability
to self-identify as a feminist is a product of the feminist collective action
she seems individually—and individualistically—to deplore.

In addition, to be able to label oneself a victim need not be a sign
of weakness: the strategies of many successful groups (take Alcoholics
Anonymous or Synanon, for example), strategies known to produce effective outcomes for many individuals, depend on explicit recognition
of a past and present problem as a first step toward solving it. That
women are angrily, rather than weakly, decrying the victim position in
which they/we have been placed is not necessarily debilitating. Rather,
naming oneself a victim, or as someone who has or could be victimized,
only becomes crippling if it is then turned into a rationalization for
inaction—if it becomes interpreted as a rationale for the perpetuation
of powerlessness.

Second, Roiphe does not simply criticize victim feminism but leans
toward blaming feminism itself for creating victims. Roiphe attributes
responsibility to feminism for a laundry list of social problems for
which it could not—logically—be the sole or even major cause. For
instance, Roiphe is concerned about the climate of sexual conservatism
in the aftermath of AIDS. But why is this traceable back to a fault of
feminism rather than relating, say, to environmental factors that our
breaking down our immune systems? Roiphe is also concerned about
the constant sense of fear she felt was engendered at Princeton by seeing
little blue lights all over the campus. (Perhaps I am especially sensitive
to this complaint since, as an undergraduate there, I helped pressure the
university to improve security measures after women were attacked on
campus.) But why not relate the need for such precautions to the reality

and complex causes of violence, especially gendered violence, in American society? Why highlight the women's movement or rape-crisis feminism alone? Last, *The Morning After* takes up the question of rigid dogmatism and judgmentalness in political movements, a concern I strongly share. Once more, though, why single out feminism? The seductive excesses of rigidly dogmatic perspectives on the world—of so-called political correctness—have affected a large number of social movements on the Left. Recently, political correctness has become a response to, and symptomatic of, the weak and defensive position in which many post-1960s social movements have found themselves for external and internal reasons, encouraging us to focus our criticisms and anger on ourselves (see chapter 1). The intense concerns within a group about political correctness seem a sign of social marginality—and then tend to reinforce this marginality in turn.

I will not spend time belaboring other methodological and theoretical flaws in *The Morning After,* as these have been pointed out by others (see, for example, an excellent essay on this subject by Katha Pollitt).[8] Suffice it to say that with regard to violence against women, for example, virtually all studies continue to show very high victimization rates.[9] One might argue about the particular figures (whether one out of four or one out of five women will experience sexual assault at some time in their lives, for instance). Clearly, we are speaking of a social problem of major proportions. In this regard, a serious shortcoming of Roiphe's work is its tendency to focus more on instances of rape that are *rare* than on those that remain *typical.*

Specifically, *The Morning After* devotes most of its critical attention to unusual and amorphous "date rape" cases, in which it seems difficult to adjudicate whether a misunderstanding took place (or could possibly have taken place); such cases, Roiphe argues, may not have involved rape at all. But far more representative of rape cases (including those involving people acquainted with one another) are the cases in which women *know* violence against them has been committed. There is no sense of ambiguity in these much more characteristic instances; as the film *The Accused* (1989) so powerfully depicts, a clear line has been crossed from what may have begun as sexual play into violence and coercion.

The problem is not the raising of ambiguous issues per se, as such ambiguities can and do exist. Rather, the grave defect in Roiphe's perspective is that it does not clarify the difference between typical and unusual incidents. In not providing such clarification, *The Morning After* blithely inclines toward reinforcing cultural attitudes that already tend to undermine the credibility of the many women who *have* been violently assaulted. Indeed, in the immediate aftermath of the book's publication, I spoke with numerous health care professionals who were concerned that the book would discourage women from reporting rape or training as peer counselors. Yet, the very fact of the all-too-frequent violence against women in American society suggests that structured issues of gender subordination are involved—not *only,* or even predominantly, individual anomalies. By not conjoining considerations of structure with those of agency (and, analogously, linking issues of sex *and* sexism), Roiphe just adds another voice, a self-identified feminist one, to the still-dominant chorus insisting that somehow these women must have desired their own violent victimization.[10] Rather than strengthening feminism, *The Morning After* seems symbolic of the defensiveness that still surrounds feminism in the mid-1990s.

Yet, despite my remarks above, I believe that some aspects of Roiphe's argument may be important to consider. This is precisely what makes the book's divisive tendencies so frustrating. When initially reading *The Morning After,* I found myself wishing it had been written from a perspective more apparently supportive of feminist concerns—rather than attacking and undermining their legitimacy. Why, I wondered, blame feminism if one's goal is not to feed the context of backlash but to move the feminist movement beyond it?

NOT DISMISSING ROIPHE'S POSITION ALTOGETHER

So, yes, *The Morning After* can be defined as part of backlash. At the same time, and just as important, to ignore certain persuasive and astute points in Roiphe's argument is to put feminism at a disadvantage. To dismiss Roiphe's perceptions entirely is to react against a reaction and thus to find oneself caught yet again within the unnecessary dichotomies of the sex debates. I believe three valid points can be pulled from Roiphe's argument, bringing us back—full circle—to the *larger* sex versus sexism debate in contemporary feminism.

First, consider *the problem of essentialism* and the related issue of sexual repressiveness. Has the assumption in any way indeed slipped back into feminism that men are by "nature" aggressive and women more passive when it comes to sex? As Cynthia Epstein clearly shows in *Deceptive Distinctions* (1988), essentialist assumptions about innate sexual differences do creep—often quite unwittingly—into feminist theory, even into apparently sociologically oriented arguments such as those made by Carol Gilligan and Nancy Chodorow.[11] From this perspective, the Antioch codes of sexual conduct become worrisome: do such codes risk reinforcing essentialist assumptions about men and corollary presumptions about women? It is important to recognize this possibility rather than blindly supporting and reproducing "biological" determinisms that feminism has little choice but to oppose if its own existence as a social movement is to be consistently persuasive.

Second, let us return to *the problem of rigidly dogmatic thinking*— of political correctness, in Roiphe's words. Are there indeed, as in other social movements, things we are afraid to say or even think as feminists because we worry that we will play into that very backlash against feminists? How can we manage to have a feminist movement, on and off college campuses, in which full dialogue and thought are possible, without a price being paid of thereafter losing our collective strength? Here, Roiphe may have been courageous, although theoretically imprecise, for it is difficult for a feminist to suggest that rape may have something to do with *sex* as well as *power*. In our understandable eagerness to redefine rape as a violent rather than a sexual crime, feminist analyses have veered away from specifying aspects of rape that may distinguish it from other forms of violence against women (say, battering). When a man rapes his wife rather than beats her, or when a woman walking down a street is raped rather than just mugged, this probably points to the association in our culture between sexual repression and relations of dominance/subordination *as well as to* the complex sources of violence more generally.

Moreover, the frequency of violence against women—and the ongoing prevalence of attitudes that hold women responsible for their/our own victimization—has made it difficult to talk about another facet of women's situation: rape *fantasies* among women. Given the dominant/subordinate character of most gender relations in our society, these fantasies may be quite common (see chapter 6 on sadomasochism in everyday life). Yet is there any way to talk about such fantasies? Or do we fear being attacked by other feminists for doing so and worry about contributing to the victim blaming that still plagues women bringing rape or other violence-related charges? Although Roiphe did not manage to raise this problem carefully herself, is there any way to insist on treating violence against women with the utmost seriousness *without* feeling compelled to repress exploration (in theory, in political discussion, in expressions of fantasy) of the complex connections between violence and eroticism in contemporary American culture?

Third, and in conclusion, *should violence against women be the major focus of feminism?* This is a point that Roiphe hints at but does not develop systematically: does the issue of violence against women (including rape, domestic violence, incest and other child abuse, as well as sexual harassment) become an isolated repository for angers that originate from a much broader sense of inequality in patriarchal society? In other words, at a time of backlash, when the promise of a holistic, multi-issued feminist movement has become more difficult to realize, does the issue of violence against women sometimes become loaded with the anger we are feeling toward a much broader set of persons, experiences, and institutions?

I am not arguing, as Roiphe does, that the issue of violence is exaggerated or that somehow it should not render us enraged and bent on change—that is preposterous. Rather, I am pointing to the danger that we will be able to bring less political and intellectual power to bear upon any single feminist issue—whether, as here, violence against women or, for that matter, pornography or beauty—*unless considered in relation to a feminist movement (and wider set of feminist issues)* overall. If we put all our energy into the *particular* issue of violence against women, we may lose sight of the relationship between violence against women and the ongoing subordination of women in general. Better, perhaps, to direct our anger against *both,* at once against the particular symptom and the general causes, and in the process move away from the defensive posture slowly developed since the 1960s. For beyond backlash, a more multifaceted and multi-issued feminist movement has already started to grow. If we can use *The Morning After* to point us even further in this direction, recognizing its serious flaws as well as the problems of which the book is partially symptomatic, an offensively oriented third wave of feminism will come closer to its own realization beyond the specious either/or divides of "victim" versus "power" feminism.

PART THREE

Feminist Futures

CHAPTER EIGHT

Beyond Gender versus Class

To students in my feminist theory classes who have piqued my curiosity with the contrast between their relative enthusiasm at reading radical feminist texts and their relative boredom at assignments drawn from Marxist and socialist feminist literature—at the same time many were also concerned about the indifference toward inequalities of economic class so characteristic of capitalism. And to Heidi Pomfret, whose provocative senior thesis on women and the FBI made me wonder exactly what it was that caused J. Edgar Hoover—for all his paranoia—to think feminism wasn't sufficiently threatening to necessitate its own branch of COINTELPRO, the counterintelligence programs he dedicated so assiduously to derailing Communists, socialists, and black nationalists (among others).

While the impact of feminism has continued to increase over the last several decades, the American Left continues to occupy a relatively much more marginal position, the latter's experience of ongoing crisis only aggravated by the dramatic collapse of the Communist world. It thus would not be surprising if many socialists are now interested in gender politics both from conviction and from a deep sense of doubt about whether traditional Marxist ideas and class-based strategies have become outdated or inadequate to the hoped-for dismantling of capitalism. Groping for alternative perspectives, some leftists and left academics have interpreted "new social movements" centered on gender, race, sexual orientation, and the environment as displaced forms of class-related contradictions; others envisage these movements as autonomous

(or relatively so) from the realm of the economic, welcoming them under the rubric of a cultural radicalism seen to offer fresh answers and
promise.[1]

On the other hand, Marxist and socialist feminism also emerged as
major theoretical and activist components of the second-wave feminist
movement. Usually involving women whose political associations originated in left as well as feminist causes, these feminisms stressed the
relevance of class and class-based differences inherited from the Marxist
model. As they incorporated feminist insights, one of their major concerns has been to hold onto class as a central analytical construct,
thereby avoiding idealizing the set of structural commonalities shared
by women as a group.[2]

But whether we consider leftists looking toward gender to resuscitate
flagging notions of class, or feminists looking toward class to more precisely analyze gender, the precise specifications of a gender/class relationship remain confused and confusing in at least one respect. Obviously, feminist-oriented socialists and socialist feminists alike agree that
both capitalism and male-dominated (or patriarchal) societies are perni-
cious; members of each group concur that any deep-seated collective
change has to uproot dominant/subordinate relationships enacted along
the lines of both sex and class. More complicated, however, is the issue
of how class- and gender-based strategies for change interrelate, especially in terms of the long-term aims of each. Is it possible to live in a
society so affected by calls for gender equality that it is in effect no
longer male-dominated, even as this society continues to be organized
around capitalist economic principles and social psychology?

The same question posed in reverse—namely, whether gender subordination would continue in a society where class inequality had been
lessened—is much less germane. For one thing, the short history of
twentieth-century communisms has already offered something of an
empirical answer, demonstrating that women's subordination in the privatized realms of sexuality and the family does not necessarily wither
away with social ownership of production or with class-conscious ideologies. As this experience has made obvious at a very concrete level,
gender is rooted in power structures that connect with, but by no means
reduce to, a function of class. However, no similar evidence exists for
our original question, since it has been the rule that social orders as we
know them were, and continue to be, generally male-dominated. Exactly how the world would look if societies, capitalist and otherwise,
ceased to be "patriarchal" remains a relevant though elusive and *neces-*

sarily theoretical question.[3] Clearly, then, it is from within capitalism—still the dominant system both in and outside the United States—that any discussion of the conceptual and practical dimensions of a gender/class relationship at present takes place.

I intend to discuss how and why realizing feminist goals might (or might not) destabilize capitalist class relations. Such an analysis must rely on how those feminist "goals" are defined. But different branches of the second-wave feminist movement have had quite varying intentions and definitions: whether their particular form is liberal, radical, Marxist or socialist, or, most recently, postmodern greatly affects the way in which feminists conceive a connection with class. For this reason, it seems appropriate to begin with an overview of the gender/class relationship from the perspective of feminism as an unfolding and multifaceted social movement. The next and concluding section, which focuses on specifying what it is that radical and socialists feminists propose to alter when they/we make critical reference to "patriarchy," speculates on the implications of replacing the overly general usage of this term (including mine) with a more concrete set of antipatriarchal goals. Here, we return to the thorny and unavoidably hypothetical issue of whether such articulated antipatriarchal demands—if met—could subvert, or would arguably be compatible with, the ongoing strength of capitalism.

My own view is that, ironically, it is the ideas of early *radical feminism*—rather than, as one might expect, those arising from Marxist and socialist forms of feminism, which explicitly underscored the importance of class—that pose the most potential trouble for the ongoing tranquillity of capitalism *on specifically gendered grounds*. I emphasize this point because if a challenge is not posed "on specifically gendered grounds," what is the difference between a feminist movement and one based on class? Unless one presupposes some clear-cut conceptual distinctions between the contents of gender- and class-based movements, the two collapse into one another, rendering the theoretical goal of this chapter rather meaningless.

It was radical feminism that promulgated the idea of women as a class, favored the restructuring of a family system based on monogamous marriage, and stressed the need to overthrow a system of male domination grounded on the commodification and colonization of women's bodies. Taken together, these beliefs have enormous, indeed mind-boggling, implications for reordering the social world and our assumptions—still often taken for granted—about the connections

between intimacy, sex, family, community, and society. And, interestingly enough, it is just these aspects of early radical feminist thought
that have vanished most from sight and memory, although feminism
has profoundly affected American society in many other respects (from
issues of work and pay equity to violence against women, among a
host of other possible examples) from the late 1960s until now. Despite
feminism's explosive cultural significance, visions of restructuring "the"
nuclear family and removing sexual controls exercised over women's
bodies, with exceptions, are still largely utopian in the United States
and elsewhere. If anything, this part of the feminist agenda has been
delegitimized and defused in the context of antifeminist "backlash" (to
use Susan Faludi's very apt term) among social and economic conservatives who harp on the importance of maintaining traditional family
values.

But it is also important to remember that just as gender is not reducible to a function of class, so too class cannot be reduced to a function
of gender. Even if radical feminist ideas, if realized, would destabilize
current structures, they do not automatically or deterministically equate
with anticapitalistic positions unless a connection between the two is
directly drawn. Indeed, the most far-reaching of specifically feminist
ideas may be manageable to some extent within the boundaries of a
capitalism that has shown itself again and again to be extraordinarily
resilient.

GENDER AND CLASS IN THE RECENT DEVELOPMENT
OF FEMINISM

As we review the gender/class relationship in feminist theory, liberal
feminism can be summarized with some rapidity. This type of feminism,
associated with liberal philosophy in general, uses the vocabulary of
post-Enlightenment thought to press for the individual rights (including
equal access to the public sphere) denied women in the development of
postindustrial societies. Liberal feminism thereby represents one pole
along a possible continuum of responses to the theoretical query posed:
according to its perspectives, equality for women *is* a potentially satis-
fiable goal within the framework of a reformed and enlightened capitalism. Since liberal feminists do not question the existence of economic
stratification, their viewpoint amounts to a belief that gender equality
is achievable *within* an unscathed framework of stratified classes.

As a matter of self-interest, the claim is not especially contradictory when we take into account the class (usually middle to upper) and race (usually white) of most liberal feminists—a limited range of backgrounds for which they have been frequently called to task. A generally liberal feminist organization like the National Organization for Women (NOW) has promoted political and economic reforms largely of benefit to its own class- and race-specific constituency. However, such an interpretation of liberal feminism is too simple and mechanistic. As Zillah Eisenstein has provocatively suggested in discussing its "radical future," liberal feminism is internally split, because its own partial interests cannot be served without reference to the structurally disenfranchised position of women as a whole.[4] Paradoxically, for middle- and upper-class women to realize a position of equity with men of their own class requires more than entree to previously closed professions and the achievement of economic parity (more than just "equal pay for equal work," in other words). In *The Second Stage* (1981), a book imbued with her characteristically liberal feminist spirit, the homemaker/career woman envisioned by Betty Friedan cannot function unless both the domestic and corporate worlds have been at least slightly reorganized to embrace her. Friedan called for businesses to provide career women (and men) with flexible hours and reasonably accessible child care in order for feminism to be practicable in and beyond the workplace.[5]

Other changes, too, would flow from a reformist demand for equality. How can women become competitive actors in the public sphere if they do not also possess reproductive rights (including, of course, abortion on demand), as well as legal and economic protection from sexual harassment, rape, and domestic violence? These problems, too, have long been and continue to be raised by NOW. Thus, liberal feminism has taken stands of eventual—though perhaps unintended—benefit to all women, even across dividing lines of race and class; in this respect, blanket criticisms of it have been unjustified. To be sure, many liberal feminists do endorse measures that would to a degree relieve the discriminatory excesses of class. For instance, it is not surprising (either in theory or practice) to find liberal feminists favoring the removal of legislative restrictions on federal funding for abortions, a class-biased measure that has been in place since the Hyde Amendment of 1976. Other liberal feminist stands approve of more generous provision of jobs and child care for women who are poor. Nonetheless, virtually by definition, liberal feminists hold that such reforms are realizable within the framework of a capitalist economy. Even if its stands may have cross-class consequences, liberal feminism is not inclined to confront capitalism head on.

But this critique of liberal feminism's limitations, and the relatively privileged class position of its proponents, is by now standard in the growing lexicon of feminist theory. Not so well known are radical feminist attitudes toward capitalism, perhaps a topic more deserving of attention since the two groups' overlapping class and race backgrounds have occasionally caused their ideas to be misleadingly aligned. For example, while bell hooks's critiques of contemporary white feminism in *Ain't I a Woman?* (1981) and *Feminist Theory* (1984) have supplied sharp and important correctives to class and race biases in liberal and radical feminist texts alike, she and other critics have sometimes too readily dismissed the importance of differences in the two strands' evaluations of capitalism.[6]

For there are three reasons for claiming that radical feminism—unlike its liberal counterpart—is, as a brand of feminist thought, at least implicitly anticapitalist and cognizant of class. First, for a number of women, association with 1970s radical feminist groups such as Redstockings and the Feminists in itself demonstrated a conviction that one was in principle against all types of oppression. Feminism's appeal was that it recognized gender as a form of dominant/subordinate relationship that other social movements—especially those of the Left—were determined to deny and with which they were often (consciously or unconsciously) in collusion. But that recognition did not render invalid those different movements' claims about class or racist or heterosexist discrimination in American society; on the contrary, for many early radical feminists, it was virtually a given that these other oppressions also had to be addressed and somehow gotten beyond.

The second reason for arguing that a latent anticapitalist orientation characterizes radical feminist thought can be culled from its early theoretical writings. An often-noted example is *The Dialectic of Sex* (1970), premised around Shulamith Firestone's assertion that a "sex class" system between men and women constitutes the deepest and most fundamental form of enslavement. Firestone came to this conclusion after having first objected to Friedrich Engels's *Origin of the Family, Private Property, and the State* in what is likewise, by now, a well-worn critique. Firestone did not take Engels to task because he emphasized class, but because his insights into class were not thoroughgoing *enough*.

Even if capitalist relations of production were overthrown, she posited in this early reading, relations of reproduction that maintain women in a secondary position would not necessarily follow suit. She argued that sexual politics are rooted in biology; they are not connected with the level of the economic by any simple relationship of causality. By extension, Marx and Engels were incorrect and indeed naive to presume that any critique based on class alone—even on the nearly universal expropriation of workers' wealth—could eliminate oppression *in general:* contrary to their imaginings, labor is not a sufficiently inclusive category to bring about this desired goal.

Instead, Firestone substituted the alternative proposition that full abolition of the sex class system would bring broader human liberation in its wake. Sexual subordination *precedes* that of labor, she reasoned, and thus may be the paradigmatic model out of which all future relations *proceed.* Why, then, wouldn't a more universal (and generalizable) radicalism be one based on calling for the complete elimination of gender as an elementary structure of social organization? With this interpretation, Firestone emerges as perhaps the first "standpoint theorist" of second-wave American feminism, convinced that the overthrowing of unacceptable conditions as experienced from the position or perspective of women would lead beyond capitalism to a genuinely more classless world.[7]

Finally, a third anticlass interpretation can be culled from radical feminism, albeit (again) indirectly. In a similar vein as Firestone, Ti-Grace Atkinson's *Amazon Odyssey* (1974) set forth the notion that women are a class by a particular set of criteria that unites this group in certain respects despite other social differentiations like economic class, race, ethnicity, nation, age, or sexual orientation. In so doing, not only did Atkinson seek to advance feminist theory, but she also rebelled from a Marxism that devalued gender by according legitimacy only to economic differentiations of "class."[8] But while Atkinson did not make the connection plain (and may not have been interested in doing so at a time when the concept of gender seemed so much more deserving of attention), the vision she associated with women-as-a-class could not be achieved unless there were also major alterations in the capitalist class system indicted by Marxists. Just as liberal feminists are forced in spite of themselves to fall back on a radical feminist concept like treating women as a group (because pressing for their partial interests requires referring to the structural situation of women generally), so a

radical feminist like Atkinson would have to invoke *economic* class—
whether or not she actually did so—for her theoretical argument in
favor of *gendered* class to be consistent.

Just as Eisenstein titled her thesis about political paradoxes within
feminism *The Radical Future of Liberal Feminism,* so I might analogously call my argument "The Socialist Future of Radical Feminism."
For if women really are in some respects conceivable politically as a
class, and feminism à la Atkinson seeks for women to be "liberated" as
such, then measures to eradicate discrimination suffered by *all* that
class's members—women across economic class, women of color,
women of different sexual orientations—would have to be included in
any genuinely radical feminist program. Given the concerns that continue to be more and more pressing in the 1990s, there can be little
doubt that such a program would have to address poverty as it affects
huge numbers of women. Logically, wouldn't it minimally have to include day care and health care made universally available at some reasonable level of quality, affordable housing guaranteed, family allowances provided to single mothers now in onerous dilemmas that
foreclose their chance to feel free, viable long-term alternatives offered
the millions of battered women who currently have nowhere to go, and
prostitution legalized and no longer frequently chosen as a matter of
economic survival? Clearly none of *this* would be possible without commitment to a fairly substantial redistribution of class resources such as
socialists.

But even if radical feminist theory is thus presumptively anticapitalist, there are good reasons to object that this position needed, and
needs, more explicit articulation. It makes little sense to recognize, as
did most radical feminists, that leftist men downplayed sexism by subordinating women's concerns to calls for class solidarity but not also to
acknowledge that radical feminism was similarly at risk of (unconsciously) subsuming class and race bias under the theoretical aegis of
women-as-a-class. In both cases, injury is done when reflexive analysis
stops short of itself, when we treat as obvious what can only become
fully clarified by being brought quite self-consciously to our attention.
Thus, allowing anticapitalist beliefs to remain largely implicit depoliti-
cizes radical feminism by contributing to an overly general and nonspe-
cific usage of the word "patriarchy." If women really are a class, then
the programmatic question of what needs to happen for all women to
enjoy a collectively greater share of social wealth is too important for
radical feminists to leave obscure or taken for granted.

A further disadvantage of leaving this issue unexamined becomes clear when we ask another question: what about men? A problem with deriving anticapitalist leanings *solely* from our third interpretation—from Atkinson's positing of women-as-a-class—is that there is then no justification for asserting that radical feminists would also support socialism because men should likewise be its beneficiaries. Would this branch of feminism advocate large-scale redistribution of income *even if* it could be shown that such a change would affect women's interests only minimally? If indeed radical feminists are opposed to all oppression, then the answer will be yes. Yet to arrive only indirectly, secondarily, at the oppressiveness of economic class leaves radical feminist theory vulnerable to a problem of essentialism also faced by other social movements that base themselves on what has come to be called "identity politics"—namely, how does one get from the interests of the part to the whole? For if a conceptual foundation for moving from specific to generally human concerns is not *explicitly* laid at a movement's inception, how will it ever arise? And how does a movement avoid maintaining or creating other forms of human suffering in the course of eradicating its own?

These issues are pertinent for any leftist—say, a male—insofar as incorporating them would also place him on firmer theoretical ground. For him, a related set of considerations includes awareness of the following. First, it cannot implicitly be presumed that other modes of discrimination like gender and race will disappear with a dissolution of class stratification. For attaining socialism cannot be counted on to dispel these other forms of discrimination more generally or in any simple manner. Second, social movements are most internally consistent when desirous of their own eventual eradication, when they wish that the "other," as a party inimical to themselves, will one day disappear. In the leftist's case, this latter consideration contains the idea of some mutual human ground being an ongoing potentiality even between "capitalists" and "workers" as currently constituted. And it might also include the open airing of concerns about excessive repression during periods of social transition, repression that should be avoided so that new rounds of resentment are not reproduced and a sense of common humanity precluded or destroyed.

An analogy can also be made between the radical feminist and a minority group member—again, perhaps, a male—who sees his primary political identification as based on race. He, too, is unable to presume that any automatic relation exists between class- and race-based forms of discrimination (or, for that matter, between gender- and race-based forms of discrimination). Clearly, eliminating the former bias relates to, but is not identical with, overcoming the latter. Yet the same pitfall arises for this person were he to support socialism *only* because it could improve the lives of minorities, and not because of advantages that bring potential benefits to all human beings across race as well. In the example of race, too, we need to find formulations that fulfill several simultaneous requirements. Certainly identity politics have legitimacy: after all, minorities and other discriminated-against groups designate "others" because they themselves have been so designated and are obviously the persons most affected by, and likely to challenge, the particular "ism" of race. But it is also important to reflect on how theories constructed in response about "race" (or "gender" or "class," for that matter) can explicitly include provisions aimed at allowing for these concepts to themselves eventually pass away.

Coming back to radical feminist thought, this analysis may itself help in clarifying this brand of feminism's general perspective on the relationship between gender and class. The promulgation of notions like a "sex class" system (Firestone) and "women-as-a-class" (Atkinson) have been crucial—probably indispensable—to feminism's theoretical development into a social movement grounded in experiences of oppression shared by women as a group. Without ideas such as these, little basis exists to distinguish the contents of gender- from class-related movements. But while most radical feminists were also implicitly anticapitalist, this opposition to economic structures needed elaboration for an insistence on ending oppression *in general* to be most consistent.

For there is always a leap required, for any social movement, between believing in particular and in general interests—between the possibility of ever forging common human ground between women and men, between the economically dispossessed and the possessors, between one subordinated race and another—which can only be resolved in one (or both) of two ways. Either a given social movement admits that being against oppression in general requires moving beyond narrow definitions of self-interest, or it redefines self-interest in a way that encompasses a general humanity. It may attempt to do both at once, though such theoretical efforts are not difficult. In this respect, a weakness of standpoint theories (whether as implied in Firestone, or later explicitly framed in the writings of Nancy Hartsock, Sandra Harding, or Patricia Hill Collins) may be a tendency to seek conceptual solutions that avoid confrontation with the apparent impossibility of ever entirely closing this gap between self-interest and the interests of an other. For it may be useless, like aiming at an infinitely regressing target, to search for the "deepest" oppression, the person who has been most victimized, or the perfect standpoint that—once eliminated or attained—will eliminate all isms in a domino effect: the problem is that some "deeper" oppression can always be found. When we come back to the instance of our gender/class relationship, therefore, it is critical to insist in this present case of radical feminism on both the validity of women-as-a-class and the recognition that *human* well-being requires a much more equitable redistribution of resources than currently exists in our class- and race-divided society. Both explicitly specified beliefs have to coexist as components of a radical feminist theory serious about its opposition to *women's and human oppression.*

But it was precisely into this relative omission within radical feminist theory—this apparent *lack* of explicitness—that Marxist and socialist feminists leapt by calling for the class side of the gender/class balance to be addressed more overtly. Without doubt, neither Marxist nor socialist feminisms can be faulted for failing to acknowledge the importance of class. On the contrary, a major goal of both strands was to compensate for the relative silence about class in the liberal and radical feminisms that came before them (one of their corollary goals, conversely, being to compensate for the absence of gender in the priorities of Marxism and socialism). Marxist as well as socialist feminists underlined a need for integrating class- and gender-related perspectives, and each agreed on what they mutually took to have been *radical* feminism's chief flaw: its inattention to issues of "historical specificity." By this they meant that radical feminist references to male-dominated societies were objectionable not so much because of any lack of specificity about "patriarchy" and its programmatic ramifications, but because the term had been employed as though universally valid to describe a transhistoric feature of societies across space and time.

Against this usage, Marxist and socialist feminists counterposed their commitment to examining how patriarchy has operated in historically specific settings, and especially how it has meshed with those societies' varying class structures. These branches have been highly influential in the history of feminist theory itself, bequeathing an emphasis on *difference* that has continued to be a dominant theme of the feminist movement as a whole in the 1980s and 1990s. In contrast to radical feminism, though, this approach concentrates less on the differing experiences that separate women-as-a-group from men and is relatively more focused on differences *between* women. In the opinion of Marxist and socialist feminists, a problem with radical feminism was that it did not discuss, as Rosemary Tong puts it, how "The wife of a Carrington (*Dynasty*) does not experience patriarchy in the same way as an Edith Bunker (*All in the Family*) or a Claire Huxtable (*The Bill Cosby Show*)."[9] Not only consciousness of class but race as well are thereby brought quite explicitly back into feminism, both by virtue of these groups' clearly anticapitalist positions and through their concern about recalling that indeed the needs of all women do not equate with the needs of those who are upper class and white.

But important differences exist between Marxist and socialist feminists themselves, as well as *within* socialist feminism. For one thing, Marxist feminism has been criticized for having gone so far in the direction of remembering class that it loses the distinctively gendered rationale for its existence. It is a criticism that seems justified insofar as Marxist feminists have taken on more class- than gender-related causes—for example, a campaign in favor of "wages for housework" and, later, the issue of comparable worth.[10]

From this theoretical angle, Marxist feminists have also been accused of recycling Engels's reductionism, which dates back to *The Origin of the Family*. Like his work, theirs echoes the claim that public ownership of property would uproot gender subordination to a greater degree than seems reasonably supportable. From this reiteration, perhaps, comes Marxist feminists' tendency to devote more attention to issues of production than to those of reproduction, sexuality, biology, and the body. And, though undoubtedly concerned about Marxism's reliance on allegedly gender-blind categories, this branch of feminism does not question the efficacy of the categories themselves. Thus, the older concept of "labor"—as opposed to sex, say, as argued by radical feminism—continues to be placed in an elevated and primary position. To be sure, Marxist feminists do incorporate earlier feminist reservations about the nuclear family into their analyses, attempting to increase the value accorded women's labor in private as well as public spheres. Still, the overall effect may have been to turn back in the direction from which radical feminism initially rebelled when it broke away from Engels and the Left. From radical feminism's vagueness about issues of class that are partially separable from those of gender, Marxist feminism reverts to lack of specificity about gendered issues that are partially separable from those of class.

I should observe that the above critique is hardly my own but one proffered by other feminists, particularly "socialist feminists" who have therefore attempted to differentiate themselves somewhat from their Marxist sisters. For many socialist feminists, a major problem of Marxist feminism was that it did not take the persistent endurance of patriarchy seriously *enough*. Within socialist feminist writings, then, one finds the development of the concept of "capitalist patriarchy," [11] employed in such a way that it serves several distinguishing functions. By reinserting the emphasis on "patriarchy" taken from radical feminist thought into its own gender/class equation, socialist feminists sought to move an unstable theoretical pendulum closer to the middle. Their desire was this time to correct for that relative inattention being paid by the *Marxist* strand to specifically gender-based notions like those set forth in earlier works by Firestone, Atkinson, or Kate Millett. [12] Probably, they suspected that to omit in-depth study of sexuality and the body—of reproductive and sexual controls exerted by men over women—stripped Marxist feminism of most of what could be dubbed distinctively (or radically) "feminist" about it.

At the same time, the idea of capitalist patriarchy attests to socialist feminists' wish to theoretically meld together the two traditions of class- and gender-based analyses, particularly since the concerns of each were thought to intersect and overlap in actual social life. Yes, patriarchal structures seemed to reappear across cultures and class systems, perhaps more repetitively than feminists intent on emphasizing "difference" admitted. But these structures nonetheless assumed historically distinct forms, with varying consequences for women and men in different positions. Consequently, the proper focus of socialist feminism ought be on patriarchy's incarnation in its specific interaction with capitalism: we live neither solely under patriarchy, nor under capitalism, but within a social system that is a hybrid form. One result of this focus is speculation within socialist feminist writings about "dual" versus "unified" systems theory—a debate that has been resonant of doctrinaire disputes, slightly reminiscent of analogous arguments over textual interpretations between (usually male) Marxists. For some, as exemplified in Juliet Mitchell's psychoanalytically influenced interpretation, patriarchy is taken to be more ideological or psychological than material in comparison to capitalism. For others, as Heidi Hartmann's account demonstrates, both patriarchy and capitalism are viewed as materially grounded structures. [13]

In addition, dual and unified systems theorists differed over the degree to which they saw patriarchy and capitalism operating together or apart. If they are so intertwined as to be inseparable, as on one side Iris Young suggests, shouldn't there be unifying concepts that reflect this merging (such as taking the term "division of labor" to describe the simultaneously class and gendered forms of work as it is experienced in both the public world of jobs and the domestic world of families)?[14] Or, as Hartmann contends, perhaps it is more significant to note that even if gender and class oppression overlap, they are still based in "dual systems. "Without this addendum, Engels's reductionism might be repeated not only among Marxist but among *socialist* feminists as well. The significance of this last point should be emphasized, since it relates to practical questions of strategy in addition to theory. An advantage of Hartmann's argument is that by insisting on a dyadic approach (and thereby on the mutual irreducibility of gender and class), socialist feminism still preserves the conceptual distinction Marxist feminism threatened to blur. And since the roots of capitalist patriarchy are taken to be dual, theoretical legitimacy is accorded the strategic tenet that feminist organizations will continue to require autonomous status for quite some time in any pre- or postsocialist society. (Paradoxically, it may be the very ease with which a given society accepts this autonomy—not just in relation to feminism but for any social movement that similarly has suffered past discrimination—that indicates preconditions for a movement's eventual *obsolescence* in a pre- or postsocialist world.)

Socialist feminism, then, deserves credit for coming closer to giving adequate expression to the two sides of a gender/class relationship than one finds in the respective versions proffered by liberal, radical, or Marxist feminisms. Liberal feminists, it may be recalled, believe gender liberation possible *within* capitalism; radical and Marxist feminists would not, though for different reasons that have different strategic implications. For radical feminists, the question is absurd because gender liberation, if achieved, would already have pointed beyond capitalism; for them, one should focus on the need to eliminate patriarchy in order to be rid of capitalism and women's subordination. Marxist feminism, however, tends to rely primarily on eliminating capitalism to overcome patriarchy's ills. For both, attacking one system *first* is hoped to bring down the other *later*. But for socialist feminists, it is *capitalist patriarchy* that must be transcended: the two systems interrelate, and therefore must be *simultaneously* and mutually opposed in order for gender-based oppression to end.

On the other hand, I am not sure that the "unhappy marriage" between Marxism and feminism, a union Hartmann and Young criticized in a volume of the same name, really ends up all that much happier after divorce and remarriage with socialist feminism. For one thing, references to the workings of "capitalist patriarchy" instead of "patriarchy" do not go very far toward a concrete definition of what it means to desire the undoing of either or both forms of social organization. It is unclear whether "patriarchy" is clarified, or made even vaguer, by being re-wed with class in a way that is arguably rather mechanical. And regardless of their undoubtedly good intentions, did socialist feminists' writings about "capitalist patriarchy" really constitute the substance of a new theory, unified or otherwise? Or perhaps instead of a whole new theory they offered a *perspective,* one constituted mostly by juxtaposing two traditions' previously more developed sets of ideas within a worldview opposed to both capitalism and patriarchy.

Moreover, it is unclear whether socialist feminist formulations in fact succeeded at redressing Marxist feminism's proclivity to place more emphasis on the "Marxist" than "feminist" part of its name. Again, such redress was certainly socialist feminists' intention. But language found in such formulations as even Hartmann's definition of patriarchy could be taken to signify otherwise: "we define patriarchy as a set of social relations which has a material base. . . . The material base of patriarchy is men's control over women's labor power. That control is maintained by excluding women from access to necessary economically productive resources *and by restricting women's sexuality.*" [15] The quotation suggests that the issue of women's sexuality is contained within that of their labor power by asserting that "restricting" the former is part of a larger project aimed at controlling the latter. But while in one sense this is true (and Hartmann immediately adds that this control includes "access to women's bodies for sex"), it is also the case that the statement's form reproduces the same subordination of gender to class that was its very purpose to avoid.

Moreover, why is patriarchy's "material basis" control over women's *labor power* rather than, say, control of and over their/our *bodies?* The implications of the two contentions would not be identical, though in a sense Hartmann is right. Sex can and does often involve women's labor. This is true indirectly, as at a workplace where harassment is experienced, but also directly: in marriage and other intimate noneconomic relations that often provide services revolving around housework and child rearing as well as "access to women's bodies"; and in economic relations (in which women are "sex workers" or models in pornographic or commercial enterprises) aimed at providing similar access.

Yet sex goes *beyond* this as well, as would the meaning of an alternative definition of patriarchy if it also included the element of controls exercised over women's *bodies*. For such controls are likewise exerted by virtue of the phenomenon of objectification, the reification of women's bodies that is the *opposite* of labor, entailing not *doing* but treatment as though one were a *thing*. Sexual domination includes what has been called the male "gaze" coming to pervade the images of, and life under, patriarchal culture; it involves delimiting women's reproductive and sexual freedom and choices, including their/our access to each other's bodies; it entails violence actual or threatened that may take place outside as well as within homes or jobs—all of which relates to, but is not exhausted through, the concept of labor. This suggests that it would have been more theoretically defensible to subsume labor under sex rather than the other way around—sex in this regard appearing to be the more overarching category. That instead sex is made once more a subset of labor (as gender had been made a subset of class) hints at socialist feminist ideas, too, having been influenced more by the dominant assumptions of traditional Marxism than by radical feminist thought. In spite of socialist feminism's criticisms of Marxist feminism and of its conscious intentions, then, even here the "socialist" half may have come to take precedence over the "feminist"—leaving the gender/class split not so equally distributed after all.

Of course, and again in socialist feminism's defense, an analysis of several authors' essays does not necessarily reveal the characteristics of a strand of feminism as a whole. Moreover, topics addressed by socialist feminists did tend to include feminist concerns related to sexual as well as economic controls, expressed not only theoretically but through political activism. A case in point was CARASA (Committee for Abortion Rights and Against Sterilization Abuse), a New York City–based socialist feminist group with which I was involved for a short period of time in the late 1970s. CARASA sought to link two issues originating obviously from more feminist than socialist concerns—the right *to* abortion and the right *not* to be sterilized—under the common rubric of guaranteed reproductive freedom for *all* women. Consciousness about gender, class, and race was thereby incorporated through the recognition that forced sterilization has very disproportionately affected poor (and minority) women, reflecting attitudes that go back in American history to the eugenicist leanings of Planned Parenthood founder Margaret Sanger herself. Simply noticing this problem markedly differentiated CARASA from pro-choice organizations of liberal feminist leanings like NOW and NARAL (then the National Abortion Rights Action League), as did the socialist feminist group's early and consistent concern about the class-skewed consequences of the halt in federal funding for Medicaid abortions.

However, while "socialist" and "feminist" impulses were both commendably apparent in such political-theoretical efforts, it again strikes me that the "socialist feminist" form is somehow intrinsically problematic. Not only does the conjunction still appear to favor the socialist side, but it also subtly dilutes the strength of its radical feminist contents. To the extent such dilution in fact takes place, it clearly does so without intention—but why does it occur at all?

I can think of two causes that may be more important, because more deeply rooted, than reasons already mentioned. The first could be characterized as more political, the second as theoretical in character. Returning to the reproductive rights activism example just cited, we might note that NARAL has had relatively greater staying power and influence over time than a group like CARASA, which dissolved. Certainly, one obvious explanation for this relative marginality is that CARASA was handicapped to some degree right from the start: neither socialism nor the plight of poor women attracts much sympathy in the United States; moreover, the comparable affluence of their constituency overall tends to accord organizations like NARAL or NOW increased social influence and power. But I believe that national groups such as NOW and NARAL reap additional benefits *simply from being built around unadulteratedly feminist platforms*. Perhaps their relatively more direct stress on issues of major concern to women, such as sexuality and sexual freedom, has worked much to their advantage.

Indeed, it is difficult to imagine some advantage *not* accruing from emphasizing women-as-a-group, particularly when feminist theory and practices are surveyed in the developmental context I have been sketching. If feminism has been distinctive in its insistence on structural characteristics of women's experience that unite women's experience across other categories like economic class, race, or ethnicity, then that very focus on *commonalities* rather than *differences* was the sine qua non for the movement's emergence and initially constituted its most radical core. After all, a fundamental criterion for becoming a movement—any movement, arguably—is escaping the influence of ideologies inculcating the belief that one's situation is merely individual, one among many outcomes, and not a sign of collective tendencies and structures that can be generalized. In the case of feminism, women had to break from the particular mythologies of patriarchy—but the same principle should hold true for any attempt to escape conditions imposed by a dominant group on subordinates who are encouraged to perceive only their separateness.

Therefore, historically speaking, the importance of having managed to achieve a common identity means that reintroducing considerations of difference would have to be undertaken with some degree of caution lest doing so reproduce, play into, or somehow (however unconsciously) feed this ideological desire of parties in power to prevent the relatively powerless from realizing their similarities with one another. In no way does this statement imply that just as careful attention ought not have been paid—as it has—to opposing interests *between* women (as in the case of divergences of class, race, or sexual orientation among various feminists themselves). To the contrary, confronting these issues is and has been a historically important necessity. Nor should this be taken to suggest that feminist theory should not be rich and diversified in the currents it contains (a very positive aspect of the evolutionary stress on difference), or that feminists do not need to organize separately in many instances precisely because women's experiences diverge in highly significant ways.

Rather, what I am contending is simply that the legitimacy of difference needs to be insisted on in such a way that the radical moment of asserting commonality is also neither lost nor diluted. In order to preserve second-wave feminism's original power, then, the women's movement may have to acknowledge (as here) its commitment *both* to ending class and race oppression *and* to an some overarching framework that continues to declare the conceptual necessity of women-as-a-group.[16] With regard to the gender/class relationship focused on here, then, there is an advantage to referring to this movement as (radically) feminist *and* socialist, rather than as relying on the labels "Marxist feminist" or "socialist feminist" per se.

Otherwise, there is a risk that in its eagerness to correct for past omissions (say, its relative inattention to issues of class, traditionally defined), the movement may also fall into an old habit of apologizing for having at last realized some sense of common cause. Ironically, for women, this "mea culpa" mode is overdetermined, reinforced by the debilitating processes of gender socialization itself. At the same time, not surprisingly, such apologies threaten to weaken feminism politically. For the 1980s and 1990s backlash so thoroughly depicted by Faludi can also be viewed as a slightly shaken male-dominated order defending itself against fledgling gains made collectively by women-as-a-class during the 1960s and 1970s; a countermovement came into being determined to deny the truth of a commonality that had been perceived and acted on.

Given this contemporary context, it seems especially critical for feminists to be sensitive toward the possibility of this enormous backlash seeping into feminism itself in extremely subtle ways. Optimally, however, it seems possible to understand "difference," politically as well as theoretically, in a way that neither (a) dilutes the power of women acting in concert for their collective interests, (b) denies the importance of accepting and politically acting on the significance of simultaneous differences, nor (c) reinforces the confidence of a male-dominated and capitalistic society in its ability to perpetuate the gender, class, and race divisions maintained between people in general that it finds so useful.

But there is one other subtle reason why, as a political matter, referring to a movement as radical *and* socialist may have advantages over the conjunction "socialist feminist." This last consideration takes us back one more time to theory and to Engels's *Origin of the Family*, as well as toward some concluding thoughts.

ENGELS AGAIN, AND NOTES TOWARD AN ANTIPATRIARCHAL CONCLUSION

That Engels's *Origin of the Family, Private Property, and the State* (1845) has been so often cited, including here, attests to the influence of its thesis on the theories about gender and class of the feminist strands investigated above. As seen, Firestone's critique of Engels served to further radical feminist ideas, while Marxist feminists agreed with and directly expanded on many of his observations. But socialist feminists too, while critical of Engels's reductionism, were affected by his position to the extent that the concept of labor came to subsume that of sex.

I would like to use Engels myself: perhaps Marxist and even socialist feminists have interpreted *The Origin of the Family* in a way that, though accurate, does not emphasize a potentially radical feminist kernel that could be culled even from Engels's own argument. Indeed, highlighting this kernel allows us to avoid the theoretical dilution of feminism that to this point has resulted from incorporating his orientation— an orientation that tends to subordinate gender to class. In offering this interpretation, I will also show its closer compatibility with radical feminism, employing this altered conception to begin to define a more specific antipatriarchal program, and to suggest a final clarification of the gender/class relation with which we began.

Let us go back to one aspect of Engels's argument, very briefly. According to Engels, women's oppression originated early on, with the amassing of surplus in the hunting sphere occupied by men. Once the embryonic basis of private property was in place because surplus now existed, men had an inheritance to provide a legitimate heir. But "legitimate" sons could only be ensured, and patrilineal/patriarchal relations embarked on, if women were forced into monogamous marriages to which they (but not necessarily their partners) remained loyal. From this came the overthrow of mother right, which, in Engels's oft-quoted description, was also "the *world historical defeat of the female sex*. The man took command in the home also; the woman was degraded and reduced to servitude; she became the slave of his lust and a mere instrument for the production of children." [17]

The theory, then, provides not only an analysis of the origins of a family form that enslaved women but also a strategic implication for how change could be accomplished. If gender subordination arises with private property, so it might end when conditions surrounding the social organization of labor and production were transformed. According to Marx and Engels's logic, women's subordination should wither as women moved out of the degraded realm of the household and into the public sphere: then, their economic dependence on men and sexual prostitution within marriage could be eliminated. And gender oppression ought also fade if, analogously, women's labor in the home (including child rearing and household chores) were socialized.

But the problem with this analysis is that once more, the concept of sexual reification has been submerged within an overly encompassing category of labor. Look closely again at Engels's words: the woman becomes a slave; she is forced to provide sexual services and to bear children. *Engels has characterized her situation more as a laborer than as an object.* As we saw when considering Hartmann's definition, however, the distinction is by no means an insignificant one. To envisage her as an object, as objectified, has quite different ramifications than seeing her as a worker in or outside the home. For one thing, woman's objectified status doesn't just go away when she moves spatially from one site to another, from domestic to public places. Rather, as previously noted, it *is* her, according to the socially constructed claims of any reifying ideology that leads to treating people more as things than as human. This tendency to reify the other as "object" has certainly been a key element of women's subordination, as Simone de Beauvoir described in *The Second Sex*. Thus, objectification may be present wherever she goes, whether on the streets or in a kitchen or office or restaurant or bar, thereby referring to a larger reality than her laboring personae alone reveal.

Second, and even more critical, the failure to emphasize woman's reification into a thing obscures a related reality—namely, that with the arrival of patriarchy, women themselves become a type and extension of private property. Given his cynicism toward marriage, it is hard to believe that Engels would dissent from this interpretation; yet significantly, the point was left mostly implicit and given relatively short shrift in the *Origin of Private Property*. Nonetheless, we can deduce from Engels's argument that male domination turns women into objects of exchange. It is not just that women are subordinated for procreative purposes (though this factor is evidently present as well), but they have also become valued possessions in themselves, a source of asserting power *between men*. Moreover, above all, it is their *bodies* that patriarchal property holders now seek to dominate, to control, and ultimately to own. Thus women are forced into constituting a major form of capital: what we might call here "sexual capital." As Pierre Bourdieu has observed, capital can clearly be incarnated in shapes other than the economic, narrowly construed—from social and cultural to bodily manifestations (see chapter 4's discussion of beauty).[18]

But for Engels, what this interpretation augurs is that his strategic blueprint for change indeed is likely to fail. If sexual capital resides in women's bodies, then it is hard to see how merely moving women into the workplace, or socializing their labor in the private sphere, could fully resolve the more complex character and origins of gender subordination. Though these changes are important in their own right, as I have been arguing all along, they nevertheless do not go to the heart of patriarchal authority. Rather, women have to take back their own identities and bodies (a collective action quite irreducible to labor, spatially or otherwise), reappropriating the sexual capital that has been expropriated from them. This conclusion is a distinctively radical feminist one, and implies that Marxist and socialist feminisms' analyses might have started to merge with the radical strand's had this latent notion in the *The Origin of the Family* been brought to the surface. That neither Engels nor Marx developed the connection between gender subordination and the objectification and commodification of women's bodies may point *both* to their writings' own historical specificity *and* to profoundly repetitive patterns of patriarchal bias through history.

With this, we arrive back at the question of the gender/class relation in feminist theory. It remains radical indeed for women to take back ownership of their/our own bodily integrity—a sense of bodily freedom still elusive, given ongoing fear of crime, the reality of violence against women, and continuing sexual objectification. Yet, to do so necessarily entails a challenge posed to both men-as-a-group and capitalism (since capitalism remains largely male-dominated worldwide). If women's bodies really have come to constitute capital—sexual capital—then a radically feminist movement intent on repossession might have a desta- bilizing effect on capital*ism* systemically just by threatening to disman- tle a property relationship so strongly desired, so still vested and in- vested in. It might well be disturbing for propertied men to feel unsure about their ability to show off "their" attractive women to one another, or to be unsure if access to women's bodies could still be proffered as a reward for, and concomitant to, entrepreneurial initiative. And what if working-class and poor women (the latter still disproportionately also minorities in the United States because of racism) were to rebel from their oppression *as women*? Might not such a rebellion catch capitalism off guard by undermining gender-based domination as a compensation for the disaffection of poor and working-class—that is, otherwise *un- propertied*—men? (Again, see chapter 4's discussion of beauty as cur- rently constructed to often comprise a form of capital in and of itself.)

By this juncture, I hope it is clear that, as I initially suggested, radical feminism's focus on women-as-a-class may have more promise than tra- ditional class politics for troubling capitalism *on specifically gendered and antipatriarchal grounds*. But making this claim less vague and gen- eral remains a complicated matter, one that deserves an essay all its own. Here it must suffice to note that the project of "taking back the body," or reclaiming sexual capital, would have to include elements familiar as well as new. Certainly, anything that involves women main- taining control of their/our bodily integrity is critical. This includes, quite obviously, continuing what perforce has become a very passionate fight to maintain abortion rights. Also significant, though little dis- cussed since CARASA, would be preventing sterilization abuse, as well as ensuring broader antipoverty measures (including universally avail- able child care) to enable women to support the children they do wish to bear. And a focus on control of our bodies just as clearly has to entail concern for lesbian rights and freedoms, both legally and culturally.

This widening circle also would have to encompass protection from sexual harassment at the workplace, as well as from sexual violence in the home. Providing *every* woman who needs it with a shelter from domestic abuse would itself take a fairly large redistribution of social resources.

Perhaps less obvious than the above measures would be those directed at combating the connection between sex and sexism, so closely intertwined in patriarchal societies as to be virtually indistinguishable. Thus, a reconstituted new wave of feminism will have *both* to be pro-sex and pro-pleasure (so that taking back our bodies is the opposite of repressing them, or reinforcing a culture in which sexual expression is denied), *and* to be bent on breaking current ties between sex and sexism. [19] This might mean using consciousness-raising groups (too infrequent since the 1960s) as well as education and demonstrations about the homogenized and age-discriminatory images of women's bodies that predominate in popular culture, from film to magazines to pornography. Women should also *own* much more of these media than yet at present, so that women themselves can increasingly determine how they are represented—again, across the board, from mainstream to pornographic images. A radical feminist movement taking back ownership of expropriated sexual capital may also wish to have far more explicit control of the sex industry itself. The resulting changes could include support for women who presently work in this industry (especially since prostitutes, or sex workers, are probably among the least protected and most ignored women in patriarchal cultures, even by other women) and, at the same time, measures to enable women to leave this industry *if* they so desired (i.e., if they originally entered not from choice but because there were no other economic options).

While these prescriptive "notes toward an antipatriarchal conclusion" are preferred in only sketchy form here, they are by no means merely utopian. In retrospect, surely many of radical feminism's ideas about gender must have seemed even more utopian in the heyday of groups such as Redstockings and the Feminists in the late 1960s and early 1970s. And while much of that early vision has not been realized, those ideas had enough impact to teach us not to frown upon dreaming. *Both* radical feminist consciousness toward women's potential as a group, *and* the explicit advocacy of socialist aims that address the depth of class and race subordination, will be required if oppression *in general* is to be opposed. Had such a consciousness existed before, the otherwise paranoid J. Edgar Hoover might not have been so secure in his

conviction that feminism posed no potential disturbance to the gendered and classed relations of power he sought illegally to protect. Yet
it is with the future that this chapter is most concerned, having been
inspired not only by a student's suspicions about Hoover's lack of interest in feminism but by many young people whose own feminist contributions remain to be felt in decades to come.

CHAPTER NINE

Third-Wave Feminisms
and Beyond

In 1991 I wrote a column in the *Village Voice* calling for a "third wave" of feminism.[1] At the time, many friends, colleagues, students, and activists with whom I discussed feminist politics shared the belief that new inspiration was needed to reverse the debilitating effects of the Reagan-Bush years. Thus, the potential of third-wave feminism was that it augured the revitalization of a movement, not merely the renaissance of a term. It symbolized the possibility of shifting from the defensive posture of the 1980s and 1990s to a collective assertiveness much more characteristic of the feminist movement during the 1960s and 1970s.

But feminist "collectivity" itself needed to evolve in the direction of broader participation and democratization. A third wave of feminism would be continuous with and yet different from its predecessors, reflecting its unique historical moment. It would not abandon but would further realize transformative hopes expressed by many early radical feminists and feminist radicals (many of whom had backgrounds more diverse in class, racial, and sexual orientation, and were concerned about these diverse forms of discrimination, than is usually recognized in dominant media depictions of an allegedly *only* middle- to upper-class women's movement).[2] Yet issues concerning race, class, and sexual discrimination would be placed at the core of a feminist program even more publicly and thoroughly than the overall movement has succeeded in doing previously;[3] its leadership would reflect a third wave's renewed determination to base itself on the concerns of *all* women (thereafter bringing immense benefits to all human beings, as befits hopes for a world in which feminism itself would eventually become unnecessary).

Simultaneously, and just as important, whereas the 1980s and 1990s witnessed a patterned splitting of sex from sexism over specifically gender-related debates on which this book centers—particularly pornography, beauty, prostitution, sadomasochism, and violence against women—third-wave feminism would incline toward developing more synthetic political positions to which large numbers of women could relate *across* other social divides. Our need for a gender-based movement continues because controls still exerted over women's bodies—from objectification in media to experiences of violence in many women's everyday lives—also *unite* persons who are exposed to such discriminations as "women." Consequently, a revitalized movement would certainly applaud the development of the varied feminisms that have grown over the last several decades; at the same time, it would not in reaction minimize or apologize for the significance of feminist convictions held in common. On the one hand, it would not hold onto an essentialized vision of "woman" as if for dear life (thereby forgetting feminism's goal of not only achieving its own eventual obsolescence but also transforming the meaning of deeply gendered binary distinctions themselves). Nor, on the other hand, would this movement simply deny that the ongoing sociological category of women exists, imposed from outside as an "identity" that still brings predictably patterned inequities in its wake. Commonalities and differences, differences and commonalities: perhaps a third wave of feminism in the future can succeed in recognizing both these dimensions of the movement's joint needs than has yet been achieved in waves of the past.

So I argued in 1991 when the notion of a "third wave" was still fresh. The phrase has since lost its novelty, lately producing a range of new associations. Some of the hopes expressed in that column have begun to be acted on and, at least in part, realized. For instance, "third-wave feminism" has come to connote a younger generation of women—age thirty-five and under—who are committed to democratizing and improving an inherited feminist legacy. The essays in *To Be Real: Telling the Truth and Changing the Face of Feminism* (1995), a volume edited by Rebecca Walker, introduced by Gloria Steinem, and concluded by Angela Davis, express a wide range of dissatisfactions with the perceived narrowness of a second-wave feminism that did not adequately reflect the complexity of diverse women's lives.[4] The contributors stress the importance of difference while also reflecting a commitment to avoiding either/or dichotomies by *also* remaining connected to the truths of earlier feminist insights. At the same time, it appears that the *relative* emphasis of this interesting volume is to underline differences rather than commonalities. Second-wave feminism sometimes seems to be under attack, not only for not fully understanding women's diversely layered social experiences but also for having asserted the importance of commonalities at all.[5]

Since 1991, too, a very different connotation of "third-wave" feminism has surfaced in references to the alleged achievements of "postfeminist" politics. For example, as detailed in previous chapters, a line of argument that differentiates Naomi Wolf's *Fire with Fire* (1993) from her earlier *Beauty Myth* (1991) is the assertion that a new burst of feminist activism ought be based on acknowledging that women have made significant gains in social, economic, and cultural power. No longer are women predominantly "victims," Wolf writes; rather, "power feminism" is a description that better suits this stage of feminist development. But have women indeed become "empowered" agents, and by what criteria? As I write these concluding words, six years after penning that *Voice* column, no basis exists for asserting that all or even most women have managed to escape structurally based experiences of dependency and victimization. The election and reelection of Bill Clinton brought certain benefits but also immense losses for women in the late 1990s. On the one hand, abortion rights were relatively secured; on the other, the federal welfare system was dismantled with nothing to replace it, exposing millions of women, men, and children who are poor and working class to even more economic impoverishment than was already part of their day-to-day lives (and posing special problems for women who, because of gender asymmetries, are left with differential responsibility for children). In this example, then, a call for an invigorated third burst of feminism—in Wolf's terminology, for "power feminism"—makes full consideration of existing *differences* among women unlikely. Whether intentionally or not, her immediate vision has the analytic effect of emphasizing a supposedly achieved *commonality,* which is presumed rather than demonstrated through a political commitment to link all women.

Thus it remains difficult to forge a renewed feminist movement that simultaneously incorporates commonalities and differences into a vision of contemporary feminist politics overall. To be sure, such joint emphases inform many women's feminist politics already, and concern for commonalities as well as differences have characterized groups and types of feminisms in the past. To overlook them is to overlook the mind-boggling growth and achievements of a national, and now an international, feminist movement of which there is tremendous reason to be proud. However, the problem of balancing the two persists insofar as tendencies toward either/or political positions continue to divide even feminists—"even," because feminist theories and practices make special, explicit efforts to think and feel outside such deeply embedded habitual dichotomies. It remains easier at present to find examples of differences receiving more attention than commonalities, or presumed commonalities stressed more than differences, than instances in which both are at once accorded equal intellectual and political emphasis. And yet, as I have been arguing throughout this book, the feminist movement may remain on the defensive and vulnerable to conservative backlash *unless* such simultaneous recognition of feminism *and* feminisms occurs. Why?

For a reader may still be wondering why such recognition is so crucial to feminism(s), and why it still is so difficult to achieve. Responding to the second question may assist in addressing the first. When looking back at the 1960s and 1970s, historians are likely to agree that for many founders of "second-wave" feminism, their original impetus arose from gender discrimination encountered in civil rights and New Left groups *already* cognizant of (and protesting) inequitable race and class "differences" in U.S. society. As chapter 8 detailed, many early radical feminists were certainly opposed to racism and capitalism while realizing that sexism persisted *within* 1960s and 1970s left and antiracist organizations. Think, for example, of Shulamith Firestone's clearly implied opposition to capitalism in *The Dialectic of Sex* (1970), where she contended that eliminating gender might go further than eliminating class toward overcoming *all* human oppressions. Thus, early feminist theory aimed at describing sexist biases experienced by women *across* different classes, races, and ethnicities, even within movements devoted to fighting other social relations based on systematic experiences of dominance and subordination.

Consequently, even though collective memory of its birth has faded, early feminist theory emerged precisely because class- and race-related theories were inadequate to understand specifically gender-based biases. These gender-based biases took wide-ranging and distinctive forms, which had not yet been fully defined when the second wave was itself freshly emerging: they varied from violence against women (including the all-too-common experiences of rape, sexual harassment, and domestic violence) to restrictions placed on women's sexual and reproductive freedom (these, too, ranging along a gamut, from what Adrienne Rich called "compulsory heterosexuality" to sterilization abuse and restrictions on abortion rights, which were never fully made available to all).

With second-wave radical feminist thought, then, the historical pendulum swung toward the immense task of defining commonality through the development of a "sexual politics" for which there was little theoretical precedent. In the process, it may have been difficult indeed to focus with equal intensity on race and class differences (even though, again, many radical, socialist, and Marxist feminists managed to do so). Still, whether some feminists succeeded more than others at incorporating multiple sociological dimensions into their perspectives, there seems little question that indispensable to second-wave thought was the act of specifying that which did not yet exist: a shared set of beliefs that would form the basis of a recognizable *feminism*, without which the later emergence of *feminisms* would literally be inconceivable. Put slightly differently, later interest in *difference* depended on a prior detailing of *commonalities;* these two moments were, as they remain, dependent for their existence on each other.

But in the initial process of defining commonalities, it is hardly surprising that questions of difference were *relatively* de-emphasized by many, though clearly not by all, feminists. Nor, for that matter, is it at all astonishing to find that later feminist works soon sought the centering of the pendulum yet again. In this dialectical sense, one effect of 1980s works authored by bell hooks and Patricia Hill Collins (among other influential feminist theorists who have called attention to differences between women) was to correct for what had already been an attempt at correction. In *Ain't I a Woman* (1981) and *Feminist Theory* (1984), hooks expressed dissatisfaction with the emphasizing of commonalities rather than differences, which started to emerge out of early second-wave feminism's own dissatisfaction with prior social movements' inadequate understanding of gender.

A major contribution of these early works by hooks and others, including Hazel Carby, Angela Davis, Paula Giddings, and Deborah Gray White,[6] was therefore to warn against still another loss of collective memory: now divergences in experience might be in danger of being forgotten, overlooked, or belittled by feminists deeply immersed in the theoretical forging of commonalities. Just as gender discrimination could not be subsumed or reduced to the workings of class or race inequities, so feminists were now reminded that race and class differences could not be subsumed or reduced to the workings of gender. Of course, this did not mean that writers like hooks and Collins did not themselves retain a strong sense of commonality while calling attention to differences (why else would Patricia Hill Collins have entitled her now well-known text *Black Feminist Thought*?), any more than many early radical feminists were completely unaware of differences between women while engaged in delineating commonalities. Once more, the theme at hand throughout these chapters is that of recurring divergences in *relative emphases,* presenting future feminisms with the challenge of regularly pursuing *several* worthwhile political and personal goals at once.

But perhaps now we are in a better position to reconsider the first question raised above—why any of this matters. Why is it critical for future feminism(s) to recognize and respect *both* commonalities *and* differences among women? And why is such simultaneous recognition important in order for "third-wave" feminism (or whatever diverse groups might wish to call it) to be able to provide renewed inspiration for a feminist movement?

Let us consider the ramifications of one possible course: placing a greater stress on *commonalities relative to differences*. Its disadvantages are clear from a contemporary example already raised above, namely, the effects of eliminating "welfare as we know it" at the end of the first Clinton administration. I believe that in order to become a movement genuinely concerned about the lives of *all* women, any satisfactory third wave would have to view a question supposedly "sexual" like reproductive rights and a supposedly "economic" issue like women's ongoing impoverishment with equal political seriousness and alarm. *Both* problems—the realizing of sexual *and* economic freedoms so that genuine choices are possible in both arenas—should be occasioning huge demonstrations and protests led by large numbers of feminists committed to bettering all women's lives. Yet, at present, it is mostly "sexual" issues with which feminism as a mass social movement is generally associated in mainstream cultural consciousness—in part because those economic issue that liberal feminists addressed in the past (such as equal pay for equal work, or glass ceilings) have often not sufficiently addressed the problems of poor and working-class women.[7] As a consequence, women who face multiple forms of discrimination may find it especially difficult to identify and defend feminism inside their own community by the 1990s, even though in other respects a gender-based movement *should* and *does* apply to problems of sexism commonly encountered in their day-to-day lives.

But what about the opposite possibility: placing relatively greater stress on *differences relative to commonalities*? If we do not retain an insistence on the importance of commonalities among women, I fear that we may also fail to recall why feminism initially emerged as an influential political movement: here, too, the result is a no-win situation. For as has been elaborated in the previous chapters, severe sexism remains an ongoing reality with deep roots in institutionalized social structures; in particular, it can be encountered in the supposed "privacy" of nuclear families that remain traditionally organized across a range of differing class, race, and ethnic situations. Another example involves the problem of sexual repressiveness: traditionally sexist controls often seek to mandate compulsory heterosexuality and double standards of sexuality for all women. Again, this problem cannot be confined in its complex effects to any one group of women. Rather, such controls aim at restricting the ability of lesbian and heterosexual women alike to enjoy sexual freedom without guilt or fear of discriminatory reprisals. Similarly, to the extent that men still hold differential and often sexist power within communities as well as households, domestic violence continues all too frequently to haunt and endanger many women's lives across an otherwise wide range of social categories. For violence against women in general—from fear of and actual experiences of rape to sexual harassment on the streets or at workplaces—still tends to create common vulnerabilities for large numbers of women. Thus, feminisms of the future need to be even more committed to understanding and transforming these deep-seated roots of violence in psyches and societies, since ongoing gendered divisions are created and re-created both in the "privacy" of nuclear families and at the "public" level of cultural images, institutional practices, and community reactions.

Commonalities clearly exist. Indeed, they remain remarkably persistent, although women experience these very commonalities differently across other social divisions such as class, race, and sexual orientation. Yet, to the extent that differences are stressed relatively more than commonalities, feminists' collective ability to argue against the structured character of sexism is likely to become politically and organizationally weakened. It may become increasingly difficult to indict sexism *in general* if claims made on behalf of "all women" are labeled as *only* class- and race-biased, all the while these claims were based on gender discrimination *as well*. For, as I am arguing, general claims about sexism are indeed also valid (even if only in part) at one and the same time. But if it becomes relatively unpopular to assert commonalities rather than differences, then "difference" can become a weakness rather than a strength of the movement. Unless we simultaneously stress commonalities, it is harder to amass precisely the kind of collective strength needed to challenge vestiges of male-dominated power that can or do affect most—and in some respects all—women's lives.

The danger is that as women become defensive about asserting commonalities, as if doing so necessarily implies that one does or cannot simultaneously understand the importance of recognizing differences, the very term "feminist" may—indeed, has—become a cause for wariness or apologia. A catchphrase of the late 1990s, used by many women on and outside college campuses, at workplaces and in communities, may in part be traced back to this asymmetry of emphases. "I'm not a feminist, but . . ." expresses a profound ambivalence. Clearly, on the one hand, the speaker perceives feminism as relevant across categories; on the other, a deeply defensive fear interferes with her ability to feel that asserting political commonalities among women is socially legitimate—which itself, ironically enough, affects the ability of feminism(s) to advocate on behalf of differing groups of women.

This defensiveness does not *only* arise from the mainstream feminist movement not yet addressing the multifaceted concerns of many working-class and poor women with sufficient commitment so that issues like welfare, child care, and jobs become—as they must—*just as important* to a third-wave vision as "traditional" feminist issues involving gender-specific problems of sexuality and control over women's bodies. But many women's hesitation to identify as feminists may *also* stem from their inner realization that somehow, some way, women who strongly assert commonalities by reaching out and across to one another are likely to be perceived as threatening.

So where does all of this leave feminism and feminisms in relation to where we began—that is, with the ongoing challenge of how to recognize differences and commonalities, commonalities and differences, simultaneously? In this revitalized movement, a number of complex political needs that transcend overly simple either/or distinctions will have to be encompassed. The next waves of feminism will have to incorporate both/and thinking and feeling even more profoundly and habitually than has already become common within many types and organizations of feminisms, in and outside the academy.

For one thing, the relationship of a feminist movement to other social movements—to class- and race-related organizations, for instance, or to gay and lesbian groups interested in queer theory and politics—is perhaps best conceived in terms of connection *and* autonomy. As suggested theoretically in chapter 8, it makes sense for future waves of feminism both to advocate the need for separate feminist politics (since gender biases cannot be subsumed within other discriminations based on class, race, and sexual orientation) *and* to advocate joint coalitions that maximize collective power to protest other forms of biases (since class, race, and homophobic biases cannot be subsumed, either, within the specific form of discrimination structured around gender).

Similarly, a revitalized movement should encompass both feminisms *and* feminism. There is no reason to think that the need for and desirability of diverse women's groups and organizations will or ought to disappear at any time in the foreseeable future. Rather, women who are lesbian and bisexual are likely to desire both connection with and autonomy from a collective movement; women of color (whether, say, groups of African American or Latina women, of Native American or Asian American women) may wish explicit association with feminisms sometimes and in some ways, while preferring to remain autonomous to varying degrees; and so on. Of course, this is already the case, as feminisms have indeed now become much more varied and inclusive— of women of different hues, desires, incomes, opinions, cultures, and nations and sometimes of just as varied men—than was generally true in the past. In each of these examples, then, one complex form of discrimination cannot simply be reduced to another. Because of complex social *differences,* the feelings and needs of some women connect with but cannot be identified with the needs and feelings of *all.* At the same time, this registering of differences need not threaten the utility of political strength amassed through the assertion of feminist commonalities. Again, commonalities exist and persist in relation to differences; logically, each renders the other possible so that both dimensions remain present even when only one is relatively emphasized.

Moreover, it is indeed the special role of a now-maturing feminist movement to inaugurate innovative modes of thinking and feeling and to imagine possibilities for a transformed society. Certainly within academic feminism, and within feminist theory, either/or categories are

already and rapidly being replaced by more creative both/and conceptions. But the time has come to ensure that this incorporation of complexity takes place outside as well as inside the academy, in public as
well as in private. It falls to a third wave to turn the second wave's now
famous adage on its head (though not, in so doing, discarding the earlier
slogan altogether). By now, many women and men, stirred by "the personal is political," have proceeded to demonstrate that power pervades
intimate, "private" relations. But isn't the political personal as well—
doesn't the inability to separate the social and structural from the psychic and individual apply both ways?

For it is not only our inner worlds that have to change but the outer
society as well. Thus the call to preserve commonalities and collective
political strength is not merely a luxury, or a theoretical nicety employed in academic investigations of people's differing experiences.
Rather, such preservation is intimately connected with the ability to
summon influence en masse, motivating large numbers of women (and
men) to believe it is in the *collective interest* of third-wave feminism
that, for example, child care and adequate income provisions are provided universally. For it strikes me that questions alleged to be only
"political," like those pertaining to welfare and child care, are just as
properly feminist, and *just as intimately personal in their ramifications,*
as any of the more obviously "private" issues with which gender has
long become itself conventionally associated.

Yet we must not overreact in the opposite direction, thereby continuing a historical process of flip-flopping from one relative emphasis to
another—in this case, away from "sexual" issues (narrowly defined) to
"economic" ones (narrowly defined). For there is no reason why a new
wave of feminism will not *also* envision a more sophisticated form of
sexual politics that incorporates understandings of both differences and
commonalities, and which conceives of "sex" economy and "political"
economy as interrelated. Nor is there any reason why, within third-
wave politics, challenges to ongoing structures of sexism cannot simultaneously respect diversities of sexual agency that differ from person to
person (see the argument made in chapter 2). Indeed, if we do not respect people's needs and rights to find happiness now, there are likely
to be rebellions against moralistic strictures. On the other hand, if we
do not equally keep in mind that some of those choices have been in-
formed by the structured constraints of sexist discriminations, previous
problems may be simply recycled rather than slowly but surely redressed.

Perhaps, then, a next wave of feminism will be able *both* to alter the economic status quo of the pornography industry, which has long remained largely under the control of men, *and* to eschew moralistic judgments of women who enjoy pornography (or who resent it, for that matter; see chapter 3). Perhaps future feminisms will manage *both* to demand changes in oppressive beauty standards that permeate cultural practices and ideals *and* to anticipate that women and men are likely to remain concerned about looks for some time to come (see chapter 4). A third wave of feminism(s) may be able *both* to call for economic assistance for all women so that sex workers are not pushed to those jobs by the lack of other options *and* to oppose the discriminatory criminalization that now endangers women because of persisting sexist realities (see chapter 5). Perhaps it will become possible *both* to protest the sadomasochistic character of a given culture *and* to understand sadomasochistic desires as they have come to shape many individuals' social psychology (see chapter 6). And, finally, perhaps it is possible *both* to protest (rather than deny) the all-too-common occurrence of actual violence against women *and* to acknowledge (rather than deny) that our fantasy lives are complex and deeply affected by the eroticization of violence in American and other still male-dominated societies (see chapter 7).

Clearly, it is not my own goal to divide feminists or feminisms from one another, though the very process of calling attention to the habitual ease of either/or distinctions runs the risk of re-creating them—again, quite unwittingly. Yet it is also a serious problem not to identify such divisions, leaving feminism in a compromised position from which there appears little possibility of escape. My hope has been that by subjecting these patterned divides to analysis and bringing them more fully to consciousness, we can avoid their recurrence in contemporary feminist politics. As this book suggests for third-wave feminism, my aim has also been to accomplish several things at once. For we have every reason to acknowledge and appreciate the achievements and courage of the many diverse feminists and feminisms who have shaped contemporary history well beyond the imaginings of most women and men only a century ago. Simultaneously, there is no reason to hold back from understanding and shaping that legacy anew, building on its serious mistakes as well as its striking successes.

But what I will certainly admit to being guilty of throughout this book is a particular kind of greed: not for money or wealth or fame, which are greed's most clichéd connotations, but for the kind of heady excitement that comes from participating in building a world better than the one left behind. I wish for myself and other women of all ages, sexualities, classes, and races that we become able to experience a sense of imagined possibilities and possible transformations—to feel convictions and shared meaning similar to, and yet different from, those experienced by participants in earlier and ongoing progressive social movements (from civil rights to the Left, from feminists to lesbian and gay rights activists).

Maybe, then, a next wave will be able to continue the process of creating such a movement by and for all women, cognizant of commonalities that weave people together while respectful of diversities that keep people apart. Such a movement will bring advantages to both sexes, benefiting all human beings whether or not men choose to participate. For it is the special gift of feminism(s) to think beyond unnecessary dichotomies, beyond commonalities *or* differences, structures *or* agencies, sex *or* sexism. We should not believe that only two options are possible—that feminists must *either* protest systematic subordinations left over from the past *or* comfort ourselves only with sexual or psychic pleasures to be found *now*. Richer and more nuanced options exist, dependent on a multifaceted awareness which the next wave of feminism is even more likely than the last to keep vibrant in our hearts, our bodies, and our minds.

Notes

INTRODUCTION: SEX VERSUS SEXISM

1. The term "sex wars" is the title of Lisa Duggan and Nan D. Hunter's recent edited collection *Sex Wars: Sexual Dissent and Political Culture* (New York: Routledge, 1995). But its usage began much earlier. See, for example, Ann Ferguson, "Sex War: The Debate between Radical and Libertarian Feminists," *Signs* 10 (1984): 106–12, written as part of that issue's forum on the sexuality debates.

2. Ferguson, "Sex Wars," summarizes what she calls this "libertarian-feminist" position in seven points, each of which stresses the importance of specifically sexual freedoms for all women (109). None of these points involves sexist injustices per se—for example, workplace discrimination or racial segregation.

3. As Ferguson describes this point on what she calls the "radical feminist" side of the debate, "In patriarchal societies sexuality becomes a tool of male domination *through* sexual objectification" ("Sex Wars," 108; my emphasis). Unlike the libertarian-feminist position, this suggests that sexuality becomes a focal concern because of its discriminatory consequences, not necessarily proclaiming sexual pleasure as a good in and of itself. However, as will be increasingly apparent, these are differences in relative emphases rather than necessarily contradictory dichotomies.

4. See, in particular, the interesting and important collection edited by Nan Bauer Maglin and Donna Perry, *"Bad Girls"/"Good Girls": Women, Sex, and Power in the Nineties* (New Brunswick, N.J.: Rutgers University Press, 1996). The editors begin their introduction by stating, "This book is an action" (xiii), and proceed clearly to explain their hope of moving feminist thought and political practice beyond an overly dichotomized impasse, an impasse with which this book is concerned as well.

5. See Wendy Chapkis, *Live Sex Acts: Women Performing Erotic Labor* (New York: Routledge, 1997), 21, but also chap. 1, "The Meaning of Sex," in its entirety.

6. Ibid. Of course, this observation regarding the unavoidability of acknowledging dualisms in the very act of calling attention to their limitations can be applied to most if not all feminist theory. The observation can be applied both to early works of feminist thought that challenged sexist gender socialization (e.g., Simone de Beauvoir's *Second Sex,* ed. and trans. H. M. Parshley [1952; rpt., New York: Vintage, 1974]), and to more recent feminist theory that challenges the binarism of "sex" itself (e.g., Judith Butler's *Gender Trouble: Feminism and the Subversion of Identity* [New York: Routledge, 1990]).

7. See Susan Faludi, *Backlash: The Undeclared War against American Women* (New York: Crown, 1991).

8. One excellent statement of the structure versus agency problem can be found in Margaret R. Somers and Gloria D. Gibson, "Reclaiming the Epistemological 'Other': Narrative and the Social Constitution of Identity," in *Social Theory and the Politics of Identity,* ed. Craig Calhoun (Cambridge, Mass.: Blackwell, 1994), 37–99.

9. This usage of "resistance" as rebellion from domination originated with the University of Birmingham Centre for Contemporary Cultural Studies in England, and has since made its way into a number of studies that focus on the "agency" side of the structure versus agency debate in contemporary cultural theory.

10. The significance of this shift from either/or to both/and modes of thought is chronicled in Joan Alway, "The Trouble with Gender: Tales of the Still-Missing Feminist Revolution in Sociological Theory," *Sociological Theory* 13 (1995): 209–28.

11. Ibid.; but see also Patricia Hill Collins, *Black Feminist Thought: Knowledge, Consciousness, and the Politics of Empowerment* (Boston: Unwin Hyman, 1990), and Dorothy Smith, *The Everyday World as Problematic: A Feminist Sociology* (Boston: Northeastern University Press, 1977). The need to go beyond "either/or" dichotomies with regard to the concept of gender per se informs other important work, including Butler, *Gender Trouble;* Marjorie Garber, *Vested Interests: Cross-Dressing and Cultural Anxiety* (New York: Routledge, 1992); Donna Haraway, *Primate Visions: Gender, Race, and Nature in the World of Modern Science* (New York: Routledge, 1989) and *Simians, Cyborgs, and Women: The Reinvention of Nature* (New York: Routledge, 1991); Judith Lorber, *Paradoxes of Gender* (New Haven: Yale University Press, 1994); and Paula Rust, *Bisexuality and the Change to Lesbian Politics* (New York: New York University Press, 1995). Lorber also deals with the problem of binary either/or distinctions in "Beyond the Binaries: Depolarizing the Categories of Sex, Sexuality, and Gender," *Sociological Inquiry* 66 (1996): 143–59.

12. Susan Bordo discusses the history of the mind/body and culture/nature dualisms that permeate the development of gender in her introduction to *Unbearable Weight: Feminism, Western Culture, and the Body* (Berkeley: University of California Press, 1993), 1–42.

13. See, in particular, bell hooks's critiques of feminism in *Ain't I a Woman:*

Black Women and Feminism (Boston: South End, 1981) and *Feminist Theory: From Margin to Center* (Boston: South End, 1984). The problem of race in relation to gender is also described in terms of developing a more complex approach to feminist theory in Collins, *Black Feminist Thought*.

14. One manifestation of this race/class debate is the stress on class found in William Julius Wilson's *Truly Disadvantaged* (Chicago: University of Chicago Press, 1987), as contrasted with the emphasis on race in Stephen Steinberg's article critiquing Wilson, "The Underclass: A Case of Color Blindness," *New Politics* 2, no. 3 (1989): 42–60.

15. Two histories of the Left that document these splits from the beginning of the century through the 1960s are John P. Diggins, *The American Left in the Twentieth Century* (New York: Harcourt Brace Jovanovich, 1973), and James Weinstein, *Ambiguous Legacy: The Left in American Politics* (New York: New Viewpoints, 1975). A general history of the sixties, which includes the emergence of black power, can be found in Peter B. Levy, *The New Left and Labor in the 1960s* (Urbana: University of Illinois Press, 1994). A classic work on the history of the civil rights movement, including the splits within it, is Clayborne Carson's *In Struggle: SNCC and the Black Awakening of the 1960s* (Cambridge, Mass.: Harvard University Press, 1981). With regard to feminism and the development of the split I have been describing in this introduction, see also Alice Echols, *Daring to Be Bad: Radical Feminism in America, 1967–1975* (Minneapolis: University of Minnesota Press, 1989).

16. See Ward Churchill and Jim Vander Wall, *The COINTELPRO Papers: Documents from the FBI's Secret Wars against Domestic Dissent* (Boston: South End, 1990). Also see the introductory note to chapter 8.

17. See Kate Millett, *Sexual Politics* (1969; rpt., New York: Simon and Schuster, 1990), 25.

18. See R. W. Connell, chap. 1, titled "Introduction: Some Facts in the Case," in *Gender and Power: Society, the Person, and Sexual Politics* (Stanford: Stanford University Press, 1987).

19. See Lorber's discussion of this point in *Paradoxes of Gender,* 3.

20. See, for example, Lynne Segal's interesting work *Straight Sex: Rethinking the Politics of Pleasure* (Berkeley: University of California Press, 1994), especially the preface and chap. 1. Segal makes a strong case for the importance of pleasure and sexual freedom in feminist politics. Questions of sexuality are the overall focus of *Straight Sex,* but, like Ellen Willis (see, e.g., *No More Nice Girls,* a set of her essays published in 1992), Segal is concerned about both "saying yes to sex" and saying "no to sexism." However, the basic orientation of her book addresses sexuality more than sexism: Segal is concerned about how to incorporate heterosexuality into a feminism from which heterosexual women and their pleasures may have been excluded in the past.

21. See Robin R. Linden, ed., *Against Sadomasochism: A Radical Feminist Analysis* (San Francisco: Frog in the Well, 1982).

22. To my knowledge, I may have been one of the first people to use the term "third-wave feminism," which later seems to have caught on. For instance, an organization of young feminists planning a "Freedom Summer 96" voter registration drive called itself *Third Wave.*

CHAPTER 1. WHY SPLIT SEX FROM SEXISM?

1. See, for example, Karen de Witt's descriptions of a recent conference in Washington, D.C., hosted by NOW and other feminist organizations to create an agenda for the 1990s: "New Cause Helps Feminists Appeal to Younger Women," *New York Times,* 5 February 1996, sec. 1, p. 10, and "Feminists Gather to Affirm Relevancy of Their Movement," *New York Times,* 3 February 1996, sec. 1, p. 9. On building greater political effectiveness, see also such recent books as Rebecca Walker, ed., *To Be Real: Telling the Truth and Changing the Face of Feminism* (New York: Anchor, 1995), especially Walker's introduction; and Naomi Wolf, *Fire with Fire: The New Female Power and How It Could Change the Twenty-first Century* (New York: Ballantine, 1993).

2. See the opening of my essay "Pornography Debates Reconsidered," *New Politics* 2, no. 1 (1988): 72–84, for a more detailed description of a conference at which this occurred.

3. See chapter 3, which discusses Strossen's book *Defending Pornography: Free Speech, Sex, and the Fight for Women's Rights* (New York: Scribner, 1995) in some detail.

4. Laurie Schrage, "Should Feminists Oppose Prostitution?" *Ethics* 99 (1989): 356–57. For the views of sex workers, see, for example, Laurie Bell, ed., *Good Girls/Bad Girls: Feminists and Sex Trade Workers Face to Face* (Seattle: Seal, 1987).

5. See especially part 3 of Wolf, *Fire with Fire.* I also discuss this problem in greater detail in chapter 7.

6. I write "even" because much feminist theory is explicitly concerned with this problem. From its beginnings, feminists have tried to explode either/or categories and binary distinctions, from nature/culture to masculinity/femininity itself.

7. See Susan Faludi, *Backlash: The Undeclared War against American Women* (New York: Crown, 1991).

8. Stuart Hall, Chas Critcher, Tony Jefferson, John Clarke, and Brian Roberts, *Policing the Crisis: Mugging, the State, and Law and Order* (London: Macmillan, 1978), 106; see also the entire chapter titled "Balancing Accounts" in this classic work.

9. In conducting over twenty-five interviews with print journalists while researching a book on high-profile crime cases, I was struck by how strongly contemporary reporters continue to believe in objectivity.

10. In this context, see Todd Gitlin's *The Whole World Is Watching: Mass Media in the Making and Unmaking of the New Left* (Berkeley: University of California Press, 1980), esp. chap. 5, "Certifying Leaders and Converting Leadership to Celebrity." *The Whole World Is Watching* argues that the focus on certain spokespersons for Students for a Democratic Society (SDS) contributed to that organization's eventual undoing.

11. See Nadine Strossen's *Defending Pornography: Free Speech, Sex, and the Fight for Women's Rights* (New York: Scribner, 1995), 82.

12. See Lisa Duggan, introduction to *Sex Wars: Sexual Dissent and Political*

Culture, ed. Lisa Duggan and Nan D. Hunter (New York: Routledge, 1995), 1–14.

13. Wendy Chapkis, *Live Sex Acts: Women Performing Erotic Labor* (New York: Routledge, 1997), 2.

14. See Clayborne Carson, *In Struggle: SNCC and the Black Awakening of the 1960s* (Cambridge, Mass.: Harvard University Press, 1981); Gitlin, *The Whole World Is Watching.*

15. See Ward Churchill and Jim Vander Wall, *The COINTELPRO Papers: Documents from the FBI's Secret Wars against Domestic Dissent* (Boston: South End, 1990), and Nelson Blackstock, *COINTELPRO: The FBI's Secret War on Political Freedom* (New York: Vintage, 1976).

16. See Douglas S. Massey and Nancy A. Denton, *American Apartheid: Segregation and the Making of the Underclass* (Cambridge, Mass.: Harvard University Press, 1993).

17. I here follow Emile Durkheim, who argued, in his famous chapter on differentiating the "normal" from the "pathological," that the creation of the other is intimately connected with creating social cohesiveness (*The Rules of Sociological Method,* trans. W. D. Halls, ed. Steven Lukes [New York: Free Press, 1982], 85–107).

18. We might note that when Bill Clinton was running for president in 1992, one of the first attacks made on Hillary Clinton charged her with being a "radical feminist": clearly, this form of feminism was the gender equivalent to the "L" word as it was used against Michael Dukakis when he ran for president as a Democrat four years earlier.

19. See the introduction. Among many others, two especially clear examples of feminist theory moving toward explicit acknowledgment of complexity, in the process incorporating both/and rather than either/or conceptions of thought, can be found in Patricia Hill Collins's *Black Feminist Thought: Knowledge, Consciousness, and the Politics of Empowerment* (Boston: Unwin Hyman, 1990) and in Dorothy Smith's *Everyday World as Problematic: A Feminist Sociology* (Boston: Northeastern University Press, 1987).

20. A good summary of postmodern theory, including its doubts about the possibility of historical agency (especially in the work of Baudrillard and Lyotard), can be found in Craig Calhoun's *Critical Social Theory* (Cambridge, Mass.: Blackwell, 1995), chap. 4.

21. See, for example, Collins, *Black Feminist Thought,* chap. 2, "Defining Black Feminist Thought."

CHAPTER 2. A PROBLEM FROM WITHIN

1. See, for example, Sara Evans, *Personal Politics: The Roots of Women's Liberation in the Civil Rights Movement and the New Left* (New York: Knopf, 1979); Alice Echols, *Daring to Be Bad: Radical Feminism in America, 1967–1975* (Minneapolis: University of Minnesota Press, 1989); and Ellen Willis, "Radical Feminism and Feminist Radicalism," in *The 60s without Apology,* ed. Sohnya Sayres et al. (Minneapolis: University of Minnesota Press, 1984), 91–118.

2. See, e.g., Shulamith Firestone, *The Dialectic of Sex: The Case for Feminist Revolution* (New York: Morrow, 1970); Kate Millett, *Sexual Politics* (Garden City, N.Y.: Doubleday, 1970); Ti-Grace Atkinson, *Amazon Odyssey* (New York: Links, 1974); and Michele Wallace, *Black Macho and the Myth of the Superwoman* (1979; rpt., London: Verso, 1990).

3. See E. Willis, "Radical Feminism."

4. See, for instance, Lise Vogel, *Woman Questions: Essays for a Materialist Feminism* (New York: Routledge, 1995), chap. 8. Louise Bernikow's *American Almanac: An Inspiring and Irreverent Women's History* (New York: Berkeley, 1997) is also helpful on this question.

5. See, in particular, Wallace, *Black Macho and the Myth of the Superwoman.*

6. See Firestone, *Dialectic of Sex,* chap. 1.

7. See Adrienne Rich, "Compulsory Heterosexuality and Lesbian Existence," *Signs* 5 (1980): 631–60.

8. See Millett, *Sexual Politics,* 33.

9. Ibid., 37.

10. See Simone de Beauvoir, *The Second Sex,* ed. and trans. H. M. Parshley (1952; rpt., New York: Vintage Books, 1974), especially chaps. 12 and 13 of book 2. On women's socialization toward cooperation and connection, see Carol Gilligan, *In a Different Voice: Psychological Theory and Women's Development* (Cambridge, Mass.: Harvard University Press, 1982).

11. For a superb analysis of the ongoing effects of dominant ideologies about "the" family, centering on the institutionalization of marriage in family law, see Martha Albertson Fineman, *The Neutered Mother, the Sexual Family, and Other Twentieth-Century Tragedies* (New York: Routledge, 1995).

12. For an excellent quantitative and qualitative account of ongoing disparities of gender, see chap. 1 of R. W. Connell, *Gender and Power: Society, the Person, and Sexual Politics* (Stanford: Stanford University Press, 1987).

13. See Firestone, *Dialectic of Sex,* chap. 1, and Millett, *Sexual Politics,* chap. 2.

14. I think here of the astute title of Jessica Benjamin's first book on psychoanalysis and gendered relations, *The Bonds of Love: Psychoanalysis, Feminism, and the Problem of Domination* (New York: Pantheon, 1988).

15. Ellen Willis begins an excellent essay on the sex debates by describing how the subtitle of Levine's work was changed from "Man-Hating and Ambivalence in Women's Lives" to "Women, Men, and the Dilemmas of Gender" when the book came out in paperback. According to Willis's account of Levine's personal explanation, "The Word had become a total conversation stopper: too many readers, including female readers, saw it, freaked out, and either refused to go near the book (as if it harbored a contagious disease) or substituted their fantasy of what the author must be saying for what she had actually said. In the interest of communication of any sort, she decided, 'manhating' had to go." Yet Levine's book was published soon after the Hill-Thomas affair had brought tremendous female rage to the surface, suggesting, Willis argues, "a troubling distortion in the public conversation about feminism." See "Villains and Vic-

tims: 'Sexual Correctness' and the Repression of Feminism," in *"Bad Girls"/ "Good Girls": Women, Sex and Power in the Nineties,* ed. Nan Bauer Maglin and Donna Perry (New Brunswick, N.J.: Rutgers University Press, 1996), 44–45.

16. See Judith Levine, *My Enemy, My Love: Man-Hating and Ambivalence in Women's Lives* (New York: Doubleday, 1992), 4.

17. An excellent discussion of the importance for all feminists of analyzing the complexity of heterosexual relationships is found in Lynne Segal, *Straight Sex: Rethinking the Politics of Pleasure* (Berkeley: University of California Press, 1994).

18. See Paula C. Rust, "The Politics of Sexual Identity: Sexual Attraction and Behavior among Lesbian and Bisexual Women," *Social Problems* 39 (1992): 375–76.

19. See the accounts provided of the relationship between de Beauvoir and Sartre both in Deirdre Bair's exhaustive biography, *Simone de Beauvoir: A Biography* (New York: Summit, 1990), and in the superb account of the intellectual context of this famous couple's interaction by Toril Moi, *Simone de Beauvoir: The Making of an Intellectual Woman* (Oxford: Blackwell, 1994).

20. See E. Willis, "Villains and Victims," 46.

21. See Connell, *Gender and Power.*

22. See Zillah Eisenstein, *The Radical Future of Liberal Feminism* (New York: Longman, 1981).

23. Joseph D. Lichtenberg and Joseph William Slap, "Notes on the Concept of Splitting and the Defense Mechanism of the Splitting of Representations," *Journal of the American Psychoanalytic Association* 21 (1973): 781, 780–81.

24. See the account of this FBI interest in Ward Churchill and Jim Vander Wall, *The COINTELPRO Papers: Documents from the FBI's Secret Wars against Domestic Dissent* (Boston: South End, 1990).

CHAPTER 3. FEMINIST OFFENSIVES

An earlier version of this essay appeared as "Feminist Offensives: Defending Pornography and the Splitting of Sex from Sexism" in the *Stanford Law Review* 48 (1996): 739. Copyright 1996 by the Board of Trustees of Leland Stanford Junior University.

1. Nadine Strossen, *Defending Pornography: Free Speech, Sex, and the Fight for Women's Rights* (New York: Scribner, 1995).

2. A history of radical feminism, including splits over sexuality, can be found in Alice Echols, *Daring to Be Bad: Radical Feminism in America, 1967– 1975* (Minnesota: University of Minnesota Press, 1989). I have also written about the politics of the Barnard conference elsewhere; in particular, see Lynn Chancer, "The Current State of the Feminist Movement," in *Socialist Perspectives,* ed. Phyllis Jacobson and Julius Jacobson (New York: Karz-Cohl, 1983), 97–117.

3. Though I am arguing that indeed real debates have existed inside feminism, Strossen's shorthand reference to a "procensorship" side is also a bit of a

misnomer. Whether or not one concurs with their views, it is not accurate to say that MacKinnon and Dworkin are in favor of censoring all sexual images, but rather only those that fit the proposed ordinances' criteria.

4. Ellen Willis was making this point as early as 1979. See her essay titled "Feminism, Moralism, and Pornography," reprinted in Snitow, Stansell, and Thompson, *Powers of Desire,* 460–67, esp. 467. An excellent and detailed description of the local politics surrounding the passage of the antipornography ordinance in Indianapolis, which gives special attention to the peculiar alliances forged in that process, is found in Donald Alexander Downs, *The New Politics of Pornography* (Chicago: University of Chicago Press, 1989), chap. 4, aptly titled "Strange Bedfellows."

5. Naomi Wolf, *Fire with Fire: The New Female Power and How It Could Change the Twenty-first Century* (New York: Ballantine, 1994); Katie Roiphe, *The Morning After: Sex, Fear, and Feminism on Campus* (New York: Little, Brown, 1993).

6. Strossen, *Defending Pornography,* 160; Deborah L. Rhode, *Speaking of Sex: The Denial of Gender Inequality* (Cambridge, Mass.: Harvard University Press, 1997), 131.

7. Strossen, *Defending Pornography,* 159; Rhode, *Speaking of Sex,* 131.

8. The idea of "mutual recognition" has been wonderfully developed in Jessica Benjamin's *Bonds of Love: Psychoanalysis. Feminism, and the Problem of Domination* (New York: Pantheon, 1988).

9. Lynn Chancer, "Pornography Debates Reconsidered," *New Politics* 2, no. 1 (1988): 75.

10. It should be noted that "anticensorship" and "procensorship," the terms Strossen uses and which I have borrowed upon here, do not precisely summarize the MacKinnon/Dworkin position and the ordinances then passed, first in Minneapolis (where it was vetoed by the mayor) and later in Indianapolis. Rather, the ordinances would censor only those instances of sexual imagery, usually classified as pornographic, that were "graphic sexually explicit subordination of women through pictures and words" (as quoted in Strossen, *Defending Pornography,* 75). While one can and should question the vagueness of such a definition, the stated intention was not to censor *all* pornography.

11. E. Willis, "Feminism, Moralism, and Pornography."

12. These arguments are considered in detail in Chancer, "The Pornography Debates Reconsidered."

13. See Strossen, *Defending Pornography,* 75–79. Strossen notes that the antipornography was first struck down by a federal trial court judge in 1984, a decision affirmed by a panel of the U.S. Court of Appeals for the Seventh Circuit in 1985 before the case reached the Supreme Court in 1986.

14. Ibid., 77. See also Downs, *The New Politics of Pornography,* chap. 4, "Strange Bedfellows: The Politics of the Ordinance in Indianapolis."

15. Strossen, *Defending Pornography,* 80, 81–82.

16. Ibid., 19, 77.

17. Ibid., 39.

18. See Jean-Paul Sartre, *Being and Nothingness,* trans. Hazel E. Barnes (New York: Philosophical Library, 1956), part 1.

19. Strossen, *Defending Pornography*, 39–40.

20. See ibid., chap. 11, "Lessons from Enforcement."

21. Rhode, *Speaking of Sex*, 131.

22. Strossen, *Defending Pornography*, 231, 234, 237.

23. I have paraphrased Strossen's last paragraphs of *Defending Pornography*, where she concludes: "The appeal of any censorship movement, including the one directed at pornography, is understandable insofar as it appears to offer a simple, inexpensive solution to complex troubling societal problems. In contrast, measures that are designed to redress the root causes of these problems are less dramatic, more cumbersome, and more costly than censorship" (279).

24. Here I again borrow from Strossen's terminology; references to the "MacDworkin" side or the "MacDworkinite movement" are scattered throughout *Defending Pornography* (e.g., see 82).

25. Rhode, *Speaking of Sex*, 134.

26. The work generally associated with Sartre's efforts at showing the *limitations* on human freedom bequeathed by social constraints, and with Marxism's influence on him, is his *Critique of Dialectical Reason* (1960).

27. I find myself thinking here of Manuel Puig's novel *Kiss of the Spider Woman* (1976) and the 1986 film version. Even when the main character is imprisoned—when he has been tortured, cut off from all external possibilities—the jailers cannot enforce total captivity on this political prisoner, because he still has the power of his imagination and dreams. Of course, suicide represents the ultimate assertion of freedom—though at the terrible cost of the self—even amid the worst horrors.

28. Stuart Hall, "The Rediscovery of 'Ideology': Return of the Repressed in Media Studies," in *Culture, Society, and the Media*, ed. Michael Gurevitch, Tony Bennett, James Curran and Janet Woollacott (New York: Routledge, 1992), 85.

29. Other visions of pornography may remain relatively subordinated by contrast, or unrealized, or even not yet able to be imagined.

30. This should not be taken as implying that *all* men have equal power. Clearly, masculinity itself is divided along complex axes that impose other forms of dominant/subordinate relationships. See, for example, R. W. Connell's recent *Masculinities* (Berkeley: University of California Press, 1995).

31. In an earlier work, I tried to describe this pattern as one that not only may make its way into pornography but pervades much of contemporary culture through common "sadomasochistic dynamics." See chaps. 2 and 5 of Lynn S. Chancer, *Sadomasochism in Everyday Life* (New Brunswick, N.J.: Rutgers University Press, 1992).

32. Catharine MacKinnon, *Only Words* (Cambridge, Mass.: Harvard University Press, 1993), 13, 31.

CHAPTER 4. THE BEAUTY CONTEXT

1. De Beauvoir begins book 2 of *The Second Sex*, ed. and trans. H. M. Parshley (1952; rpt., New York: Vintage, 1974) with this statement, as she

begins to chronicle the development of the young girl through myriad life stages and social influences (301).

2. See Emile Durkheim, "What Is a Social Fact?" in *The Rules of Sociological Method,* trans. W. D. Halls, ed. Steven Lukes (New York: Free Press, 1982), 50–59.

3. See, for instance, Susan Bordo's essay on anorexia nervosa, in which she cites three axes that influence social concerns about this particular form of appearance expectations: the "control axis" affects men as well as women because the insecurities that cause it cross gender lines (*Unbearable Weight: Feminism, Western Culture, and the Body* [Berkeley: University of California Press, 1993], 148–54).

4. By this I mean the disproportionate importance placed on marriage and coupledom for women (see de Beauvoir's chapter "The Married Woman," in *The Second Sex,* 475–540). The point is also clearly made in Adrienne Rich's classic essay, "Compulsory Heterosexuality and Lesbian Existence," *Signs* 5 (1980): 631–60.

5. This claim that looks and traditional expectations determine women's lives is in general analytically apt—even if it varies to some extent depending on the position of a particular woman. At one end of the socioeconomic spectrum, the rich woman may be able to evade this imperative; at another, the poor or racialized man may be subject to it. But these exceptions do not undermine the rule itself. As we will see later in more detail, men of differing classes and races feel a common right to evaluate women's bodies. Simultaneously, and ironically, men facing class and race discrimination are more likely to find that they are assessed too much in terms of bodily endowments. see, on this point, Robert Connell's discussion of these difference in *Masculinities* (Berkeley: University of California Press 1995), esp. chaps. 3, 8, and 10.

6. Michael A. Messner, for example, in *Power at Play: Sports and the Problem of Masculinity* (Boston: Beacon, 1992), shows the different ramifications of looks for men relative to a particular man's class and race position in society. Thus, in certain circumstances, men may find themselves not only judges (of women's beauty) but judged themselves. See also Sandra Bartky, "Narcissism, Femininity, and Alienation," in *Femininity and Domination* (New York: Routledge, 1990), 40; and Naomi Wolf, *The Beauty Myth: How Images of Beauty Are Used against Women* (New York: Morrow, 1991).

7. Bordo, *Unbearable Weight,* 140, 154.

8. See Becky Wangsgaard Thompson, " 'A Way Outa No Way': Eating Problems among African-American, Latina, and White Women," *Gender and Society* 6 (1992): 546–61.

9. See Thompson, " 'A Way Outa No Way,'" and *A Hunger So Wide and So Deep: American Women Speak Out on Eating Problems* (Minneapolis: University of Minnesota Press, 1994). Racism is cited not only by Thompson but by several of my students in papers for undergraduate courses.

10. Bordo, *Unbearable Weight,* 61. In this essay, "Whose Body Is This?" Bordo writes that "this is a culture in which rigorous dieting and exercise are being engaged in by more and younger girls all the time—girls as young as seven or eight, according to some studies."

11. Ibid., 154.

12. Mary Pipher, *Reviving Ophelia: Saving the Selves of Adolescent Girls* (New York: Ballantine, 1995), 27, 28, 184, 185.

13. Kate Peirce, "A Feminist Theoretical Perspective on the Socialization of Teenage Girls through *Seventeen* Magazine," *Sex Roles* 23 (1990): 491–500.

14. Susan Faludi, *Backlash: The Undeclared War on American Women* (New York: Crown, 1991), 217; Wolf, *The Beauty Myth*, 251.

15. See Kathy Davis's overview of this boom in *Reshaping the Female Body: The Dilemma of Cosmetic Surgery* (New York: Routledge, 1995), 20–21.

16. Ibid., 21.

17. See Eugenia Kaw, "Medicalization of Racial Features: Asian American Women and Cosmetic Surgery," *Medical Anthropological Quarterly* 7 (1993): 74–89.

18. Naomi Murakawa, "The Politics of Looking: Unveiling Asian Blepharoplasty and Exposing the Fallacies of Liberal Choice" (senior thesis, Columbia College, 1995).

19. In the introduction to *Reshaping the Female Body,* Kathy Davis describes the research opportunity she saw when, after the Netherlands had covered cosmetic surgery in its national health insurance plan for many years, budgetary considerations led policy makers to seek cuts in insurance coverage: how would these be made, and on what basis? Observing this decision-making process became part of Davis's research.

20. Ibid., 3.

21. For a good overview of ongoing class stratification among women in the United States, see Ruth Sidel, *Women and Children Last: The Plight of Poor Women in Affluent America* (New York: Penguin, 1987).

22. An exception to the exception, however, may be found among those women who quite reasonably discover that their jobs seems to demand such surgery: say, a newscaster or actor moving into her forties and fifties whose very livelihood demands looking still young.

23. See Edwin M. Schur, *Labeling Women Deviant: Gender, Stigma, and Social Control* (New York: Random House, 1984), 77.

24. Wolf, *The Beauty Myth*, 17.

25. See the introduction; also, see Lisa Duggan and Nan D. Hunter, *Sex Wars: Sexual Dissent and Political Culture* (New York: Routledge, 1995).

26. See chapter 7.

27. Cathy Schwichtenberg, "Madonna's Postmodern Feminism: Bringing the Margins to the Center," in *The Madonna Connection: Representational Politics, Subcultural Identities, and Cultural Theory,* ed. Cathy Schwichtenberg (Boulder: Westview, 1993), 141.

28. Susan Bordo, " 'Material Girl': The Effacements of Postmodern Culture," in Schwichtenberg, *The Madonna Connection,* 285, 288.

29. Ibid., 288–89.

30. Davis, *Reshaping the Female Body,* 174, and more generally 174–81. See Kathryn Pauly Morgan, "Women and the Knife: Cosmetic Surgery and the Colonization of Women's Bodies," *Hypatia* 6, no. 3 (1991): 25–53.

31. See, for instance, Lily Burana, "Bend Me, Shape Me," *New York,* 15

July 1996, 28–34, in which a clearly beautiful reporter describes being told she nevertheless needed $20,000 worth of cosmetic surgery reforms; and Charles Siebert, "The Cuts That Go Deeper," *New York Times Magazine,* 7 July 1996, 20–35, in which the author attempts to interpret rises in cosmetic surgical operations performed on both men and women. Around the same time, National Public Radio did an hour-long program on the subject of beauty and its meaning for feminists across class and race as well as gendered lines.

32. See Holly Brubach, "The Athletic Esthetic," *New York Times Magazine,* 23 June 1996, 48–51, written this same summer.

33. Nancy Friday, *The Power of Beauty* (New York: HarperCollins, 1996), 320–21, 337.

34. Geoffrey Cowley, "The Biology of Beauty: What Science Has Discovered about Sex Appeal," *Newsweek,* 3 June 1996, 65, 66.

35. It should be emphasized that Davis herself, in treating cosmetic surgery, wishes to avoid such dichotomizing (even if her position eventually becomes perceived, despite her intentions, as taking sides in the debate).

36. See the section on the professional beauty qualification, from the "Work" chapter in Wolf's *Beauty Myth,* esp. 27–48.

37. Paul E. Willis writes of "lads" who "penetrate" their own situation in *Learning to Labour: How Working Class Kids Get Working Class Jobs* (New York: Columbia University Press, 1981). But why wouldn't such penetration be possible for women, and perhaps to other groups in situations across gender lines?

38. See the useful work of R. W. Connell in this regard, both in *Gender and Power: Society, the Person, and Sexual Politics* (Stanford: Stanford University Press, 1987) and *Masculinities.*

39. Regarding the immensity of this cultural influence, see, for example, two recent articles: Melissa K. Rich and Thomas F. Cash, "The American Image of Beauty: Media Representations of Hair Color for Four Decades," *Sex Roles* 29 (1993): 113–23, and Barry Vacker and Wayne R. Key, "Beauty and the Beholder: The Pursuit of Beauty through Commodities," *Psychology and Marketing* 10 (1993): 471–93.

40. A good summation of this literature is found in Bryan S. Turner, *The Body and Society: Explorations in Social Theory* (New York: Blackwell, 1984).

41. See Steven Goldberg, *The Inevitability of Patriarchy* (New York: Morrow, 1973), and Norman Mailer, *The Prisoner of Sex* (New York: Little, Brown, 1971), chap. 3, esp. 93–95.

42. See Lois Banner, *In Full Power: Aging Women, Power, and Sexuality* (New York: Knopf, 1992).

43. Emily Martin, "Science and Women's Bodies: Forms of Anthropological Knowledge," in *Body/Politics: Women and the Discourses of Science,* ed. Mary Jacobus, Evelyn Fox Keller, and Sally Shuttleworth (New York: Routledge, 1990), 69.

44. See chapter 3, especially with regard to how a hegemonic pornography can come to dominate a given society.

45. Bartky, "Narcissism, Femininity, and Alienation."

46. Wolf, *The Beauty Myth,* 17 (my emphases); for the $10 billion figure,

see Nadine Strossen, *Defending Pornography: Free Speech, Sex, and the Fight for Women's Rights* (New York: Scribner, 1995), 160.

47. See John Kenneth Galbraith, *The Affluent Society,* 4th ed. (New York: New American Library, 1985).

48. In this context, see especially Michel Foucault's *Discipline and Punish,* trans. Alan Sheridan (New York: Pantheon, 1977) and *History of Sexuality,* vol. 1, *An Introduction,* trans. Robert Hurley (New York: Pantheon, 1978).

49. See Stanley Aronowitz and William DiFazio, *The Jobless Future: Sci-Tech and the Dogma of Work* (Minneapolis: University of Minnesota Press, 1994).

50. I mean "distinction" in the sense used by Pierre Bourdieu in *Distinction: A Social Critique of the Judgement of Taste,* trans. Richard Nice (Cambridge, Mass.: Harvard University Press, 1984).

51. See the overview concerning the inadequate exploration of race in classic sociological theory provided by Robert Blauner at the opening of *Racial Oppression in America* (New York: Harper and Row, 1972). Also, see Max Weber, *Economy and Society* (1922; rpt., Berkeley: University of California Press, 1978).

52. See Connell's explanation of the distinction between hegemonic and marginalized masculinities in *Masculinities,* chaps. 3, 8, 10.

53. Banner, *In Full Power.*

54. See Connell, *Masculinities,* chap. 3, in which hegemonic and marginalized forms of masculinities are distinguished.

55. Jessica Benjamin noted this beautifully when describing the relation between Stephen and Rene, characters in *The Story of O.* See chap. 2, "Master and Slave," in *The Bonds of Love: Psychoanalysis, Feminism, and the Problem of Domination* (New York: Pantheon Books, 1988).

56. To be sure, in many cases a woman's attraction to a man is indeed primarily based upon looks. However, the man *with* power but without good looks is able to translate that combination into attractiveness to women far more easily than a woman likely can who has power *without* good looks.

57. See Pierre Bourdieu, "Social Space and the Genesis of Groups," *Theory and Society* 14 (1985): 723–44.

58. Talcott Parsons, *Social Systems and the Evolution of Action Theory* (New York: Free Press, 1977).

59. Murakawa, "The Politics of Looking."

60. The irony for the many men who fall into this category is especially acute, because (as we have seen) throughout their lives such values of physical attractiveness were not equally important for them as for women.

61. For that matter, if I am a man whose race or class position makes such constructed "bodily capital" only differentially available to him (perhaps a young man of color for whom sports may seem the only way out of the ghetto, given the relative inaccessibility of other forms of social capital), I may find myself suffering from a similar sense of poignant obsolescence and possibilities forever lost as I age—even if gender's own insidious effects allow me some comforts, in terms of the relative power I still have over women.

62. For an explanation of performativity, see Judith Butler, *Gender Trouble:*

Feminism and the Subversion of Identity (New York: Routledge, 1990), esp. 24–25.

63. Wolf, *The Beauty Myth*, 10–11.

64. Connell does a good job of summing up this lack of progress in "Introduction: Some Facts in the Case," in *Gender and Power*, 1–11.

65. Again, an important exception to viewing beauty only as a feminist issue can be found in the writings of Becky Thompson.

66. Let me be clear that I fervently believe in the political validity and necessity of affirmative action, *especially* since the larger class and economic structures of American society have remained largely unaltered despite the existence of legal equality. Yet the same argument I am making about looks-ism holds here too: the strong reaction against affirmative action may in part be because social movements have fought for gender- and race-related interests within too narrowly challenged economic limits.

67. On "mutual recognition," see Benjamin, *The Bonds of Love*, chap. 1.

68. I think here of a speech given by Betty Friedan on a panel organized by Amitai Etzioni at the American Sociological Association meetings in August 1995. Friedan argued that it had been a mistake for feminists to keep emphasizing distinctively gender-specific issues like violence against women: she proposed taking a recess from doing so. But this is an unfortunately either/or proposition in itself: why can't women press for class-related reforms at the same time they unapologetically keep issues about gender at the surface of public consciousness?

69. Many feminists are already recognizing the need to act on several fronts at once: in political terms, see Kristal Brent Zook, "A Manifesto of Sorts for a Black Feminist Movement," *New York Times Magazine*, 12 November 1995, 86–89; in academic terms, see Joan Alway, "The Trouble with Gender: Tales of the Still-Missing Feminist Revolution in Sociological Theory," *Sociological Theory* 13 (1995): 209–28.

70. See the introduction to Aronowitz and DiFazio, *The Jobless Future*.

71. See Messner, *Power at Play*, and Connell, *Masculinities*.

72. Bordo discusses the control axis in her essay on anorexia nervosa in *Unbearable Weight*, 142, 148–54.

73. See Butler's *Gender Trouble* for a critique of speciously separating "gender" from "sex" in feminist analyses (e.g., 6–7).

74. I do not mean to imply that no one manages to minimize the effects of looks-ism—but even defining oneself against the beauty system is to acknowledge its prior effects and to admit it is something against which one had to make very strenuous efforts to rebel.

75. I realize, of course, that men experience this split between the sexual and intellectual too: it is simply a part of life that one feels sexual at some moments, intent on projects that have little to do with being sexual at others. But for women, as the discussion of Faludi and Wolf above makes clear, the ability to experience one *and* the other—intellectuality and sexuality—is often compromised, so that too often a woman feels she must be entirely one *or* the other in a society structured to be at once sexist *and* looks-ist.

76. The sociological necessity for which I am arguing is made clear in Rich, "Compulsory Heterosexuality and Lesbian Existence," as well as more generally in the writings of Durkheim.

77. See the "methodology" of life stage development that de Beauvoir approached in parts 4 and 5 of *The Second Sex*.

78. See, for example, the interesting analysis of this complex question found in Holly Devor's *Gender Blending: Confronting the Limits of Duality* (Bloomington: Indiana University Press, 1989), esp. chaps. 4–7.

79. An excellent description of these projected fantasies can be found in chaps. 5 and 6 of Diana Scully, *Understanding Sexual Violence: A Study of Convicted Rapists* (New York: Routledge, 1994). Scully shows that convicted rapists were convinced that the women they assaulted had really "wanted it"; she lists the varied mythologies regarding women's sexuality which that projected belief entailed.

80. See, in particular, chap. 3 in Cecilie Hoigard and Liv Finstad, *Backstreets: Prostitution, Money, and Love* (College Park: University of Pennsylvania State University Press, 1992), esp. 69–75, 90, 95–97.

81. Ibid.

82. My analysis here is indebted to the analysis of sociological distinctions that is found in Bourdieu's *Distinctions*. Obviously, I intend to illuminate only the specific question of beauty distinctions in the contemporary U.S. context.

83. See, for example, Patricia Hill Collins, *Black Feminist Thought: Knowledge, Consciousness, and the Politics of Empowerment* (Boston: Unwin Hyman, 1990), and Deborah Gray White, *Ar'n' I a Woman: Female Slaves in the Plantation South* (New York: Norton, 1985).

84. See bell hooks, *Ain't I a Woman: Black Women and Feminism* (Boston: South End, 1981), 33.

85. Ibid.

86. See Malcolm X, *The Autobiography of Malcolm X,* as told to Alex Haley (New York: Ballantine Books, 1964); Eldridge Cleaver, *Soul on Ice* (1968; rpt., New York: Laurel/Dell, 1992); and Michele Wallace, *Black Macho and the Myth of the Superwoman* (1979; rpt., London: Verso, 1990).

87. See Suzanna Danuta Walters, *Lives Together/Worlds Apart: Mothers and Daughters in Popular Culture* (Berkeley: University of California Press, 1992), for an account of mothers and daughters that offers an entirely different and much more mutually supportive conception of this relationship. Walters shows that a negative depiction of mother/daughter relationships has frequently characterized popular cultural representations: it has been imposed from without, even though the actual experiences of many mothers and daughters are quite different.

88. In researching other topics, I have carried out several interviews in Los Angeles among women who seek acting jobs after entering their mid-forties and fifties. Their experience of age discrimination is frequently worse than for their male peers.

89. See, for example, reports on a Washington conference attended by 3,000 feminists: Karen de Witt, "New Cause Helps Feminists Appeal to

Younger Women," *New York Times,* 5 February 1996, sec. 1, p. 10, and "Feminists Gather to Affirm Relevancy of Their Movement," *New York Times,* 3 February 1996, sec. 1, p. 9.

90. Nancy Chodorow's best-known work is *The Reproduction of Mothering: Psychoanalysis and the Sociology of Gender* (Berkeley: University of California Press, 1978).

91. See not only ibid., especially Chodorow's description of hypersymbiosis as may often affect the development of young girls and their relationships with primary caretakers (usually mothers; 100), but also chaps. 1, 5, and 6 of Benjamin, *The Bonds of Love.*

92. Suzanna Danuta Walters, *Material Girls: Making Sense of Feminist Cultural Theory* (Berkeley: University of California Press, 1995), 30–31.

93. "No More Miss America!" is taken from the section titled "Historical Documents" in *Sisterhood Is Powerful: An Anthology of Writings from the Women's Liberation Movement,* ed. Robin Morgan (New York: Vintage, 1970), 584–88. To this reprint, Morgan added a note: "Bras were never burned. Bra-burning was a whole-cloth invention of the media."

94. Interview with Lila Karp, who was in the early 1970s a member of the Feminists. For a more specific history of these groups, see, e.g., Alice Echols's *Daring to Be Bad: Radical Feminism in America, 1967–1975* (Minneapolis: University of Minnesota Press, 1989) and a theoretically and historically important essay by Ellen Willis, "Radical Feminism and Feminist Radicalism," in *The 60s without Apology,* ed. Sohnya Sayres et al. (Minneapolis: University of Minnesota Press, 1984), 91–118.

95. "No More Miss America!" 584–85, 586, 587–88.

96. For a good description of current debates over such usages of "woman," see Judith Grant, *Fundamental Feminism: Contesting the Core Concepts of Feminist Theory* (New York: Routledge, 1993), especially the first two chapters; for a more detailed argument for the term's necessity in historical contexts, see chapter 8 of this volume.

97. Kate Millett, *Sexual Politics* (Garden City, N.Y.: Doubleday, 1970); Shulamith Firestone, *The Dialectic of Sex: The Case for Feminist Revolution* (New York: Morrow, 1970); and Ti-Grace Atkinson, *Amazon Odyssey* (New York: Links, 1974).

98. These essays themselves respond to the dominant psychological approach that characterizes the "medical model's" approach to anorexia, an individualized lens that ignores the relevance of more sociological and feminist interpretations that stress social construction. See Bordo, *Unbearable Weight,* 139–65, 185–215. See also Kim Chernin, *The Obsession: Reflections on the Tyranny of Slenderness* (New York: Perennial Library, 1982), 139–64.

99. On obesity see, in addition to Thompson's works, Marcia Millman, *Such a Pretty Face: Being Fat in America* (New York: Norton, 1980), and Susie Orbach, *Fat Is a Feminist Issue: The Anti-Diet Guide to Permanent Weight Loss* (1978; rpt., New York: Berkley, 1990). For a sense of the main positions on cosmetic surgery and the relationship between them, see K. Morgan, "Women and the Knife," and Kathy Davis, "Remaking the She-Devil: A Critical Look at Feminist Approaches to Beauty," *Hypatia* 6, no. 2 (1991): 21–43.

100. I have shamelessly lifted the title of this section from chap. 1 of Walters, *Material Girls.*

101. See, e.g., Laura Mulvey, *Visual and Other Pleasures* (Bloomington: Indiana University Press, 1989); Tania Modleski, *Loving with a Vengeance: Mass-Produced Fantasies for Women* (Hamden, Conn.: Archon, 1982), and Teresa de Lauretis, *Alice Doesn't: Feminism, Semiotics, Cinema* (Bloomington: Indiana University Press, 1984).

102. Walters, *Material Girls,* esp. chap. 3.

103. Ibid., 143, 155.

104. Karl Marx, "Concerning Feuerbach," in *Early Writings* (New York: Vintage, 1975), 423.

105. See Collins, *Black Feminist Thought,* chap. 4.

106. Bartky focuses on narcissism in "Narcissism, Femininity, and Alienation," 33–44.

107. Robin Tolmach Lakoff and Raquel L. Scherr, *Face Value: The Politics of Beauty* (Boston: Routledge and Kegan Paul, 1984), and Wendy Chapkis, *Beauty Secrets: Women and the Politics of Appearance* (Boston: South End, 1986).

108. See Naomi Wolf, *Fire with Fire: The New Female Power and How to Use It* (New York: Ballantine, 1993), esp. part 3, "Victim Feminism versus Power Feminism." See also chapter 7 of this volume.

109. See "Beyond the Beauty Myth," which concludes Wolf's *Beauty Myth;* chap. 5, "Toward a More Colorful Revolution," which ends Chapkis's *Beauty Secrets;* and chap. 10, "Some Final Thoughts," in Lakoff and Scherr, *Face Value.*

110. See, in their entireties, Sara Halprin, *"Look at My Ugly Face"! Myths and Musings on Beauty and Other Perilous Obsessions with Women's Appearance* (New York: Penguin, 1995), and Ellen Zetzel Lambert, *The Face of Love: Feminism and the Beauty Question* (Boston: Beacon, 1995).

CHAPTER 5. PROSTITUTION AND FEMINIST THEORY

An earlier version of this essay appeared as "Prostitution, Feminist Theory, and Ambivalence: Notes from the Sociological Underground" in *Social Text* 37 (vol 11, no. 4, Winter 1993): 143–72. Copyright 1993, Duke University Press.

1. See Judith Rollins, *Between Women: Domestics and Their Employers* (Philadelphia: Temple University Press, 1985); Terry Williams, *The Cocaine Kids: The Inside Story of a Teenage Drug Ring* (New York: Addison-Wesley, 1989), and *Crack House* (New York: Addison-Wesley, 1992); Martin Sanchez Jankowski, *Islands in the Street: Gangs and American Urban Society* (Berkeley: University of California Press, 1991); and Loic J. D. Wacquant, "Corps et âme: notes ethnographiques d'un apprenti-boxeur," *Actes de la recherch en sciences sociales* 80 (November 1989): 33–67.

2. My friend Eric, an economics Ph.D. candidate, arrived for dinner while I was beginning this essay, read these first paragraphs, and remarked: "What is this, a joke? She's a whore, right? I'd give her a job right now—lying down." Another guest, a Legal Aid lawyer, also suddenly reverted to the state of a

sexually embarrassed and rather mindless fourteen-year-old, adding with a laugh, "Ditto—I disagree with you, Lynn, there'd be lots of openings for *her* (hee hee) . . ."

3. Of course, works cited do not exhaust or complete include all studies of prostitution in the United States. However, those mentioned are a good sampling of the more academic, frequently cited, and better-known writings I found on the subject.

4. See Judith Walkowitz, *Prostitution and Victorian Society: Women, Class, and the State* (Cambridge: Cambridge University Press, 1980); Ruth Rosen, *The Lost Sisterhood: Prostitution in America, 1900–1918* (Baltimore: Johns Hopkins University Press, 1982); Anne Butler, *Daughters of Joy, Sisters of Misery: Prostitution in the American West* (Urbana: University of Illinois Press, 1985); Barbara Meil Hobson, *Uneasy Virtue: The Politics of Prostitution and the American Reform Tradition* (New York: Basic Books, 1987); and Alain Corbin, *Women for Hire: Prostitution and Sexuality in France after 1850* (Cambridge, Mass.: Harvard University Press, 1990).

5. Laurie Bell, ed., *Good Girls/Bad Girls: Feminists and Sex Trade Workers Face to Face* (Seattle: Seal, 1987); Frederique Delacoste and Priscilla Alexander, eds., *Sex Work: Writings by Women in the Sex Industry* (Pittsburgh: Cleis, 1987); and Gail Pheterson, ed., *A Vindication of the Rights of Whores* (Seattle: Seal, 1989).

6. Kathleen Barry, *Female Sexual Slavery* (New York: New York University Press, 1979); see also Laurie Schrage, "Should Feminists Oppose Prostitution?" *Ethics* 99 (1989): 347–61.

7. On feminists, see Michael Musheno and Kathryn Seely, "Prostitution Policy and the Women's Movement: Historical Analyses of Feminist Thought and Organization," *Contemporary Crises* 10 (1986): 237–55; on college students, see Bell, *Good Girls/Bad Girls.*

8. Lena Dominelli, "The Power of the Powerless: Prostitution and the Reinforcement of Submissive Femininity," *Sociological Review* 34 (1986): 65–92. On images of prostitution, see Valerie Jenness, "From Sex as Sin to Sex as Work: COYOTE and the Reorganization of Prostitution as a Social Problem," *Social Problems* 37 (1990): 403–20; on feminists' failure to effect significant change, see Ronald Weitzer, "Prostitutes' Rights in the United States: The Failure of a Movement," *Sociological Quarterly* 32 (1991): 23–41.

9. See Gayle Rubin, "The Traffic in Women: Notes on the 'Political Economy' of Sex," in *Toward an Anthropology of Women*, ed. Rayna Reiter (New York: Monthly Review, 1975), 157–210.

10. Charles Winick and Paul M. Kinsie, *The Lively Commerce: Prostitution in the United States* (Chicago: Quadrangle, 1971), 57, 29.

11. Barbara Sherman Heyl, *The Madam as Entrepreneur: Career Management in House Prostitution* (New Brunswick, N.J.: Transaction, 1979).

12. Eleanor M. Miller, *Street Woman* (Philadelphia: Temple University Press), 10, 25.

13. Arlene Carmen and Howard Moody, *Working Women: The Subterranean World of Street Prostitution* (New York: Harper and Row, 1985).

14. Ibid., xi.

15. Ibid., 12–13.

16. Ibid., 27.

17. Cecelie Hoigard and Liv Finstad, *Backstreets: Prostitution, Money, and Love* (University Park: Pennsylvania State University Press, 1992).

18. I would include films here as well: Lizzie Borden's *Working Girls* (Miramax Films, 1988) comes to mind as an example of the same misleading equation operative within a cinematic representation.

19. Edwin Schur defined prostitution as one of three "victimless crimes" in his book *Crimes without Victims* (Englewood Cliffs, N.J.: Prentice-Hall, 1965).

20. Here, the reader might wish to reflect on the interesting question, again in the realm of fantasy, of whether a male sociologist undertaking a participant observation of male customers (again in Amsterdam, say) would fare any better at an ASA conference, or worse, than the hypothetical feminist sociologist with whom I commenced. He, too, would have to be brave indeed.

21. See Erving Goffman, *Stigma: Notes on the Management of Spoiled Identity* (Englewood Cliffs, N.J.: Prentice-Hall, 1963).

22. While it is certainly possible that a male might choose to do a study of prostitutes, participant observation à la the Amsterdam scenario would be unlikely, since most prostitutes appear to be women. As for our hypothetical sociologist being feminist, this seems a fair assumption for two reasons: not only would an interest in a participant observation study imply a preexisting sympathy with the subjects, but the ethnographic process itself would probably forge empathy and some collective sense of identification among women.

23. Shrage, "Should Feminists Oppose Prostitution?" 347, 356–57 (my emphasis).

24. See, for instance, Catharine A. MacKinnon, *Feminism Unmodified: Discourses on Life and Law* (Cambridge, Mass.: Harvard University Press, 1987).

25. In an interview with a high-level New York City Police Department official conducted in connection with general research I am undertaking on rape cases, I was told that if a prostitute were raped in Central Park, her case would be unlikely ever to receive much public attention. However, if I were raped, this official continued, it would be different since I'm a professor.

26. See Helen Benedict, *The Virgin and the Vamp: How the Press Covers Sex Crimes* (New York: Oxford University Press, 1992).

27. See Lynn S. Chancer, "New Bedford, Massachusetts, 6 March 1983–22 March 1984: The 'Before and After' of a Group Rape," *Gender and Society* 1 (1987): 239–60, and Diana Scully, *Understanding Sexual Violence: A Study of Convicted Rapists* (New York: Routledge, 1994), esp. 171–82.

28. Adrienne Rich, "Compulsory Heterosexuality and Lesbian Existence," *Signs* 5 (1980): 631–60.

29. Weitzer, "Prostitutes' Rights in the United States"; quotation, 36.

30. Naomi Wolf, *The Beauty Myth: How Images of Beauty Are Used against Women* (New York: Morrow, 1991).

31. Walkowitz, *Prostitution and Victorian Society;* Rosen, *The Lost Sisterhood;* and Carmen and Moody, *Working Women.*

32. A feminist pro-choice banner I noticed displayed at several abortion rights demonstrations comes to mind here: it said that if men could get pregnant, abortion would be a sacrament.

33. This may change under certain conditions, e.g., when "family values" campaigns aim at arresting anyone, male or female, who is involved. Sometimes, too, male political figures are discredited for associating with prostitutes, e.g., the case of Marion Barry in Washington, D.C. For the most part, however, prostitutes are still the parties most likely to be prosecuted for prostitution.

34. See Mercer L. Sullivan, *Getting Paid: Youth, Crime, and Work in the Inner City* (Ithaca, N.Y.: Cornell University Press, 1989). In his well-known essay, "Social Structure and Anomie" (in *Social Theory and Social Structure* [Glencoe, Ill.: Free Press, 1957]), sociologist Robert Merton defined an innovator as someone who feels compelled to turn to illegal means in order to obtain the goal of wealth that is allegedly available to all in the U.S. social context.

35. It is interesting that the only female member of the group of "cocaine kids" studied by Williams, Kitty, was employed in making contacts with prostitutes for clients (see *Cocaine Kids,* 111–13). In merging drugs with sex, her job reflected a typically gendered division of labor.

36. Rollins, *Between Women,* 168–70; and Hoigard and Finstad, *Backstreets,* 74, 90–91.

37. Jankowski, *Islands in the Street,* and Sullivan, *Getting Paid.*

38. Paul Willis, *Learning to Labour: How Working Class Kids Get Working Class Jobs* (1977; rpt., New York: Columbia University Press, 1981).

39. See Wendy Chapkis, *Live Sex Acts: Women Performing Erotic Labor* (New York: Routledge, 1997), 6–7.

40. Ibid., viii.

CHAPTER 6. FEMINISM AND SADOMASOCHISM

1. Melinda Blau, "Ordinary People," *New York,* 28 November 1994, 38–46.

2. See, in particular, Erich Fromm, *Escape from Freedom* (New York: Holt, Rinehart, and Winston, 1941), and Jessica Benjamin, *The Bonds of Love: Psychoanalysis, Feminism, and the Problem of Domination* (New York: Pantheon, 1988).

3. See, e.g., a prominently displayed article by Louis Uchitelle, "Insecurity Forever: The Rise of the Losing Class," *New York Times,* 20 November 1994, sec. 4, p. 1. For a more theoretical account of why economic insecurities may be rising, see also Stanley Aronowitz and William DiFazio, *The Jobless Future: Sci-Tech and the Dogma of Work* (Minneapolis: University of Minnesota Press, 1994), esp. the introduction.

4. See, for instance, Ruth Sidel's latest work that documents the increasing stigmatization of poor women on welfare, *Keeping Women and Children Last: America's War against the Poor* (New York: Penguin, 1996).

5. See Lynn S. Chancer, *Sadomasochism in Everyday Life* (New Brunswick, N.J.: Rutgers University Press, 1992).

6. See, for example, Pat Califia, "Feminism and Sadomasochism" and

"Genderbending: Playing with Roles and Reversals," in *Public Sex: The Culture of Radical Sex* (Pittsburgh: Cleis, 1994), 165–74, 175–82.

7. Ibid., e.g., 168.

8. For feminist writings on social sadomasochism, see the essays in Robin R. Linden, ed., *Against Sadomasochism: A Radical Feminist Analysis* (San Francisco: Frog in the Well, 1982). On sexual sadomasochism, see Califia, *Public Sex;* also, noting that the stress on sexuality links women of diverse sexual orientation, hetero- and bisexual as well as lesbian, see Sallie Tisdale's *Talk Dirty to Me: An Intimate Philosophy of Sex* (New York: Doubleday, 1994), esp. 147–66, where Tisdale takes issue with the Dworkin/Mackinnon approach to "sex debates."

9. See Linden, *Against Sadomasochism; Coming to Power: Writings and Graphics on Lesbian S/M* (San Francisco: Samois, 1981); and *Powers of Desire: The Politics of Sexuality*, ed. Ann Snitow, Christine Stansell, and Sharon Thompson (New York: Monthly Review, 1983).

10. The implicit argument I am about to make could be drawn out of a radical feminist work such as Kate Millett's *Sexual Politics* (New York: Doubleday, 1970); compare the overt association of sadomasochism with oppression that we find in a text like Andrea Dworkin's *Letters from a War Zone* (New York: Lawrence Hill, 1993), e.g., 81.

11. Millett, *Sexual Politics*, 24–26.

12. See Sherry B. Ortner, "Is Female to Male as Nature Is to Culture?" in *Women, Culture, and Society*, ed. Michelle Zimbalist Rosaldo and Louise Lamphere (Stanford: Stanford University Press, 1974), 67–87.

13. Andrea Dworkin, "Wuthering Heights," in *Letters from a War Zone*, 81.

14. Sigmund Freud, *Three Essays on the Theory of Sexuality*, trans. and ed. James Strachey (New York: Basic Books, 1962). He specified three types of masochism, of which feminine masochism was the second, in "The Economic Problem of Masochism," in *Standard Edition of the Complete Psychological Works of Sigmund Freud*, ed. James Strachey (London: Hogarth Press, 1964), 164–69.

15. See Helene Deutsch, *The Psychology of Women: A Psychoanalytic Interpretation*, 2 vols. (New York: Grune and Stratton, 1944–45).

16. Pat Califia, *Sapphistry: The Book of Lesbian Sexuality*, 3d ed. (Tallahassee, Fla.: Naiad, 1988), 118.

17. Ibid., 119.

18. For a fuller description, see the interpretation of sadomasochism found in Freud, *Three Essays on Sexuality*, 25.

19. Chancer, *Sadomasochism in Everyday Life;* see chap. 2, "A Basic Dynamic." In addition to Pauline Réage's *Story of O* (New York: Ballantine Books, 1965) and Leopold von Sacher-Masoch's *Venus in Furs* (New York: Sylvan, 1947) the other examples from which I drew the definition about to be provided (which uses the conventional associations of sadomasochism with a specifically sexual example to glean more generally applicable possible conclusions) were Sade's *Juliette*, trans. Austryn Wainhouse (New York: Grove Press, 1968), Jenni Diski's *Nothing Natural* (London: Methuen, 1986) and Elizabeth

McNeill's *Nine and a Half Weeks: A Memoir of a Love Affair* (New York: Dutton, 1978).

20. The terms "secondary" and "inessential" link this analysis with that made by Simone de Beauvoir in *The Second Sex*, ed. and trans. H. M. Parshley (1952; rpt., New York: Vintage, 1974), which immediately brings up the *particular* application of this theoretical perspective to the world of gender.

21. I am indebted here to Jessica Benjamin, who used "mutual recognition" to describe this state of simultaneously acknowledged dependence on, and independence of, two parties in relation to one another. See esp. "The First Bond," chap. 1 of *The Bonds of Love: Psychoanalysis, Feminism, and the Problem of Domination* (New York: Pantheon, 1988).

22. See Arlie Russell Hochschild, *The Managed Heart: Commercialization of Human Feelings* (Berkeley: University of California Press, 1983), 11, 25. See the Delta training seminar described on 25.

23. Judith Rollins, *Between Women: Domestics and Their Employers* (Philadelphia: Temple University Press, 1985), 182–83.

24. See, e.g., L. N. Newell, *Contemporary Industrial/Organizational Psychology* (St. Paul, Minn.: West, 1983). I elaborate this dynamic in greater detail in *Sadomasochism in Everyday Life*, chap. 4, "Employing Chains of Command."

25. Michael Lewis, *Liar's Poker* (New York: Penguin, 1989), 43, 46–47.

26. See, for example, Robin Norwood, *Women Who Love Too Much* (New York: Pocket, 1986); Kevin Leman, *The Pleasers: Women Who Can't Say No— And the Men Who Control Them* (New York: Bantam Doubleday Dell, 1987); and Brenda Schaeffer, *Is It Love or Is It Addiction?: Falling into Healthy Love* (New York: Harper/Hazelton, 1987). I describe these examples in greater detail in *Sadomasochism in Everyday Life*, chap. 5, "Engendering Sadomasochism."

27. See Chancer, *Sadomasochism in Everyday Life*, chap. 5, "Engendering Sadomasochism."

CHAPTER 7. VICTIM FEMINISM OR NO FEMINISM?

1. Katie Roiphe, *The Morning After: Sex, Fear and Feminism on Campus* (Boston: Little, Brown, 1993), 5–6.

2. See Susan Brownmiller, *Against Our Will: Men, Women, and Rape* (New York: Simon and Schuster, 1975).

3. Naomi Wolf, *Fire with Fire: The New Female Power and How to Use It* (New York: Ballantine Books, 1993), 135.

4. Ibid., 135–36.

5. Ibid., 137–38, 136–37, 65, 120–21.

6. See Susan Faludi, *Backlash: The Undeclared War against American Women* (New York: Crown, 1991).

7. Alice Echols's *Daring to Be Bad: Radical Feminism in America, 1967– 1975* (Minneapolis: University of Minnesota Press, 1989) provides one of the best historical chronicles available of the boldness that characterized early radical feminism. One can also sense the flavor of the period from original docu-

ments of the time, collected in *Sisterhood Is Powerful,* ed. Robin Morgan (New York: Vintage, 1970).

8. Katha Pollitt, *"The Morning After,"* *New Yorker,* 4 October 1993, 220–24.

9. See, for example, Diana Scully, *Understanding Sexual Violence: A Study of Convicted Rapists* (New York: Routledge, 1994), chap. 2; Julie A. Allison and Lawrence S. Wrightsman, *Rape: The Misunderstood Crime* (Newbury Park, Calif.: Sage, 1993), chap. 1; Diana E. H. Russell, *The Politics of Rape: The Victim's Perspective* (New York: Stein and Day, 1975), and *Rape in Marriage* (Bloomington: Indiana University Press, 1990), esp. chap. 1.

10. See Scully's *Understanding Sexual Violence,* regarding a troubling correspondence she found between the attitudes of convicted rapists (their stereotyped views of women and their rationalizing tendency to hold their victims partly or fully responsible for the violence they commit) *and* stereotypical attitudes still dominant in American culture on the whole.

11. See Cynthia Epstein, *Deceptive Distinctions: Sex, Gender, and the Social Order* (New Haven: Yale University Press; New York: Russell Sage Foundation, 1988).

CHAPTER 8. BEYOND GENDER VERSUS CLASS

An earlier version of this essay appeared as "The Socialist Future of Radical Feminism" in *Socialism: Crisis and Renewal,* ed. Chronis Polychroniou (Westport, Conn.: Praeger, an imprint of Greenwood Publishing Group, Inc., 1993).

1. See, for example, Stanley Aronowitz, *The Crisis of Historical Materialism* (New York: Praeger, 1983).

2. Numerous summaries of Marxist and socialist feminisms have stressed this point. Two excellent such accounts are Rosemarie Tong, *Feminist Thought: A Comprehensive Introduction* (Boulder, Colo.: Westview, 1989), and an older book by Alison M. Jaggar, *Feminist Politics and Human Nature* (Totowa, N.J.: Rowman and Allanheld, 1983).

3. Many socialists would object that the communist societies that have hitherto existed have not corresponded to a genuinely democratic vision of socialism or communism, and thus should not be taken to illustrate much of anything. To this, I would respond that however flawed (and I believe that they were—fatally so), there are historical examples of states that were at least *consciously* "Communist"; there have been no such entities structured on a consciously "Antipatriarchal" ideology. Had more genuinely socialist societies existed, though, they would have been more likely to recognize that feminism's autonomy from class-based movements is defensible on both theoretical and empirical grounds.

4. See Zillah R. Eisenstein, *The Radical Future of Liberal Feminism* (New York: Longman, 1981), esp. 3–8.

5. See Betty Friedan, *The Second Stage* (New York: Summit, 1981).

6. See bell hooks, *Ain't I a Woman: Black Women and Feminism* (Boston: South End, 1981), and *Feminist Theory: From Margin to Center* (Boston: South End, 1984).

7. See Shulamith Firestone, *The Dialectic of Sex: The Case for Feminist Revolution* (New York: Morrow, 1970). I am contending that Firestone took a standpoint perspective much earlier than that position became better known in the socialist feminist writings of Nancy Hartsock and Sandra Harding, as well as in black feminist thought as clearly presented by Patricia Hill Collins. For those later views, see Hartsock, *Money, Sex, and Power: Toward a Feminist Historical Materialism* (1983; rpt., Boston: Northeastern University Press, 1985); Harding, *Whose Science? Whose Knowledge? Thinking from Women's Lives* (Ithaca, N.Y.: Cornell University Press, 1991); and Collins, *Black Feminist Thought: Knowledge, Consciousness, and the Politics of Empowerment* (Boston: Unwin Hyman, 1990).

8. Ti-Grace Atkinson, *Amazon Odyssey* (New York: Links Books, 1974).

9. Tong, *Feminist Thought* 182.

10. Ibid., 58–61.

11. See, e.g., the set of essays in *Capitalist Patriarchy and the Case for Socialist Feminism,* ed. Zillah Eisenstein (New York: Monthly Review, 1979).

12. In addition to the already-discussed works by Firestone and Atkinson, see Kate Millett, *Sexual Politics* (Garden City, N.Y.: Doubleday, 1970).

13. See Juliet Mitchell's *Psychoanalysis and Feminism* (New York: Vintage, 1974), and Heidi Hartmann's essay, "The Unhappy Marriage of Marxism and Feminism: Towards a More Progressive Union," in *Women and Revolution: A Discussion of the Unhappy Marriage of Marxism and Feminism,* ed. Lydia Sargent (Boston: South End, 1981), 1–41.

14. See Iris Young, "Beyond the Unhappy Marriage: A Critique of the Dual Systems Theory," in Sargent, *Women and Revolution,* 43–69.

15. Hartmann, "The Unhappy Marriage," 18; my emphasis.

16. I do not mean that women should be politically organized in a way that subordinates race or class to gender, nor, as I have already made clear, that the work of groups of women subdivided along whatever lines is not important. I am simply emphasizing the point that if commonality as well as difference is not asserted, then the rationale for feminism's existence is in danger of being lost.

17. Friedrich Engels, *The Origin of the Family, Private Property, and the State,* trans. Alec West (1942; rpt., New York: International, 1972), 120–21.

18. See Pierre Bourdieu, "Social Space and the Genesis of Groups," *Theory and Society* 14 (1985): 723–44.

19. See chapter 9.

CHAPTER 9. THIRD-WAVE FEMINISMS AND BEYOND

1. Lynn S. Chancer, "Third Wave Feminism," *Village Voice,* 21 May 1991, 28.

2. See, for example, the account provided by Louise Bernikow in *The American Woman's Almanac: An Inspiring and Irreverent Women's History* (New York: Berkeley, 1997).

3. As noted in earlier chapter, the women's movement is often stereotyped as having been more "white" and "upper class" in the backgrounds and con-

cerns of its participants than is historically accurate. See the important corrective provided by, among others, Lise Vogel in *Woman Questions: Essays for a Materialist Feminism* (New York: Routledge, 1995), chap. 8.

4. See *To Be Real: Telling the Truth and Changing the Face of Feminism,* ed. Rebecca Walker (New York: Anchor, 1995), esp. the introduction, foreword, and afterword.

5. Ibid. Perhaps reflecting this problem, Gloria Steinem in her introduction seems both to support and to feel a bit of discomfort with some of the volume's essays. At points, she appears respectful of but slightly puzzled by younger feminists' perception of second-wave feminism as a movement that necessarily *subordinated* differences as it asserted commonalities.

6. In an interesting *Village Voice* article written in 1995, Michele Wallace argued for the importance of crediting a number of black intellectuals, including Carby, Davis, Giddings, and others, with influencing a move toward incorporating race into feminist analysis. See Wallace, "For Whom the Bell Tolls: Why We Can't Deal with Black Intellectuals," *Village Voice,* 7 November 1995, ss 19–24.

7. Indeed, the issue of reproductive rights is not even itself adequately secured for women of unequal class resources. The aim of ensuring reproductive freedom for all women therefore remains relevant, as it was in the early 1970s when the New York City–based organization CARASA (Committee for Abortion Rights and Against Sterilization Abuse) attempted to connect difficulties encountered by women when desiring *not to bear* a child with the hardships suffered by women forcibly sterilized when wishing *to bear* a child.

Bibliography

Allison, Julie A., and Lawrence S. Wrightsman. *Rape: The Misunderstood Crime.* Newbury Park, Calif.: Sage, 1993.

Alway, Joan. "The Trouble with Gender: Tales of the Still-Missing Feminist Revolution in Sociological Theory." *Sociological Theory* 13 (1995): 209–28.

Aronowitz, Stanley. *The Crisis of Historical Materialism.* New York: Praeger, 1983.

Aronowitz, Stanley, and William diFazio. *The Jobless Future: Sci-Tech and the Dogma of Work.* Minneapolis: University of Minnesota Press, 1994.

Atkinson, Ti-Grace. *Amazon Odyssey.* New York: Links, 1974.

Bair, Deirdre. *Simone de Beauvoir: A Biography.* New York: Summit, 1990.

Banner, Lois. *In Full Power: Aging Women, Power, and Sexuality.* New York: Knopf, 1992.

Barry, Kathleen. *Female Sexual Slavery.* New York: New York University Press, 1979.

Bartky, Sandra. "Narcissism, Femininity, and Alienation." In *Femininity and Domination.* New York: Routledge, 1990.

Beauvoir, Simone de. *The Second Sex,* edited and translated by H. M. Parshley. 1952. Reprint, New York: Vintage, 1974.

Bell, Laurie, ed. *Good Girls/Bad Girls: Feminists and Sex Trade Workers Face to Face.* Seattle: Seal, 1987.

Benedict, Helen. *The Virgin and the Vamp: How the Press Covers Sex Crimes.* New York: Oxford University Press, 1992.

Benjamin, Jessica. *The Bonds of Love: Psychoanalysis, Feminism, and the Problem of Domination.* New York: Pantheon, 1988.

Bernikow, Louise. *The American Almanac: An Inspiring and Irreverent Women's History.* New York: Berkeley, 1997.

Blackstock, Nelson. *COINTELPRO: The FBI's Secret War on Political Freedom.* New York: Vintage, 1976.

Blauner, Robert. *Racial Oppression in America*. New York: Harper and Row, 1972.

Bordo, Susan. " 'Material Girl': The Effacements of Postmodern Culture." In *The Madonna Connection: Representational Politics, Subcultural Identities, and Cultural Theory*, edited by Cathy Schwichtenberg. Boulder: Westview, 1993.

―――. *Unbearable Weight: Feminism, Western Culture, and the Body*. Berkeley: University of California Press, 1993.

Bourdieu, Pierre. *Distinction: A Social Critique of the Judgment of Taste*, translated by Richard Nice. Cambridge, Mass.: Harvard University Press, 1984.

―――. "Social Space and the Genesis of Groups." *Theory and Society* 14 (1985): 723–44.

Brownmiller, Susan. *Against Our Will: Men, Women, and Rape*. New York: Simon and Schuster, 1975.

Brubach, Holly. "The Athletic Esthetic." *New York Times Magazine*, 23 June 1996, 48–51.

Burana, Lily. "Bend Me, Shape Me." *New York Times Magazine*, 15 July 1996, 28–34.

Butler, Anne. *Daughters of Joy, Sisters of Misery: Prostitution in the American West*. Urbana: University of Illinois Press, 1985.

Butler, Judith. *Gender Trouble: Feminism and the Subversion of Identity*. New York: Routledge, 1990.

Calhoun, Craig. *Critical Social Theory*. Cambridge, Mass.: Blackwell, 1995.

Califia, Pat. *Public Sex: The Culture of Radical Sex*. Pittsburgh: Cleis, 1994.

―――. *Sapphistry: The Book of Lesbian Sexuality*. 3d ed. Tallahassee, Fla.: Naiad, 1988.

Carmen, Arlene, and Howard Moody. *Working Women: The Subterranean World of Street Prostitution*. New York: Harper and Row, 1985.

Carson, Clayborne. *In Struggle: SNCC and the Black Awakening of the 1960s*. Cambridge, Mass.: Harvard University Press, 1981.

Chancer, Lynn. "The Current State of the Feminist Movement." In *Socialist Perspectives*, edited by Phyllis Jacobson and Julius Jacobson. New York: Karz-Cohl, 1983.

―――. "New Bedford, Massachusetts, 6 March 1983–22 March 1984: The 'Before and After' of a Group Rape." *Gender and Society* 1 (1987): 239–60.

―――. "Pornography Debates Reconsidered." *New Politics* 2, no. 1 (1988): 72–84.

―――. *Sadomasochism in Everyday Life*. New Brunswick, N.J.: Rutgers University Press, 1992.

―――. "Third Wave Feminism." *Village Voice*, 21 May 1991, 28.

Chapkis, Wendy. *Beauty Secrets: Women and the Politics of Appearance*. Boston: South End, 1986.

―――. *Live Sex Acts: Women Performing Erotic Labor*. New York: Routledge, 1997.

Chernin, Kim. *The Obsession: Reflections on the Tyranny of Slenderness*. New York: Perennial Library, 1982.

Chodorow, Nancy. *The Reproduction of Mothering: Psychoanalysis and the Sociology of Gender.* Berkeley: University of California Press, 1978.

Churchill, Ward, and Jim Vander Wall. *The COINTELPRO Papers: Documents from the FBI's Secret Wars against Domestic Dissent.* Boston: South End, 1990.

Cleaver, Eldridge. *Soul on Ice.* 1967. Reprint, New York: Laurel/Dell, 1992.

Clough, Patricia Ticineto. *Feminist Thought.* Cambridge, Mass.: Blackwell, 1994.

Collins, Patricia Hill. *Black Feminist Thought: Knowledge, Consciousness, and the Politics of Empowerment.* Boston: Unwin Hyman, 1990.

Coming to Power: Writings and Graphics on Lesbian S/M. San Francisco: Samois, 1981.

Connell, R. W. *Gender and Power: Society, the Person, and Sexual Politics.* Stanford: Stanford University Press, 1987.

———. *Masculinities.* Berkeley: University of California Press, 1995.

Corbin, Alain. *Women for Hire: Prostitution and Sexuality in France after 1850.* Cambridge, Mass.: Harvard University Press, 1990.

Cowley, Geoffrey. "The Biology of Beauty: What Science Has Discovered about Sex Appeal." *Newsweek,* 3 June 1996, 61–66.

Davis, Kathy. "Remaking the She-Devil: A Critical Look at Feminist Approaches to Beauty." *Hypatia* 6, no. 2 (1991): 21–43.

———. *Reshaping the Female Body: The Dilemma of Cosmetic Surgery.* New York: Routledge, 1995.

Delacoste, Frederique, and Priscilla Alexander, eds. *Sex Work: Writings by Women in the Sex Industry.* Pittsburgh: Cleis, 1987.

de Lauretis, Teresa. *Alice Doesn't: Feminism, Semiotics, Cinema.* Bloomington: Indiana University Press, 1984.

Deutsch, Helene. *The Psychology of Women: A Psychoanalytic Interpretation.* 2 vols. New York: Grune and Stratton, 1944–45.

Devor, Holly. *Gender Blending: Confronting the Limits of Duality.* Bloomington: Indiana University Press, 1989.

Diggins, John P. *The American Left in the Twentieth Century.* New York: Harcourt Brace Jovanovich, 1973.

Diski, Jenni. *Nothing Natural.* London: Methuen, 1986.

Dominelli, Lena. "The Power of the Powerless: Prostitution and the Reinforcement of Submissive Femininity." *Sociological Review* 34 (1986): 65–92.

Downs, Donald Alexander. *The New Politics of Pornography.* Chicago: University of Chicago Press, 1989.

Duggan, Lisa, and Nan D. Hunter. *Sex Wars: Sexual Dissent and Political Culture.* New York: Routledge, 1995.

Durkheim, Emile. *The Rules of Sociological Method,* translated by W. D. Halls, edited by Steven Lukes. New York: Free Press, 1982.

Dworkin, Andrea. *Letters from a War Zone.* New York: Lawrence Hill, 1993.

Echols, Alice. *Daring to Be Bad: Radical Feminism in America, 1967–1975.* Minneapolis: University of Minnesota Press, 1989.

Eisenstein, Zillah. *The Radical Future of Liberal Feminism.* New York: Longman, 1981.

———, ed. *Capitalist Patriarchy and the Case for Socialist Feminism*. New York: Monthly Review, 1979.

Engels, Friedrich. *The Origin of the Family, Private Property, and the State* (1845), translated by Alec West. 1942. Reprint, New York: International, 1972.

Epstein, Cynthia. *Deceptive Distinctions: Sex, Gender, and the Social Order*. New Haven: Yale University Press; New York: Russell Sage Foundation, 1988.

Evans, Sara. *Personal Politics: The Roots of Women's Liberation in the Civil Rights Movement and the New Left*. New York: Knopf, 1979.

Faludi, Susan. *Backlash: The Undeclared War against American Women*. New York: Crown, 1991.

Ferguson, Ann. "Sex War: The Debate between Radical and Libertarian Feminists." *Signs* 10 (1984): 106–12.

Fineman, Martha Albertson. *The Neutered Mother, the Sexual Family, and Other Twentieth-Century Tragedies*. New York: Routledge, 1995.

Firestone, Shulamith. *The Dialectic of Sex: The Case for Feminist Revolution*. New York: Morrow, 1970.

Foucault, Michel. *Discipline and Punish*, translated by Alan Sheridan. New York: Pantheon, 1977.

———. *The History of Sexuality*. Vol. 1, *An Introduction*, translated by Robert Hurley. New York: Pantheon, 1978.

Freud, Sigmund. "The Economic Problem of Masochism" (1924). In vol. 19 of *Standard Edition of the Complete Psychological Works of Sigmund Freud*, edited by James Strachey. London: Hogarth Press, 1964.

———. *Three Essays on the Theory of Sexuality*, translated and edited by James Strachey. New York: Basic Books, 1962.

Friday, Nancy. *The Power of Beauty*. New York: HarperCollins, 1996.

Friedan, Betty. *The Second Stage*. New York: Summit, 1981.

Fromm, Erich. *Escape from Freedom*. New York: Holt, Rinehart, and Winston, 1941.

Galbraith, John Kenneth. *The Affluent Society*. 4th ed. New York: New American Library, 1985.

Garber, Marjorie. *Vested Interests: Cross-Dressing and Cultural Anxiety*. New York: Routledge, 1992.

Gilligan, Carol. *In a Different Voice: Psychological Theory and Women's Development*. Cambridge, Mass.: Harvard University Press, 1982.

Gitlin, Todd. *The Whole World Is Watching: Mass Media in the Making and Unmaking of the New Left*. Berkeley: University of California Press, 1980.

Goffman, Erving. *Stigma: Notes on the Management of Spoiled Identity*. Englewood Cliffs, N.J.: Prentice-Hall, 1963.

Goldberg, Steven. *The Inevitability of Patriarchy*. New York: Morrow, 1973.

Grant, Judith. *Fundamental Feminism: Contesting the Core Concepts of Feminist Theory*. New York: Routledge, 1993.

Hall, Stuart. "The Rediscovery of 'Ideology': Return of the Repressed in Media Studies." In *Culture, Society and the Media*, edited by Michael Gurevitch,

Tony Bennett, James Curran, and Janet Woollacott. New York: Routledge, 1992.

Hall, Stuart, Chas Critcher, Tony Jefferson, John Clarke, and Brian Roberts. *Policing the Crisis: Mugging, the State, and Law and Order.* London: Macmillan, 1978.

Halprin, Sara. *"Look at My Ugly Face!": Myths and Musings on Beauty and Other Perilous Obsessions with Women's Appearance.* New York: Penguin, 1995.

Haraway, Donna. *Primate Visions: Gender, Race, and Nature in the World of Modern Science.* New York: Routledge, 1989.

———. *Simians, Cyborgs, and Women: The Reinvention of Nature.* New York: Routledge, 1991.

Harding, Sandra. *Whose Science? Whose Knowledge? Thinking from Women's Lives.* Ithaca, N.Y.: Cornell University Press, 1991.

Hartmann, Heidi. "The Unhappy Marriage of Marxism and Feminism: Towards a More Progressive Union" In *Women and Revolution: A Discussion of the Unhappy Marriage of Marxism and Feminism,* edited by Lydia Sargent. Boston: South End, 1981.

Hartsock, Nancy. *Money, Sex, and Power: Toward a Feminist Historical Materialism.* 1983. Reprint, Boston: Northeastern University Press, 1985.

Heyl, Barbara Sherman. *The Madam as Entrepreneur: Career Management in House Prostitution.* New Brunswick, N.J.: Transaction, 1979.

Hobson, Barbara Meil. *Uneasy Virtue: The Politics of Prostitution and the American Reform Tradition.* New York: Basic Books, 1987.

Hochschild, Arlie Russell. *The Managed Heart: Commercialization of Human Feelings.* Berkeley: University of California Press, 1983.

Hoigard, Cecilie, and Liv Finstad. *Backstreets: Prostitution, Money, and Love,* translated by Katherine Hanson, Nancy Sipe, and Barbara Wilson. University Park: Pennsylvania State University Press, 1992.

hooks, bell. *Ain't I a Woman: Black Women and Feminism.* Boston: South End, 1981.

———. *Feminist Theory: From Margin to Center.* Boston: South End, 1984.

Jaggar, Alison M. *Feminist Politics and Human Nature.* Totowa, N.J.: Rowman and Allanheld, 1983.

Jankowski, Martin Sanchez. *Islands in the Street: Gangs and American Urban Society.* Berkeley: University of California Press, 1991.

Jenness, Valerie. "From Sex as Sin to Sex as Work: COYOTE and the Reorganization of Prostitution as a Social Problem." *Social Problems* 37 (1990): 403–20.

Kaw, Eugenia. "Medicalization of Racial Features: Asian American Women and Cosmetic Surgery." *Medical Anthropological Quarterly* 7 (1993): 74–89.

Kimmel, Michael. *Men Confront Pornography.* New York: Meridian, 1991.

Lakoff, Robin Tolmach, and Raquel L. Scherr. *Face Value: The Politics of Beauty.* Boston: Routledge and Kegan Paul, 1984.

Lambert, Ellen Zetzel. *The Face of Love: Feminism and the Beauty Question.* Boston: Beacon, 1995.

Leman, Kevin. *The Pleasers: Women Who Can't Say No—And the Men Who Control Them.* New York: Bantam Doubleday Dell, 1987.

Levine, Judith. *My Enemy, My Love: Man-Hating and Ambivalence in Women's Lives.* New York: Doubleday, 1992.

Levy, Peter B. *The New Left and Labor in the 1960s.* Urbana: University of Illinois Press, 1994.

Lewis, Michael. *Liar's Poker.* New York: Penguin, 1989.

Lichtenberg, Joseph D., and Joseph William Slap. "Notes on the Concept of Splitting and the Defense Mechanism of the Splitting of Representations." *Journal of the American Psychoanalytic Association* 21 (1973): 772–87.

Linden, Robin R., ed. *Against Sadomasochism: A Radical Feminist Analysis.* San Francisco: Frog in the Well, 1982.

Lorber, Judith. "Beyond the Binaries: Depolarizing the Categories of Sex, Sexuality, and Gender." *Sociological Inquiry* 66 (1996): 143–59.

———. *Paradoxes of Gender.* New Haven: Yale University Press, 1994.

MacKinnon, Catharine. *Feminism Unmodified: Discourses on Life and Law.* Cambridge, Mass.: Harvard University Press, 1987.

———. *Only Words.* Cambridge, Mass.: Harvard University Press, 1993.

Maglin, Nan Bauer, and Donna Perry, eds. *"Bad Girls"/"Good Girls": Women, Sex, and Power in the Nineties.* New Brunswick, N.J.: Rutgers University Press, 1996.

Mailer, Norman. *The Prisoner of Sex.* New York: Little, Brown, 1971.

Malcolm X. *The Autobiography of Malcolm X,* as told to Alex Haley. New York: Ballantine, 1964.

Martin, Emily. "Science and Women's Bodies: Forms of Anthropological Knowledge." In *Body/Politics: Women and the Discourses of Science,* edited by Mary Jacobus, Evelyn Fox Keller, and Sally Shuttleworth. New York: Routledge, 1990.

Marx, Karl. *Early Writings,* translated by Rodney Livingstone and Gregor Benton. New York: Vintage, 1974.

Massey, Douglas S., and Nancy A. Denton. *American Apartheid: Segregation and the Making of the Underclass.* Cambridge, Mass.: Harvard University Press, 1993.

McNeill, Elizabeth. *Nine and a Half Weeks: A Memoir of a Love Affair.* New York: Dutton, 1978.

Merton, Robert K. "Social Structure and Anomie." In *Social Theory and Social Structure.* Glencoe, Ill.: Free Press, 1957.

Messner, Michael A. *Power at Play: Sports and the Problem of Masculinity.* Boston: Beacon Press, 1992.

Miller, Eleanor M. *Street Woman.* Philadelphia: Temple University Press, 1986.

Millett, Kate. *Sexual Politics.* Garden City, N.Y.: Doubleday, 1970.

Millman, Marcia. *Such a Pretty Face: Being Fat in America.* New York: Norton, 1980.

Mitchell, Juliet. *Psychoanalysis and Feminism.* New York: Vintage, 1974.

Modleski, Tania. *Loving with a Vengeance: Mass-Produced Fantasies for Women.* Hamden, Conn.: Archon, 1982.

Moi, Toril. *Simone de Beauvoir: The Making of an Intellectual Woman.* Oxford: Blackwell, 1994.

Morgan, Kathryn Pauly. "Women and the Knife: Cosmetic Surgery and the Colonization of Women's Bodies." *Hypatia* 6, no. 3 (1991): 25–53.

Morgan, Robin, ed. *Sisterhood Is Powerful: An Anthology of Writings from the Women's Liberation Movement.* New York: Vintage, 1970.

Mulvey, Laura. *Visual and Other Pleasures.* Bloomington: Indiana University Press, 1989.

Murakawa, Naomi. "The Politics of Looking: Unveiling Asian Blepharoplasty and Exposing the Fallacies of Liberal Choice." Senior thesis, Columbia College, 1995.

Musheno, Michael, and Kathryn Seely. "Prostitution Policy and the Women's Movement: Historical Analyses of Feminist Thought and Organization." *Contemporary Crises* 10 (1986): 237–55.

Newell, L. N. *Contemporary Industrial/Organizational Psychology.* St. Paul, Minn.: West, 1983.

Norwood, Robin. *Women Who Love Too Much.* New York: Pocket, 1986.

Orbach, Susie. *Fat Is a Feminist Issue: The Anti-Diet Guide to Permanent Weight Loss.* 1978. Reprint, New York: Berkley, 1990.

Ortner, Sherry B. "Is Female to Male as Nature Is to Culture?" In *Women, Culture, and Society,* edited by Michelle Zimbalist Rosaldo and Louise Lamphere. Stanford: Stanford University Press, 1974.

Parsons, Talcott. *Social Systems and the Evolution of Action Theory.* New York: Free Press, 1977.

Peirce, Kate. "A Feminist Theoretical Perspective on the Socialization of Teenage Girls through *Seventeen* Magazine." *Sex Roles* 23 (1990): 491–500.

Pheterson, Gail, ed. *A Vindication of the Rights of Whores.* Seattle: Seal, 1989.

Pipher, Mary. *Reviving Ophelia: Saving the Selves of Adolescent Girls.* New York: Ballantine, 1995.

Pollitt, Katha. "*The Morning After.*" *New Yorker,* 4 October 1993, 220–24.

Réage, Pauline. *The Story of O.* New York: Ballantine, 1965.

Rich, Adrienne. "Compulsory Heterosexuality and Lesbian Existence." *Signs* 5 (1980): 631–60.

Rich, Melissa K., and Thomas F. Cash. "The American Image of Beauty: Media Representations of Hair Color for Four Decades." *Sex Roles* 29 (1993): 113–23.

Rhode, Deborah. *Speaking of Sex: The Denial of Gender Inequality.* Cambridge, Mass.: Harvard University Press, 1997.

Roiphe, Katie. *The Morning After: Sex, Fear, and Feminism on Campus.* New York: Little, Brown, 1993.

Rollins, Judith. *Between Women: Domestics and Their Employers.* Philadelphia: Temple University Press, 1985.

Rosen, Ruth. *The Lost Sisterhood: Prostitution in America, 1900–1918.* Baltimore: Johns Hopkins University Press, 1982.

Rubin, Gayle. "The Traffic in Women: Notes on the 'Political Economy' of Sex." In *Toward an Anthropology of Women,* edited by Rayna Reiter. New York: Monthly Review, 1975.

Russell, Diana E. H. *The Politics of Rape: The Victim's Perspective.* New York: Stein and Day, 1975.
———. *Rape in Marriage.* Bloomington: Indiana University Press, 1990.
Rust, Paula C. *Bisexuality and the Change to Lesbian Politics.* New York: New York University Press, 1995.
———. "The Politics of Sexual Identity: Sexual Attraction and Behavior among Lesbian and Bisexual Women." *Social Problems* 39 (1992): 366–86.
Sacher-Masoch, Leopold von. *Venus in Furs.* New York: Sylvan, 1947.
Sade, Marquis de. *Juliette* (1797), translated by Austryn Wainhouse. New York: Grove Press, 1968.
Sartre, Jean-Paul. *Being and Nothingness,* translated by Hazel E. Barnes. New York: Philosophical Library, 1956.
Schaeffer, Brenda. *Is It Love or Is It Addiction?: Falling into Healthy Love.* New York: Harper/Hazelton, 1987.
Schrage, Laurie. "Should Feminists Oppose Prostitution?" *Ethics* 99 (1989): 347–61.
Schur, Edwin. *Crimes without Victims.* Englewood Cliffs, N.J.: Prentice-Hall, 1965.
———. *Labeling Women Deviant: Gender, Stigma, and Social Control.* New York: Random House, 1984.
Schwichtenberg, Cathy. "Madonna's Postmodern Feminism: Bringing the Margins to the Center." In *The Madonna Connection: Representational Politics, Subcultural Identities, and Cultural Theory,* edited by Cathy Schwichtenberg. Boulder: Westview, 1993.
Scully, Diana. *Understanding Sexual Violence: A Study of Convicted Rapists.* New York: Routledge, 1994.
Segal, Lynne. *Straight Sex: Rethinking the Politics of Pleasure.* Berkeley: University of California Press, 1994.
Sidel, Ruth. *Keeping Women and Children Last: America's War against the Poor.* New York: Penguin, 1996.
———. *Women and Children Last: The Plight of Poor Women in Affluent America.* New York: Penguin, 1987.
Siebert, Charles. "The Cuts That Go Deeper." *New York Times Magazine,* 23 June 1996, 20–25.
Smith, Dorothy. *The Everyday World as Problematic: A Feminist Sociology.* Boston: Northeastern University Press, 1987.
Somers, Margaret R., and Gloria D. Gibson. "Reclaiming the Epistemological 'Other': Narrative and the Social Constitution of Identity." In *Social Theory and the Politics of Identity,* edited by Craig Calhoun. Cambridge, Mass.: Blackwell, 1994.
Steinberg, Stephen. "The Underclass: A Case of Color Blindness." *New Politics* 2, no. 3 (1989): 42–60.
Strossen, Nadine. *Defending Pornography: Free Speech, Sex, and the Fight for Women's Rights.* New York: Scribner, 1995.
Sullivan, Mercer L. *Getting Paid: Youth, Crime, and Work in the Inner City.* Ithaca, N.Y.: Cornell University Press, 1989.
Thompson, Becky Wangsgaard. *A Hunger So Wide and So Deep: American*

Women Speak Out on Eating Problems. Minneapolis: University of Minnesota Press, 1994.

———. " 'A Way Outa No Way': Eating Problems among African-American, Latina, and White Women." *Gender and Society* 6 (1992): 546–61.

Tisdale, Sallie. *Talk Dirty to Me: An Intimate Philosophy of Sex.* New York: Doubleday, 1994.

Tong, Rosemarie. *Feminist Thought: A Comprehensive Introduction.* Boulder: Westview, 1989.

Turner, Bryan S. *The Body and Society: Explorations in Social Theory.* New York: Blackwell, 1984.

Uchitelle, Louis. "Insecurity Forever: The Rise of the Losing Class." *New York Times,* 20 November 1994, sec. 4, p. 1.

Vacker, Barry, and Wayne R. Key. "Beauty and the Beholder: The Pursuit of Beauty through Commodities." *Psychology and Marketing* 10 (1993): 471–93.

Vogel, Lise. *Woman Questions: Essays for a Materialist Feminism.* New York: Routledge, 1995.

Wacquant, Loic J. D. "Corps et âme: notes ethnographiques d'un apprenti-boxeur." *Actes de la recherche en sciences sociales* 80 (November 1989): 33–67.

Walker, Rebecca. *To Be Real: Telling the Truth and Changing the Face of Feminism.* New York: Anchor, 1995.

Walkowitz, Judith. *Prostitution and Victorian Society: Women, Class, and the State.* Cambridge: Cambridge University Press, 1980.

Wallace, Michele. *Black Macho and the Myth of the Superwoman.* 1979. Reprint, London: Verso, 1990.

———. "For Whom the Bell Tolls: Why We Can't Deal with Black Intellectuals." *Village Voice,* 7 November 1995, ss 19–24.

Walters, Suzanna Danuta. *Lives Together/Worlds Apart: Mothers and Daughters in Popular Culture.* Berkeley: University of California Press, 1992.

———. *Material Girls: Making Sense of Feminist Cultural Theory.* Berkeley: University of California Press, 1995.

Weber, Max. *Economy and Society.* 1922. Reprint, Berkeley: University of California Press, 1978.

Weinstein, James. *Ambiguous Legacy: The Left in American Politics.* New York: New Viewpoints, 1975.

Weitzer, Ronald. "Prostitutes' Rights in the United States: The Failure of a Movement" *Sociological Quarterly* 32 (1991): 23–41.

White, Deborah Gray. *Ar'n'I a Woman: Female Slaves in the Plantation South.* New York: Norton, 1985.

Williams, Terry. *The Cocaine Kids: The Inside Story of a Teenage Drug Ring.* New York: Addison-Wesley, 1989.

———. *Crack House.* New York: Addison-Wesley, 1992.

Willis, Ellen. "Feminism, Moralism, and Pornography." In *Powers of Desire: The Politics of Sexuality,* Ann Snitow, Christine Stansell, and Sharon Thompson. New York: Monthly Review, 1983.

———. *No More Nice Girls*. Hanover, N.H.: University Press of New England for Wesleyan University Press, 1992.

———. "Radical Feminism and Feminist Radicalism." In *The 60s without Apology*, edited by Sohnya Sayres et al. Minneapolis: University of Minnesota Press, 1984.

———. "Villains and Victims: 'Sexual Correctness' and the Repression of Feminism." In *"Bad Girls"/"Good Girls": Women, Sex and Power in the Nineties*, edited by Nan Bauer Maglin and Donna Perry. New Brunswick, N.J.: Rutgers University Press, 1996.

Willis, Paul. *Learning to Labour: How Working Class Kids Get Working Class Jobs*. 1977. Reprint, New York: Columbia University Press, 1981.

Wilson, William Julius. *The Truly Disadvantaged*. Chicago: University of Chicago Press, 1987.

Winick, Charles, and Paul M. Kinsie. *The Lively Commerce: Prostitution in the United States*. Chicago: Quadrangle, 1971.

Witt, Karen de. "Feminists Gather to Affirm Relevancy of Their Movement." *New York Times*, 3 February 1996, sec. 1, p. 9.

———. "New Cause Helps Feminists Appeal to Younger Women." *New York Times*, 5 February 1996, sec. 1, p. 10.

Wolf, Naomi. *The Beauty Myth: How Images of Beauty Are Used against Women*. New York: Morrow, 1991.

———. *Fire with Fire: The New Female Power and How It Could Change the Twenty-first Century*. New York: Ballantine, 1993.

Young, Iris. "Beyond the Unhappy Marriage: A Critique of the Dual Systems Theory." In *Women and Revolution: A Discussion of the Unhappy Marriage of Marxism and Feminism*, edited by Lydia Sargent. Boston: South End, 1981.

Zook, Kristal Brent. "A Manifesto of Sorts for a Black Feminist Movement." *New York Times Magazine*, 12 November 1995, 86–89.

Index

Abortion rights, 267, 296n32; backlash and, 19, 125; CARASA and, 256–257; feminism and, 33, 48, 245, 269; *Roe v. Wade* and, 68. *See also* Reproductive rights
Accused, The, 235
Adult videos, 64
Advertising, 111
Affirmative action, 290n66
African Americans, 30, 144, 145, 147, 148–149, 301n6
Against Our Will (Brownmiller), 230
Against Sadomasochism, 11, 207, 208
Age discrimination: looks-ism and, 96, 122–123, 137, 149–155; media and, 150–151, 263; of men vs. women, 84, 99, 150–151, 291n88
Aging: cosmetic surgery and, 87, 96, 135, 287n22; fear of, 87, 119–120, 135, 289n61; sexuality and, 65, 84, 99, 102, 135, 150–151
AIDS, 234
Ain't I a Woman? (hooks), 246, 269
Alcoholics Anonymous, 234
Amazon Odyssey (Atkinson), 160, 247–248
"American apartheid," 22, 38
American Booksellers Association v. Hudnut, 68

American Psycho (Easton), 72
American Society of Criminology, 183
Anorexia, 85–86, 160, 286n3
Antioch College, 229, 237
Asian American women, 87, 119
Atkinson, Ti-Grace, 29; on beauty, 160, 163; on marriage as prostitution, 178; Marxist feminism and, 253; on sadomasochism, 207; on traditional families, 34; on women as a class, 247–249, 250
Attraction: beauty vs., 90–91, 157, 165–167, 170–171; biologically-based, 95–96, 101–108, 167; as dynamic, 168–169, 170–171; looks-based, 97–101, 289n56; physical vs. social, 113–117
Autobiography of Malcolm X, 147

Backlash, 281n18; conservatism and, 19, 51, 55, 124–125, 244; defensiveness of feminism and, 19, 238, 268; defined, 233; within feminism, 10, 19, 55–57, 259; looks-ism and, 124–129; as male-dominated countermovement, 258–259; man-hating and, 45; media on, 19–20; *Morning After* (Roiphe) as part of, 12–13, 232–236; sex debates influenced by, 4, 7, 10, 18, 19–20, 62

Backlash (Faludi), 19, 55, 87, 92, 124–125, 233
Backstreets (Hoigard and Finstad), 180–181, 182, 193–194
Barnard College, Scholar and the Feminist Conference, 11, 62, 67, 207–208, 211
Barry, Kathleen, 177
Barry, Marion, 296
Bartky, Sandra, 84, 108, 162
Baudrillard, Jean, 161
Beauty: achieved, 118–120, 121, 129; attraction vs., 90–91, 157, 165–167, 170–171; biologically based, 95–96, 101–108, 167; control and, 91, 131; as cultural capital, 117–121, 126; fear of loss of, 65; health and, 91, 118, 167; images of, 8, 65, 150, 161–162, 169–170, 263; inexplicable, 99–100; intelligence and, 134–135; love and, 171; men's evaluations of, 99–100, 286n6; as physical trait, 166–167, 168, 169; pleasures of recognition vs., 167–168; race and, 87, 145–149, 162; self-worth and, 113–114, 120–121, 129, 152; technology and, 118–119, 131; third-wave feminism and, 275. *See also* Looks-ism
Beauty industry, 89, 108–111
Beauty Myth (Wolf): on backlash, 124–126; on beauty, 124–128, 157; on cosmetic surgery, 87; *Fire with Fire* (Wolf) vs., 163–164, 230, 267; limitations of argument in, 127–128; as political work, 162; popularity of, 92, 124; *Power of Beauty* (Friday) vs., 95, 157
Beauty Secrets (Chapkis), 162
Beauvoir, Simone de: on attraction, 98; on beauty, 159–160; as a feminist, 45; on marriage as prostitution, 178; on objectification of women, 82, 261; relationship with Sartre, 43–44; "second sex" described by, 209; on socialization of gender, 34, 35, 107, 226–227
Being and Nothingness (Sartre), 69
Bell Curve (Herrnstein and Murray), 96
Bellingham (Washington), antipornography laws in, 68
Benjamin, Jessica, 153, 201, 289n55, 298n21
Between Women (Rollins), 193, 222
Biological determinism: in beauty, 95–96, 101–108, 167; gender differences and, 237; gender subordination and, 31; in sadomasochism, 211–213
Birth control, 71

Bisexuality, 2, 3, 42, 273. *See also* Sexual orientation
Black Feminist Thought (Collins), 162, 270
Black Macho and the Myth of the Superwoman (Wallace), 30, 147
Blepharoplasty, 87, 119
Bly, Robert, 19
Body/Politics (ed. Martin), 107–108
Body vs. mind, 25, 100
Bordo, Susan, 84–85, 91, 93–94, 131, 160, 286n3, 286n10
Bourdieu, Pierre, 117, 119, 121, 193, 261
Bra-burning, 292n93
Brontë, Emily, 210–211
Brownmiller, Susan, 230, 231
Buchanan, Pat, 128
Bulimia, 85
Butler, Anne, 176
Butler, Judith, 121
Butler v. the Queen, 68, 71

Califia, Pat, 11, 207, 212–213, 217
California, prostitutes' rights in, 176–177
Cambridge (Massachusetts), antipornography laws in, 68
Canada, antipornography laws in, 9, 64, 68, 71–72
Capital: bodily, 117, 289n61; cultural, 117–121, 126; sexual, 193, 195, 261–263
Capitalism: beauty industry and, 109–111; gender/class relationships within, 13, 242–243, 262–263; global, 128–129; liberal feminism on, 244–246, 254; as male-dominated, 242–243, 262; Marxist feminism on, 254–256; radical feminism against, 246–251, 262–263, 268; sadomasochistic character of, 221–222, 227; socialist feminism on, 253–256; social movements against, 241–242; women as property in, 260–261
CARASA (Committee for Abortion Rights and Against Sterilization Abuse), 256–257, 262, 301n7
Carby, Hazel, 269
Carmen, Arlene, 179–180, 184, 190, 196
Carmichael, Stokely, 30
Censorship: of popular culture, 72; Supreme Court on, 69; used against women, 70–71
Center for the Study of Anorexia and Bulimia (New York), 84–85
Chancer, Lynn, 11, 213–214

Chapkis, Wendy: on beauty, 162–163, 164, 165; on feminist divisions, 3–4, 21; sex workers studied by, 21, 198, 199
Chernin, Kim, 160
Child care, 48, 245, 248, 274
Chodorow, Nancy, 153, 154, 237
Civil rights, 6, 21–22, 268
Class: death and, 122; good woman/bad woman dichotomies and, 140–143; of liberal feminists, 245–246, 300–301n3; looks-ism and, 83–84, 91–92, 112–123, 132–144, 154–156, 171–172, 286n5, 290n74; postmodernism and, 243; prostitution and, 195; race and, 6, 145–146, 249–250; women as a, 31–32, 47–48, 242, 243–244, 246–249, 250, 262–263
Class discrimination, 6, 26, 35–36, 37–38, 249–250, 273
Cleaver, Eldridge, 30, 147
Cleveland Art Museum, 71
Clinique, 109
Clinton, Bill, 128, 267, 270, 281n18
Clinton, Hillary Rodham, 55, 281n18
Cocaine Kids (Williams), 193, 296n35
Codependency, 225
COINTELPRO (Counter Intelligence Program), 22, 241
Collins, Patricia Hill, 52, 162, 250, 269–270, 300n7
Coming to Power, 207
Committee for Abortion Rights and Against Sterilization Abuse (CARASA), 256–257, 262, 301n7
Communism, 21, 112, 241, 243, 299n3
Comparable worth, 252
Connell, R. W., 7, 115, 129–130, 141
Conservatism, 162; backlash and, 19, 51, 55, 124–125, 244; pornography and, 21, 63–64, 68, 69, 73; sadomasochism and, 203, 227–228
Corbin, Alain, 176
Cosmetics, 88–89, 158
Cosmetic surgery: to achieve beauty, 118–119; aging and, 87, 96, 135, 287n22; judging women who elect, 129; prevalence of, 87–88; racial discrimination and, 87; sex debates on, 9–10, 50, 94–95, 96, 156, 287–288n31, 288n35
Counter Intelligence Program (COINTELPRO), 22, 241
Cowley, Geoffrey, 95–96
COYOTE (Call Off Your Old Tired Ethics), 177
Crime, organized, 220–221

Critique of Dialectical Reason (Sartre), 285n26
Cultural feminism, 161–162
Culture. See Imagery; Media; Popular culture

Date rape, 12, 186, 229–230, 235–236
Daughters, mothers and, 151–154, 291n87
Davis, Angela, 266, 269
Davis, Kathy: on cosmetic surgery, 9–10, 87, 88, 94, 118, 135, 156, 287n19, 288n35; Morgan vs., 94, 156
Death: class and, 122; fear of, 106–107, 119–120, 122, 131; sadomasochism and, 204–205
Deceptive Deceptions (Epstein), 236–237
Deconstructionism, 161
Defending Pornography (Strossen), 9, 21, 62–64, 65–66, 67–74, 80
de Lauretis, Teresa, 161
Denton, Nancy, 22, 38
Depression, 85–86
Deutsch, Helene, 211–212
Diagnostic and Statistical Manual, 200
Dialectic of Sex, The (Firestone), 37, 160, 246–247, 268
Dieting, 89, 131, 286n10
Discrimination. See Age discrimination; Class discrimination; Gender discrimination; Oppression; Racial discrimination
Domestic violence: feminism and, 269, 271; heterosexuality and, 42–43, 49; resources for, 47, 263; as sadomasochistic dynamic, 224–225. See also Violence against women
Domestic workers, 193, 222–223
Dominelli, Lena, 177
Double standards, 2, 140–143
Drug dealing, 193, 195, 197, 296n35
Duggan, Lisa, 21
Durkheim, Emile, 75, 83, 166, 281n17
Dworkin, Andrea: antipornography laws inspired by, 64, 68, 71, 72, 284n10; conservatism and, 63–64, 73; critics of, 23, 75; demonization of, 81; on imagery, 80, 283–284n3; on pornography, 9, 10–11, 63–64, 66–67, 73, 79, 81, 231, 283–284n3; radical feminism and, 20, 66–67, 81; on sadomasochism, 207, 210–211, 212; supporters of, 66–67, 73–74, 78; on "Uncle Toms," 18; victim feminism and, 231

Easton, Bret Ellis, 72
Eating disorders, 85–86, 160, 286n2

Echols, Alice, 9, 207–208, 232
Eisenstein, Zillah, 51, 245, 248
"Emotional labor," 221
Employment, fear of losing, 221
Engels, Friedrich: on elimination of op-
    pression, 247; Firestone on, 246–247,
    259; on gender subordination, 260,
    261–262; on labeling women as ma-
    donnas or whores, 189; on marriage as
    prostitution, 178; Marxist feminism
    and, 252, 254, 259; radical feminism
    and, 259–262
Epstein, Cynthia, 236–237
Equality, liberal feminism on, 244–246,
    270
Essentialism, 12, 215, 236–237, 249
Eulenspiegel society, 217
Evans, Sarah, 30
Existentialism, 70–71, 75
Eyelid surgery, 87, 119

Face of Love (Lambert), 165
Face Value (Scherr), 162–163, 164
FACT (Feminist Anti-Censorship Task-
    force), 64, 67
Faludi, Susan: on backlash, 10, 19, 55,
    124–126, 127, 244, 258–259; on
    beauty, 124–128; on cosmetic surgery,
    87; popularity of, 92
Families: ideology of, 33–36; radical femi-
    nism on, 31, 33–36, 243–244; sexism
    within, 271; single parent, 35–36,
    248
Family values, 19, 35, 125, 244, 296n33
Fashion-beauty complex, 84, 108–109,
    162
FBI, 6, 22, 56, 241
Female Sexual Slavery (Barry), 177
Femininity, masculinity vs., 6, 25, 136
Feminism: ambivalence over, 272; back-
    lash within, 10, 19, 55–57, 259; as col-
    lective movement, 17–18, 48–51, 265–
    266, 271–272; commonalities vs. dif-
    ferences among women in, 25–26, 29,
    31–32, 35–36, 37, 40–41, 48–50, 257–
    258, 267–274, 300n16; connection
    and autonomy of, 273; cultural, 161–
    162; defensiveness of, 4, 17, 19, 29,
    66, 236, 238, 265, 268; economic vs.
    sexual issues in, 66, 80–81, 267, 270–
    271, 274, 300–301n3; either/or dichot-
    omies in, 56, 66, 73, 268, 272–274,
    275, 277n4, 278n6, 280n6; gender sub-
    ordination and, 28–29; generational
    solidarity in, 151–152; history of, 29–
    36, 268–269; lesbians and, 187, 273;
    libertarian, 277n2–3; man-hating in,

40–41, 45, 282n15; media influenced
    by, 86; polarization of positions in,
    18–19; postmodernism and, 19, 25–
    26; rape-crisis, 234–235; relative em-
    phases in, 3–4, 17, 62, 267, 270, 274;
    social movements and, 13, 30, 243,
    273; splitting within, 21–24, 28–29,
    51–58; structure vs. agency in, 4–5,
    24–25, 46–52, 57; in theory vs. prac-
    tice of, 5, 24–25, 46–52; weakening of,
    13–14, 41, 258–259, 271–272; women
    of color in, 30, 273. See also Liberal
    feminism; Marxist feminism; Power
    feminism; Radical feminism; Second-
    wave feminism; Sex debates; Social
    feminism; Third-wave feminism; Vic-
    tim feminism
Feminist Anti-Censorship Taskforce
    (FACT), 64, 67
Feminists, The, 158, 246, 263
Feminist Theory (hooks), 246, 269
Ferguson, Ann, 277n1–3
Film industry, 150–151, 291n88
Finstad, Liv, 180–181, 191, 193–194
Firestone, Shulamith, 29; on beauty, 160,
    163; on capitalism, 268; on Engels,
    246–247, 259; on gender as "deepest"
    form of oppression, 37; on marriage as
    prostitution, 178; Marxist feminism
    and, 253; as standpoint theorist, 247,
    300n7; on women as a class, 31, 247,
    250
Fire with Fire (Wolf), 18, 61, 163–164,
    230–231, 267
Fitness, 91, 118
Fitzgerald, F. Scott, 168
Foucault, Michel, 82, 161, 200–201,
    202, 203
Fraser, Donald, 68
Freedom of Information Act (FOIA),
    22
Freud, Sigmund, 154, 211, 212, 215,
    297n14
Friday, Nancy, 95, 157
Friedan, Betty, 245, 290n68
Fromm, Erich, 201

Galbraith, John Kenneth, 109
Gangs, 174, 175, 193, 195
Gender/class relationship, 13, 242–243,
    262–263. See also Class
Gender differences, 236–237
Gender discrimination, 6, 24, 249–250,
    271–272, 273. See also Gender subor-
    dination; Sexism
Gender gap, 50
Gender relations: clichés in, 114; domi-

nant/subordinate character of, 237; sadomasochistic dynamics in, 224–227. *See also* Heterosexuality
Gender subordination: biological determinism and, 31; feminism and, 28–29; heterosexuality and, 7, 37, 38–39; labor and, 254, 255–256, 260; objectification of women and, 260–262; private property and, 260–261; race/class discrimination and, 35–36; radical feminism on, 32–33
Gender Trouble (Butler), 121
Germany, cosmetic surgery in, 87
Giddings, Paula, 269
Gilligan, Carol, 237
Gingrich, Newt, 201, 202, 203
Glamour, 85
Goldberg, Stephen, 105
Goldman, Emma, 71
Good Girls/Bad Girls, 177
Good woman/bad woman dichotomies: class and, 140–143; heterosexuality and, 140–143; looks-ism and, 140–143; male fantasies and, 141–142, 226, 291n79; prostitution and, 188–191, 195, 197; racial discrimination and, 144–146, 162; sadomasochism and, 226
Gramsci, Antonio, 76, 77
Great Britain: cosmetic surgery in, 87; prostitution in, 177
Great Gatsby, The (Fitzgerald), 168

Hall, Stuart, 19, 20, 75–76
Halprin, Sara, 165
Handsomeness, 115
Harding, Sandra, 250, 300n7
Hartmann, Heidi, 253–255, 260
Hartsock, Nancy, 52, 250, 300n7
Health, 91, 118, 167
Health care, 248
Hegemony, 76, 77; beauty imagery and, 75–76; masculinity and, 115, 136; in pornography, 77–78, 79, 80
Herrnstein, Richard, 96
Heterosexuality: compulsory, 33, 137–138, 139, 269, 271; domestic violence and, 42–43, 49; double standards in, 2, 140–143; gender subordination and, 7, 37, 38–39; good woman/bad woman dichotomies in, 140–143; looks-ism and, 8, 84, 136–140; pornography and, 78; radical feminism on, 37, 39, 45–46; relationships in, 3, 37, 38–40, 42–46, 47, 48–49; reproduction and, 102–103; second-wave feminism on, 31. *See also* Gender relations

Heyl, Barbara, 178
Hill, Anita, 282n15
Hobson, Barbara, 176
Hochschild, Arlie Russell, 221
Hoigard, Cecilie, 180–181, 191, 193–194
Homosexuality. *See* Lesbians
hooks, bell, 52, 144, 246, 269–270
Hoover, J. Edgar, 6, 13, 23, 56, 241, 263–264
Hustler, 64
Hyde Amendment of 1976, 245

Image, women as, 161–162
Imagery: of beauty, 8, 65, 150, 161–162, 169–170, 263; clichés in, 114; effects of, 75, 76–77, 80; hegemony and, 75–76; in popular culture, 8, 75–76, 80, 161–162; in pornography, 67, 75–77, 80; transforming, 161, 164, 169–170. *See also* Media
Indianapolis, antipornography laws in, 68, 284n10
Individualism, 205
Inland Books, 71
Intelligence, sexuality and, 134–135, 290n75
Is It Love or Is It Addiction? (Schaeffer), 225

Jungle Fever, 148

Kaw, Eugenia, 87
Kinsie, Paul, 178, 179–180
Kiss of the Spider Woman, 219, 285n27
Koedt, Anne, 29, 163

Labeling Women Deviant (Schur), 89
Labor, 254, 255–256, 260
Lakoff, Robin, 162–163, 164, 165
Lambert, Ellen Zetzel, 165
Learning to Labor (P. Willis), 194
Lee, Spike, 148, 149
Leftist social movements, 6, 21–24, 241, 246
Lesbians: discrimination against, 2, 3, 40; feminism and, 187, 273; looks-ism and, 138–140; in pornography, 78; relationships with men, 41–42; rights of, 48, 262. *See also* Sexual orientation
Levine, Judith, 40–41, 282n15
Lewis, Michael, 223
Liberal feminism: backlash and, 51, 55; on capitalism, 244–246, 254; class and, 245–246, 300–301n3; on equality, 244–246, 270; radical feminism vs., 51, 55, 247

Libertarian-feminism, 277n2–3
Lively Commerce (Winick and Kinsie), 178, 182
Live Sex Acts (Chapkis), 21, 198
Look at My Ugly Face! (Halprin), 165
Looks-ism: age discrimination and, 96, 122–123, 137, 149–155; backlash and, 124–129; as class system, 83–84, 91–92, 112–123, 132–144, 154–156, 171–172, 286n5, 290n74; cultural feminism on, 161–162; as damaging, 97, 164–165; defined, 83–84; eating disorders and, 85–86, 160, 286n3; economic class and, 142–144; fears of death and, 106–107, 119–120, 122, 131; feminist influences on, 92, 124; feminist protests against, 157–159; between generations of women, 151–154; good woman/bad woman dichotomies in, 140–143; heterosexuality and, 8, 84, 136–140; masculinity and, 114–116, 129–130; men vs. women and, 83–84, 115–117, 126–130, 164–165, 289n56, 289n60; mind vs. body in, 100; persistence of, 121–124; political feminist works on, 162–166; racial discrimination and, 87, 145–149, 162, 290n66; radical feminism on, 157–160; sex debates on, 9–10, 92–97, 155–156, 157; sexual orientation and, 8, 84, 138–140; as social fact, 83–84, 111, 121, 124, 136, 156, 166; socialist feminism on, 162; socialization of, 104–105, 107–108, 111–112; types of, 160; worsening of, 82–83, 84–90, 124, 128–131, 163. *See also* Beauty
Lorber, Judith, 7
Love, 112, 171
Lyotard, Jean-François, 161

MacDworkinism, 18, 21, 70, 74, 285n24
MacKinnon, Catherine, 29; antipornography laws inspired by, 64, 68, 71, 284n10; conservatism and, 21, 63–64, 73; critics of, 21, 23, 75; on debating feminists, 20–21, 52–53; demonization of, 23, 81; on imagery, 80, 283–284n3; on pornography, 9, 10–11, 21, 63–64, 66–67, 73, 79, 81, 283–284n3; on prostitution, 186; radical feminism and, 20, 23, 66–67, 81; on rape correlated with pornography, 70; supporters of, 66–67, 73–74, 78; on "Uncle Toms," 18, 23, 67; victim feminism and, 231
Madam as Entrepreneur (Heyl), 178, 181, 200

Madonna, 9, 93–94, 96, 122, 157, 195, 200
Madonna Connection, The, 93
Mailer, Norman, 105
Makeup. *See* Cosmetics
Malcolm X, 30, 147
Male-dominated societies: capitalism and, 242–243, 262; patriarchy vs., 7; sexuality and sexism in, 3. *See also* Patriarchy
Managed Heart, The (Hochschild), 221
Man-hating, 40–41, 45, 282n15
Mapplethorpe, Robert, 71
Marriage, 34, 38, 178, 255, 260, 286n4
Martin, Emily, 107–108
Marx, Karl: on class, 166, 247; on elimination of oppression, 247; on gender subordination, 260, 261–262; on social change, 162; on social psychology, 221–222
Marxism: beauty industry and, 109, 111; inadequacy of, 241; postmodernism vs., 49; sadomasochism and, 221–222, 226; on social distinctions, 121
Marxist feminism: on capitalism, 254–256; on comparable worth, 252; criticism of, 252; differences between women emphasized in, 251–252; emergence of, 242; Engels and, 252, 254, 259; race and, 252; radical feminism vs., 251–252; socialist feminism vs., 252–256, 258, 259
Masculinity, 13; dominant/subordinate relationships in, 285n30; femininity vs., 6, 25, 136; feminism and, 126; hegemonic, 115, 136; looks-ism and, 114–116, 129–130; marginalized, 129–130; sadism and, 209. *See also* Men
Masochism, 211–213, 215–216. *See also* Sadomasochism
Massey, Douglas, 22, 38
Material Girls (Walters), 158, 161
Media: advertising, 111; age discrimination and, 150–151, 263; on backlash, 19–20; family ideals in, 34; feminist influences on, 86; images of women in, 161–162; objectivity of, 19–20, 280n9; sadomasochism in, 200–201, 202–203, 206, 225; on sex debates, 12, 19–21, 62, 230, 287–288n31; women's control of, 263. *See also* Imagery; Popular culture
Medicaid, 257
Meese Commission, 64
Men: aging and, 84, 99, 150–151, 291n88; on beauty, 99–100, 286n6;

fantasies of, 78, 141–142, 226, 291n79; feminism and, 126; as head of households, 35; looks-ism and, 83–84, 115–117, 126–130, 164–165, 289n56, 289n60; naturally aggressive, 236–237; power of, 285n30; propertied, 262; prostitution arrests of, 181, 190–191, 296n33; prostitution by, 181; prostitution studies of, 181–182; socialism and, 249; in third-wave feminism, 13. *See also* Masculinity

Men's movement, 19

Men's studies, 164–165, 182

Merton, Robert, 193

Miller, Eleanor, 178–179, 183

Millett, Kate, 29; on beauty, 159–160; on gender as "deepest" form of oppression, 37; Mailer on, 105; on male dominance, 208; on marriage as prostitution, 178; Marxist feminism and, 253; on patriarchy, 7; on traditional families, 34

Millman, Marcia, 160

Mind vs. body, 25, 100

Minneapolis (Minnesota), antipornography legislation in, 68, 284n10

Miss America Pageant, 158–159, 162

Mitchell, Juliet, 253

Mobilization theories, 188

Modleski, Tania, 161

Moody, Howard, 179–180, 184, 190, 196

Morgan, Kathryn, 94, 156, 163

Morning After (Roiphe): as backlash, 12–13, 232–236; media attention paid to, 12, 20, 229, 230; methodological and theoretical flaws in, 235; structure vs. agency in, 233; on victim feminism, 229–232; on violence against women, 12–13, 229–230, 236–238; Wolf on, 230–231

Mortality. *See* Death

Mothers: daughters and, 151–154, 291n87; single, 35–36, 248

Mulvey, Laura, 161

Mundane sexism, 46

Murakawa, Naomi, 87

Murray, Charles, 96

My Enemy, My Love (Levine), 40–41

National Abortion Rights Action League (NARAL), 256–257

National Organization for Women (NOW), 187, 245, 256–257

Netherlands: cosmetic surgery in, 87, 88, 287n19; prostitution in, 191

Nevada, prostitution in, 191

Newsweek, 95–96

New York, antipornography laws in, 68

New York Center for the Study of Anorexia and Bulimia, 84–85

New York magazine, 200, 202–203, 206, 225, 228

New York Times, 20

New York University conference (1987), 67

"No More Miss America," 158–159, 162

Norway, prostitution studied in, 180–181

NOW (National Organization for Women), 187, 245, 256–257

Obesity, 167

Objectification of women, 8, 82, 157, 256, 260–262

Ohrbach, Susie, 160

Only Words (MacKinnon), 80

Oppression: elimination of, 247, 248–251, 258, 263, 268; ranking, 30, 37, 251

Organized crime, 220–221

Origin of the Family, Private Property, and the State (Engels), 246–247, 252, 259–262

Ortner, Sherry, 208–209

Paglia, Camille, 95

Parsons, Talcott, 118, 119

Patriarchy: capitalist, 253–256; defined, 208, 255; male-dominated societies vs., 7; pornography and, 76–77, 79; rape and, 230; sadomasochistic, 206, 208–213, 227; sex and sexism within, 263; sexual repression under, 32–33; sexual vs. economic controls under, 255–256; structural enormity of, 54; structure vs. agency in, 25; usage of term, 243, 248, 251, 255; women as property under, 260–261. *See also* Male-dominated societies

Pay equity, 126, 244, 245

Peirce, Kate, 86

Penthouse, 64

Personal Politics (Evans), 30

Pheterson, Gail, 185

Pipher, Mary, 85–86

Planned Parenthood, 256

Playboy, 64

Pleasers, The (Leman), 225

Political correctness, 207, 229, 235, 237

Pollitt, Katha, 235

Popular culture: censorship of, 72; imagery in, 8, 75–76, 80, 161–162; pornog-

Popular culture *(continued)*
  raphy in, 75–77; sadomasochism in,
  200–201, 225, 228. *See also* Media
Pornography: alienation of women by,
  64, 78–79; anticensorship views and,
  66, 67–74, 79–80; civil liberties threatened by censorship of, 65, 70–71; conservatism and, 21, 63–64, 68, 69, 73;
  domination/subordination in, 77–78;
  effects of, 69–70, 73, 75, 76–77; enjoyed by women, 74; hegemonic, 77–
  78, 79, 80; heterosexuality and, 78; imagery in, 67, 75–77, 80; laws against,
  64, 65–66, 68–69, 71–72, 73, 284n10,
  284n13; lesbians in, 78; as male-dominated business, 9, 64, 77–78; male fantasies depicted in, 78; objectionable,
  74, 76–77, 79; patriarchal character
  of, 76–77, 79; in popular culture, 75–
  77; procensorship views and, 63–64,
  66, 73–74, 75–79; rape correlated
  with, 70; sadomasochistic dynamics in,
  285n31; sex debates on, 9, 20, 50, 62–
  67, 77, 80–81; sexual orientation and,
  8; sexual repression by censorship of,
  63, 67–68, 70–71; as single issue in
  feminism, 68, 71–72, 73–74, 80–81;
  third-wave feminism and, 275; videos,
  64; women's control of, 48, 77–78,
  80–81
Pornography (Dworkin), 72
Pornography Victims' Compensation
  Act, 68
Postmodernism: class and, 243; feminism
  and, 19, 25–26; Marxism vs., 49; sadomasochism and, 202
Poverty, 248, 262
Power, sadomasochism and, 214–215,
  218–219, 223–224, 226
Power feminism: defined, 231; third-
  wave feminism as, 267; victim feminism vs., 18, 163–164, 230–231, 238,
  267
Power of Beauty (Friday), 95, 157
Powers of Desire, 207
Princeton University, 234
Programme for the Reform of the Law
  on Soliciting, 177
Property: gender subordination and,
  260–261; women as, 260–261
Prostitutes' rights movement, 188
Prostitution: as alienating, 180; ambivalence over, 176, 177, 183–184, 185–
  188, 195–196; as antifeminist, 185–
  186; arrests in, 181, 190–191, 296n33;
  class and, 195; dangers in, 174–175;
  decriminalization of, 10, 177, 180,

190–192, 196; economically motivated, 193, 196, 296n34; in feminist
  theory, 175–176, 177, 185–188, 190–
  192; gay liberation vs., 187–188; good
  woman/bad woman dichotomies and,
  188–191, 195, 197; literature review
  of, 176–184; male, 181; male clients
  studied in, 181–182, 295n22; marriage
  as, 178; participant observation research on, 10, 173–175, 179, 184–
  185, 197, 198–199, 295n20, 295n22;
  power in, 193–194; professionalization
  of, 192; prostitutes judged in, 179,
  180, 194, 195–196; prostitutes' writings on, 10, 176–177; rape and, 186–
  187, 295n25; sex debates on, 10–11,
  177, 185–188; sex-economic exchanges in, 191–196; socialist feminism on, 177–178; sociological studies
  of, 173–176, 177–184, 194–195, 198–
  199; studies of vs. studies of prostitutes, 181, 182–183, 186, 196–197;
  United States studies of, 180, 182, 198,
  294n3; venereal diseases and, 179–
  180; as victimless crime, 295n19. *See
  also* Sex work; Sex workers
Prostitution and Feminist Theory (Chancer), 197
Psychology of Women (Deutsch), 211–
  212
Puig, Manuel, 285n27

Quayle, Dan, 73

Race: beauty and, 87, 145–149, 162;
  class and, 6, 145–146, 249–250; gender vs., 24, 270; Marxist and socialist
  feminism on, 252
Racial discrimination: cosmetic surgery
  and, 87; gender discrimination and,
  24, 26, 37–38, 270; gender subordination and, 35–36; good woman/bad
  woman dichotomies and, 144–146,
  162; looks-ism and, 87, 145–149, 162,
  290n66
Racial segregation, 22, 38
Radical feminism: on beauty, 157–160;
  against capitalism, 246–251, 262–263,
  268; emergence of, 30–32; Engels and,
  259–262; essentialism and, 249; on
  families, 31, 33–36, 243–244; on gender subordination, 32–33; on heterosexuality, 37, 39, 45–46; history of,
  232–233, 268–269; liberal feminism
  vs., 51, 55, 247; MacKinnon and
  Dworkin associated with, 20, 23, 66–
  67, 81; man-hating in, 45; Marxist and

socialist feminism vs., 251–252; against oppression, 248–251, 258, 263, 268; "personal is political" in, 43; on rape, 230; sadomasochism and, 210; sex radical feminism vs., 3–4; in theory vs. practice of, 46–52; as victim feminism, 230; women as a class in, 31–32, 47–48, 242, 243–244, 246–249, 250, 262–263. *See also* Second-wave feminism

Radical Future of Liberal Feminism, The (Eisenstein), 51, 248

Rape: date, 12, 186, 229–230, 235–236; fantasies among women, 237–238; patriarchy and, 230; pornography correlated with, 70; prostitution and, 186–187, 295n25; radical feminism on, 230; rapists' attitudes on, 291n79, 299n10; victim blaming in, 237–238; as violent vs. sexual crime, 235, 237. *See also* Violence against women

Rape-crisis feminism, 234–235

Réage, Pauline, 207, 216, 289n55

Redstockings, 158, 246, 263

Reproduction, 31, 102–103, 211–212

"Reproduction of mothering," 153–154

Reproductive rights, 13–14, 48, 51, 245, 256–257, 268–269, 301n7

Reshaping the Female Body (K. Davis), 9–10, 94

Reviving Ophelia (Pipher), 85–86

Rhode, Deborah, 75

Rich, Adrienne, 33, 137, 139, 187, 269

Right to Life movement, 125

Roe v. Wade, 68

Roiphe, Katie: on Brownmiller, 230; on date rape, 229–230, 235; media attention to, 12, 20, 229, 230; as symbolic of backlash against feminism, 12–13, 232–236; on victim feminism, 229–232; on violence against women, 12–13, 229–230, 236–238; Wolf on, 230–231

Rollins, Judith, 174, 193, 222

Romance novels, 225

Rosen, Ruth, 176, 190

Roth, Philip, 146

Rubin, Gayle, 11, 177–178, 181, 207, 217

Rust, Paula, 42

Sacher-Masoch, Leopold von, 216

Sadism, 209–211. *See also* Sadomasochism

Sadomasochism: biological determinism and, 211–213; in capitalism, 221–222, 227; conservatism and, 203, 227–228; death and, 204–205; defined, 214–216; desires in, 12, 204–205, 228; dual character of, 201–205; essentialism and, 215; in everyday life, 11–12, 204, 213–227; good woman/bad woman dichotomies and, 226; Mapplethorpe and, 71; Marxism and, 221–222, 226; masochism in, 211–213, 215–216; in media, 200–201, 202–203, 206, 225; patriarchy and, 206, 208–213, 227; in popular culture, 200–201, 225, 228; postmodernism and, 202; radical feminism and, 210; sadism in, 209–211; sex debates on, 11–12, 203, 204, 206–214, 227–228; sexual orientation and, 3, 8; sexual repression and, 207–208; sexual vs. social, 201–214, 227–228; in social theories, 201; third-wave feminism and, 275; victimization of women and, 215–216

Sadomasochism in Everyday Life (Chancer), 11, 213–214

Sadomasochistic dynamics: characteristics of, 216–220; defined, 214; dependency in, 204–205, 217–219, 220, 225, 226–227; domestic violence as, 224–225; in gender relations, 224–227; hierarchical relationships in, 216–217, 220–221, 298n20; internally transformable, 215–216, 218–219, 222–223, 226; mutual recognition in, 219–220, 223–224, 226–227, 298n21; in pornography, 285n31; power relations in, 214–215, 218–219, 223–224, 226; push/pull character of, 219, 225–226, 227; sexual harassment as, 221; threats as underlying, 217, 221, 224–225; in workplace, 220–224

Samois, 207–208

Sanchez-Jankowski, Martin, 174, 194

Sanger, Margaret, 71, 256

Sartre, Jean-Paul, 43–44, 69, 75, 285n26

Scherr, Raquel, 162–163, 164, 165

Scholar and the Feminist Conference (Barnard College), 11, 62, 67, 207–208, 211

Schrage, Laurie, 185–186, 187, 191

Schur, Edwin, 89, 295n19

Schwichtenberg, Cathy, 93

Scully, Diana, 291n79, 299n10

Second Sex, The (Beauvoir): on beauty, 159–160; feminism since, 82; on objectification, 261; Sartre's encouragement of, 43–44; on socialization of gender, 34, 35, 226–227

Second Stage, The (Friedan), 245

Second-wave feminism: criticism of, 266–
    267; emergence of, 30–32, 128, 268;
    on heterosexuality, 31; history of, 232–
    233; standpoint theories in, 247, 250–
    251, 300n7; third-wave feminism on,
    266–267. *See also* Radical feminism
Segal, Lynne, 279n20
Self-esteem, 164
Senate Judiciary Committee, 68
Service industry, 221
Seventeen magazine, 86
Sex, labor and, 255–256
Sex (Madonna), 93, 200
Sex debates: backlash and, 4, 7, 10, 18,
    19–20, 62; bridging over, 3–4, 8–9,
    25–27; on cosmetic surgery, 9–10, 50,
    94–95, 96, 156, 287–288n31, 288n35;
    economic issues vs., 66, 80–81, 270–
    271, 274; either/or dichotomies in, 5–
    6, 18–19, 24–25; emergence of, 46; em-
    phases in, 3–4, 17, 62, 267, 270, 274;
    feminism weakened by, 13–14; issues
    in, 7–8; on looks-ism, 9–10, 92–97,
    155–156, 157; media on, 12, 19–21,
    62, 230, 287–288n31; on pornogra-
    phy, 9, 50, 62–67, 77, 80–81; on prosti-
    tution, 10–11, 177, 185–188; on sado-
    masochism, 11–12, 203, 204, 206–
    214, 227–228; sexism strengthened by,
    10; on sexual freedom vs. sexism, 1–4,
    8–9, 52, 61–62, 65, 277n1–3; sexual
    orientation and, 3; on sex work, 10–
    11; splitting in, 18, 21–24; structure
    vs. agency in, 4–5, 8, 18, 24–25, 233;
    in third-wave feminism, 266, 275; on
    victim feminism, 230–231; on violence
    against women, 12–13, 230, 238
Sexism: as commonality among women,
    271–272; in families, 271; mundane,
    46; sexual freedom vs., 1–4, 8–9, 52,
    61–62, 65, 277n1–3. *See also* Sex de-
    bates
"Sex radical feminism," 3–4
Sex therapy, 192
Sexual assault. *See* Rape
Sexual capital, 193, 195, 261–263
Sexual freedom, sexism vs., 1–4, 8–9, 52,
    61–62, 65, 277n1–3. *See also* Sex de-
    bates; Sexual repression
Sexual harassment, 186, 221, 255, 263,
    269, 271
Sexuality: aging and, 65, 84, 99, 102,
    135, 150–151; intelligence and, 134–
    135, 290n75; pleasure and, 103–104,
    279n20; racism and, 144; reproduction
    vs., 102–103; socialist feminism on,
    253; studies on, 197–199

Sexual Liberals and the Attack on Radi-
    cal Feminism conference, 67
Sexual orientation: commonalities among
    women vs., 41; individual experiences
    of, 48–49; looks-ism and, 8, 84, 138–
    140; pornography and, 8; relationships
    with men and, 41–42; reproduction
    and, 102–103; sadomasochism and, 3,
    8; sex debates and, 3. *See also* Lesbians
Sexual Politics (Millett), 37, 105, 159–
    160
Sexual repression: by censorship of por-
    nography, 63, 67–68, 70–71; under pa-
    triarchy, 32–33; sadomasochism and,
    207–208
Sex wars, 277n1. *See also* Sex debates
*Sex Wars: Sexual Dissent and Political
    Culture* (ed. Duggan), 21
Sex work: as male-dominated business,
    64, 77–78; sex debates on, 10–11; stud-
    ies on, 21, 175, 182–183, 197–199;
    third-wave feminism and, 275; wom-
    en's control of, 77–78, 80–81. *See also*
    Pornography; Prostitution; Sex
    workers
*Sex Work: Writings by Women in the Sex
    Industry,* 177
Sex workers, 255; class and, 142–143;
    degradation of, 185; employer/em-
    ployee relationships of, 193–194; good
    woman/bad woman dichotomies and,
    141–143; as professionals, 192; sup-
    port for, 50, 74, 263; third-wave femi-
    nism and, 275. *See also* Pornography;
    Prostitution; Sex work
Single mothers, 35–36, 248
Slavery, 38, 144
Smith, William Kennedy, 12
Snitow, Ann, 64
Soap operas, 225
Socialism, 249–250, 299n3
Socialist feminism: on beauty, 162; on
    capitalist patriarchy, 253–256; dual vs.
    unified theories in, 253–254; emer-
    gence of, 242; on Engels, 259; Marxist
    feminism vs., 252–256, 258, 259; on
    prostitution, 177–178; radical femi-
    nism vs., 251–252; on reproductive
    rights, 256–257; on sexuality, 253
Social movements: against capitalism,
    241–242; class- vs. gender-based, 243;
    defensiveness of, 235; feminism and,
    13, 30, 243, 273; gender and race in,
    24; infiltration of, 6, 22, 56; Leftist, 6,
    21–24, 241, 246; marginalization of,
    22, 23; against oppression in general,
    248–251, 263, 268; sexism within,

268; splitting within, 6, 18, 21–24, 54–55; structure vs. agency in, 4–5, 278n9
Sociology, prostitution studies in, 173–176, 177–184, 194–195, 198–199
Soul on Ice (Cleaver), 147
South Africa, apartheid in, 38
Speaking of Sex (Rhode), 75
Steinem, Gloria, 95, 266, 301n5
Sterilization abuse, 13–14, 48, 256, 262, 301n7
Story of O (Réage), 207, 216, 289n55
Street Woman (Miller), 178–179, 183
Strossen, Nadine: on censorship used against women, 70–71; on imagery, 76; on MacDworkinism, 18, 21, 70, 74, 285n24; on pornography, 9, 62–74, 79, 80, 81, 283–284n3, 284n10, 284n13
Students for a Democratic Society, 22
Suffolk County (New York), antipornography laws in, 68
Suicide, 285n27
Sullivan, Mercer, 194
Supreme Court (Canada), 9, 68
Supreme Court (United States), 68, 69, 284n13
Sweeney, John, 128
Synanon, 234

Take Back the Night demonstrations, 234
Third-wave feminism: commonalities and differences among women in, 13–14, 266–268, 270, 274–276; democratization in, 265; men in, 13; power feminism as, 267; as revitalization of feminism, 27, 57–58, 265–266, 275–276; on second-wave feminism, 266–267; sex debates in, 266, 275; sexual and economic issues in, 274–275; usage of term, 266–267, 279n22; younger generation and, 266–267
Thomas, Clarence, 282n15
Thompson, Becky, 85, 87, 160
Three Essays on the Theory of Sexuality (Freud), 211, 215
To Be Real (ed. Walker), 266–267
Tong, Rosemary, 252
Two Live Crew, 71
Tyson, Mike, 12

Unbearable Weight (Bordo), 84–85, 131
Unions, 221

Vance, Carol, 9, 64, 207
Venereal disease, 179–180

Venus in Furs (Sacher-Masoch), 216
Victim feminism: defined, 230, 231; power feminism vs., 18, 163–164, 230–231, 238, 267; radical feminism as, 230; sex debates on, 230–231; violence against women and, 12, 230, 234–236
Victimization, sadomasochism and, 215–216
Videos, adult, 64
Vindication of the Rights of Whores, A (Pheterson), 177, 185
Violence against women: domestic, 42–43, 47, 49, 224–225, 263, 269, 271; essentialism and, 12, 236–237; feminism and, 244, 268–269, 271; as focus of feminism, 12, 238; laws against, 8; prevalence of, 235; sex debates on, 12–13, 230, 238; third-wave feminism and, 275; victim feminism and, 12, 230, 234–236. *See also* Rape

Wacquant, Loic J. D., 174
Walker, Rebecca, 266
Walkowitz, Judith, 176, 190
Wallace, Michele, 29, 30, 147, 301n6
Walters, Suzanna Danuta, 158, 161, 164, 291n87
WAP (Women Against Pornography), 63, 190, 207
Washington, antipornography laws in, 68
Weathermen, 21–22
Weber, Max, 112
Weitzer, Ronald, 188
Welfare, 48, 51, 66, 80–81, 267, 270, 274
White, Deborah Gray, 269
Whore (term), 189
Williams, Terry, 174, 193, 194, 196, 296n35
Willis, Ellen, 29, 67, 282n15; on mundane sexism, 46; on pornography, 9, 63–64, 67; on sadomasochism, 207–208
Willis, Paul, 99, 194
Winick, Charles, 178, 179–180
Wolf, Naomi: as attractive, 97–98, 163–164; on backlash, 124–126, 127; on beauty, 84, 124–128, 157, 162–164, 165, 189; on beauty industry, 89, 109; on cosmetic surgery, 87, 89, 109, 118; Friday vs., 95, 157; popularity of, 92; on pornography, 64; on post-victim feminism, 61; on power vs. victim feminism, 18, 163–164, 230–231, 267; on Roiphe, 230–231

Women Against Pornography (WAP), 63,
    190, 207
Women Who Love Too Much (Nor-
    wood), 225, 226
Working Women (Carmen and Moody),
    179–180, 181

Workplace, sadomasochistic dynamics in,
    220–224
Wuthering Heights (Brontë), 210

Young, Iris, 52, 254–255

Zaftig, 146

Indexer: Amy Harper
Compositor: Maple-Vail Book Manufacturing Group
Text: 10/13 Sabon
Display: Sabon
Printer and binder: Maple-Vail Book Manufacturing Group